PSYCHOLOGY SURVEY 5

EDITED BY

JOHN NICHOLSON AND HALLA BELOFF

THE BRITISH PSYCHOLOGICAL SOCIETY

First edition
ISBN 0 901715 27 1

British Library Cataloguing in Publication Data

Psychology survey.
5
1. Psychology
I. Nicholson, John II. Beloff, Halla
150 BF121

ISBN 0-901715-27-1

Published by The British Psychological Society,
St Andrews House, 48 Princess Road East, Leicester LE1 7DR

Distributed by The Distribution Centre,
Blackhorse Road, Letchworth Herts SG6 1HN

PRINTED IN GREAT BRITAIN BY A. WHEATON & CO. LTD., EXETER

CONTENTS

Page

Introduction 1

1. Absent-mindedness 3
James Reason
Department of Pyschology, University of Manchester

2. Visual Word Identification 32
John M. Wilding
Department of Psychology, Bedford College, London

3. Diurnal Rhythms in Cognitive Performance 63
Maureen Marks and Simon Folkard
MRC Applied Psychology Unit, University of Sussex

4. Computational Vision 95
M.J. Morgan
Department of Psychology, University College, London

5. Drugs and Human Information Processing 129
D.M. Warburton and K. Wesnes
Department of Psychology, University of Reading

6. The Relation between Thought and Language in Young Children 156
George Butterworth
Department of Psychology, University of Southampton

7. Personality Dimensions: an overview of modern trait psychology 175
Chris Brand
Department of Psychology, University of Edinburgh

8. Core Concepts in Attribution Theory 210
Charles Antaki
Department of Psychology, University of Lancaster

9. Political Ideology 234
Michael Billig
Department of Social Science, University of Loughborough

10. Psychological and Social Stress 265
J. Michael Innes
Department of Psychology, University of Adelaide

11. Cognitive Approaches to Clinical Psychology 290
Ivy M. Blackburn
MRC Brain Metabolism Unit, Royal Edinburgh Hospital

12. Women and Mental Illness 320
Jennifer A. Williams
Department of Psychology, University of Exeter

13. Counselling Psychology 345
Stephen Murgatroyd
The Open University in Wales, Cardiff

14. Contemporary Approaches to the Understanding, Assessment and Treatment of Delinquency 369
Norman Tutt
Department of Social Administration, University of Lancaster

15. Assessment Procedures in Organizations 397
Peter Herriot
Department of Occupational Psychology, Birkbeck College, London

Index 417

INTRODUCTION

The fifth volume in the 'Psychology Survey' series has the same objectives as its predecessors: to encourage and provide the means for psychologists and psychology students to keep in touch with new developments in a wide variety of areas of psychological research and practice. If the choice of subjects is eclectic, we have tried to play safe in our choice of authors by going for people who have not only made a significant contribution to the area they are reviewing but have also demonstrated a flair for making their expertise accessible to non-specialists. They have not been instructed to write for non-psychologists (although there is little in 'Psychology Survey 5' which will be beyond the understanding of the intelligent and determined layperson). They have however been given a brief to produce a contribution which will be comprehensible to a mid-course psychology student, rather than to their peers and colleagues.

As before, the contents of the current volume can be divided into: core subjects, that is, those which lie at the centre of teaching in British psychology departments; for example, cognition, social and developmental psychology, and individual differences: optional subjects, that is, the sort of topic found in Final Honours courses directed towards specific careers in psychology (occupational or clinical psychology, for example): and those subjects, which, although they may not be central to conventional courses, are of special interest to, and often the subject of controversy among, psychologists.

The present volume has an unusually strong cognitive flavour. Since neither of the editors could be described as a cognitive psychologist, this emphasis can only be attributed to the recent revival in the fortunes of this approach to psychology. Chapters 1 to 6 all describe advances in areas near to the heart of traditional experimental psychology - learning, perception and memory. Chapter 7 reviews developments in an area of the study of personality where British psychologists have been unusually dominant. Chapters 8 and 9 deal with areas of social psychology where recent discoveries have led to significant progress on both the theoretical and applied fronts. Chapters 10 to 13 discuss topics bearing on clinical psychology and psychotherapy from viewpoints which range from the psychosomatic to - once again - the cognitive. In Chapter 14, an ex-DHSS-researcher turned academic reviews recent developments in the treatment of delinquency, while the book concludes (Chapter 15) with a timely evaluation of what psychology can offer industry by way of assessment techniques.

Like its immediate predecessor, 'Psychology Survey 5' is being produced by the publishing/production team at the British Psychological Society's headquarters in Leicester, under the aegis of the BPS Books and Special Projects Group. Both current editors serve on this group. For the future it is planned that each volume in the 'Psychology Survey' series will be edited by one of the editors of the previous volume and one newcomer. In this way we hope to maintain a regular infusion of new ideas for topics and authors without having to undertake the editorial equivalent of reinventing the wheel every time. The present intention is to produce a new 'Psychology Survey' every other year, although the BPS, like every responsible publisher, will periodically review the situation, in the light of supply of ideas, authors and editors and demand for the books.

John Nicholson
Halla Beloff

ABSENT-MINDEDNESS

James Reason

Absent-mindedness is not an easy condition to define since it presumes the absence of something which itself eludes adequate description. Taking a wide perspective upon human fallibility, it is possible to distinguish two broad classes of error: **mistakes** and **slips**. A series of planned actions may fail to achieve their desired outcome either because the plan is inadequate (mistakes), or because the actions did not go as planned (slips). Both, of course, can co-exist in the same behavioural sequence. Although it is likely that absent-mindedness, in its most general sense, is implicated in both types of error, the primary focus of this review is upon slips rather than mistakes. Slips have been studied for over a century, and though there is still much to be resolved, far more is known about their nature and underlying mechanisms than is the case for mistakes - despite recent successes in identifying the heuristics mediating faulty inference and judgement (see Nisbett and Ross, 1980; Kahneman, Slovic and Tversky, 1982).

Within the slips category, it is convenient to distinguish a further sub-class: **lapses**. These differ in their manifestations rather than their origins. Whereas slips are potentially observable as externalized actions-not-as-planned (slips of the tongue, slips of the pen, slips of action, etc.), the term 'lapse' will be reserved for more covert error forms, largely involving failures of memory, which do not necessarily reveal themselves in actual behaviour, and which may only be evident, if at all, to the person who suffers them. Typical lapses are the temporary inability to retrieve the name of a known individual, or the forgetting of an intention to say or do something.

This chapter is primarily concerned with surveying the empirical evidence accumulated over the past few years relating to both slips of action, and to some of the more obvious and commonplace lapses (for example, memory blocks associated with the 'tip-of-the-tongue' state). Excluded from it will be any detailed consideration of verbal slips, since these have been extensively reviewed in a number of recent texts (Fromkin, 1973; Fromkin, 1980; Frith, 1980; Cutler, 1982).

As the early psychologists well understood (see Sully, 1881; James, 1890; Bawden, 1900; Jastrow, 1905), a close study of the nature and circumstances of systematic errors can yield important clues to hidden control processes, and especially those which guide the largely routine activities of daily life. This has become an even more urgent pursuit since the mid-1970s, when cognitive scientists such as Minsky (1975), Rumelhart (1975) and Norman (Norman and Bobrow, 1975) disinterred the Bartlettian notion of the 'schema' (Bartlett, 1932), and began to provide a theoretical substrate upon which to build adequate explanations of both correct performance and of these unintended yet coherent actions.

The bulk of this chapter is most conveniently organized around the principal techniques used in the investigation of absent-minded errors. Accordingly, the empirical findings will be discussed under four major headings:

Naturalistic corpus-gathering
Questionnaire studies
Laboratory studies
Case studies.

The final section will touch upon the wider theoretical implications of this work.

NATURALISTIC CORPUS-GATHERING

The collection and analysis of naturally-occuring events is an essential preliminary to the process of classification and theory building. It has the great advantage of capturing the richness and variety of real-world phenomena, and, given a large enough corpus, offers the chance of netting most of the available species of error. From such a collection, it is possible to identify recurrent error patterns within aspects of mental life that in the laboratory, are often treated in relative isolation.

The methods used in recording naturally-occurring slips range from the inspired self-observation employed by Freud in 'The Psychopathology of Everyday Life' (1914) to ingenious attempts to bring the rigour of laboratory measurement into the realm of everyday life (Wilkins and Baddeley, 1978). Three sets of studies will be discussed briefly below:

1. Norman's analysis of slips of action;
2. The Manchester extended diary studies of action slips and memory blocks;

3. Laboratory-derived investigations of everyday memory failures carried out at the Applied Psychology Unit, Cambridge.

1. Norman's slips of action corpus

Norman (1981) constructed a sophisticated conceptual classification based upon some 1,000 action slips, collected both by himself and by others. A key concept in this categorization was that of the schema:

> We assume that the human information processing system is mediated by means of many processing structures, each of which can do only simple operations, but each of which is coupled to numerous other structures. We call these structures schemas ... (Norman, 1982, p. 12)

Norman's taxonomy is given in Table 1, page 6.

Norman's action slip taxonomy is organized around three primary headings, each corresponding to a different phase in the initiation and guidance of action, and each contributing distinct types of slip. These three phases are the formation of the intention, and the activation and triggering of schemata. Norman's classification has the great merit of linking the idea of schemata (concerned with the detailed control of largely automatic processes in all cognitive domains) with the observation that most slips take the form of organized segments of familiar behaviour, albeit unintended ones. Schemata may be triggered (that is, have their activation level raised above some threshold value) by a variety of agencies: specific intentions, influences from neighbouring schemata, past activity, and by environmental circumstances. The taxonomy thus neatly accommodates the occurrence of both intended and unintended actions.

2. The Manchester diary studies

Slips of action. In a preliminary diary study (Reason, 1979), 36 volunteer subjects were asked to note down, over a continuous period of four weeks, whenever their actions deviated from their intentions. On each occasion, they were required to record the date and time of the slip, what they had intended to do, what they actually did, and the circumstances prevailing at the time. A second study (Reason and Mycielska, 1982) involved a more elaborate, or 'extended', diary form, kept over a two-week period by 63 subjects. In addition to providing the basic details of the

Table 1. Norman's (1981) classification of slips

1. **Slips in the formation of the intention.**

   A. Mode errors: erroneous classification of the situation.

   B. Description errors: ambiguous or incomplete specification of the intention.

II. **Slips that result from faulty activation of schemas.**

   A. Unintentional activation.
   1. Capture errors: when the intended sequence is similar to another better learned or more frequent sequence, the latter may gain control.
   2. Data-driven activation: external events activate schemas.
   3. Associative activation: currently active schemas activate others with which they are associated.

   B. Loss of activation.
   1. Forgetting an intention (but continuing with the sequence).
   2. Misordering the components of a sequence.
   3. Leaving out steps in a sequence.
   4. Repeating steps in a sequence.

III. **Slips that result from faulty triggering of active schemas.**

   A. False triggering: a properly activated schema is triggered at an inappropriate time.
   1. Spoonerisms: reversals of event components.
   2. Blends: combinations of components from two competing schemas.
   3. Thoughts leading to actions: triggering of schemas only meant to be thought, not executed.
   4. Premature triggering.

   B. Failure to trigger.
   1. The action was pre-empted by competing schemas.
   2. There was insufficient activation.
   3. The trigger conditions failed to match.

From D.A. Norman (1981) Categorization of action slips. 'Psychological Review', 88.

slips, as indicated above, the diarists were required to mark a set of standardized rating scales in regard to each slip recorded. Only the main findings are summarized below; for more detailed information regarding the samples, the rating scales and the statistical analyses, the reader should consult the primary sources (Reason, 1979; Reason and Mycielska, 1982).

1. Slips of action were most likely to occur in highly familiar surroundings during the performance of frequently and recently executed tasks in which a considerable degree of automaticity had been achieved.

2. Their occurrence was most commonly associated with states of attentional 'capture', either by some pressing internal preoccupation or by an external distractor.

3. A large proportion of these slips (40 per cent in the extended diary study) took the form of intact, well-organized action sequences that were judged as recognizably belonging to some other task or activity, not then being carried out. These 'other activities' were consistently rated as being recently and frequently executed, and as sharing similar locations, movements and objects with the intended actions. In short, the majority of action slips were strong habit intrusions.

4. Two further types of action slip, other than strong habit intrusions, could be identified in the corpus: place-losing errors, mostly involving omissions or unnecessary repetitions, where slips result from a wrong assessment of the current position in the sequence, and are often associated with unexpected interruptions: and blends and reversals, in which errors appear to arise from 'crosstalk' between two currently active but different tasks (blends), or between elements of the same task (reversals or behavioural spoonerisms). In this case, the actions are correct, but the objects to which they are applied become partially or completely transposed.

Although this corpus of slips did not itself bear directly upon the matter, there is a wealth of both introspective and clinical evidence (see Hamilton and Warburton, 1980) to show that emotional factors can also trigger unwanted thoughts and actions. Marked similarities exist between the strong habit intrusions observed in slips of action and the 'strong emotion' intrusions of thinking experienced in states of grief and depression. In both cases, the consciously planned guidance of action or thought is apparently usurped by largely automatic controlling agencies, or 'schemata', that have been 'fired up' by one or a combination of non-intentional activating factors, of which prior use, environmental context, shared features, and strong needs or emotions seem especially potent.

Memory blocks. A variant of the extended diary technique was subsequently used to investigate naturally occurring memory blocks, or 'tip-of-the-tongue' states (TOTs), in which people find themselves temporarily unable to retrieve known items, most usually names, from memory (Reason and Lucas, 1984a). These studies were carried out in the naturalistic tradition of Woodworth (1938) and Wenzl (1936), and represented a departure from more recent laboratory investigations involving the artificial induction of TOT states (Brown and McNeill, 1966; Yarmey, 1973; Koriat and Lieblich, 1974; Rubin, 1975; Gruneberg and Sykes, 1978; Williams and Hollan, 1981; Williams and Santa-Williams, 1982). The purpose of the first study was to confirm Freud's observation (Freud, 1914) that these deliberate and often laborious memory searches involve the dredging up of incorrect solutions, or substitute items which 'although immediately recognized as false, <u>nevertheless obtrude themselves with great tenacity</u>' (author's emphasis). The hypothesis was that these substitutes, or 'recurrent blockers', constituted strong habit intrusions in the process of non-automatic memory retrieval.

As before, the diarists were required to answer a set of standardized questions regarding each resolved TOT state experienced over a four-week period during the course of everyday life. The first diary study netted a total of 75 resolved TOTs, an average of 2.5 per diarist (N=32) over the recording period. Nearly 70 per cent of the diarists reported having at least one TOT state involving recurrent 'blockers'. These 'blockers' were encountered in 53.3 per cent of the recorded TOT states. The 40 TOTs ('blocked' TOTs) involving recurrent 'blockers' were found to differ significantly from 35 'non-blocker' TOTs in the following respects:

1. Whereas most 'non-blocked' states were resolved through the use of internal strategies (for example, alphabetical search, recall of contextual information, generation of similar items, etc.), the majority of 'blocked' TOTs were resolved through external factors (asking others, looking it up, being accidentally cued by TV, books, etc.). In both TOT forms, approximately 30 per cent of the states were resolved through spontaneous 'pop-ups', occurring at some variable time after the last search period, and usually during the performance of some routine activity.

2. The only internal strategy to be used with any success in the

resolution of 'blocked' TOTs was the generation of similar words or names. By contrast, a variety of consciously employed strategies proved successful in ending 'non-blocked' states.

3. Sixty-eight per cent of the 'non-blocked' TOTs were resolved after only one search, whereas 57.5 per cent of the 'blocked' TOTs required more than one deliberate search before the item was retrieved.

4. Diarists experiencing 'blocked' TOTs knew more features of the target than did those having 'non-blocked' states.

This study established that Freud was correct in his assertion that a substantial proportion of everyday TOT states are characterized by the presence of recurrent 'blocking' intermediates; that is, wrong items which are called to mind whenever a conscious attempt is made to retrieve the target. The next step was to determine whether these 'blockers' could be regarded as strong habit intrusions: words or names that are judged by the diarists to be more familiar and more in keeping with the circumstances of the search than either the particular target or the 'non-blocking' intermediates that arose during the TOT state.

A second study was carried out in which the diary form was similar to that used before, except that it included an additional section concerned with assessing the relative recency and frequency of 'blocking' intermediates, 'non-blocking' intermediates and targets. Sixteen subjects kept these modified diaries over a four-week period, and the study yielded 40 resolved TOT states. Fifteen of the diarists reported having at least one 'blocked' TOT state, and 70 per cent of the TOTs involved 'blocking' intermediates.

The findings supported the notion that 'blocking' intermediates represent strong habit intrusions. They were judged by the diarists as being more recently and more frequently used than either the targets or the 'non-blocking' intermediates. Subjects also rated the 'blocking' intermediates as being more closely associated with the target than were the other intermediates generated during that particular TOT state. These findings therefore conform to the general principle of error production found in other cognitive domains (Reason and Mycielska, 1982): unintended deviations from plan tend to take the form of responses that are more probable, more expected, and more in keeping with both the prevailing circumstances and established knowledge structures than those intended for that time.

3. Remembering to do things

In most laboratory studies of memory performance, subjects are required to recall previously learned material at the experimenter's bidding. But 'prompted recall' of this kind rarely occurs in everyday life. In executing real-life plans, people not only have to perform intended actions at specified times, but they also have to generate for themselves the cues which prompt these actions. Omitting to carry out items in a plan constitutes one of the commonest types of everyday memory failure (Reason and Mycielska, 1982).

An activity which places heavy demands on this self-cueing aspect of everyday memory is taking medication at set times. Wilkins and Baddeley (1978) used an analogue of pill-taking in which, instead of taking pills, the 31 female subjects (aged between 35 and 49) were required to push a button on a miniature print-out clock at four pre-arranged times (8.30 am, 1.00 pm, 5.30 pm, and 10.00 pm) each day for a week. The subjects were also requested to note down whenever they were aware of not pushing the button at the target time.

None of the subjects responded more than the required four times per day. Thirty per cent of them, however, forgot to push the button on one or more occasions, and, most interestingly, were apparently unaware of these omissions. That they were truly unaware, rather than simply forgetting to record such omissions, was suggested by their diligence in noting any other inappropriate responses. Subjects rarely, if ever, forgot that they had pushed the button if they had actually done so, no matter how 'off-target' it was. The results also indicated that laboratory tests of free recall generalize poorly to the real world, since subjects with high free recall scores (previously obtained) responded less accurately than those with lower scores.

Harris and Wilkins (1982) have proposed a useful descriptive framework within which to accommodate the important parameters implicated in forgetting to remember. This is the Test-Wait-Test-Exit (TWTE) cycle, based upon the TOTE unit of Miller, Galanter and Pribram (1960).

In the now familiar example of a TOTE-driven activity, that of hammering a nail into wood, the test phase relates continuously to the previous operations of the tester, so that there is little opportunity for forgetting. But in many everyday activities, such as preparing a meal, the monitoring phase is independent of the tester's own activity. The operations are carried out automatically by devices such as ovens or toasters, and only require the cook to check upon their progress. If, having performed a check, the cook decides that more cooking is required, it is then necessary to specify a time at which this subsequent test should take place. Discontinuous monitoring tasks are thus characterized by test-wait cycles, followed by a test-exit sequence, and are especially prone to memory failure. By specifying the important elements of these everyday tasks, the TWTE notion permits ecologically valid simulations of failure-prone activities to be created in the laboratory.

QUESTIONNAIRE STUDIES

Another way of obtaining data concerning everyday absent-mindedness is through self-report questionnaires. Most commonly, they present subjects with descriptions (and/or examples) of different slips and lapses, and ask them to give ratings of how often they have experienced each one during some specified time period. Of course, the subjects can only respond with general impressions, and these are liable to various types of distortion. Nevertheless, such questionnaires can yield interesting data with regard to individual differences in absent-mindedness, the relatedness of different error forms, and the organization of the underlying control mechanisms. In addition, they can provide a crude indication of how people perceive the relative frequencies of particular kinds of cognitive failure. As such, they offer a valuable supplement to the extended diary mode of naturalistic investigation.

Questionnaire techniques have been used by several research groups over the past few years to investigate the beliefs people hold about their everyday cognitive failures (see Herrmann, 1982). Many of these studies have focused upon memory performance, while others have been concerned with more varied forms of error proneness. For a thorough critique of this work, the reader is directed to Herrmann's excellent review article (Herrmann, 1982). The scope of the present chapter permits only a brief summary of the major findings of these questionnaire studies. There are, however, some significant points of agreement which hold true irrespective of the particular questionnaire form used or the type of cognitive failure investigated.

1. Summarizing the questionnaire findings

1. Error proneness questionnaires reveal wide and consistent individual differences in liability to minor cognitive

failures, or absent-mindedness. Split-half and test-retest reliabilities (over several months) are in the region of 0.7-0.8 and sometimes higher (see Broadbent et al., 1982; Herrmann, 1982).

2. The Oxford group (Broadbent et al., 1982) obtained significant correlations between ratings of cognitive failure by spouses and self-reports as measured by the Cognitive Failures Questionnaire (CFQ). Thus, the respondent's own view of his or her liability to cognitive failure tends to be shared by someone else (the marital partner) with a good opportunity to judge actual performance. At worst, this indicates that responses to the CFQ are not greatly influenced by a person's wish to present himself (or herself) as largely infallible when this is not actually the case. At best, it suggests that there is some genuine correspondence between self-reports of error-liability and everyday behaviour.

3. Responses to questionnaire items are usually positively correlated. Thus, those individuals who acknowledge themselves to be particularly liable to one kind of cognitive failure (for example, memory lapses) also report a high degree of susceptibility to other forms of failure (for example, action slips), and conversely. This suggests that error proneness is not specific to any one cognitive domain, but operates more or less uniformly across all types of mental function (see Broadbent et al., 1982; Reason and Mycielska, 1982). It appears, therefore, that susceptibility to these minor failures is determined by some universal control process that operates independently of the particular cognitive activities in which these errors reveal themselves.

4. This conclusion is further endorsed by the finding that the total scores derived from different forms of these error proneness questionnaires correlate highly one with another, regardless of the particular cognitive domain to which they are directed (see Broadbent et al., 1982). Few other relationships of any significance have yet been established. In short, these questionnaire measures of failure liability appear to be tapping some function that is not readily assessed by existing psychometrics.

5. The exception to this pattern is that the CFQ has been found to correlate significantly with the number of current psychiatric symptoms as assessed by the Middlesex Hospital Questionnaire (MHQ). In one study involving student nurses, a significant relationship was obtained between prior CFQ scores and scores

on the MHQ following a six-week period of stressful ward training (Broadbent et al., 1982). No such relationship was found with nurses who had spent an equivalent period on low stress wards. One interpretation of these findings is that a high level of everyday slips and lapses is associated with an increased vulnerability to stress. It is not so much that stress induces a high rate of cognitive failure (though it may indeed be so), but that the general control factor which determines error liability is also involved in coping with stress. There are also data which hint at a relationship between unusually low error rates and obsessionality (Broadbent et al., 1982; Reason and Mycielska, 1982).

2. What do these questionnaires measure?

One possible answer is that the ratings elicited by all of these questionnaire items are coloured by the respondents' global impressions of their overall error proneness, and that these broadly-based metacognitive beliefs are reasonably accurate reflections of the characteristic efficiency with which they manage their cognitive affairs. A likely candidate for this general management function is the attentional control resource described by a number of cognitive theorists (Kahneman, 1973; Norman and Bobrow, 1975; Navon and Gopher, 1979). In their most basic form, these theories argue that attention can be usefully regarded as a finite reservoir of information processing resources which is equally available to all mental operations.

In what ways could people vary in regard to this attentional resource? Taking the metaphor of a reservoir rather literally, it could be argued that individuals differ in the total amount of their endowment. But the available evidence suggests otherwise. If attention is indeed a universal control resource, one would expect that those people possessing a lesser quantity would show not only a high rate of cognitive failures, but also fairly marked deficits in a wide range of intellectual activities. Yet there is no relationship between self-reported absent-mindedness and either intelligence or educational attainment (Reason and Mycielska, 1982; Broadbent et al., 1982). Although this possibility cannot be ruled out altogether, it does not appear to be a very promising line of speculation.

A more feasible proposition is that people vary characteristically in the efficiency with which they deploy this control resource in order to cope with competing informational demands. Some recent empirical support for this idea has been provided by Martin and

Jones (1983), who found that people with high levels of everyday cognitive failure (as measured by the CFQ) tended to be poor at executing two tasks concurrently, but not when the same tasks were performed separately.

So far, a tentative case has been presented for trait-like variations in the efficiency of attentional deployment, or resource management. Such a view would be in accord with the observed relationship between a high cognitive failure rate and increased vulnerability to stress. Cognitive coping strategies are liable to make heavy demands upon the limited attentional resource. For those individuals in whom a chronically high level of slips and lapses indicates a characteristically inefficient allocation of attention, the availability of this limited resource may well be less than that necessary to sustain effective coping strategies. And, as Lazarus (1966) pointed out, psychiatric symptoms emerge when coping strategies begin to crumble.

It is also well known (see Hockey, 1973; Hamilton and Warburton, 1979) that attentional mobility diminishes under stress. One possible way of representing both state and trait variation in cognitive resource management is along a dimension, varying from extreme attentional fixedness at one end, to a high degree of flexibility at the other. Two further assumptions are needed. First, that individuals differ in their typical position along this dimension. Second, that situational or life event stresses will act to shift everyone some way towards the fixedness end of the dimension. The extent and the duration of this shift will depend upon the complex interplay of many factors, including the severity of the stress, the effectiveness of the coping strategies, and the individual's characteristic position on the dimension. It is reasonable to assume that a stress-induced shift toward a state of attentional fixedness will reveal itself in a variety of ways: by the presence of intrusive ruminations (as in grief or depression), by an increased rate of minor cognitive failures, and by a more pronounced degree of 'routinization' in the performance of both physical and mental activities.

3. Absent-mindedness in shops

Some indirect support for these ideas comes from an analysis of letters written by people (N=67) who felt themselves to have been wrongly accused of shoplifting, and a related questionnaire investigation (N=150) of the incidence of various slips and lapses while shopping (Reason and Lucas, 1984b). The latter was designed to provide normative data against which to evaluate the accounts given by the accused group of the circumstances leading up to their prosecutions.

Fifty-three per cent of the accused group specifically cited absent-mindedness, mental 'blanks' or confusion as the primary cause of their predicaments. Sixty-nine per cent mentioned being distracted or preoccupied when the incident occurred. Twenty-three per cent were receiving medical treatment at the time of the incident, and 50 per cent were involved in negative life events (for example, divorce, separation, discovery of a spouse's infidelity, bereavement, seriously ill children, etc.). For nearly a third of the accused, these life crises were present in truly diabolical combinations.

This analysis suggested that most of these critical lapses happened while the shopper's attentional resource was heavily engaged by something other than the immediate task. In nearly a quarter of the sample, this tendency towards attentional fixedness was likely to have been further exacerbated by medication. An additional factor in many cases was the employment of some unwise practice, mostly involving the transfer of goods from the store's container to a personal receptacle. This was done to separate items of different size or for different people, to make carrying more convenient, or simply through inadvertence. The shopper then failed to declare these goods at the checkout.

A hundred-and-fifty men and women (not involved in shop-lifting charges) were asked how often they had experienced each of 24 different slips and lapses while shopping. Six of these errors (risky lapses) could lead to accusations of shop theft (for example, transferring goods out of trolley, leaving without paying, etc.), the remaining 18 items were relatively trivial in their consequences. The most important finding was that the six risky lapses were all judged as having occurred far less frequently than other error forms. Nevertheless, 18 per cent of the sample had at some time inadvertently left a store with an article they had not paid for.

One interpretation of these findings is that under normal circumstances (that is, when not worried, unhappy or ill), shoppers, being well aware that they may be under observation by security staff, deliberately avoid any actions that could be interpreted as furtive or suspect. Thus, they appear to allocate some part of the attentional resource to guard against the making of potentially risky errors. Supermarkets are evidently places that promote self-consciousness rather than absent-mindedness, at least in regard to risky slips. So why do they happen?

The attentional resource is a limited commodity. As the accounts of the accused group revealed, certain states of mind have the power to tie this resource down so fixedly that there are no custodial reserves to spare. Under these conditions, people are no longer able to monitor their largely routine actions with sufficient vigilance, and risky errors pass unnoticed (cf. Baars, 1980). Moreover, since the layout of supermarkets is specifically designed to elicit taking-behaviour, it is not unreasonable to suppose that such environmental factors also play a part in 'shaping' unintended actions. The diary studies indicated how potent these contextual factors are in eliciting unwanted but routinized actions.

LABORATORY STUDIES

The relative merits of the naturalistic and experimental modes of enquiry, and their mutual interdependence were concisely expressed by Motley (1980) as follows:

> Without naturalistic facts, experimental work may become narrow and blind: but without experimental research, the naturalistic approach runs the danger of being shallow and uncertain.

MacKay (1980) argued that the most appropriate strategy was to use a detailed analysis of naturally occurring slips and lapses to develop a model of the underlying mechanisms, and then to subject the assumptions and predictions of this model to laboratory test. Some examples of this approach are considered below.

1. Inducing speech errors

An ingenious technique for eliciting predictable speech errors has been used with considerable theoretical profit by Baars and his colleagues over the past few years (see Baars, 1980). Since this work has been extensively reviewed elsewhere (see Fromkin, 1980), only its main features are discussed below.

The rationale for the various slip-provoking methods employed by this group is most succinctly expressed in the 'competing plans hypothesis' (Baars, 1980). This states that subjects can be induced to make predictable and involuntary speech errors in the laboratory if (a) they are given two competing plans for one utterance, and (b) they are denied sufficient time to 'sort out' these plans. A brief description of the original technique, termed SLIP (Spoonerisms of Laboratory-Induced Predisposition), will serve to convey the type of manipulations employed by the family of methods as a whole.

Word pairs are presented to the subjects one at a time for about 1 second each. They are instructed to read them silently, with the exception of certain target pairs that are cued to be spoken aloud. The targets are preceded by interference pairs, designed to resemble more closely the phonology of the desired spoonerism than the phonology of the intended target. For example, the target 'darn bore', expected to spoonerize into 'barn door', is preceded by the following interference items: 'ball doze', 'bash door', 'bean deck', 'bell dark'. After the target pair ('darn bore') has disappeared from sight, the subjects are cued with a RESPOND signal which requires them to say out loud the immediately preceding pair of words as quickly as possible.

It has been found that between 10 to 30 per cent of responses to these unexpected target pairs will be spoonerisms. This result has been obtained over a variety of phonetic, lexical or nonsense patterns, and a range of word-pair exposure times from 0.5 to 3 seconds. Related techniques, also based upon the competing plans hypothesis, have been used to elicit word switches between two syntactically parallel phases (for example, starting with the sentence 'She touched her nose and cut a flower', it is possible to induce the error: 'She cut her nose and touched a flower'), word blends (for example, 'ghastly' plus 'grizzly' produces the blend 'gistli'), and active-passive transforms (for example, subjects are given the sentence 'John hit the ball' followed by the cue ACTIVE or the cue PASSIVE, eliciting errors like 'Ball hit the ball' and 'Ball hit the John').

By establishing 'base error rates', a fine-grained analysis of the comparative effects of various error determinants can be carried out by noting how the base-rates are influenced by different experimental manipulations. A considerable amount of evidence has now been accumulated to suggest that semantic as well as phonological and lexical criteria are employed by the speaker in the pre-articulatory editing process (see Motley, 1980). Error frequencies are affected by linguistic and semantic factors that are independent of the characteristics of the intended utterances. With induced spoonerisms, for example, frequencies increase according to the lexical legitimacy of the target, being greater for lexical combinations (for example, 'barn door') than for nonsense ones (for example, 'bad goof' to 'gad boof'), regardless of the lexical status of the targets. This effect only holds however when the prior context contains lexical rather than nonsense interference items. In addition, spoonerism frequences have been shown to increase according to the transitional probability of the initial phoneme sequence of the error (Motley and Baars, 1975).

An extremely interesting finding (particularly in the light of the previous discussion of high-risk shopping lapses) is that subjects are generally reluctant to produce salacious speech errors. For example, the error rate of neutral sentential errors, of the kind 'She cut a flower and touched her nose', is about twice that for errors involving some potentially blush-making element (for example, 'She picked her nose and touched the flower', induced by reading the sentence 'She touched her nose and picked a flower' with a subsequent cue to reverse the phrases). Likewise, it is harder to induce salacious spoonerisms (for example, target = 'tool kit' or 'fuzzy duck') than neutral ones (for example, target = 'darn bore').

These observations provide further support for the notion that some part of the attentional resource is held in reserve to guard against damaging errors. In the speech context, it suggests that the editing process brackets both sides of the articulatory program. The incomplete articulatory program may be subject to invasion by unwanted linguistic elements so long as they satisfy the phonetic and/or lexical criteria of the editor. But the apparent censoring of embarrassing outputs indicates that editing continues after the program has been formed, and before it is uttered. Subjects appear to anticipate the semantically or socially anomalous errors and suppress them.

However, the fact that such damaging errors can occur, albeit infrequently, indicates that there are occasions when the editing is inadequate. If, as seems reasonable, one identifies this editing function with some part of the attentional control resource, then it is probable that speech errors, like action slips, occur when attention has been 'captured' elsewhere. If just a small part of this monitoring capacity has been diverted, then only the best camouflaged (that is, phonetically and lexically possible) words can evade the slightly relaxed vigilance of the editor. But the editing function needs to be a good deal more depleted to permit salacious or socially damaging slips to escape into speech. The same appears to be the case with potentially risky action slips or memory lapses in shops.

2. Inducing memory blocks

A well-known example of the laboratory elicitation of memory lapses is Brown and McNeill's (1966) tip-of-the-tongue (TOT) study. This now classic experiment has given rise to several investigations of a similar kind (Yarmey, 1973; Koriat and Lieblich, 1974, 1976; Rubin, 1975; Gruneberg and Sykes, 1978; Gruneberg, 1978). Other paradigms used to induce retrieval blocks have been part-list cueing (Mueller and Watkins, 1977) and paired-associate interference (see Crowder, 1976). This work on blocking in episodic and semantic memory has been recently reviewed (Roediger and Neely, 1982), and will not be discussed further.

We will focus instead upon efforts to test the hypothesis (generated by the TOT diary studies described earlier) that memory retrieval can be blocked by 'strong-habit intrusions', that is, by words that share similar characteristics to the sought-for items, but which are more extensively used in the course of daily life. Such a notion is not novel. Ebbinghaus (1885), for example, cited Delboeuf, who explained forgetting 'by the theory that one memory might hinder another from appearing'.

Naturalistic data derived from the various extended diary studies suggest that schemata (for actions or words) can be brought into play by non-intentional factors such as frequency and recency of use, context, and shared properties (see earlier discussion). Such a view is also supported by the artificial elicitation of speech errors, discussed earlier. The question at issue is: which of these possible 'priming' factors is most involved in prolonging memory blocks?

A recent study by Lucas (1984) required subjects to give synonyms to moderate-frequency cue words presented on a VDU. These cue words were immediately preceded by a priming word which could be of one of four kinds:

1. A high-frequency, semantically related word.
2. A low-frequency, semantically related word.
3. A moderate-frequency, semantically unrelated word.
4. An orthograpically similar word (that is, one sharing a first syllable with the cue word).

As predicted, the greatest incidence of blocks (operationally defined as responses taking longer than six seconds) and the slowest average responses occurred when the cue words were immediately preceded by semantically related, high-frequency primers. There was also a statistically insignificant tendency for orthographically similar priming words to delay retrieval slightly. There was no difference between the two control conditions (that is, low frequency, semantically related primers and moderate frequency, unrelated primers). This suggests the influence of a complex interaction between frequency and semantic relatedness in the priming of retrieval blockers. Such a result is in keeping with Brown's (1979) finding of inhibition in retrieval from semantic memory produced by presentation of semantically related primers (see also Roediger, Neely and Blaxton, 1983), and presents some difficulties for spreading activation models of semantic memory (for example, Collins and Loftus, 1975).

3. Inducing place-losing errors

Relatively common among naturally-occurring slips of action are those errors which stem from a failure to keep track of one's current position in a sequence of planned actions (Reason, 1979; Reason and Mycielska, 1982). At a behavioural level, these slips can show themselves in a variety of ways:

* as unnecessary repetitions of previously completed actions (for example, attempting to pour a second kettle of water into a pot of freshly made tea);

* as omissions (for example, attempting to drive away before turning on the ignition);

* most profoundly, as 'blanks' (for example, not recalling whether or not one has washed one's hair in the shower).

Possible mechanisms for these errors have been discussed at length elsewhere (see Reason and Mycielska, 1982).

Analysis of everyday place-losing errors suggests that they are often contingent upon some unexpected interruption of the planned sequence of actions. This notion was examined experimentally by Lucas (1984), using recitation of multiplication tables as the primary task. It was assumed that place-losing errors could be induced by interrupting the subjects at various points during this activity, requiring them to solve arithmetic problems, and then asking for the task to be resumed at the point at which it was left off.

Errors were produced on 69 (19 per cent) out of a total of 363 test trials, and each subject made between 0 and 6 errors over the 11 test trials encountered per person. Fifty of the 69 errors involved place-losing. Of these, 42 per cent were omissions, and 26 per cent repetitions. These relative proportions were in accord with those found by Wing and Baddeley (1980) in analyzing slips of the pen in examination scripts, and with the neuropsychological observations of Chedru and Geschwind (1972). In 4 per cent of the cases, the subjects suffered complete 'blanks', and in 19 of the 69 errors, the subjects could not recall which table they had been reciting.

It was also found that the probability of making a place-losing error varied according to the point in the multiplication table at which the interruption occurred. Errors were significantly more likely to be induced in the middle of the sequence than at either the beginning or the end. Similar inverted-U functions have been observed by both Mandler (1964) with irrelevant-word interruptions of learnt sentences, and by Wing and Baddeley (1980). One possible explanation is that the beginning and the end of the multiplication table is less subject to interference from neighbouring items. Alternatively, it could be argued that the middle of a table is relatively devoid of salient 'landmarks' by which to judge one's position (von Restorff, 1933). This issue needs to be resolved by further experiments.

Rabbitt and his colleagues have carried out some elegant studies of place-losing errors in old people (Rabbitt and Vyas, 1980; Rabbitt, 1981). Their results indicate that the elderly are less efficient at using recently acquired information to check their current position relative to the plan, and so are particularly prone to place-losing. This is especially marked in social gatherings where they are unable to keep a record of a number of different conversational themes. To cope with this deficiency, they are inclined to conduct a monologue, since they have an excellent recall for what they themselves have said previously. What many people are inclined to attribute to the cussedness of the elderly may simply be adaptive social strategy to compensate for the defects of working memory.

CASE STUDIES

The detailed historical study of the single case can yield valuable information about the circumstances leading up to catastrophic errors. Where sufficient evidence is available, it is possible to study the interaction of the various contributing factors over an extended period in a way that would be impossible for the inconsequential errors of everyday life. Although any one catastrophe may result from the unhappy conjunction of several distinct causal chains, and hence be a truly unique event, the effects of particular combinations of contributing factors reveal something about the limits of human performance that cannot be obtained from either the laboratory or from naturalistic observations.

One of the important lessons to be learned from such case studies is that disasters are rarely the product of a single isolated error. Usually they involve a series of errors, committed either by one individual or, more often, by several. Another is that the errors contributing to serious man-made disasters recognizably belong to the familiar body of slips and mistakes to which everyone is prone during the course of daily living (see Dixon 1976; Hall, 1980; Reason and Mycielska, 1982). The case studies presented briefly below were chosen to illustrate how familiar and normally inconsequential absent-minded lapses can, in unforgiving circumstances, lead to injurious or damaging outcomes.

1. Signalmen's errors

In his comprehensive account of British railway disasters, Rolt (1978) made the following observation:

> The mistake which has probably caused more serious accidents in the last sixty years than any other is that of a signalman forgetting, especially at night, that he has a train standing near his box. (p. 194)

A particularly terrible example was the collision at Quintinshill on the Carlisle-Glasgow line in 1915 between a heavily laden troop train coming from the north and a stationary local train. It was Britain's worst rail disaster: 226 people were killed. The primary cause was that the relief signalman forgot there was a stationary train on the up-line, even though he himself had just got off it and it was in plain view just outside his box. A contributing factor was that the signalman previously on duty had failed to attach the reminder collars to the signal levers. If noticed, these would have alerted the relief to the presence of the stationary train.

2. The Tenerife runway collision

A multitude of factors combined to produce the world's worst air disaster, a runway crash between two Boeing 747s at Tenerife in 1977: bomb scares, diverted flights, fatigue, absence of ground radar, thick fog and taxiing errors by the Pan Am crew. The most immediate of them, however, was the KLM captain's commencement of his take-off run after receiving airways clearance (giving airways instructions), but before obtaining take-off clearance. A Working Party of the American Airline Pilots Association (Roitsch, Babcock and Edmunds, 1978) noted that this captain's principal job within KLM was as head of the Flight Training Department. During the preceding six years, he had spent some 1,500 hours in the flight training simulator, and had not actually flown for 12 weeks prior to the Tenerife catastrophe. The Working Party judged as highly significant that, in the simulator, the instructor issued airways and take-off clearance at the same time. To reduce operating costs, simulator pilots were never required to hold position awaiting take-off clearance. As a consequence of the many stresses associated with the unscheduled landing at Tenerife, the KLM captain may have reverted to a preprogrammed mode of action (strong-habit intrusion) derived from long experience with the predictable world of the simulator.

3. The Pontypool bus disaster

In the summer of 1982, a double-decker bus on a country route in South Wales sheared off its top deck when attempting to pass through a low bridge, killing six people. At the inquest, the driver explained that he normally drove a single-decker on that route. On this trip, he 'forgot' that he was driving a double-decker.

4. The Wildenrath Sidewinder incident

During an exercise over West Germany in May 1982, the pilot of a Royal Air Force Phantom accidentally fired a live Sidewinder missile up the exhaust pipe of a Royal Air Force Jaguar aircraft. The pilot ejected safely, but a £7 million aircraft was destroyed. At his court martial, the Phantom pilot attributed his expensive error to the fact that, at the time of firing, he had completely forgotten about the missiles and believed himself to be on the kind of routine training mission he had been flying for the past eight years. He acknowledged that he had known of the live missiles beforehand. In his defence, a senior officer argued that combat procedures were dinned so intensively into pilots that they reacted automatically.

Other contributing errors noted at the court martial were the failure by the ground crew to mark the master arms switch with red warning tape and to remove the gunsight with its attached camera: both being required procedures when flying with live missiles. These omissions would undoubtedly have made it easier for the crew to forget that they were flying with armed weapons. Without these indicators, the cockpit environment would have been no different from the general run of training missions in which interceptions were recorded by the gunsight camera.

THEORETICAL IMPLICATIONS

Although a number of models of action control have been derived from error data (Norman and Shallice, 1980; McRuer, Clement and Allen, 1980; Rasmussen, 1982; Reason, 1984b), it would be premature in the present state of the art, as well as inappropriate for a brief survey of this kind, to focus too closely upon their details. Such models were in any case designed to serve a variety of different functions, and even where these are comparable (for example, Norman and Shallice, 1980; Rasmussen, 1982; Reason, 1984b), it is not possible to choose between them on the basis of the available evidence. Instead, this concluding section will be restricted to considering a few of the central issues that have been raised by the error studies reviewed in this chapter, and which need to be addressed by any adequate theory of cognitive control.

As Freud (1914) was one of the first to point out, absent-minded errors are not random events. They show remarkable regularities of form across a wide range of cognitive domains, though not necessarily in the way that Freud himself indicated (see Timpanaro, 1976). As such, they demand a more global level of cognitive theorizing than has hitherto been derived from laboratory studies dealing with highly specific features of memory, attention, motor control, and the like.

Most commonly, these errors appear not as the unwitting signs of socially unacceptable impulses (that is, Freudian slips), but in the more prosaic guise of 'strong-habit intrusions', intact and highly organized sequences of thought or action that are more familiar and more in keeping with the prevailing circumstances than those which were intended. The impression gained from considering a large number of these errors is that the more frequently a particular routine is set in motion and achieves its desired ends, the more likely it is to recur unbidden as a slip of habit. Absent-minded errors demonstrate misapplied competence rather than incompetence.

The circumstances as well as the form of absent-minded errors pose problems for cognitive theory. For example, the slips of action data suggest that all mental and physical activities, no matter how apparently automatic, make some demands upon the attentional resource. Strong-habit intrusions invariably occur when attention is 'captured' by something other than the task in hand. From this, it can be inferred that some part of the attentional resource is necessary to suppress those activated but unwanted schemata that would otherwise claim a piece of the action (see Reason and

Mycielska, 1982; Reason, 1984). A further implication is that the attentional control resource extends beyond the reaches of direct awareness. Traditionally, it has been more usual to regard attention as a region of sharpened awareness within the boundaries of consciousness (for example, 'The field of consciousness ... is wider than that of attention', Sully, 1884, p.73). However, the slips of action findings strongly suggest that this inclusiveness relationship is reversed, and that consciousness is in fact a subset of the attentional resource (see Reason, 1984).

Finally, it is worth pointing out that the circumstances provoking absent-minded errors also challenge aspects of contemporary cognitive theories. For example, in their widely cited theory of controlled and automatic information processing, Shiffrin and Schneider (1977) stated:

> Memory is conceived to be a large and permanent collection of nodes, which become complexly and increasingly interassociated and interrelated through learning. Most of these nodes are normally passive and inactive and termed 'long-term store', or LTS, when in the inactive state. The set of currently activated nodes is termed short-term store, or STS. LTS is thus a permanent, passive repository for information. (p.155, author's emphasis.)

While there can be little dispute about the size of the LTS, or about the permanence and interrelatedness of the knowledge structures within it, the error data clearly deny their passivity. The only way to account for the appearance of organized yet unwanted action sequences is to assume that their underlying control structures (schemata) can be independently activated by influences other than those emanating from some central executive, or the STS (in Shiffrin and Schneider's terms). As indicated earlier, the most important of these non-intentional activating factors seem to be the extent and recency of previous employment, the prevailing need state, the present environment, and the features shared with other schemata.

Acknowledgements

My special thanks are due to Deborah Lucas for her data, ideas, and helpful comments on the draft versions of this chapter. I am also indebted to the Economic and Social Research Council for supporting our own research in this area over the past five years (Research grants, HR 6290 and HR 7755).

REFERENCES

BAARS, B.J. (1980) On elicing predictable speech errors in the laboratory. In: V. Fromkin (ed.) **Errors in Linguistic Performance: Slips of the Tongue, Ear, Pen and Hand.** New York: Academic Press

BARTLETT, F.C. (1932) **Remembering.** Cambridge: CUP

BROADBENT, D.E., COOPER, P.F., FITZGERALD, P. and PARKES, K.R. (1982) The Cognitive Failures Questionnaire (CFQ) and its correlates. **British Journal of Clinical Psychology, 21,** 1-16

BROWN, A.S. (1979) Inhibition in cued recall. **Journal of Experimental Psychology: Human Learning and Memory, 7,** 204-215

BROWN, R. and McNEILL, D. (1966) The 'tip of the tongue' phenomenon. **Journal of Verbal Learning and Verbal Behavior, 5,** 325-337

BAWDEN, H.H. (1900) A study of lapses. **Psychological Review: Monograph Supplements, 3,** 1-122

CHEDRU, F. and GESCHWIND, N. (1972) Writing disturbances in acute confusional states. **Neuropsychologia, 10,** 343-353

COLLINS, A.M. and LOFTUS, E.F.A. (1975) A spreading activation theory of semantic processing. **Psychological Review, 82,** 407-428

CROWDER, R. (1976) **Principles of Learning and Memory.** Hillsdale, NJ: Erlbaum

CUTLER, A. (1982) **Slips of the Tongue.** Amsterdam: Mouton

DIXON, N.F. (1976) **On the Psychology of Military Incompetence.** London: Jonathan Cape

EBBINGHAUS, H. (1885) **Uber das Gedachtnis.** Leipzig: Duncker (Trans. H. Ruger and C.E. Bussenius, 1913)

FREUD, S. (1914) **The Psychopathology of Everyday Life.** London: Ernest Benn

FRITH, U. (1980) **Cognitive Processes in Spelling.** London: Academic Press

FROMKIN, V.A. (1973) **Speech Errors as Linguistic Evidence.** The Hague: Mouton

FROMKIN, V.A. (1980) **Errors in Linguistic Performance.** New York: Academic Press

GRUNEBERG, M. (1978) Memory blocks and memory aids. In: M. Gruneberg and P. Morris (eds) **Aspects of Memory.** London: Methuen

GRUNEBERG, M. and SYKES, R.N. (1978) Knowledge and retention: the feeling of knowing and reminiscence. In: M. Gruneberg, P. Morris and R. Sykes (eds) **Practical Aspects of Memory.** London: Academic Press

HALL, P. (1980) **Great Planning Disasters.** London: Weidenfeld and Nicolson

HAMILTON, V. and WARBURTON, D. (1980) **Human Stress and Cognition.** Chichester: Wiley

HARRIS, J.E. and WILKINS, A. (1982) Remembering to do things: a theoretical framework and an illustrative experiment. **Human Learning, 1,** 123-136

HERRMANN, D.J. (1982) Know thy memory: the use of questionnaires to assess and study memory. **Psychological Bulletin, 92,** 434-452

HOCKEY, G.R.J. (1973) Changes in information selection patterns in multi-source monitoring as a function of induced arousal shifts. **Journal of Experimental Psychology, 101,** 35-42

JAMES, W. (1890) **The Principles of Psychology.** New York: Holt

JASTROW, J. (1905) The lapses of consciousness. **The Popular Science Monthly, 67,** 481-502

KAHNEMAN, D. (1973) **Attention and Effort.** Englewood Cliffs,NJ: Prentice-Hall

KAHNEMAN, D., SLOVIC, P. and TVERSKY, A. (1982) **Judgement Under Uncertainty: Heuristics and Biases.** Cambridge: CUP

KORIAT, A. and LIEBLICH, I. (1974) What does a person in a 'TOT' state know that a person in a 'don't know' state doesn't know? **Memory and Cognition, 2,** 647-655

LAZARUS, R.S. (1966) **Psychological Stress and the Coping Press.** New York: McGraw-Hill

LUCAS, D. (1984) **Everyday Memory Lapses.** PhD thesis, University of Manchester

MACKAY, D.G. (1980) Speech errors: retrospect and prospect. In: V. Fromkin (ed.) **Errors in Linguistic Performance: Slips of the Tongue, Ear, Pen, and Hand.** New York: Academic Press

McRUER, D.T., CLEMENT, W.F. and ALLEN, R.W. (1980) **A Theory of Human Error.** (Technical report no. 1156-1.) Hawthorne, Ca.: Systems Technology Inc.

MANDLER, G. (1964) The interruption of behavior. In: D. Levine (ed.) **Nebraska Symposium on Motivation.** Lincoln, Neb: University of Nebraska Press

MARTIN, M. and JONES, G.V. (1983) Distribution of attention in cognitive failure. **Human Learning, 2,** 221-226

MILLER, G.A., GALANTER, E. and PRIBRAM, K.H. (1960) **Plans and The Structure of Behavior.** London: Holt, Rinehart and Winston

MINSKY, M. (1975) A framework for representing knowledge. In: P.H. Winston (ed.) **The Psychology of Computer Vision.** New York: McGraw-Hill

MOTLEY, M.T. (1980) Verification of 'Freudian slips' and semantic prearticulatory editing via laboratory-induced spoonerisms. In: V. Fromkin (ed.) **Errors in Linguistic Performance: Slips of the Tongue, Ear, Pen, and Hand.** New York: Academic Press

MOTLEY, M.T. and BAARS, B.J. (1975) Encoding sensitivities to phonological markedness and transitional probability: evidence from spoonerisms. **Human Communication Research, 2,** 351-361

MOTLEY, M.T. and BAARS, B.J. (1976) Laboratory induction of verbal slips: a new method for psycholinguistic research. **Communication Quarterly, 24,** 28-34

MUELLER, C. and WATKINS, M. (1977) Inhibition from part-set cueing: a cue-overload interpretation. **Journal of Verbal Learning and Verbal Behavior, 16,** 699-710

NAVON, D. and GOPHER, D. (1979) On the economy of the human processing system. **Psychological Review, 86,** 214-255

NISBETT, R. and ROSS, L. (1980) **Human Inference: Strategies and Shortcomings of Social Judgement.** Englewood Cliffs, NJ: Prentice-Hall

NORMAN, D.A. (1981) Categorization of action slips. **Psychological Review, 88,** 1-15

NORMAN, D.A. (1982) Some observations on mental models. In: D Gentner and A. Stevens (eds) **Mental Models.** Hillsdale, NJ: Erlbaum

NORMAN, D.A. and BOBROW, D.G. (1975) On data-limited and resource-limited processes. **Cognitive Psychology, 7,** 44-64

NORMAN, D.A. and BOBROW, D.G. (1975) **Representation and Understanding: Studies in Cognitive Science.** New York: Academic Press

NORMAN, D.A. and SHALLICE, T. (1980) Attention to action: willed and automatic control of behavior. **CHIP 99** (University of California, San Diego: Center for Human Information Processing)

RABBITT, P.M.A. (1981) Talking to the old. **New Society, 22 Jan.** 140-141

RABBITT, P.M.A. and VYAS, S.M. (1980) Selective anticipation for events in old age. **Journal of Gerontology, 35,** 913-919

RASMUSSEN, J. (1982) Human errors: a taxonomy for describing human malfunction in industrial installations. **Journal of Occupational Accidents, 4,** 311-333

REASON, J.T. (1979) Actions not as planned: the price of automatization. In: G. Underwood and R. Stevens (eds) **Aspects of Consciousness, Volume I: Psychological Issues.** London: Wiley

REASON, J.T. (1984) Absent-mindedness and cognitive control. In: J. Harris and P. Morris (eds) **Everyday Memory, Actions and Absent-Mindedness.** London: Academic Press

REASON, J.T. and LUCAS, D. (1984a) Using cognitive diaries to investigate naturally occurring memory blocks. In: J. Harris and P.

Morris (eds) **Everyday Memory, Actions and Absent-Mindedness.** London: Academic Press

REASON, J.T. and LUCAS, D. (1984b) Absent-mindedness in shops: its correlates and consequences. **British Journal of Clinical Psychology, 23,** 121-131

REASON, J.T. and MYCIELSKA, K. (1982) **Absent-Minded? The Psychology of Mental Lapses and Everyday Errors.** Englewood Cliffs, NJ: Prentice-Hall

ROEDIGER, H.L. and NEELY, J.H. (1982) Retrieval blocks in episodic and semantic memory. **Canadian Journal of Psychology, 36,** 213-242

ROEDIGER, H.L., NEELY, J.H. and BLAXTON, T.A. (1983) Inhibition from related primes in semantic memory retrieval: a reappraisal of Brown's (1979) paradigm. **Journal of Experimental Psychology: Learning, Memory, and Cognition, 9,** 478-485

ROITSCH, P.A., BABCOCK, G.L. and EDMUNDS, W.W. (1978) **Human Factors Report on the Tenerife Accident.** Washington DC: Engineering and Air Safety (Air Line Pilots Association Study Group Report)

ROLT, L.T.C. (1978) **Red for Danger.** London: Pan Books

RUBIN, D.C. (1975) Within word structure in the tip of the tongue. **Journal of Verbal Learning and Verbal Behavior, 14,** 392-397

RUMELHART, D.E. (1975) Notes on a schema for stories. In: D. Bobrow and A. Collins (eds) **Representation and Understanding: Studies in Cognitive Science.** New York: Academic Press

SHIFFRIN, R.M. and SCHNEIDER, W. (1977) Controlled and automatic human information processing: II. Perceptual learning, automatic attending, and a general theory. **Psychological Review, 84,** 155-171

SULLY, J. (1881) **Illusions: A Psychological Study.** London: Kegan Paul

SULLY, J. (1884) **Outlines of Psychology.** London: Longmans Green and Co.

TIMPANARO, S. (1976) **The Freudian Slip.** London: NLB

VON RESTORFF, H. (1933) Uber die Wirkung von Bereichsbildungen in Spurenfeld. **Psychologisch Forschung, 18,** 299-342

WENZL, A. (1936) Empirische und theoretische Beitrage zur Erinnerungsarbeit bei erschwerter Wortfindung. **Archiv fur die gesamte Psychologie, 97,** 294-318

WILKINS, A. and BADDELEY, A.D. (1978) Remembering to recall in everyday life: an approach to absent-mindedness. In: M. Gruneberg, P. Morris and R. Sykes (eds) **Practical Aspects of Memory.** London: Academic Press

WILLIAMS, M. and HOLLAN, J. (1981) The process of retrieval from very long-term memory. **Cognitive Science, 5,** 87-119

WILLIAMS, M. and SANTA-WILLIAMS, S. (1982) A method for exploring retrieval processes using verbal protocols. In: R.S. Nickerson (ed.) **Attention and Performance: XIII.** Hillsdale, NJ: Erlbaum

WING, A. and BADDELEY, A.D. (1980) Spelling errors in handwriting. In: U. Frith (ed.) **Cognitive Processes in Spelling.** London: Academic Press

WOODWORTH, R.S. (1938) **Experimental Psychology.** New York: Holt

YARMEY, A.D. (1973) I recognise your face but I can't remember your name: further evidence on the tip-of-the-tongue phenomenon. **Memory and Cognition, 1,** 287-290

VISUAL WORD IDENTIFICATION

John M. Wilding

Why should some patients who have impaired reading ability due to brain injury be totally unable to read simple non-words, while their reading of words is nearly perfect, and why should others have little difficulty with non-words but mispronounce many common English words, especially where the spelling does not exactly represent the sound? These are two of the more intriguing phenomena which an adequate model of the reading of words has to explain. But such a model must naturally be well-grounded on observation of the abilities of normal competent readers and it is with such abilities that I shall be initially concerned in this chapter. Though the process of reading continuous text clearly involves much more than just reading words, a study of the reading of single words has the merits of being more manageable and involving the earliest and most fundamental of the reading processes, with relevance both to early learning and later breakdown.

Information processing models envisage reading, like many other cognitive processes, as requiring the activation by a visual input of internal representations or codes, sometimes directly and sometimes by a succession of intervening transformations of the input. Thus normal reading for meaning is seen as requiring activation of <u>semantic</u> codes which carry information about the meaning of words, perhaps in the form of a list of semantic features such as:

animate / inanimate
human / nonhuman
male / female

Reading aloud requires activation of an <u>articulatory</u> code which can control the relevant muscles. A model of word processing requires an understanding of the different codes involved, the way in which they are linked together and the processes of translating from one to another.

Investigations typically try to discover the effects of different variables on tasks which are believed to incorporate different combinations of codes and discover whether anticipated effects occur. For example, the regularity of spelling-to-sound correspondence might be expected to affect tasks which require translation from visual input to an articulatory code. However a task which strictly speaking requires only one code to be derived from print may often in fact involve others, either as necessary links or simply because they are automatically activated due to long practice. Thus reading aloud will normally involve not only an articulatory code but also a semantic one because we understand what we are reading. Deciding whether a letter sequence is a word requires access to a lexical code but not necessarily to the associated semantic information, and there is a dispute as to whether a phonological code is involved in access to the lexical code or not. It has proved quite difficult to devise experiments which provide clear answers on which codes are involved in which tasks. Most of the discussion in this limited survey will centre around the apparently straightforward questions about which tasks require which codes and the way in which codes are linked.

The following codes have been suggested, mainly on the basis of the many different things which fluent readers can do with words:

letter codes: letters can be named

graphemic codes: these are sometimes regarded as visual patterns of the whole word but recent evidence suggests there is a more abstract representation which can be activated by different written versions of the same word such as upper case, lower case and handwritten versions, so we should probably distinguish visual codes specific to a distinct written version from the more abstract graphemic code.

phonological codes: stress pattern and sound can be judged, as in making rhyme judgements. These codes are often difficult to distinguish experimentally from ...

articulatory codes: words can be pronounced aloud

lexical codes: known words can be distinguished from unknown words or non-words. These codes are closely related to but not exactly the same as ...

semantic codes: category membership, synonymy and many other aspects of meaning can be judged

graphological codes: words can be written

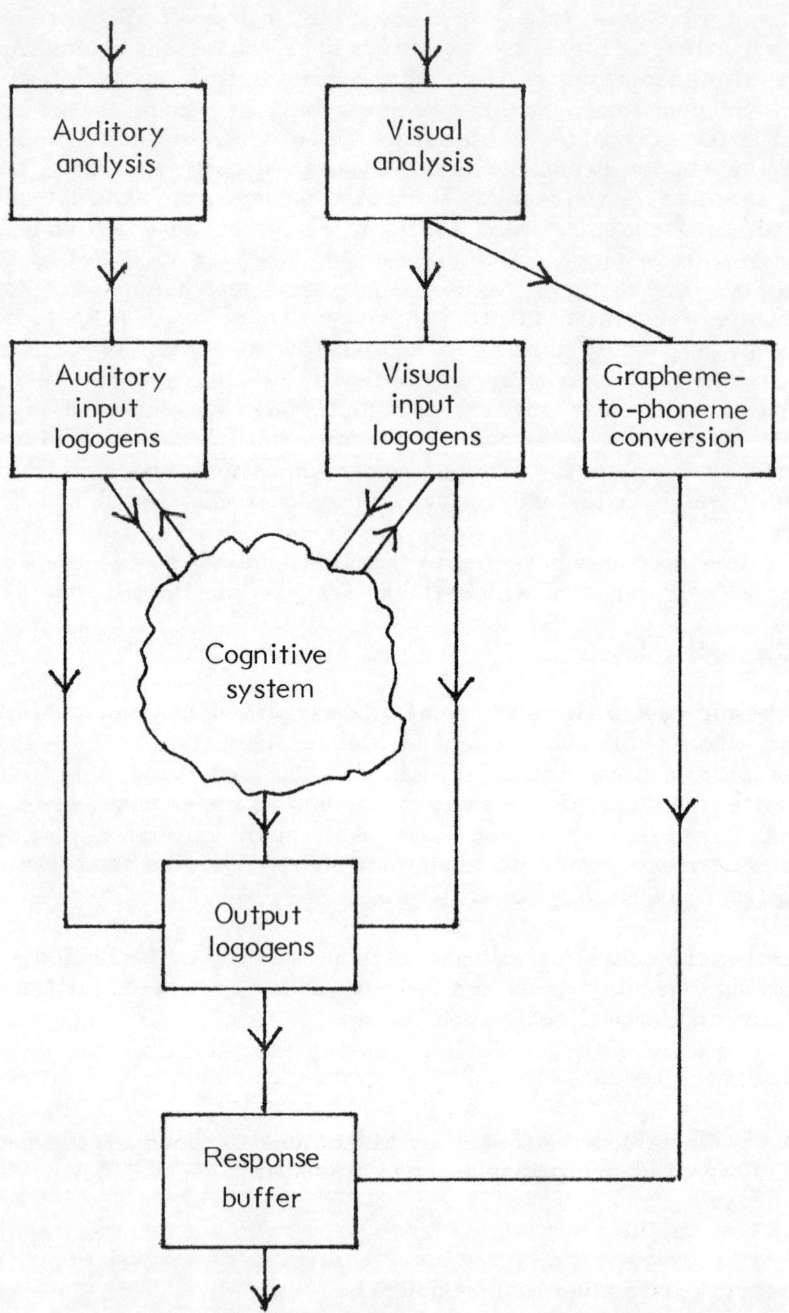

Figure 1. Morton's logogen model re-drawn. (From M.Coltheart, K.Patterson and J.C.Marshall (eds) 'Deep Dyslexia'. London: Routledge & Kegan Paul.)

A general model

Morton's (1979) logogen model provides a useful initial framework for our discussion. It is a general model of the verbal cognitive system and the most recent version is shown in Figure 1. It assumes logogen units which represent each known word and are activated by appropriate inputs. Separate logogen systems exist for auditory and visual inputs of words and there is also a separate output logogen system. The reason for separating the auditory and visual systems is that hearing a word does not make it much easier to identify it when it is later presented visually (and vice versa) but seeing it does help markedly even if the visual form is different (Clarke and Morton, 1983).

Most of the codes listed above can be easily assigned to different parts of the logogen model, though Morton uses different labels. His 'visual input logogens' are equivalent to what I have called graphemic codes and also serve to distinguish words from non-words, so they function as lexical codes. The 'output logogens' are like articulatory codes. Grapheme-to-phoneme conversion will activate phonological codes, though these are not shown separately, and semantic information is contained in the cognitive system. Letter codes, though not overtly represented, are presumably involved in the visual analysis before the visual logogen. Morton also accepts that other input systems (for pictures, for example) and output systems, such as a writing system, exist in a more comprehensive model.

We can now consider tasks which might require the involvement of different parts of this system and variables which might affect them. The tachistoscopic identification task tests how much of a word can be seen in a brief exposure and involves mainly visual analysis and activation of the logogen system. In the lexical decision task the reader has to decide whether a string of letters is a word or not; in Morton's model this decision can be based simply on the firing of a logogen.

Several variables are found to affect one or both of these tasks, with improved performance when items are:

* more legible

* are words rather than non-words

* are frequent rather than infrequent words in the language

* are recently-seen rather than new words

* and are preceded (or primed) by related rather than unrelated words.

Legibility is assumed to affect initial visual analysis and lexicality (being a word) to determine the existence of a logogen unit. Frequency, repetition and priming are assumed by Morton to affect the threshold or sensitivity of the logogen units, because every time a unit fires its sensitivity is increased and then gradually returns to the previous level. Priming by a related word is assumed to act through the cognitive system. Later I shall consider the adequacy of these explanations.

Reading aloud in the model can proceed either via the cognitive system as when reading for meaning, or by grapheme-to-phoneme conversion (GPC) as when reading new words. A direct connection from input to output logogens is also shown, but for the sake of simplicity I ignore this, and also because it is suggested by just one observed case of dyslexia discussed later. Hence we cannot always know whether the cognitive system is involved when reading aloud, but we can devise other tasks to ensure this such as judging whether a word belongs to a specified category. Access from visual logogen units to the cognitive system occurs without any mediation from phonological codes, which are only involved in reading by the GPC route. Thus variables which affect access to phonological codes should not affect reading by the cognitive route; furthermore, variables such as those mentioned above which Morton believes affect access to logogens should not affect reading by the GPC route, since it bypasses the logogens.

I will now discuss the early stages of visual analysis which enable access to the logogen (or in other words activate a graphemic code) and later consider the role of phonological codes in reading. The discussion of visual analysis is mainly concerned with specifying the processes in more detail than is contained in the very general outline of the logogen model.

VISUAL ANALYSIS

The word superiority effects

The greater ease of reporting words than non-words was noticed many years ago. Recently Reicher (1969) and Wheeler (1970) have also shown that single letters may be more easily identified in the context of words than when presented on their own. These authors briefly presented a single letter or word (such as D or WORD) then asked which of two letters had been present at one of the positions (for example, D or K at the final position). Thus the number of choices was controlled and both possibilities always formed a word. Non-words spelled more like real words (pseudo-words) also yielded better performance than those which were different from real words (Baron and Thurston, 1973). These results suggest that in some sense the word is processed as a whole, or that all letters are processed in parallel and that less information is needed to identify any one of them when they form a word. Other possible explanations are that some letters are identified and together with knowledge about English words this knowledge is used to guide decisions about the rest, or that the memory traces of words may be more durable or robust than those surviving from letters (see Henderson, 1982, for a full discussion of these theories).

Some of these suggestions are easily rejected. Superiority for letters in words occurs even when the type founts are mixed in the words (McClelland, 1976; Adams, 1979). Since this destroyed the normal visual pattern of the words, these findings show that features which extend over several letters are not important. However the effect does require words to be treated as wholes rather than separate letters, since it vanishes when the letters are widely spaced (Purcell and Stanovich, 1982), or (usually) if a warning is given on which position will be tested (Henderson, 1982, p.264).

The advantage of letters in pseudo-words over non-words does not vary when the frequency of adjacent pairs of letters in normal English is varied (McClelland and Johnston, 1977), and words still yield superior performance to non-words when a limited set of each is used and the possible letters at each position are known (Purcell and Stanovich, 1982); hence, an explanation which suggests that knowledge of letter sequences in English is important can also be rejected.

Thus there remain the explanations which suggest that letter codes are not readily available to awareness, either because the input is organized so that only the most inclusive or highest code enters awareness (Gleitman and Rozin, 1977) or because lower level modes are more vulnerable to interference and hence are lost from memory (Henderson and Chard, 1980). One piece of evidence in favour of this approach is that the superiority of letters in words over single letters seems to require use of a randomly-patterned masking field immediately after the stimulus, and letters are more vulnerable to such masks (Johnston and McClelland, 1973; Massaro and Klitzke, 1979). However the superiority of words and pseudo-words over non-words occurs without masking and Henderson (1982, p.284) explains this by suggesting that it is difficult to derive a stable memory code for non-words. These explanations amount to little more than a restatement of the effect.

Marcel (1983) provides a more detailed theory. He argues that the perceptual system tries to construct the most inclusive description possible of the input using features extracted by lower level mechanisms and that only this inclusive description enters awareness. Thus we are directly aware of words but only indirectly aware of separate letters in them. However this suggests that letters presented alone should also enter awareness directly and be seen as readily as words and better than letters in words.

The most convincing explanation of word superiority effects to date is provided by McClelland and Rumelhart (1981), following up earlier work by Johnston and McClelland. They developed a hierarchical model in which feature detectors (for lines, curves, etc.) feed into letter detectors which feed into word detectors. Words activate units at all three levels and letters activate units at feature and letter levels. A masking stimulus made of letter features feeds random information to previously active letter units and deactivates them, but an already active word unit remains unaffected because no letter units remain active to produce competing information, once the mask has occurred. Johnston and McClelland (1980) showed that a mask consisting of letters only slightly affected letter detection but greatly impaired word detection and thus reduced the word superiority effect. The theory predicted this because these masks would feed random letter information to word detectors and deactivate them.

The graphemic code

McClelland and Rumelhart's model provides an elaboration of the 'visual analysis' stage in the logogen model; each letter is identified separately and word units are activated by specific letter combinations. These word units can be activated by a variety of physical forms, including a mixture of type founts. This has been further shown by priming effects when the primer and the following word differ physically. Both handwritten and printed forms of a word served to prime the identification of a printed form presented some time later (Clarke and Morton, 1983). However these effects seem to be located at a stage involving a semantic code since visual similarity without similarity of meaning is inadequate. SEEN primes the identification of SEES but SEED does not (Murrell and Morton, 1974). Priming effects over briefer intervals are more relevant to visual analysis and show that similarity of letter sequence (graphemic code) without physical similarity can produce priming. Evett and Humphreys (1981) showed that lower case versions of words presented too rapidly for identification could aid identification of the same words in upper case presented immediately afterwards. Graphemically similar words had a similar though weaker effect and it was irrelevant whether these were similar in pronunciation or not. (TOUCH and POUCH primed COUCH equally well.) Non-words primed identification of graphemically similar words as effectively as words did. These effects could be occurring at the level of letter codes or sub-word units or graphemic units for whole words before these are matched to the logogen entries. Alternatively, though Morton does not envisage this, non-words may partially activate logogen units for similar words.

Factors affecting access to the logogens

Theorists have had considerable difficulty in resolving some apparent inconsistencies in the combined effects of legibility and the lexical factors of frequency, repetition and semantic priming which Morton believes affect the threshold of the logogen units. By testing the effects of combinations of these variables on a task we hope to discover whether they affect a common process or different ones. Sternberg (1969) has suggested that if the combined effects of two variables are equal to the sum of their separate effects (are additive) it is likely that they affect separate stages of processing; whereas, if their combined effects are greater than the sum of the separate effects (that is, if they interact) it is likely that they affect a common stage. There are, however, several doubts about the validity of this argument (see Wilding, 1982, for a discussion).

More simply, we would expect two variables which are supposed to exercise their effect in the same way (frequency and priming are both assumed to alter logogen threshold, for example) to combine in the same way with the effects of another (legibility, for example, which can be varied by superimposing random patterns over a word). More specifically, if illegibility slows the rate at which information accrues from the input, logogens with low thresholds (frequent, primed or repeated words) should be less affected. This result has been found when variation in legibility is combined with variation in priming or repetition in lexical decision tasks (Meyer et al., 1975; Becker and Killion, 1977; Besner and Swan, 1982), but not when legibility and frequency are varied together, when the effects of legibility were the same whatever the word frequency (Stanners et al., 1975; Becker and Killion, 1977). Repetition and frequency also interact (Scarborough et al., 1977), supporting the view that they act similarly, despite the differences in the way they combine with legibility, but no data are available for the combinations of priming and frequency or priming and repetition. Morton could argue that legibility affects the early analysis and frequency the matching of the input to the logogen units, but he cannot then explain why legibility interacts with both priming and repetition, which are supposed to act like frequency.

An alternative model of lexical access, Becker's verification model (Becker, 1979) also has problems. In this model, a set of hypotheses (the sensory set) is first derived from the input and in the verification stage a description is constructed for each and matched against the physical description of the stimulus in iconic memory. More frequent words are tested earlier, but if the prior context has suggested other words (the semantic set) these are tested before the sensory set.

Becker can explain the additive effect of legibility and frequency by assuming that legibility affects an early stage while frequency affects the order of testing the sensory set. Repetition should also presumably affect the testing process (Becker is not explicit on this) and not interact with legibility, but Besner and Swan (1982) did find such an interaction. Repeated items, like primed items, were less affected by reduced legibility than non-repeated or unprimed ones. Becker could explain this by saying that repeated and primed items are in the semantic set and only the sensory set is affected by legibility. However the interaction of frequency and repetition is then unexplained.

Besner and Swan, in attempting to resolve these problems, suggest that repetition must have two effects, one producing the interaction with legibility and the other the interaction with frequency. They also found an interaction of legibility and repetition for non-words, which causes problems for Morton, since the effect should occur in the logogen system and it is odd to assume that one presentation of a non-word causes it to acquire a logogen. They offer a modification of Becker's model, that appears to make it virtually indistinguishable from the logogen model. They abandon the notion of a semantic set, assume parallel matching of sensory set and physical description to avoid predicting an interaction of frequency and legibility, and suggest there are both transient and more permanent effects of repetition. Legibility interacts with repetition because 'not all items which are presented for verification have the same evidence criteria', which seems identical with Morton's criterion change; but no explanation of frequency effects is offered. However the sugestion that repetition (to which I would add, though less convincingly, priming by prior context) can have two effects does seem to provide a key to the puzzle. The short-lived effect, like Evett and Humphrey's priming effect from graphemically similar words, can be taken to affect visual analysis and the more permanent effect is on the criterion settings or sensitivity of the logogen units.

Earlier I remarked that logogen units function both as graphemic and lexical codes. A distinction has now been forced upon us in an effort to explain the observed interactions, with some effects assigned to a graphemic code and others to the lexical code. In the following sections I shall be concerned with the connection between these two levels.

ACCESS TO THE LEXICON

Role of the phonological code

The importance of phonology in learning to read has been stressed by several theorists (Gleitman and Rozin, 1977; Bradley and Bryant, 1983). Children with poor phonological skills have difficulty in learning to read. However the way in which learning occurs may be quite different from the strategy eventually used by the skilled reader.

Morton and Becker both assume that there is direct access from a visual code to the lexicon and thence to semantic memory and articulation (which I shall call the visual route). Morton also assumes two paths to articulation outside the cognitive system: one for words (which I shall ignore) and the other for pronouncing non-words. Other theorists have argued that a phonological code is a necessary link between graphemes and the lexicon (Rubinstein et al., 1971; Smith and Spoehr, 1974), or that it provides a second path to the lexicon, which I shall call phonological (Forster and Chambers, 1973), in addition to being necessary for pronouncing non words. Yet others, however, argue that all inputs, whether words or non-words, access the lexicon visually (Glushko, 1979; Marcel, 1980; Henderson, 1982). Before discussing these different possibilities I will consider the nature of different writing systems, because they can represent language in different ways and require different methods of processing to derive meaning.

Writing systems

Some complex and sophisticated categorizations of different types of written language have been advanced (see Henderson, 1982, for a detailed discussion). No simple scheme covers all the known variety but I confine myself here to a basic distinction between scripts which represent meaning and scripts which represent sound. The former range from fairly direct pictorial representation (pictographs) through stylized pictures to quite arbitrary symbols which are known as ideographs or logographs.

As the relation between logograph and meaning becomes more fixed in a language there is necessarily also a relation between logograph and sound and sometimes the same logograph may then be used also for a word with different meaning but the same sound. However the reader faced with a novel logograph cannot derive meaning or sound, and reading requires the acquisition of many arbitrary connections as in learning Chinese or the Kanji characters of Japanese, which were borrowed from China. It becomes possible to derive sound from a new visual pattern only when the writing system uses separate symbols for a limited number of component sounds. These symbols can represent syllables as in the Kana form of Japanese writing, or still smaller sound units known as phonemes*. In some languages each letter or letter group represents only one phoneme, but not in English.

English orthography and its relations to phonology

In English we have pictographs (road signs and washing labels), logographs (numerals, £, %, etc.) and for some words the spelling represents sound directly. However, much English spelling is inconsistent, with the same letter combinations representing different sounds on different occasions and the same sound represented by several letter combinations. There are many reasons for this. In many cases the written form of a word indicates not the pronunciation of that word but its relation to another word which is pronounced like the spelling. The change in pronunciation is usually due to change in stress pattern as a suffix is added, for example, TELEGRAPH and TELEGRAPHY. The common spelling signals the common root even though in the second case the E is pronounced like the A in CANADIAN, which in turn signals its connection with CANADA. Other reasons for the peculiarities of English spelling are survivals from other languages and changes of pronunciation while spelling reflects the old form.

** Phonemes are the smallest sound units which change word meaning when altered, as when a change from /z/ to /s/ changes 'eyes' to 'ice' in English.*

The difficulty of deriving pronunciation from spelling rules suggests to some theorists that all or some reading of English might be like reading logographs. Others argue that a large proportion of English words (the regularly spelled words) could be pronounced by using rules, but the exact proportion depends on the complexity of the rules and the frequency of the words included, since common words are the most irregular in their spelling. Only empirical study can discover what actually happens while reading. I will discuss first theories which claim that access to meaning occurs only via phonology; next those which claim it can occur by both routes; then those which claim it is always visual.

1. Lexical access via phonology only

This view cannot explain how we distinguish words which sound alike but are spelled differently (homophones), except by adding a visual spelling check, nor how we identify logographs and irregularly spelled words for which no rules exist relating visual pattern to sound. People also often find it difficult to identify the words which match non-words which sound like words (pseudohomophones like PHLIE, ROAG, WEERED, REQ), even after pronouncing them.

2. Two routes to the lexicon

Two-route theories assume that access to a lexical code can occur either directly from a graphemic code or indirectly from a phonological code which is first activated by the graphemic code. As the logogen model does not distinguish graphemic and lexical codes, this cannot be mapped directly on to Figure 1. Phonological codes used to gain access to the lexicon are called prelexical while those derived after lexical access are called postlexical. Hence phonological codes for non-words must be prelexical, those for logographs and irregularly spelled words which can only be pronounced correctly on the basis of previous knowledge must be postlexical, and those for regularly spelled words can be of either type. Coltheart (1978, 1980a) argues that no experiments are needed to show there is direct visual access to the lexicon as we can read logographs and irregularly spelled words; or to show phonological access, as we can identify the real word which sounds like PHOCKS; or to show a phonological route to articulation since we can pronounce non-words. The critical questions, he suggests, are when these different processes are used and how we can decide this.

Demonstrations that words are read aloud faster than non-words and regularly spelled words faster than irregularly spelled words may not be directly relevant to questions of lexical access. Reading aloud may sometimes occur without lexical access since Forster and Chambers, 1973, found that the frequency effect was smaller in reading aloud than in lexical decision.) Alternatively, the effects may occur at articulation. What is needed, says Coltheart, is evidence of similar effects in lexical decision and semantic processing tasks where lexical access is occurring.

We should note that Coltheart ignores the possibility that the tasks he cites in support of a two-route theory may be carried out in other ways. Secondly, he admits elsewhere that the phonological route may be affected by lexical information so is not strictly independent. Thirdly, Gough and Cosky (1977) showed that if subjects were allowed a delay before pronouncing words, the regularity effect vanished, suggesting it was occurring at lexical access rather than articulation, so evidence from reading aloud can be relevant if suitable control conditions are employed.

I will consider the data which Coltheart considers relevant before discussing in detail how two-route theories are assumed to account for the effect of spelling regularity and the reading of non-words.

(i) Lexical decision tasks. Rubinstein et al. (1971) showed that pseudohomophones produced slow negative decisions, which suggested phonological coding in accessing the lexicon. However this may be due to their visual similarity to words (Martin, 1982) and does not prove how words are processed. Furthermore the presence of non-words and especially pseudohomophones may change the normal reading strategy. Davelaar et al. (1978) found that subjects were slower to decide that a rare homophone (for example, THYME) was a word when the non-words contained no pseudohomophones, but decision times dropped to the same as those for control words when pseudohomophones were present. This suggested that phonological coding was used in the first case when it was not confusing, but was dropped when it was likely to produce errors (see also McQuaide, 1981), though it is not clear why decisions on homophones should be slower when phonological coding is used.

Another source of relevant evidence is the effect of spelling regularity in lexical decision. Faster reading aloud of regular words can be explained by the two-route theories as due to the possibility of reading them by either route, while irregularly spelled words can only be read by the visual route. (Later I discuss some problems with this proposal.) If a similar effect of spelling regularity occurred in lexical decisions it would implicate two routes in lexical access. Coltheart et al. (1979) and Bauer and Stanovich (1980) claimed to find no effects of regularity in lexical decisions, implying that only the visual route was used, but Parkin (1982) reclassified their words, using a stricter system of separating words of exceptional pronuncation from mildly irregular and regular words, and found longer latencies for exception words in their data and his own. Parkin and Ellingham (1983) also found a similar result even when pseudohomophones were included among the non-words, and the effect survived even when the slower responding to the pseudohomophones had almost disappeared after practice. If this disappearance was due to reduced use of phonological coding, why did the effect of spelling regularity persist?

(ii) Semantic classification tasks. Meyer and Gutschera (1975) gave a category name followed by a word to be classified as a member or non-member. Some words were homophones of category members (FRUIT - pair) and responses to these were slowed. In another version of the task, words which sounded like category members were to be categorized as belonging; positive responses were faster than in the first task where only correctly spelled words were acceptable. Both these findings imply phonological coding, as does an experiment by Baron (1973) in which subjects had to decide whether phrases like TIE THE NOT made sense. More errors were made when the phrases sounded right than when they did not (TIE THE BUT). However none of these results compels us to accept that the phonological effects occurred <u>before</u> lexical access. They could reflect use of a phonological code in some later stage of these complex tasks.

(iii) Articulatory suppression. One further possibility for deciding whether a phonological code is used in lexical access is to impose some interfering task which would impair such coding if it were present. A subject may be asked to recite some sequence aloud which imposes little memory load, such as counting to ten repeatedly or repeating a single word. This technique (articulatory suppression) is given theoretical significance by the working memory model of Baddeley and Hitch (1974), who demonstrated that it had little effect on several cognitive processes and suggested that it merely occupied a subsidiary articulatory loop which could hold a small amount of material for a brief time and recirculate it by rehearsal. There is no obvious reason why it should affect prelexical phonological codes in this case, but nevertheless Kleiman (1975) showed that the rather more complex task of repeating back heard digits interfered more with making rhyme judgements than with judging visual similarity or synonymity of words. Since the latter two tasks were affected to the same degree and since visual judgements should not require a phonological code, he concluded that synonymity judgements did not require such a code either.

He also showed that deciding whether phrases made sense was affected by shadowing, suggesting that a phonological code is needed for storing sequences of words. However the results might all be due to the general interfering effects of the shadowing task, rather than simply impaired access to such codes. Moreover there was no guarantee that interference with rhyme judgements was due to an effect on a prelexical phonological code rather than the postlexical one which was presumably used in phrase evaluation. It might be that the synonyms task does involve a prelexical code which is not impaired by shadowing.

In an attempt to establish the effect of suppression on prelexical phonology Baddeley and Lewis (1981) and Baddeley, Eldridge and Lewis (1981) examined its effects on tasks requiring access to the phonology of non-words (homophony and rhyme judgements) and found only slight effects on accuracy and speed. They did, however, like Kleiman, find an effect of suppression on decisions as to whether sentences made sense. Besner et al. (1981) compared the effects of suppression on word and non-word rhyme judgements and on non-word homophony judgements. Suppression slowed performance on words and caused more errors, but had only the latter effect on non-word judgements. (The authors claim that the results for rhyme judgements and homophony judgements differed, but the reported results were similar.) They also found that the effects vanished when a slower rate of articulation was required and argue that general interference is the main cause rather than specifically phonological interference. However it seems equally possible that a slow rate of suppression permits interleaving of the two tasks.

So far it appears that suppression has only minor effects on access to prelexical phonology (non-words) and more effect on access to postlexical phonology (words and phrases). In terms of Figure 1 this suggests an effect on the output logogens. However Wilding and White (in press)found similar interfering effects on rhyme judgements of silent or overt suppression or chewing a peanut, while hearing another voice or tapping a foot had little effect. Though the effects were somewhat smaller for non-words, the differences between the effects on words and non-words were not significant. Since all the words were inconsistently spelled, postlexical articulation and phonology were required and the results suggest that rhyme judgements for words are based on a postlexical articulatory code (or such a code is needed to access phonology).

The finding does not of course prove that words and non-words are processed in the same way (the effects could be on the response buffer in Figure 1) but it does refute any suggestion that suppression enables a distinction to be drawn between postlexical and prelexical phonology, with only the former being vulnerable to suppression. This last suggestion is also refuted by Kimura and Bryant (1983; also Kimura, 1984) who have shown that in Japanese readers suppression interfered with reading syllabic Kana characters for meaning, but not logographic Kanji characters. English children reading words for meaning behaved like Japanese reading Kanji, supporting Kleiman's conclusion that no phonological coding is involved. Visual confusability impaired reading of Kanji and English words.

Adequacy of a two-route model

The evidence discussed so far does not provide striking support for a two-route model for reading English words for meaning, apart from the demonstration of a regularity effect in both delayed pronunciation and lexical decision. However the latter effect has not been obtained consistently and may be explicable in other ways. We now have to decide how well the two-route theories can account for such an effect if it does occur. Henderson (1982) has considered the adequacy of the two-route theories in detail and my discussion is closely related to his.

Relation between the two routes: the regularity effect

A two-route theory could assume that only the visual route normally operates or that it always operates more quickly, which Coltheart et al. (1979) argued from the absence of a spelling regularity effect on lexical decision. The phonological route would only be used for non-words. Words would therefore be read more quickly than non-words and no effect of regularity should occur. The regularity effect in reading aloud is assumed to be due to postlexical effects on, for example, accessing an articulatory code. However, the regularity effect which has subsequently been reported in lexical decision tasks cannot be explained in this way.

Alternatively the phonological route might be the sole or faster route. Problems with this view have been discussed above. We may note also that it predicts frequent mispronunciations of irregularly spelled words when regularization produces another word which is acceptable as a lexical entry (for example BREAD pronounced as BREED).

Since no way of directing inputs to the appropriate route without already knowing the nature of the input is apparent, the remaining possibility is that both routes always operate and vary in speed such that either may be faster on any occasion (Forster and Chambers, 1973). It is usually assumed that the visual route is more often the faster (for example, Coltheart, 1978, p.197), but Henderson (1982) points out that exception words and pseudo-words have similar pronunciation latencies, suggesting there is little difference. The advantage of regular words must therefore be ascribed to access occurring by whichever route operates more quickly on each occasion. This still predicts some mispronunciations of exception words which yield another word when regularized. These occur infrequently, and probably sufficiently infrequently to contradict the theory, and leave it with no way of explaining regularity effects. Data are needed to decide this issue.

Visual-phonological conversion

How does conversion of visual to phonological or articulatory codes occur? Coltheart (1978) has argued that it must work at the level of grapheme-to-phoneme conversion rather than on larger units, but admits that 'the GPC approach is not entirely free from theoretical difficulties' given the extensive variability in letter-sound correspondences. He also admits that 'nonlexical should not be taken to mean that this mechanism makes no use of lexical information when determining pronunciation', but this implies that the prelexical phonological code could not be sufficiently accurate to access the lexicon reliably, before such lexically-based improvements could occur.

Thus there are serious deficiencies in the ability of a two-route theory to provide a coherent account of the processes it assumes. I shall now discuss one-route theories of lexical access before describing some modifications which attempt to provide a compromise between the two-route and one-route approaches.

3. Visual access only to the lexicon

Some compelling evidence against two-route theories of reading aloud was provided by Glushko (1979). He showed that it was not just exception words which were pronounced more slowly, but any words containing spelling which is not always pronounced in the same way (inconsistent words). Thus the existence of the single exception PINT slowed pronunciation of MINT, HINT, etc., compared with consistent words like MILL, HILL etc. Moreover non-words which look like consistent words (LILL, NILL) were pronounced more quickly than non-words which look like inconsistent words (FINT, RINT). Phonologically-based theories assume rules which produce the standard pronunciation and are unaffected by the existence of a few exceptions and non-word pronunciation should be likewise immune. Glushko argued that 'words and pseudo-words are pronounced using ... the pronunciation of words that resemble them'. Thus several visually similar words are activated by an input and consistent words have orthographic neighbours with the same pronunciation, while inconsistent words activate neighbours with conflicting pronunciations (but it is unclear from Glushko's statement how the correct pronunciation could be retrieved in these cases). Non-words require segmentation of components and resynthesis but Glushko is vague about the details. Since the theory ascribes the effects of consistency to conflict over pronunciation, it has problems explaining regularity effects in lexical decision, though Henderson (1982, p.331) points out that regular and irregular words may differ in other ways such as age of acquisition and that a phonological 'echo' from orthographic neighbours may facilitate lexical activation of regularly spelled words and impede that of irregular ones. Neither suggestion is supported by any evidence.

Glushko's findings present a severe problem for two-route theories, as Coltheart (1981) acknowledges, though Glushko's own explanation is not entirely satisfactory and I will consider a development of his approach later. Some comfort for two-route theories is provided by Parkin (1983) who found that the effect of consistency was not reliable and only <u>exception</u> words took longer in pronunciation and lexical decision (which two-route theories claim to explain by the availability of only one route for such words). Glushko's consistency effect may have been due in part to conflict from earlier competing pronunciations in the list (such as PINT preceding HINT). However this would show lexical influence on the phonological route and this has been further demonstrated by Kay and Marcel (1981) and Campbell and Besner (1981), who showed that the pronunciation of non-words is affected by that of preceding words or syntactic context. These effects present major difficulties for any two-route theory which allows only the fixed application of rules to derive phonology from visual input. Once some lexical influence on the process is admitted, the case for a separate route becomes hard to defend.

THE DYSLEXIAS

The final body of evidence to be considered is that from cases of dyslexia due to brain damage in previously competent readers, where specific components of normal reading appear to be missing. These present the strongest evidence for two distinct routes in reading aloud, though we should be cautious in concluding that they illustrate unchanged functioning of part of the normal reading system rather than new strategies to cope with the disability.

A renewed interest in classifying varieties of reading deficit following brain damage stems from Marshall and Newcombe's (1973) pioneering analysis distinguishing two syndromes which they labelled **deep dyslexia** and **surface dyslexia.** The deep dyslexic (see Coltheart et al., 1980) is unable to read (pronounce aloud) non-words, has severe problems with function words, sometimes substituting one for another, and often responds to real words with a word of related meaning (a semantic paralexia). Surface dyslexics (Coltheart et al., 1983; Shallice et al., 1983) can read non-words (not perfectly) and at least shorter regular words but have difficulty with words of irregular spelling and may regularize the pronunciation (BROAD may be pronounced BRODE). Japanese parallels to deep dyslexia have been reported who can read Kanji logographs but not the Kana syllabary and also some examples of the reverse pattern resembling surface dyslexia (Sasanuma, 1980). It should be added that the defects are specific to reading, ability to repeat spoken words being adequate.

A variety of other defects have been reported but I confine myself to only two other patterns which have been reported with any consistency. One is **phonological dyslexia** (Funnell, 1983; Temple and Marshall, 1983), which shows in a purer form the deep dyslexic's ability to read words but not non-words, without the semantic paralexias and sometimes without problems over function words. Finally letter-by-letter reading (Patterson and Kay, 1983) illustrates a method of access to the lexicon which I have not considered as it bears little relation to normal reading. Letters are named one by one and a word derived from these names. Presumably this demonstrates use of pre-logogen codes for individual letters which cannot be combined into a higher order unit, but can activate the lexical code by another route.

At first sight deep dyslexia suggests loss of a phonological route to meaning and pronunciation, producing inability to read non-words and imprecise specifications of real words. However the semantic paralexias imply very imprecise lexical access by the visual route and the existence of phonological dyslexics, who can read most words accurately but not non-words, shows that loss of the phonological route does not necessarily produce imprecise lexical access. Coltheart (1980b) noting the extensive left hemisphere damage in deep dyslexia, suggests that deep dyslexic performance reflects the functioning of a subsidiary right hemisphere reading system which has little direct relevance to normal reading. However Besner (1983) casts some doubt on this suggestion.

Phonological and surface dyslexia seem to be neatly explained by loss of the phonological and visual routes respectively, but a close examination of the errors made suggests some doubts. Also in some cases the reading is very slow, though others show normal speed. Kay and Marcel (1981) point out that phonological dyslexics do often show difficulty in reading function words (and also suffixes) and are better at reading pseudohomophones than other non-words, implying that there is no simple dissociation between words and non-words.

As yet, no 'perfect' case of surface dyslexia has been described, showing perfect reading of non-words and all errors on words due to regularization of pronunciation. Errors usually occur which imply impairment of the assumed phonological route as well as of the visual route, but as Marcel (1980) demonstrates in detail these are often inconsistent with each other in their use of suppose GPC rules and include additions and deletions of letters which no such rules could explain. Coltheart et al. (1983) have described two more cases which reinforce this argument. Different errors in the reported corpus seem to illustrate a variety of types such as visual confusions between letters (DUEL - /diəl /, TROUGH - /θrɒŋ/, pronunciation based on visually similar but phonologically different words (TROUGH - /θrʊ /, THOROUGH - /θərʌf/ BOROUGH /brʌf /) and one patient frequently produced no response at all. Effects of grammatical class, frequency and concreteness have been observed in surface dyslexics and one of these recently described cases read non-words very poorly. None of these observations is consonant with reading solely by a functional GPC route, which would produce regularized mispronunciations.

A more plausible explanation has been offered by Marcel (1980) and a similar one by Shallice and Warrington (1980), who suggest that larger units than graphemes are normally employed in reading non-words. In Marcel's model (Figure 2) these are segmented by visual analysis before accessing a visual input lexicon (equivalent to the logogen system of Figure 1). Shallice and Warrington see these units as available in a store and activated by the input. The largest (highest level) units are assumed to control articulation so that words activate a whole-word pronunciation, while non-words

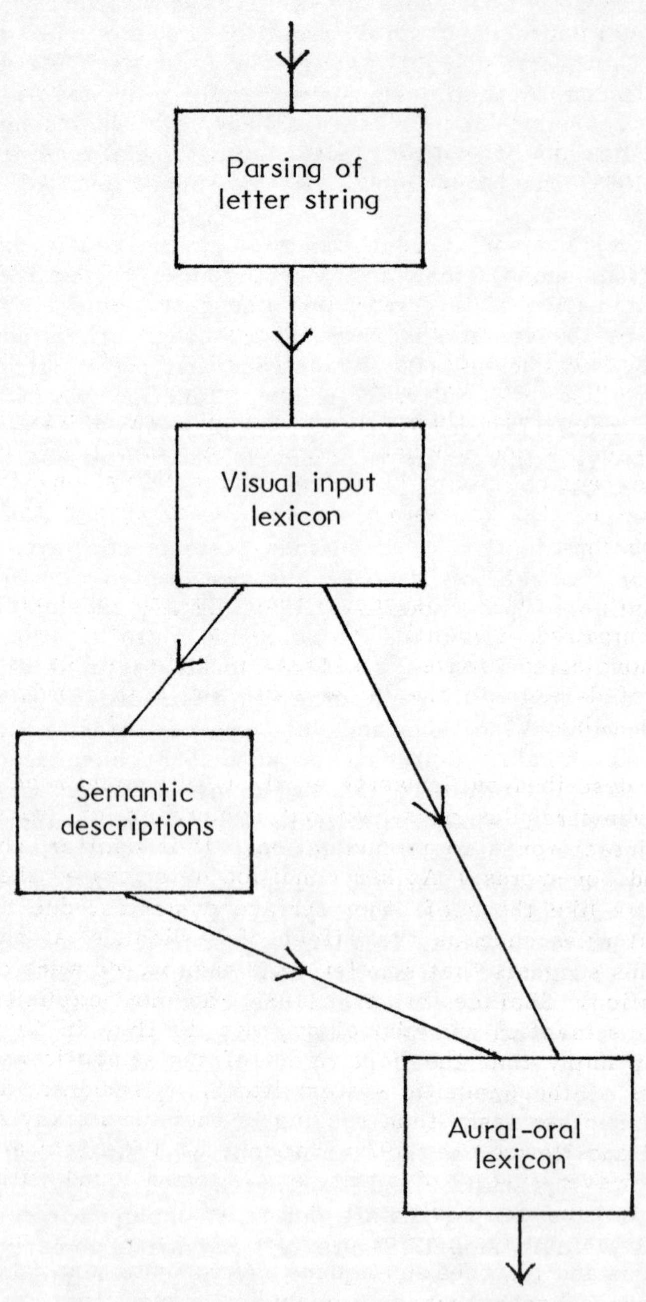

Figure 2. Marcel's model for oral reading. (After Marcel, 1980, Fig. 11.2)

activate parts of known words, which will often lead to mispronunciations due to the lack of constraints from the wider context of the word. Regularity effects are explained by conflict between the pronunciation specified by units of different sizes in the case of inconsistent and exception words, but note that again this only explains regularity effects in pronunciation and not in lexical access. Coltheart (1981) has no strong arguments against these suggestions.

Marcel (Figure 2) envisages two routes to pronunciation: one direct from the visual input lexicon and one passing via a semantic lexicon. No phonological route to the latter is envisaged and Marcel sees his model as an elaboration of Glushko's analogy theory. Shallice and Warrington, on the other hand, see theirs as an extended two-route theory in which whole words either access the lexicon visually and thence articulation, or, like the smaller units, they activate only phonology and articulation. Presumably the lexicon is also accessible via this route though they are not explicit on this.

Shallice et al. (1983) suggest that surface dyslexics have a 'grossly impaired semantic (i.e. visual) route and relatively intact phonological route' but that in different cases different amounts of damage to the latter exist and higher-order units are more vulnerable.

One case described by Schwartz et al. (1980) could read nearly all words, even irregular ones, without comprehension, so seemed to have an intact route to pronunciation. (It is unclear whether she could read non-words.) As her condition deteriorated she began to show errors like those of other surface dyslexics, due to ignoring contextual rules such as the effect of a silent 'e' at the ends of words. This suggests that smaller units than words were controlling pronunciation. Shallice et al. (1983) do not explicitly accept access to semantics via phonology, nor do they in fact need to since they imply that the impairment of the semantic route is due to defects of the semantic system itself, as semantic difficulties appeared in other tasks than reading in their own study and others (Marshall and Newcombe, 1973; Warrington, 1975; Schwartz et al., 1980). However surface dyslexia may also be found without other semantic impairment (Coltheart et al., 1983), and Coltheart (1981) points out that letters may be read out correctly but comprehension is erroneous and matches subsequent mispronunciation. Thus at least some cases suggest that a phonological route to the lexicon is operating.

Nevertheless Shallice and Warrington do have to postulate <u>two</u>

defects in the great majority of cases of surface dyslexia: one to the semantic system or visual route to it and the other some degree of damage to the phonological route. Only the case described by Schwartz et al. seems to have had only the first defect. Marcel's model can explain these facts more economically. Surface dyslexia is due to the loss of orthographic addresses for words in the visual input system, leaving only lower-order units which will activate erroneous pronunciations and sometimes cause false responses in the semantic system. Correct reading of letters with errors of pronunciation and comprehension is explained by the availability of letter identities prior to the processs which segment units in the visual input lexicon, though these are not used to achieve lexical access, and the case described by Schwartz et al. can be explained simply by the malfunctioning semantic system.

What then of phonological dyslexia? Marcel, having pointed out the problems with the two-route explanation mentioned above, suggests that ability to segment an input may be impaired. Several phonological dyslexics read some non-words as visually similar words, which would be explicable if words in the semantic system are activated by visually similar non-words. Funnell (1983) argued against the segmentation explanation because her case, WB, could usually segment spoken words and pronounce parts of them, though with some difficulty. However he was quite unable to pronounce non-words consisting of combined words (such as TUGANT) and did poorly even when told to read only parts of them. This supports Marcel's suggestion and data are needed from other cases.

In conclusion, the clinical evidence offers no great support for the simpler versions of the two-route theories and can be adequately explained by postulating only visual access to the lexicon. However, nearly all the evidence is drawn from studies of reading aloud. Deep dyslexics can discriminate words from non-words fairly reliably. Presumably surface dyslexics categorize items according to whether they pronounce them as words or not. One phonological dyslexic (Patterson, 1982) performed satisfactorily on a lexical decision task. However finer details of performance such as the effects of spelling regularity and frequency on such decisions are as yet unknown.

Developmental dyslexias

The relation between acquired dyslexias due to brain damage in adulthood and developmental dyslexias in the child learning to read is under debate. Developmental cases analogous to both surface and phonological dyslexia have been described and some of the evidence cited above was drawn from such cases (Holmes, 1978; Coltheart et al., 1983; Temple and Marshall, 1983).

Seymour and MacGregor (in press) provide a more systematic attempt to consider causes underlying developmental dyslexia within a more elaborate processing framework than the one I have been using. They argue that learning to read involves overlapping stages of establishing grapheme-phoneme correspondences (alphabetic stage), whole-word discrimination (a logographic lexicon) and units involving combinations of letters (an orthographic lexicon). Weaknesses in different component processes are predicted to have different consequences for reading and separate tests were made of the different components.

Sample cases are described of a phonological dyslexic, assumed to have difficulty in establishing grapheme-sound correspondences, though logographic units could be established; a morphemic (surface) dyslexic, assumed to have difficulty in constructing the holistic logographic units, and a third syndrome exhibiting problems when the visual input was distorted and use of the holistic process was thus impeded, so that the analytic processes were required but functioned inadequately. These analyses have a broad similarity to those I have discussed above, but Seymour and MacGregor suggest that phonological dyslexia is due primarily to an impairment of the phonological processor which would be detectable also in non-reading tasks. Evidence for this suggestion is not available as yet.

CONCLUSIONS

The approach to visual word identification which currently seems most promising requires some adjustments to Figure 1. The processes of visual analysis need to be specified in more detail, including stages of letter analysis and combination of letters into units of various sizes. Whole-word units have a special status (which could be the existence of logogen units or lexical codes) as only they can activate entries in the cognitive or semantic system. However they can also activate articulation via a GPC route, as can non-words and parts of words.

Surface dyslexia is most plausibly attributed to loss of whole-word units and phonological dyslexia to problems in segmenting the input. The additional difficulty with function words and suffixes in the latter syndrome is often ascribed to the nature of lexical organization. It has been suggested that lexical entries may be root morphemes and that suffixes and function words may require phonological processing (see Coltheart, 1981, for a discussion of this view).

REFERENCES

ADAMS, M.J. (1979) Models of word recognition. **Cognitive Psychology, 11,** 133-176

BADDELEY, A.D. and HITCH, G. (1974) Working memory. In: G.H. Bower (ed.) **The Psychology of Learning and Motivation, Vol.8.** New York: Academic Press

BADDELEY, A.D., ELDRIDGE, M. and LEWIS, V.L. (1981) The role of sub-vocalization in reading. **Quarterly Journal of Experimental Psychology, 33A,** 439-454

BADDELEY, A.D. and LEWIS, V.L. (1981) Inner active processes in reading: the inner voice, the inner ear and the inner eye. In: A.M. Lesgold and C.A. Perfetti (eds) **Interactive Processes in Reading.** Hillsdale, NJ: Erlbaum

BARON, J. (1973) Phonemic stage not necessary for reading. **Quarterly Journal of Experimental Psychology, 25,** 241-246

BARON, J. and THURSTON, I. (1973) An analysis of the word superiority effect. **Cognitive Psychology, 4,** 207-228

BAUER, D.W. and STANOVICH, K.E. (1980) Lexical access and the spelling-to-sound regularity effect. **Memory and Cognition, 8,** 424-432

BECKER, C.A. (1979) Semantic context and word frequency effects in visual word recognition. **Journal of Experimental Psychology: Human Perception and Performance, 5,** 252-259

BECKER, C.A. and KILLION, T.H. (1977) Interaction of visual and cognitive effects in word recognition. **Journal of Experimental Psychology: Human Perception and Performance, 3,** 389-401

BESNER, D. (1983) Deep dyslexia and the right hemisphere hypothesis: evidence from the USA and USSR. **Canadian Journal of Psychology, 37,** 565-571

BESNER, D. and SWAN, M. (1982) Models of lexical access in visual word recognition. **Quarterly Journal of Experimental Psychology, 34A,** 313-325

BESNER, D., DAVIES, J. and DANIELS, S. (1981) Reading for meaning: the effects of concurrent articulation. **Quarterly Journal of Experimental Psychology, 33A,** 415-437

BRADLEY, L. and BRYANT, P.E. (1983) Categorizing sounds and learning to read: a causal connection. **Nature, 301, (5899),** 419-421

CAMPBELL, R. and BESNER, D. (1981) This and thap - constraints on the pronunciation of new, written words. **Quarterly Journal of Experimental Psychology, 33A,** 375-396

CLARKE, R. and MORTON, J. (1983) Gross modality facilitation in tachistoscopic word recognition. **Quarterly Journal of Experimental Psychology, 35A,** 79-96

COLTHEART, M. (1978) Lexical access in simple reading tasks. In: G. Underwood (ed.) **Strategies of Information Processing.** London: Academic Press

COLTHEART, M. (1980a) Reading, phonological coding, and deep dyslexia. In: M. Coltheart, K. Patterson and J.C. Marshall (eds) **Deep Dyslexia.** London: Routledge and Kegan Paul

COLTHEART, M. (1980b) Deep dyslexia: a right hemisphere hypothesis. In: M. Coltheart, K. Patterson and J.C. Marshall (eds) **Deep Dyslexia.** London: Routledge and Kegan Paul

COLTHEART, M. (1981) Disorders of reading and their implications for models of normal reading. **Visible Language, 15,** 245-286

COLTHEART, M., BESNER, D., JONASSON, J.T. and DAVELAAR, E. (1979) Phonological coding in the lexical decision task. **Quarterly Journal of Experimental Psychology, 31,** 489-507

COLTHEART, M., MASTERSON, J., BYNG, S., PRIOR, M. and RIDDOCH, J. (1983) Surface dyslexia. **Quarterly Journal of Experimental Psychology, 35A,** 469-495

COLTHEART, M., PATTERSON, K. and MARSHALL, J.C. (1980) **Deep Dyslexia.** London: Routledge and Kegan Paul

DAVELAAR, E., COLTHEART, M., BESNER, D. and JONASSON, J.T. (1978) Phonological recoding and lexical access. **Memory and Cognition, 6,** 391-402

EVETT, L. and HUMPHREYS, G.W. (1981) The use of abstract graphemic information in lexical access. **Quarterly Journal of Experimental Psychology, 33A,** 325-350

FORSTER, K.I. and CHAMBERS, S.M. (1973) Lexical access and naming time. **Journal of Verbal Learning and Verbal Behaviour, 12,** 627-635

FUNNELL, E. (1983) Phonological processes in reading: new evidence from acquired dyslexia. **British Journal of Psychology, 74,** 159-180

GLEITMAN, L.R. and ROZIN, P. (1977) The structure and acquisition of reading I: relations between orthographies and the structure of language. In: A.S. Reber and D.L. Scarborough (eds) **Toward a Psychology of Reading.** Hillsdale, NJ: Erlbaum

GLUSHKO, R.J. (1979) The organization and activation of orthographic knowledge in reading aloud. **Journal of Experimental Psychology: Human Perception and Performance, 5,** 674-691

GOUGH, P.B. and COSKY, M.J. (1977) One second of reading again. In: N.J. Castellan, D.B. Pisoni and G.R. Potts (eds) **Cognitive Theory, Vol.2.** Hillsdale, NJ: Erlbaum

HENDERSON, L. (1982) **Orthography and Word Recognition in Reading.** London: Academic Press

HENDERSON, L. and CHARD, M.J. (1980) The reader's implicit knowledge of orthographic structure. In: U. Frith (ed.) **Cognitive Processes in Spelling.** London: Academic Press

HOLMES, J.M. (1978) Regression and reading breakdown. In: A. Caramazza and E.B. Zurif (eds) **Language Acquisition and Language Breakdown: Parallels and Divergencies.** Baltimore: John Hopkins Press

JOHNSTON, J.C. and McCLELLAND, J.L. (1973) Visual factors in word perception. **Perception and Psychophysics, 14,** 365-370

JOHNSTON, J.C. and McCLELLAND, J.L. (1980) Experimental tests of a hierarchical model of word identification. **Journal of Verbal Learning and Verbal Behaviour, 19,** 503-524

KAY, J. and MARCEL, A.J. (1981) One process, not two, in reading aloud: lexical analogies do the work of non-lexical rules. **Quarterly Journal of Experimental Psychology, 33A,** 397-413

KIMURA, Y. (1984) Concurrent visual interference: its effects on Kana and Kanji. **Quarterly Journal of Experimental Psychology, 36A,** 117-132

KIMURA, Y. and BRYANT, P. (1983) Reading and writing in English and Japanese: a cross cultural study of young children. **British Journal of Developmental Psychology, 1,** 143-154

KLEIMAN, G.M. (1975) Speech recoding in reading. **Journal of Verbal Learning and Verbal Behaviour, 24,** 323-339

McCLELLAND, J.L. (1976) Preliminary letter identification in the perception of words and non-words. **Journal of Experimental Psychology: Human Perception and Performance, 2,** 80-91

McCLELLAND, J.L. and JOHNSTON, J.C. (1977) The role of familiar units in perception of words and non-words. **Perception and Psychophysics, 22,** 249-261

McCLELLAND, J.L. and RUMELHART, D.E. (1981) An interactive activation model of context effects in letter perception: Part 1. An account of basic findings. **Psychological Review, 88,** 375-407

McQUAIDE, D.V. (1981) Variable reliance on phonological information in visual word recognition. **Language and Speech, 24,** 99-109

MARCEL, A.J. (1980) Surface dyslexia and beginning reading. In: M. Coltheart, K. Patterson and J.C. Marshall (eds) **Deep Dyslexia.** London: Routledge and Kegan Paul

MARCEL, A.J. (1983) Conscious and unconscious perception: an approach to the relations between phenomenal experiences and perceptual processes. **Cognitive Psychology, 15,** 238-300

MARSHALL, J.C. and NEWCOMBE, F. (1973) Patterns of paralexia: a psycholinguistic approach. **Journal of Psycholinguistic Research, 2,** 175-199

MARTIN, R.C. (1982) The pseudohomophone effect; the role of visual similarity in non-word decisions. **Quarterly Journal of Experimental Psychology, 34A,** 395-409

MASSARO, D.M. and KLITZKE, D. (1979) The role of lateral masking and orthographic structure in letter and word recognition. **Acta Psychologica, 43,** 413-426

MEYER, D.E. and GUTSCHERA, K. (1975) Orthographic versus phonemic processing of printed words. Paper presented at Psychonomic Society Meeing, Denver, Colorado

MEYER, D.E., SCHWANEVELDT, R.W. and RUDDY, R.G. (1975) Loci of contextual effects on visual word recognition. In: P.M.A. Rabbitt and S. Dornic (eds) **Attention and Performance 5.** London: Academic Press

MORTON, J. (1979) Facilitation on word recognition: experiments causing change in the logogen model. In: P.A. Kolers, M. Wrolstad and H. Bouma (eds) **Processing of Visible Language, 1.** New York: Plenum

MURRELL, G. and MORTON, J. (1974) Word recognition and morphemic structure. **Journal of Experimental Psychology, 102,** 963-968

PARKIN, A.J. (1982) Phonological recoding in lexical decision: effects of spelling-to-sound regularity depend on how regularity is defined. **Memory and Cognition, 10,** 43-53

PARKIN, A.J. (1983) Regularity versus consistency in pronouncing single words: a tale of two theories. Paper presented at Experimental Psychology Meeting, Oxford

PARKIN, A.J. and ELLINGHAM, R. (1983) Phonological recoding in lexical decision: the influence of pseudohomophones. **Language and Speech, 26,** 81-90

PATTERSON, K.E. (1982) The relation between reading and phonological coding: further neuropsychological observations. In: A.W. Ellis (ed.) **Normality and Pathology in Cognitive Functions.** London: Academic Press

PATTERSON, K. and KAY, J. (1983) Letter-by-letter reading: psychological descriptions of a neurological syndrome. **Quarterly Journal of Experimental Psychology, 34A,** 411-441

PURCELL, D.G. and STANOVICH, K.E. (1982) Some boundary conditions for a word superiority effect. **Quarterly Journal of Experimental Psychology, 34A,** 117-134

REICHER, G.M. (1969) Perceptual recognition as a function of meaningfulness of stimulus material. **Journal of Experimental Psychology, 81,** 274-280

RUBINSTEIN, H., LEWIS, S.S. and RUBINSTEIN, M.A. (1971) Evidence for phonemic recoding in visual word recognition. **Journal of Verbal Learning and Verbal Behaviour, 10,** 645-657

SASANUMA, S. (1980) Acquired dyslexia in Japanese: clinical features and underlying mechanisms. In: M. Coltheart, K. Patterson and J.C. Marshall (eds) **Deep Dyslexia.** London: Routledge and Kegan Paul

SCARBOROUGH, D.L., CORTESE, C. and SCARBOROUGH H.S. (1977) Frequency and repetition effects in lexical memory. **Journal of Experimental Psychology: Human Perception and Performance, 3,** 1-17

SCHWARTZ, M.F., SAFFRAN, E.M. and MARIN, O.S.M. (1980) Fractionating the reading process in dementia. In: M. Coltheart, K. Patterson and J.C. Marshall (eds) **Deep Dyslexia.** London: Routledge and Kegan Paul

SEYMOUR, P.H.K. and MacGREGOR C.J. (1984) Developmental dyslexia: a cognitive experimental analysis of phonological, morphemic and visual impairments. **Cognitive Neuropsychology** (in press)

SHALLICE, T. and WARRINGTON, E.K. (1980) Single and multiple component central dyslexic syndromes. In: M. Coltheart, K. Patterson and J.C. Marshall (eds) **Deep Dyslexia.** London: Routledge and Kegan Paul

SHALLICE, T., WARRINGTON, E.K. and McCARTHY, R. (1983) Reading without semantics. **Quarterly Journal of Experimental Psychology, 35A,** 111-138

SMITH, E.E. and SPOEHR, K.T. (1974) The perception of printed English: a theoretical perspective. In: B.H. Kantowitz (ed.) **Human Information Processing: Tutorials in Performance and Cogition.** Potomac Md: Erlbaum

STANNERS, R.F., JASTRZEMBSKI, J.E. and WESTBROOK, A. (1975) Frequency and visual quality in a word-nonword classification task. **Journal of Verbal Learning and Verbal Behaviour, 14,** 259-264

STERNBERG, S. (1969) The discovery of processing stages: extensions of Donders' method. In: W.G. Koster (ed.) **Attention and Performance, 2.** Amsterdam: North Holland

TEMPLE, C.M. and MARSHALL, J.C. (1983) A case study of developmental phonological dyslexia. **British Journal of Psychology, 74,** 517-533

WARRINGTON, E.K. (1975) The selective impairment of semantic memory. **Quarterly Journal of Experimental Psychology, 27,** 635-657

WHEELER, D.D. (1970) Processes in word recognition. **Cognitive Psychology, 1,** 59-85

WILDING, J.M. (1982) **Perception: From Sense to Object.** London: Hutchinson

WILDING, J.M. and WHITE, W. (1985) Impairment of rhyme judgements of words by silent and overt articulatory suppression. **Quarterly Journal of Experimental Psychology** (in press)

DIURNAL RHYTHMS IN COGNITIVE PERFORMANCE

Maureen Marks and Simon Folkard

The presence of a circadian rhythm, that is, consistent, cyclical variations over a period of about 24 hours, in many human physiological processes has been well documented. 'There is hardly a tissue or function that has not been shown to have some 24-hour variation (Aschoff and Wever, 1981 p.311).' Indeed, rhythmicity in general is a ubiquitous characteristic of living systems. In the human it is evident within the single cell, in individual behaviour and at the population level. It occurs across a range of frequencies extending from one cycle per millisecond to a cycle every several years. For example, DNA replication is an oscillatory process and hence the growth and division of single cells follows a periodic time course. There is a 90 to 100 minute cycle in the occurrence of REM sleep (Kleitman, 1963). Ultradian rhythms of this type (that is, those with frequencies of less than a day; see Broughton (1975) for a review) have been demonstrated in many physiological and behavioural processes: for example, renal excretion, heart rate and oral activity. Rhythms with frequencies greater than a day (infradian) include of course the 28-day menstrual cycle. A 21-day rhythm in male testosterone excretion has also been demonstrated (Doehring et al., 1975). For a review of processes which exhibit annual rhythms, for example, suicide, conception and mortality rates, see Aschoff (1981a).

Here we are concerned with the demonstration of diurnal (waking day) rhythms in human cognition. Given the reliability and consistency of the physical circadian system, the question to be addressed in this chapter concerns the existence of consistent variations in cognitive performance during the normal waking day. Does the time at which we carry out a particular cognitive task make a difference to how well we do the task? In short, the answer appears to be a qualified yes. However, before we address this qualification, and in order to do so, we need to examine the theoretical framework informing 'time of day' research.

THEORETICAL FRAMEWORK

Our current understanding of the effects of diurnal rhythms in human performance comes from three main research areas, each with somewhat different aims and theoretical emphases. At one end of the scale we have studies carried out in temporal isolation, at the other 'applied' studies of the effects of abnormal living routines due to, for example, shift-work or time-zone transitions. Laboratory studies lie somewhere in between. The starting point for laboratory research is a theoretical notion of the human cognitive system and then, ideally, a systematic examination of time of day effects on the various components said to contribute to this system. Most laboratory studies have been confined to the 'normal' day (from about 08.00 to 23.00 hours). In these experiments, variations in performance due to endogenous (natural) circadian factors are confounded with those associated with the exogenous masking effects of living on a normal day-oriented routine. From a practical point of view, such a distinction may be relatively unimportant. But it becomes more important when we are trying to determine to what extent the results are indeed due to an underlying circadian factor.

Early research

At the turn of this century a number of investigators were interested in mapping out the pattern over the day of performance variations on a variety of cognitive tasks. These researchers were interested in the applied aspects of their research. What was the best time of day for scheduling school subjects? How did continuous work and its associated fatigue affect the output of workers over the day? There seemed to be little agreement between research findings and the conclusions drawn by these investigators concerning the effects of time of day on the performance of mental work (see Freeman and Hovland, 1934, for a review). One of the main problems encountered when assessing the findings of these early workers is the difficulty in comparing across the wide variety of tasks used as performance measures. Most were tasks which involved a number of cognitive processes. Furthermore, the conclusions cited were based on trends arrived at by averaging across performance on many different tasks. In some cases the individual performance measures showed a pattern over the day which was quite different from the average trend.

These early researchers explained their findings either in terms of increasing fatigue over the day (for example, Laird, 1925) or when their observations suggested increasingly enhanced performance, in terms of a progressive recovery over the day of the brain from the effects of sleep (for example, Gates, 1916a). This latter account was taken up by more recent researchers. A well-documented increase over the day in body temperature was said to be associated with decreasing 'sleepiness' as the day progressed.

The body temperature rhythm

Body temperature shows a consistent 24-hour periodicity, with a peak around 20.00 to 21.00 hours and a trough at 04.00 to 05.00 hours. It is the physiological variable used most often as an indicator of circadian variations in the internal state of a subject. This tends to be so for pragmatic reasons: body temperature is easy to measure. But it is also because there is a remarkable consistency and stability in circadian variations in body temperature. They appear with normal daily activity, during continuous bed rest and during sleep deprivation. Although bed rest and sleep deprivation reduce the range of variation, that is, the amplitude of the daily cycle, the general shape of the trend over the day and the times at which peaks and troughs occur remain the same. (See Aschoff, 1981b, and Aschoff and Wever, 1981, for summaries of experimental findings.) This suggests that temperature rhythms are not due to the normal daily alternation in activity and rest or the result of sleep per se. However, if the sleep-wake cycle is inverted, that is, shifted by 12 hours so that sleep occurs during the day and activity at night, body temperature rhythms may also invert. During rotating shifts, on the other hand, when subjects work for, say, four hours then rest for four hours over the 24-hour day, the temperature rhythm persists, albeit in a flattened form due to decreased day values (Colquhoun, Blake and Edwards, 1968a).

Although it was once thought that the sleep-wake cycle 'entrained' (that is, controlled the phase of) other circadian rhythms, including that of body temperature, the contemporary view is that while the sleep-wake cycle has an influence on the circadian system, it is itself influenced by endogenous rhythms such as the circadian rhythm in body temperature. For example, sleep time and time of waking can be predicted from body temperature. When the rhythms of free-running subjects (subjects isolated from external time-cues) become desynchronized so that the temperature rhythm has a different periodicity from that of the sleep-wake cycle (and hence sleep time is always at a different phase of the temperature cycle) the duration and the onset of sleep are still related to the temperature rhythm. Long sleep times occur when temperature is dropping, short sleep times as temperature increases. Sleep starts some 6 to 7 hours before minimum temperature, the phase of the temperature cycle when synchronized subjects are most likely to sleep (Aschoff, 1981b).

The evidence to date therefore indicates that circadian variations in temperature are related to endogenous factors, despite the fact that exogenous variables such as sleep timing can affect the temperature rhythm. It is against the background of variations over the day in body temperature that circadian variations in human performance have been examined for the last 20 years.

Kleitman (1963) argued that an observed parallelism between body temperature and performance efficiency on a number of tasks throughout the day indicated a causal relationship between circadian variations in temperature and performance. For mental tasks this relationship was said to be due to the possibility that either (a) mental processes are themselves chemical reactions, or (b) an increase in the temperature of cells in the cerebral cortex (in conjunction with a general rise in body temperature) will speed up metabolic activity of these cells and hence the speed of thinking. Kleitman provides a body of empirical evidence of circadian variations in a number of tasks, for example, simple reaction time, hand steadiness and body sway; and evidence of even greater variations over the day in tasks involving mental activity such as card dealing and sorting, code transcription, multiplication and choice reaction time. However, his evidence for a causal relationship between temperature and performance is limited to observations of a correlation between these two variables on only two tasks, that is, reaction time (simple and choice) and colour naming response speed.

The 'sleepiness rhythm'

Colquhoun (1971) agreed that 'diurnal fluctuations in performance (where observed) are in general associated with concomitant variations in body temperature' (p.146). But he was at pains to point out that this does not necessarily indicate a causal relationship between the two. Colquhoun discusses at some length doubts concerning the generality of Kleitman's conclusions, based as they are on data from only six subjects, and the fact that invoking a causal relationship between temperature variations and performance variations ignores certain discrepancies observed in both Kleitman's research and his own, in particular, the 'post-lunch dip' phenomenon. This is a temporary fall in performance efficiency in the early afternoon which is not usually accompanied by a fall in temperature and which has been reported by several researchers (for example, Blake, 1967; Colquhoun, 1971). It should be noted, however, that 'post-lunch dip' is a misnomer. Evidence suggests that this early afternoon dip in performance is unrelated to the ingestion of food. It appears whether or not subjects have eaten lunch (Craig, Baer and Diekmann, 1981). However, as Blake (1971) has suggested, it is possible that the dip is a conditioned response associated with the habit of eating a mid-day meal and will therefore appear even when lunch is missed on occasion, as was the case for the subjects in this latter experiment. Nonetheless, in 'free-running' subjects the periodicity of the dip has been observed to be different from that of meal timing (Wever, 1979), which suggests that the phenomenon may be something more than a conditioned response.

Colquhoun suggests that diurnal performance variations may be explained in terms of changes over the day in 'basal arousal level' or 'sleepiness', such that the 'general level of sleepiness falls (that is, arousal rises) during the waking day to reach a minimum somewhere in the evening' (p.51) and that the post-lunch dip in performance represents a transient drop in arousal. Invoking arousal theory, which relates arousal and efficiency via an inverted U-shaped function (Freeman, 1948), Colquhoun argues that when subjects are sleep deprived (hence under-aroused) the effects of circadian changes in arousal on performance efficiency will be more marked. Thus, Alluisi and Chiles (1967) found that diurnal variations in 'watch-keeping' appeared when subjects had been deprived of sleep for 40 to 44 hours, but not if subjects had slept normally. Unfortunately, Colquhoun's explanation for time of day effects on performance is as unsuccessful as Kleitman's. For example, in attempting to account for the fact that the 'post-lunch dip' in performance is unaccompanied by a similar dip in temperature, Colquhoun suggests, with obvious circularity, that 'we cannot take body temperature as an index of the level of arousal throughout the day <u>except at times when changes in the former happen to coincide with the latter'</u> (p.51, our emphasis). Secondly, in a recent experiment Craig, Baer and Diekmann (1981) report a 12.00 hours (end of session) to 13.00 hours (beginning of session) dip in temperature. Curiously, while this temperature change was positively correlated with changes in detection performance for subjects who had <u>not</u> eaten lunch, it was negatively correlated with performance variation when subjects had consumed a meal between the two test sessions.

There are too a number of other findings which cannot be incorporated in an arousal explanation for time of day effects which rests almost completely on the performance-temperature parallelism. For example, it has been shown that when the effects of circadian rhythms on temperature are controlled for, there is no correlation between choice reaction time and temperature (Rutenfranz, Aschoff and Mann, 1972). Monk (1982) attempted to fit a mathematical model of the arousal/performance relationship to serial search data (Folkard et al., 1976). He reported that two arousal rhythms, with a three-hour phase difference between them, were required to account for the data!

In addition, the phase maps of various other indices of arousal do not show the same pattern over the day as that of temperature. Self-ratings of alertness peak several hours before temperature (for example, Monk et al., 1983) around the time when self-ratings of 'sleepiness' are lowest (Akerstedt and Gillberg, 1981). Adrenalin secretion peaks at 12.00 hours (Klein et al., 1977); catecholamine levels (said to be directly related to alertness) have been shown to peak before noon (for example, Patkai, 1971) and in the afternoon (Akerstedt and Levi, 1978). It is difficult to ignore this sort of evidence, which suggests that if there is a circadian variation in base-level arousal, then the peak in arousal appears to be sometime around mid-day, rather than mid-evening as suggested by temperature measures.

Despite its inadequacy, the unidimensional arousal explanation became the framework for research into time of day effects on cognitive performance. A single underlying process, said to mediate both temperature and performance variations over the day, described as 'basal arousal', was postulated to account for the empirical data. Some extensive research has been carried out to demonstrate that there are similarities between the effects of time of presentation on performance and those of other variables said to affect arousal levels; to show that when time of day is paired with another 'arousal' variable interactions sometimes appear; and to demonstrate circadian variations in various physiological indices of arousal in addition to that of temperature. But it is body temperature which has been used most consistently as an index of arousal, and the concomitant effects on the temperature and behavioural rhythms of various environmental factors which have been cited as evidence for the the notion that temperature and performance rhythms are mediated by the same underlying process.

Eysenck (1982) suggests that perhaps body temperature is an indirect measure of basic metabolic processes rather than arousal (which sounds very like Kleitman's, 1963, explanation of the relationship between temperature and performance rhythms); or alternatively that there are two separate arousal systems - one which is indexed by temperature and peaks in the evening, the other peaking around mid-day, as indicated by the remaining arousal measures. The evidence does not support Eysenck's first suggestion: Miners and Waterhouse (1981) point out that in studies within which changes in metabolic rate are kept to a minimum (for example, constant routine or complete bed rest), the circadian rhythm in body temperature persists and 'the variations in metabolic rate seen in these circumstances are far too small to affect heat gain and thus body temperature by anything like the required amount' (p. 34). Eysenck's second hypothesis is clearly circular, unless one can find some way to separate the two systems which is independent of the physiological indices to which he refers.

TRENDS OVER THE DAY

Most of the more systematic studies carried out have examined the effects of time of day on various aspects of the memory system. The evidence suggests that different components of the information processing system may show different trends over the day such that the observed trend for a given task will reflect the combination of trends for the various cognitive components involved in that task.

Memory load

Memory load is one component which has been shown to affect the trend. Folkard et al. (1976) varied the memory load of a visual search task. This task involves looking for a character or set of characters in sections of prose or alphanumeric characters. One of the more reliable findings in the area is that the speed with which subjects perform this task when only one character is to be detected improves steadily over the day (with a possible post-lunch dip) and peaks mid-evening, at around 20.00 hours as illustrated in Figure 1. However, when the memory load is manipulated by varying the number of characters which must be searched for, it has been shown that the precise trend in performance over the day is a function of load. Thus with a high load (a target of six characters) performance was fastest at midnight, a low load (two targets) fastest at 16.40 and an intermediate load (four targets) fastest at 08.40. In the one character case cited above, the memory load component is minimal and the trend in performance over the day probably reflects processing throughput.

Articulatory loop

A number of studies have examined the effects of time of presentation on the recall of lists of words. The trend in performance on this task appears to be a function of serial position. For words presented early in the list there is an improvement in immediate free recall from 08.00 to mid-morning and then a decrease over the rest of the day (Folkard and Monk, 1979).

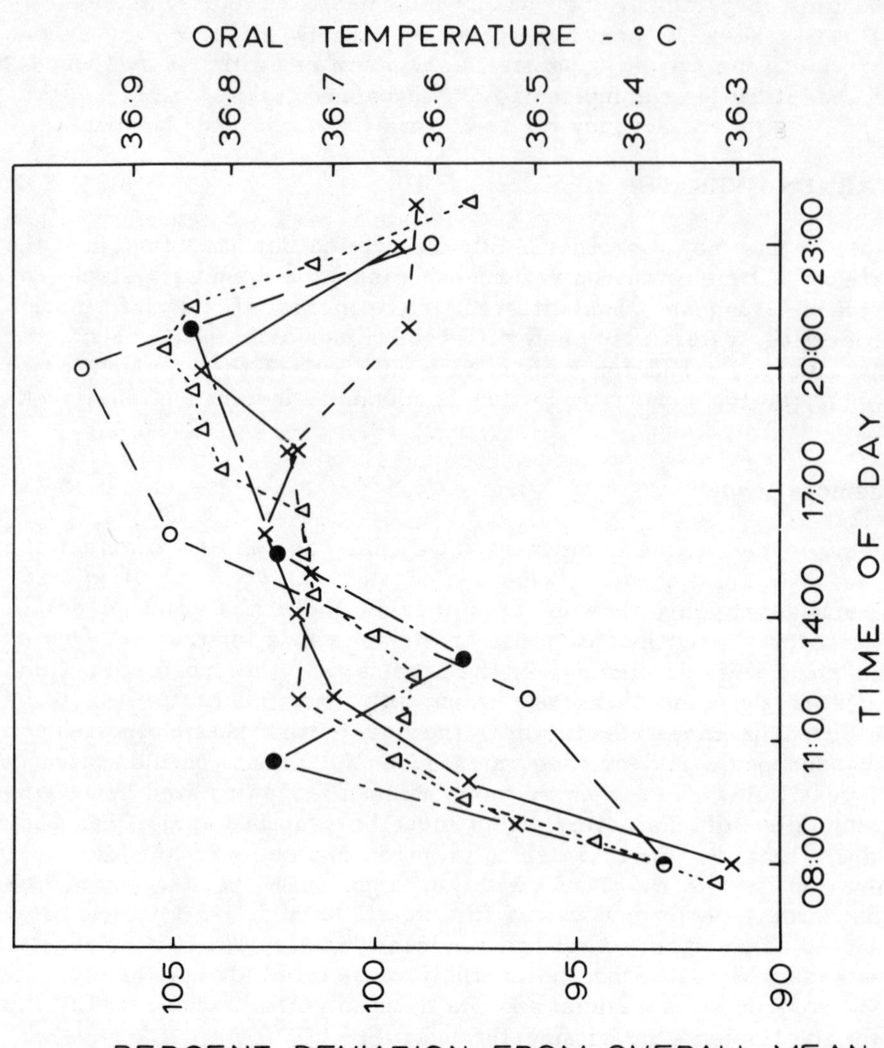

Figure 1. Performance speed on visual search tasks as a function of time of day. Blake (1967) (●- - -●), Fort and Mills (1976) (X——X), Hughs and Folkard (1976) (O— —O), and Klein, Wegmann and Hunt (1972) (X- - - -X). Also shown is the trend for oral temperature after Colquhoun, Blake and Edwards (1968a) (Δ- - -Δ).

This pattern is similar to that observed in digit span experiments (see Figure 2). The memory span, a relatively 'pure' measure of one memory component, improves from early to mid-morning and then declines over the rest of the day (Gates, 1916a; Blake, 1967, 1971). The memory span is said to reflect the use of an articulatory loop component of the memory system (Hitch, 1980). Learning of pre-recency items in word lists, too, has been shown to involve rehearsal (Rundus, 1971). This suggests that the time of day trends described here may reflect a decline over the day in the use of sub-vocal rehearsal. More direct evidence for this hypothesis has been provided by Folkard and Monk (1979). They showed that when subjects are prevented from rehearsing during list presentation (by being forced to count aloud from 1 to 10), immediate recall of pre-recency items is reduced with morning presentation, but not in the afternoon. In addition, Folkard (1979) has shown that acoustic similarity has a detrimental effect on the immediate recall of word lists in the morning (10.00 hours) but not the afternoon (19.00 hours). The converse was the case for the delayed recall of semantically similar words: impairment with afternoon presentation, but not in the morning.

Working memory

In the studies discussed above subjects were required to memorize lists of digits or words presented under external time pressure. In addition, after the items had been presented they were asked to recall as many of them as possible. In the experiments discussed in this section, however, the subject's task involved holding in short-term memory a limited number of items (within the memory span) and manipulating those items in some way. Each set of items was dealt with one at a time so that, unlike the task in the experiments discussed earlier, memory capacity was not continuously overloaded and time pressure was self-imposed. Various studies report time of day effects in the performance of tasks such as these, which are said to involve the concomitant use of short-term storage and other information processing mechanisms: in short, that group of memory mechanisms together referred to as 'working' memory (Baddeley and Hitch, 1974; Hitch, 1980). The trend for arithmetic reasoning has been examined by many researchers. It was a favourite task in some of the studies carried out early this century. While most findings suggest an improvement from early to late morning, the pattern for the rest of the day is less than clear, with some studies reporting a rise (Gates, 1916a; Blake, 1967), others a decline (Laird, 1925). One study has examined verbal reasoning (Folkard, 1975). On two tasks (logical syllogisms and Baddeley's, 1968, A-B reasoning), performance improved until about mid-day and then declined.

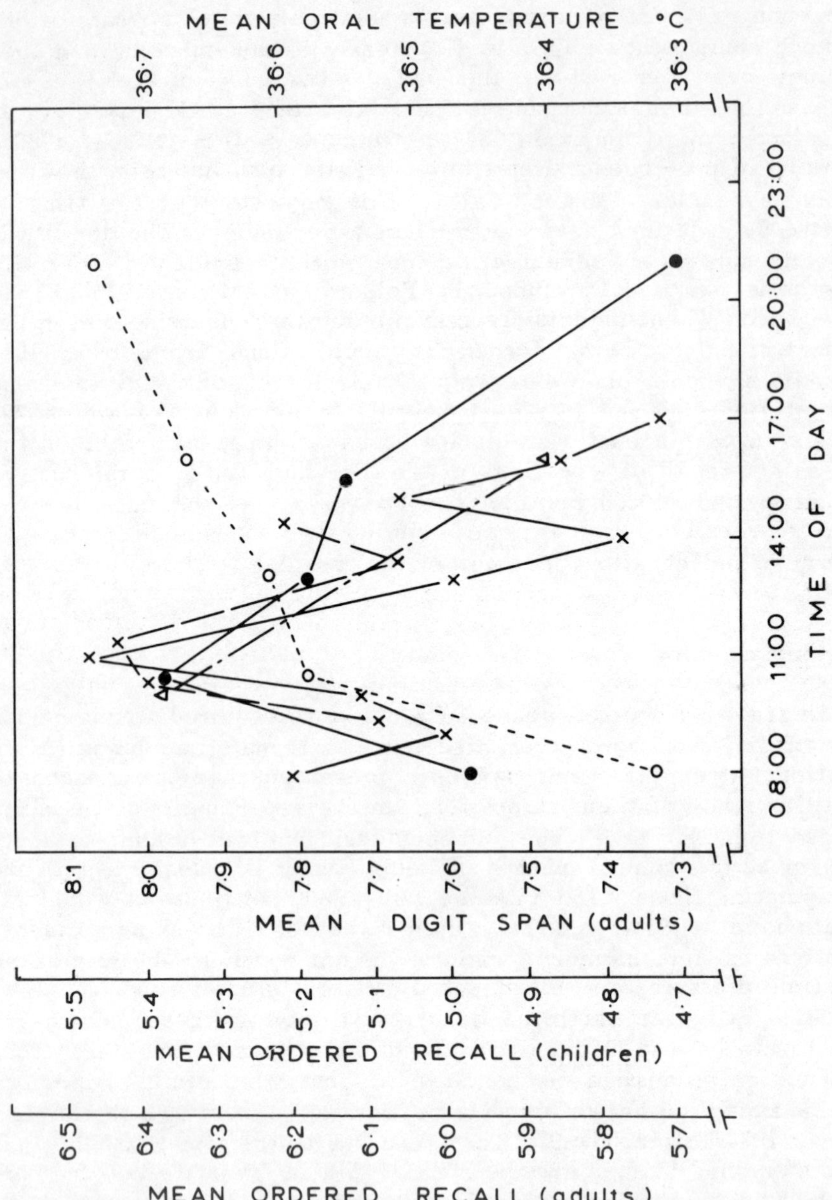

Figure 2. The trend over the day in digit-span/sequence performance. Baddley et al. (1970) (Δ---Δ), Blake (1967) (●——●), Gates (1916a) (×——×), and Gates (1916b) (×— —×). Also shown is the trend for oral temperature after Blake (1971) (○----○).

It is also possible that the trend in performance on tasks such as these may be a function of practice level (Folkard, 1983). In the Blake (1967) study the subjects were highly practised. Results from a study carried out by Colquhoun, Blake and Edwards (1968a) suggest that peak performance on a similar task occurred at a later time of day with practice. Winch (1911) too reports that 'mental work involving reasoning ... appears to be less and less affected by fatigue engendered by the school day as the children rise in age and mental capacity' (p.341). This possible change in trend with practice may be related to a reduction in the effective memory load. As we saw earlier, peak performance times get later as the memory load of a task decreases. It should be noted, too, that this suggests that individual differences in age, intelligence and practice level may well influence the precise trend over the day for any given task.

Immediate memory for realistic material

Bearing in mind that there may be many different cognitive processes involved in carrying out complex 'real world' tasks, performance on such tasks has been shown to vary systematically over the day. A number of researchers have investigated time of day effects on the recall of information from realistic material, including stories, magazine articles, film, lectures and television news programmes.

Two studies have demonstrated that the immediate recall of information from prose passages declines progressively over the day with a trend similar to that observed in digit span experiments (see Figure 3). Laird (1925) tested immediate and delayed (40 minutes) free recall of 'ideas' after subjects had read text 'intentionally to remember'. Subjects were tested seven times (08.00 to 22.00 hours). There was a decrease in immediate recall over the day, except for a slight rise after lunch, to a trough at 20.00. Folkard and Monk (1980, experiment I) report a similar pattern for immediate recall of information 'read for comprehension' during an allowed three minutes. In their experiment subjects read as much as they could of a different 1,500-word 'New Scientist' article six times (08.00 to 23.00 hours). Recall was tested using multiple choice questions. The trend in immediate memory showed a decrease over the day, a post-lunch increment at 14.00 and poorest performance at 20.00.

Additional evidence that immediate memory for realistic events is better in the morning than the afternoon is provided by studies which have tested subjects at two times of the day. Folkard et al.

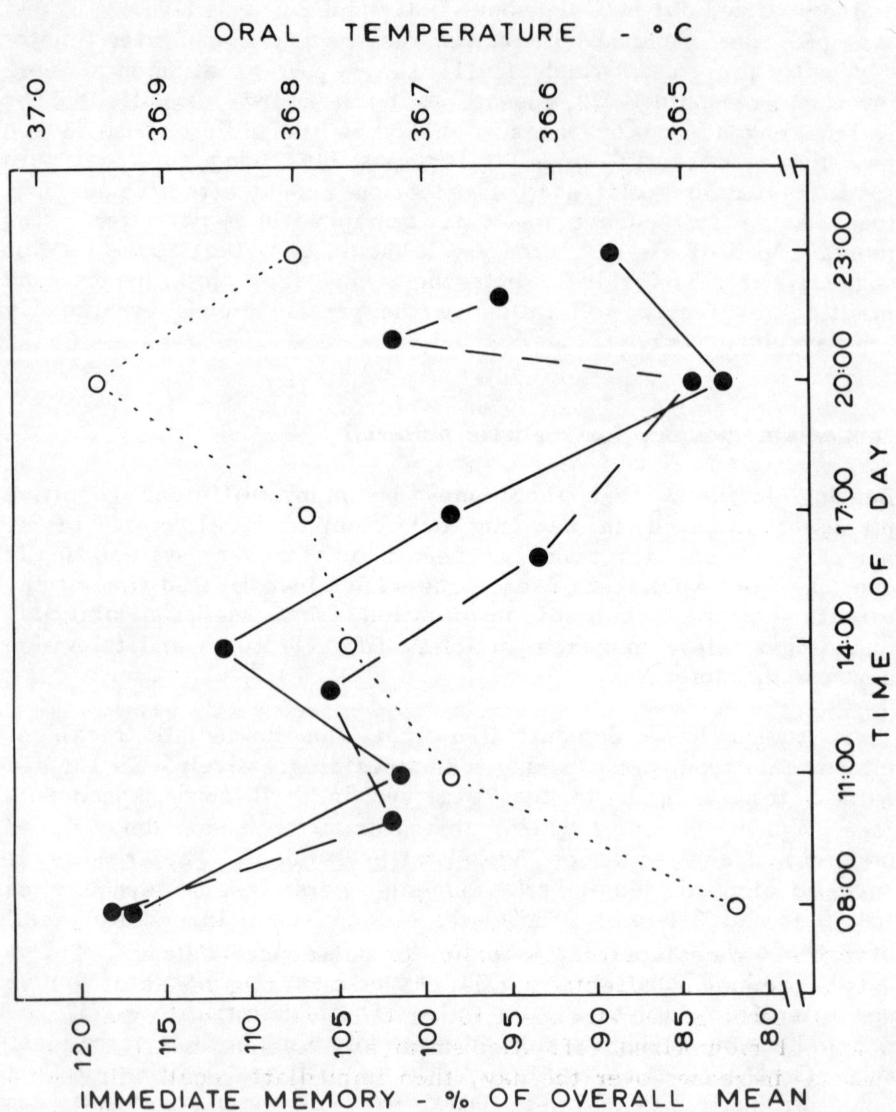

Figure 3. Immediate memory for information presented in prose as a function of time of day. Folkard and Monk (1980) (●——●), Gates (1916a) (×——×), and Laird (1925) (●— —●). Also shown is the trend in oral temperature after Folkard and Monk (1980) (○⋯⋯○).

(1977) read a story to independent groups of schoolchildren at 09.00 and 15.00 hours. Memory was tested using a four-choice multiple choice questionnaire. Subjects were told to 'listen carefully since they would be asked some questions about it'. Morning immediate recall was superior to afternoon performance.

Folkard and Monk (1980, experiment II) presented a ten-minute film to night nurses at 20.30 and 04.00 hours and tested immediate recall using 15 open-ended questions (requiring a single word or short phrase to answer) and five multiple (four) choice questions. There was no effect of time of presentation on immediate recall. However, when 'adjustment' to night work (as indicated by temperature rhythm) was taken into account, for poor adjusters 04.00 hours immediate recall was superior to recall at 20.30 hours, whereas for good adjusters immediate memory was superior at 20.30 hours. In this latter study 'poor adjusters' were those whose circadian rhythms had not become entrained to the late night shift and hence would be less aroused at 04.00 than at 20.30 hours. 'Good adjusters' on the other hand, were those whose rhythms had become entrained to the new sleep-wake cycle of the shift and would therefore be less aroused at 20.30 than at 04.00 hours.

Gunter, Jarrett and Furnham (in press) report a similar trend for the immediate recall of television news information: a decline across the three times of day tested (09.00, 13.00 and 17.00). Two studies have failed to demonstrate time of day effects on the amount of information remembered from lectures (Holloway, 1967; Adam, 1983). There is some evidence, however, that there may be an improvement over the day in our ability to extract the main theme from expository discourse (Adam, 1983).

These results have been attributed to increases over the day in subject arousal. Findings from the general memory and arousal area suggest that increasing arousal appears to be associated with impaired immediate recall, while for subsequent delayed recall it has the opposite effect: that is, with increasing levels of arousal during learning we can expect to see improved delayed recall of the material memorized (cf. Kleinsmith and Kaplan, 1963). Thus, if arousal increases over the day, then immediate recall will decline (as we have seen is often the case), but the trend for later delayed recall will be a progressive improvement.

Delayed recall

Many of the studies cited above have also examined the trend for delayed memory. Hockey et al. (1972) report that the amount forgotten from lists of words after a five-hour delay was greater after morning presentation than evening. Folkard and Monk (1979) tested delayed (20 minutes) free recall of lists presented at 11.00, 14.00, 17.00 and 20.00 hours and reported that the pattern of recall for recency and pre-recency items was a mirror image of that observed in immediate tests. Laird's (1925) study included an examination of the effects of time of presentation on the delayed (40 minutes) recall of ideas from text. However, apart from a steady increase in delayed recall from 08.00 to 13.00 hours, the pattern of recall was similar to that observed in the immediate test.

On the other hand, Folkard et al. (1977), in the study mentioned earlier, reported superior delayed (one week) recall by the 15.00 hours group compared to the 09.00 hours group, as would be predicted by an arousal explanation. The strongest evidence against an arousal explanation for the effects of time of day on delayed memory comes from Folkard and Monk's (1980) night nurse study. In this study, delayed (28 day) recall of information presented in a film was higher following presentation at 20.30 than at 04.00 hours, independent of level of adjustment, that is, independent of subject arousal.

Finally, in an unpublished study by Monk et al. (1980), subjects read 1,500-word 'New Scientist' articles for a timed 10 minutes at six times (08.00 to 23.00 hours). Recall was tested after a delay of one week, using multiple choice questionnaires. Between 11.00 and 23.00 hours, the pattern of performance paralleled that observed for temperature, as one would predict in arousal theory terms. However, recall was best at 08.00 hours (and followed by a sharp drop in performance at 11.00 hours). This superiority of delayed recall at a time when arousal due to time of day is said to be low is inconsistent with the arousal model, and may have been related to slower reading rates at this time, or alternatively, due to the fact that the 08.00 hours session, unlike other sessions, is separated from testing times by a night of sleep.

Retrieval

One other aspect of the memory process which has been ignored so far is that of retrieval. The design of the studies of Folkard et al. (1977), Folkard and Monk (1980) and Adam (1983) was such that time of retrieval effects in delayed retention could be separated from those of time of presentation. In none of these studies was any evidence obtained for a main effect of time of retrieval. Adam (1983), however, reports a small state-dependent effect. In this study for early morning test times, retrieval of information from text was better at the same time as the original presentation. This however could well have been a context-dependent effect and not due to the time of day factor, since the early morning test session was for many subjects an unusual hour for them to be 'up and working'. Neither of the two other studies mentioned found state-dependent effects.

There is some evidence of an effect of time of retrieval on category instance recognition. This task, which may be more sensitive to fine differences in retrieval, requires that subjects recognize dominant (for example, 'apple') or non-dominant (for example 'mango') instances of a category ('fruit'). Performance speed on this task has been found to improve over most of the normal day (Millar, Styles and Wastell, 1980; Tilley and Warren, 1983), and to decrease over the night to reach a minimum at about 04.00 hours (Tilley and Warren, 1984). Further, these latter studies have found the effect of dominance on recognition latency to reduce over the day, and to increase subsequently over the night to reach a maximum at about 04.00 hours. This effect of dominance has been argued to reflect changes in retrieval efficiency over the day, such that retrieval is most efficient in the evening.

Strategy changes

More recent attempts to account for the effects of time of day on cognitive performance have invoked the notion of variations over the day in the way material is encoded. Evidence that subvocal rehearsal may decline concomitant with an increasing reliance on semantic processing over the day came from word recall experiments detailed earlier. Additional evidence is provided by studies involving the recall of more realistic material, especially those which examine both immediate and delayed recall.

Folkard (1980) re-analysed data from a study cited earlier (Folkard et al., 1977), in which childrens' immediate recall of information presented in a story was higher in the morning than the afternoon, but after a week's delay recall by the afternoon group was better than the morning group. He found that the superior immediate recall of the morning group was due to better recall of unimportant information and that over the week between presentation and the second recall test, morning subjects forgot more unimportant information. Folkard suggested that the results are consistent with the view that arousal (that is, afternoon performance) 'biases attention to more dominant or important information' (p.96); hence the effect of importance on afternoon immediate recall, but not on morning recall. He further argued that the greater forgetting of unimportant information by the morning group may be attributable to the type of processing that morning subjects rely on, viz., 'maintenance processing that takes no account of the meaning of information'.

In a series of experiments which examined the effects of time of presentation on immediate and delayed recall of information from lectures and expository text, Adam (1983) showed that there is an improvement over the day in delayed recall of important compared to unimportant information from text. This effect appeared to be related to an improvement with time of day in the ability to construct a representation of text which incorporates the text's hierarchical structure.

There is additional evidence from studies involving tasks of little or no memory load that time of day effects may be related to strategy changes. Craig, Wilkinson and Colquhoun (1981) examined five vigilance studies to find that changes over the day in discrimination efficiency (d') were negligible. Instead, the trend appeared to be one of increasing riskiness. Thus, for example Craig (1979) reports that while there was no effect of time of day (08.00 and 20.00 hours) on performance of a binary discrimination task, responses were more confident at the later time. This finding was substantiated in a later study (Craig and Condon, in press) which examined discrimination at six times of day (08.00 to 23.00 hours). Speed (a measure of 'inspection time') and confidence ('certain' reports) increased over the day while detectability (d') declined. There was no criterion shift with time of day. The authors suggest that time of day effects on performance might reflect changes in attitude or approach to the task from one of conservatism towards one of risk: performance got faster, decisions more confident and yet actual efficiency declined.

Monk and Leng (1982) have also argued that strategy changes over the day account for their data. On a task with a large motor component (card sorting) tested at six times (08.00 to 23.00 hours), while 'actual' performance increased to 11.00 hours and then declined, 'subjective' performance (ratings by subjects as to how well they thought they performed) peaked at about 17.00 hours. That is, from about 11.00 hours, when actual performance peaked, subjects thought they were getting better at the task where in fact actual performance was declining.

Thus, while in general speed in performance on such tasks as simple serial search or signal detection may indeed improve over most of the day, parallel with the trend for temperature, this improvement in speed may represent a progressive shift in the speed-accuracy trade-off. Secondly, it is possible that the heterogeneity in trends over the day observed for various repetitive tasks with low information processing load but high sensory or motor components (for example, manual dexterity, choice reaction time, tapping; see Monk and Leng, 1982, for a review) is the outcome of different effects of such strategy changes over the day on different types of task. However, we first need to disentangle the various cognitive and motor components which must contribute to the performance of tasks such as these, as is beginning to be done in the memory area, before we can even start to understand how time of day related strategy changes might affect the overall trend for any given task.

INDIVIDUAL DIFFERENCES

It was mentioned earlier that inter-individual differences may affect the diurnal trend in performance. There is some evidence for personality and age related differences.

Morning and evening types

The most substantial contributor to personality differences appears to be diurnal type, as measured by, for example, the Horne and Ostberg (1976) 'Morningness-Eveningness Questionnaire'. Extreme morning-types are characteristically tired in the evening, go to bed early and wake in the morning feeling alert. Evening types conversely perform best in the evening, go to bed late and feel tired on waking. These differences may be due to a phase advance of the circadian system. Morning-types peak up to some two or more hours earlier than evening-types on a number of variables, for example, temperature, alertness ratings and catecholamine excretion (see Kerkhof (in press) for a review). The size of the phase difference tends to be greater when the measures concerned are psychological rather than physiological. These phase differences in arousal measures are reflected in performance data. For example, on a choice reaction time morning-types are better than evening-types in the morning but evening-types better than morning-types in the evening (Patkai, 1970).

Extraversion-Introversion

The 'Extraversion-Introversion' factor is also said to be associated wth diurnal differences. Extraverts are thought to be less aroused than Introverts (Eysenck, 1967). The combination of the two sources of arousal (time of day and this personality factor) was seen to contribute to possible differences in the overt diurnal trend on a number of measures for introverts and extraverts. Thus, for example Colquhoun (1960) and Blake (1971) have demonstrated different patterns of performance at different time of day as a function of the 'Introversion-Extraversion'. It was thought that there may be a phase difference of about two hours in temperature function. The introvert temperature rhythm was said to be phase advanced with respect to that of extraverts resulting in higher early day temperatures, an earlier peak and a subsequent earlier drop (Blake, 1971). The pattern of performance for introverts was said to reflect this phase advance in temperature rhythm. Thus, for example, detection of changes in visual stimuli was shown to be positively correlated with introversion in the morning but negatively correlated with introversion in the afternoon (Colquhoun, 1960), and letter detection positively correlated with introversion at 08.00 but negatively at 21.00 hours (Blake, 1971).

While these findings could indeed be explained in arousal theory terms, the more recent suggestion that the differences may be attributable to the impulsivity component of the extraversion dimension (Revelle et al., 1980) complicates the picture. These researchers examined performance on a number of cognitive tasks (analogies, antonyms, sentence completion, abstract reasoning) as a function of time of day and the two sub-components (sociability and impulsivity) said to make up the 'Introversion-Extraversion' factor. High impulsives performed worse than low impulsives in the morning (09.00 hours) but better than low impulsives in the evening (19.00 hours).

Kerkhof (in press) suggests that differences in sleep-wake behaviour may be the determining factor, rather than a phase difference in an underlying circadian arousal rhythm. As he points out, bed-times are influenced not only by endogenous clock mechanisms but also psychosocial influences. Thus, there may be differences between extraverts and introverts in such factors as length of sleep and regularity of sleep, possibly attributable to social influences, which are likely to have masking effects on the overt rhythms.

Age

Age differences have also been observed. At birth there is no sleep-wake rhythm. How soon one appears depends on the extent to which the baby is exposed to external time cues. Palmer (1976) cites a study of one infant who was allowed to determine its own sleep-wake schedule. At about the fourth week a 25-hour period appeared (similar to the free-running period of temporally isolated subjects). By about the eighteenth week the sleep-wake cycle was entrained to the 'normal' 24 hours.

As middle age is reached the circadian system appears to become less synchronized, possibly because the coupling between rhythms becomes weakened (Wever, 1979). In temporal isolation the temperature and sleep-wake cycles of older subjects are more likely to become desynchronized (Wever, 1979). In addition rhythm amplitudes tend to decrease with increasing age. Older subjects are more likely to lie along the morningness end of the diurnal type dimension (Akerstedt and Torsvall, 1981). As Kerkhof (in press) has pointed out, this may be related to a phase advance in the temperature rhythm of older subjects with respect to the sleep-wake cycle and to external 'Zeitgeber'.

The effect of these age related changes on performance rhythms has yet to be determined, although some shift-work studies have found that there is a decreasing tolerance of shift-work with age.

Sex

As with age, there is some evidence for sex differences in the circadian system but little evidence to suggest that these differences will be reflected in cognitive performance. The free running rhythms of temporarily isolated females are on average some 28 minutes shorter than those of males (Wever, 1983.) The difference appears to be related to the activity rhythm: when the sleep-wake cycle of females becomes desynchronized (see later discussion) it is more likely to become so by shortening than that of males (Wever, in press). There have been some attempts to demonstrate sex differences in cognitive performance over the day but any differences which have been reported tend to be those involving some other factor as well as the time of day variable (for example, Loeb, Holding and Baker, 1982).

CHANGES TO THE DAILY ROUTINE

What happens to cognitive performance when the circadian system has to adjust to changes in the normal living routine? There has been some extensive applied research into this question, which has involved investigating the effects of, for example, changes associated with shift-work or rapid time-zone transitions. One focus of these studies has been the rate of adjustment of various parameters to phase shifts, another the direction of adjustment. That is, if an individual's living routine is inverted so that work takes place at night and sleep during the day; or if (because of a time-zone transition) the (external) clock is moved on (the phase is delayed) or moved back (the phase is advanced), how long does it take for the rhythm of a particular variable to adjust to this change, and hence show a normal pattern of variation across the new activity routine? Secondly, was the adjustment made by a 'stretching out', or lengthening, of the rhythm's 'normal' period (phase delay) or by a shortening (phase advance)? Findings from this type of research have obvious practical implications. We have a better idea now of which of the various possible types of shift system is less likely to disrupt the circadian system and which types of task are most likely to be affected by routine changes. We know too that moving forward through shifts (for example, morning-evening-night) or westwards through time-zones is more likely to be adjusted to quickly than if the shifts are moved back (for example, morning-night-evening) or flights are eastward (see Monk and Folkard, 1983, for a review).

In addition, by allowing the identification of groups of variables which are affected by phase changes in a similar way, studies such as these may give us some understanding of the mechanisms which might underlie the normal synchronized circadian system. It was once thought that phase adjustment of the temperature and performance rhythms took place at the same rate (for example, Colquhoun, Blake and Edwards, 1968a,b). This observation was used as evidence for the arousal-performance link said to mediate circadian variations in performance. However, these studies used relatively simple tasks. More recent studies have shown that the adjustment of the performance rhythm for more complex tasks can occur at a quite different rate from that of temperature. Furthermore, the rate of adjustment for a particular task may be a function of the memory load involved: tasks with a high memory load appear to adjust more rapidly than those which have a minimal load. Thus, for example, Hughes and Folkard (1976) report that performance on verbal reasoning and double digit addition (said to be 'working memory' tasks) showed greater adjustments, after 10 days, to an eight-hour shift in the sleep-wake cycle, than performance on a visual search or manual dexterity task. Similarly Monk et al. (1978) showed that performance on the high memory load version of a visual search task adjusted more quickly to changes in the sleep-wake cycle than did performance on the low-load version of the task. Folkard and Monk (1982) re-examined data from a rapid time-zone transition study by Klein, Wegmann and Hunt (1972). They showed that working memory performance (additions) adjusted more rapidly to the phase change than either temperature or immediate processing (symbol cancellation).

The implications of findings such as these for the arousal explanation of time of day effects on performance are clear: the unidimensional model which rests on a link between performance and temperature cannot account for the differing effects of phase changes on the phase adjustment of the performance rhythms of different types of task. Folkard and Monk (1982) conclude that perhaps the circadian rhythm in arousal mediates only some performance rhythms; for example, those on tasks which largely consist of immediate processing, and that another mechanism may be responsible for circadian rhythms in short-term, immediate and working memory.

TEMPORAL ISOLATION

Additional support for the idea that more than one underlying process must control circadian rhythms in cognitive peformance comes from temporal isolation studies. These studies are mainly concerned with locating and describing the so-called 'clock' or 'clocks' said to control the circadian system. Two related theoretical questions underpin this line of research. Firstly, to what extent is any given overt rhythm determined by factors external to the organism (for example, the alternation of light and dark) and to what extent is the rhythm endogenously controlled, either by some other internal rhythm or by a superordinate 'biological clock'? Secondly, given the existence of a multiplicity of rhythms with their different phases, what is the mechanism whereby these rhythms are synchronized? One method of investigating these questions has involved placing subjects in temporal isolátion, such that the influence of all external time cues ('Zeitgeber') is eliminated, and observing the subsequent course of various rhythms when they are allowed to 'free-run' or when they are influenced by experimentally provided time cues with a periodicity different from the normal 24-hour day.

Most of the more recent studies of this type have been carried out by Wever, Aschoff and their associates in Munich (see Wever, 1979, 1982; Aschoff and Wever, 1981) and Moore-Ede and his colleagues in the USA (see Moore-Ede, Sulzman and Fuller, 1982). These studies have shown that when there are no external time cues, and rhythms are left free to adopt their own periodicity, they usually remain synchronized to one another at a periodicity slightly longer than that observed in nychthermal (normal day) subjects. Sometimes, however, the rhythms become desynchronized and the rhythms of two or more variables adopt widely different periodicities. For example, the sleep-wake cycle might follow a period of 30 hours while the temperature rhythm continues to run at 25 hours. When such internal desynchronization occurs, performance rhythms can adopt the period of either the activity (sleep-wake) rhythm or of temperature. However, if the isolated subjects are exposed to a strong 'Zeitgeber' (for example, periodic absolute darkness signalled by a gong) the period of which is changed continuously, for example, lengthened or shortened progressively, by, say, four hours over several weeks, then various functions will separate out at different periodicities. This phenomenon appears to be due to the fact that different rhythms have different ranges of 'entrainment'. Any rhythm is able to adjust to a period which is different from that which would be followed if the rhythm was completely unaffected by all external factors, either from the environment or from some other internal variable. However, the range of periodicities which any particular rhythm can adopt is different for different functions. The 'range of entrainment' for temperature appears to be about 22.3 to 26.9 hours (Wever, 1982). The sleep-wake cycle on the other hand can adopt a much wider range. Thus, when the artificial 'Zeitgeber' is progressively lengthened or shortened, various functions split off as the limit to their range of entrainment is reached, and continue to run at a periodicity within this range which may be different from that of the artificial 'Zeitgeber' and different from those of various other functions which have split off at earlier or later stages.

On the basis of evidence such as this Wever (1979) proposed that there may be two, or possibly more than two 'clocks' or oscillators controlling the circadian system. One he associates with temperature variations, the other with the sleep-wake cycle. Any particular overt rhythm may be controlled to some extent by both oscillators, but in general the effect of one of the oscillators would dominate.

Temporal isolation research has gone a long way towards elucidating the nature of the circadian system, but until recently such research has focused on physiological rather than behavioural variations. Comparable studies are now being run in which the response of performance rhythms during desynchronizing conditions is being monitored. Early findings from these studies suggest that at least two oscillators are also required to account for the cognitive data.

Folkard and Monk (1982) examined the response of the circadian rhythms in high and low load memory performance during temporal isolation when the normal eight-hour daily sleep was replaced with an unusual sleep schedule of four hours a night and four further hours at different times of what would have been the waking day. With this sleep disruption the two performance rhythms became desynchronized: the low memory load rhythm adopted a period of 24.6 hours while the high memory load followed a period of 22.7 hours. These authors also point out that the results from another study (Froberg, 1979) show a similar pattern of dissociation between immediate processing and memory loaded tasks. In this latter study, 15 subjects were sleep deprived for 72 hours, without knowledge of the clock time. Performance on a coding task adopted a period of 25.2 hours while performance on a digit span task followed 20.6 hours.

A similar finding is reported by Folkard, Wever and Wildgruber (1983). Under conditions of induced desynchronization, in all seven subjects symbol cancellation performance followed the temperature rhythm but in three of them verbal reasoning separated from both the temperature and sleep-wake cycle to adopt a period of about 21 hours. In addition, in two subjects given low and high memory load versions of a serial search task, rhythms separated out such that the low load version followed the temperature rhythm, the high memory load task a period of, again, approximately 21 hours. Monk et al. (1983) induced desynchronization in a temporally isolated subject such that the temperature rhythm was following a period of 24.8 hours within an imposed activity rhythm of 25.8 hours. The performance rhythm of a manual dexterity task (putting pegs into a pegboard) appeared to be influenced solely by the temperature rhythm. The pattern for performance on a verbal reasoning task was less clear. Best performance on the manual dexterity task occurred when temperature was highest, best performance on the reasoning task soon after waking.

While the use of techniques such as these in the search for cognitive 'clocks' is at an early stage, the findings obtained so far provide further evidence for the notion that more than one 'clock' must be responsible for circadian rhythms in cognitive performance. For obvious reasons, however, it is not possible to measure cognitive performance while subjects are asleep. And even during the waking day, it is difficult to obtain continuous measures of cognitive activity. This means that while many studies have reported significant variations in performance at different times of the day, few have sampled performance at close enough intervals to provide the sort of data required to map out the rhythm in performance or give any precise estimate of such parameters as the rhythm amplitude or the timing of its peaks and troughs.

CONCLUSION

The search for daily rhythms in cognitive performance has been continuing since the nineteenth century. Today we are only just beginning to understand the mechanisms which might be responsible for these rhythms. It is clear that a postulated circadian variation in arousal cannot alone account for the trends observed. A second possible mediating factor, one which has been given little attention by recent researchers, is a reduction over the day in motivation or effort expenditure due to increasing fatigue. Thus while there may indeed be a speeding up of some processes, associated with arousal increases, this may be sometimes offset by concomitant decreases in the amount of effort subjects are prepared to invest in the task. This suggests that there will be an increase in performance efficiency over the day on automatic tasks which require little or no effort to execute (cf. Posner and Snyder, 1975; Shiffrin and Schneider, 1977) whereas performance will decline over the day on tasks which are effortful. Hartley and Shirley (1976) showed that interference on a colour-name Stroop task increased over most of the day to peak at 20.00. As Posner and Snyder (1975) have pointed out, interference on a Stroop task is due to the unconscious activation of automatic processes. There is some evidence for diurnal variation in effort expenditure. Time of day effects on performance are reduced if subjects are told to try harder (Chiles, Alluisi, Adams, 1968) or each subject's score announced to the whole group after each test session (Blake, 1971). Breen-Lewis and Wilding (1984) varied test-expectations at two times of the day. Subjects were told to expect either a recall or recognition test before learning lists of words and then given a recall test. (Recall instructions are said to be associated with more active encoding strategies than recognition instructions). Test expectation had no effect in the morning, perhaps because in the morning subjects were trying hard anyway, whereas in the afternoon 'recall' instructed subjects remembered more than the recognition group. Finally, the extent to which a process is automatic is seen to be inversely related to stimulus load (see Hasher and Zacks, 1979). It is possible that the effects of memory load on performance rhythms observed in both diurnal and desynchronization studies discussed above may be related to the extent to which the task is automatic or effortful, rather than memory load per se. Future research in the area is required to decide this question.

Recent findings from the applied area, particularly studies of the effects of abnormal living routines, and from temporal isolation studies in which desynchronization of the circadian system has occurred, all suggest that at least two and possibly more cognitive 'clocks' are required to account for the data. The current view (for example, Folkard and Monk, 1982; Folkard, Wever and Wildgruber, 1983) is that one of these clocks or oscillators may be responsible for the circadian variation in some immediate processing tasks. Because of its association with the temperature rhythm, this oscillator is seen to be relatively resistant to external influences, and to have a 'natural' period of slightly more than 24 hours. It may be responsible, too, for circadian variations in arousal. A second oscillator, which is somewhat labile, relatively easily influenced by exogenous variables, and with a natural periodicity of about 21 hours, is required to account for the immediate and working memory data.

In general, the research findings suggest that performance on a number of different cognitive tasks varies over the day. However, the observed trend for a particular task appears to be the result of a combination of many different rhythms reflecting the various cognitive functions which contribute to overt performance. Current research efforts are being directed towards describing how these different components of the human information processing system may change over the day. The effect of possible diurnal variations in 'higher level' aspects of the system, for example, the motivational and decision-making processes, is also yet to be determined.

REFERENCES

ADAM, M.N. (1983) Time of day effects in memory for text. DPhil thesis, University of Sussex

AKERSTEDT, T. and GILLBERG, M. (1981) The circadian pattern of unrestricted sleep and its relation to body temperature, hormones and alertness. In: L.C. Johnson, D.I. Tepas, W.P. Colquhoun and M.J. Colligan (eds) **The Twenty-Four Hour Workday: Proceedings of a Symposium on Variables in Work-Sleep Schedules.** Cincinatti, Ohio: NIOSH

AKERSTEDT, T. and LEVI, L. (1978) Circadian rhythms in the secretion of cortisol, adrenalin and noradrenalin. **European Journal of Clinical Investigation, 8,** 57-58

AKERSTEDT, T. and TORSVALL, L. (1981) Shift work. Shift-dependent well-being and individual differences. **Ergonomics, 24,** 265-273

ALLUISI, E.A. and CHILES, W.D. (1967) Sustained performance, work-rest scheduling and diurnal rhythms in man. **Acta Psychologica, 27,** 436-442

ASCHOFF, J. (1981a) Annual rhythms of man. In: J. Aschoff (ed.) **Handook of Behavioural Neurobiology, Volume 4: Biological Rhythms.** New York/London: Plenum Press

ASCHOFF, J. (1981b) Circadian rhythms: interference with and dependence on work-rest schedules. In: L.C. Johnson, D.I. Tepas, W.P. Colquhoun and M.J. Colligan (eds) **The Twenty-Four Hour Workday: Proceedings of a Symposium on Variables in Work-Sleep Schedules.** Cincinatti, Ohio: NIOSH

ASCHOFF, J. and WEVER, R. (1981) The circadian system in man. In: J. Aschoff (ed.) **Handbook of Behavioural Neurobiology, Volume 4: Biological Rhythms.** New York: Plenum Press

BADDELEY, A.D. (1968) A 3-min. reasoning test based on grammatical transformation. **Psychonomic Science, 10,** 341-342

BADDLELEY, A.D., HATTER, J.E, SCOTT, D. and SNASHALL, A. (1970) Memory and time of day. **Quarterly Journal of Experimental Psychology, 22,** 605-609

BADDELEY, A.D. and HITCH, G.J. (1974) Working memory. In: G. Bower (ed.) **The Psychology of Learning and Motivation: Advances in Research and Theory, Volume 8.** New York: Academic Press

BLAKE, M.J.F. (1967) Time of day effects on performance in a range of tasks. **Psychonomic Science, 9,** 349-350

BLAKE, M.J.F. (1971) Temperament and time of day. In: W.P. Colquhoun (ed.) **Biological Rhythms and Human Performance.** London: Academic Press

BREEN-LEWIS, K. and WILDING, J. (1984) Noise, time of day and test expectations in recall and recognition. **British Journal of Psychology, 75,** 51-63

BROUGHTON, R. (1975) Biorhythmic variations in consciousness and psychological functions. **Canadian Psychological Review, 16,** 217-239

CHILES, W.D., ALLUISI, E.A. and ADAMS, O. (1968) Work schedules and performance during confinement. **Human Factors, 10,** 143-196

COLQUHOUN, W.P. (1960) Temperament, inspection efficiency, and time of day. **Ergonomics, 3,** 377

COLQUHOUN, W.P. (1971) Circadian variations in mental efficiency. In: W.P. Colquhoun (ed.) **Biological Rhythms and Human Performance.** London: Academic Press

COLQUHOUN, W.P., BLAKE, M.J.F. and EDWARDS, R.S. (1968a) Experimental studies of shiftwork. 1: a comparison of rotating and stabilized 4-hour shift systems. **Ergonomics, 11,** 437-453

COLQUHOUN, W.P., BLAKE, M.J.F. and EDWARDS, R.S. (1968b) Experimental studies of shiftwork. 2: stabilized 8-hour shift system. **Ergonomics, 11,** 527-546

CRAIG, A. (1979) Discrimination, temperature and time of day. **Human Factors, 21,** 61-68

CRAIG, A., BAER, K. and DIEKMANN, A. (1981) The effects of lunch on sensory-perceptual functioning in man. **International Archives of Occupational and Environmental Health, 49,** 105-114

CRAIG, A. and CONDON, R. (in press) Speed-accuracy trade-off and time of day. **Acta Psychologica**

CRAIG, A., WILKINSON, R.T., COLQUHOUN, W.P. (1981) Diurnal variation in vigilance efficiency. **Ergonomics, 24,** 641-651

DOEHRING, C.H., KRAEMER, H.C., KEITH, H., BRODIE, H. and HAMBURG, D.A. (1975). A cycle of plasma testosterone in the human male. **Journal of Clinical Endocrinology and Metabolism, 40,** 492-500

EYSENCK, H.J. (1967) **The Biological Basis of Personality.** Springfield, Illinois: Charles C. Thomas Publishers

EYSENCK, M.W. (1982) **Attention and Arousal: Cognition and Performance.** Berlin: Springer-Verlag

FOLKARD, S. (1975) Diurnal variation in logical reasoning. **British Journal of Psychology, 66,** 1-8

FOLKARD, S. (1979) Time of day and level of processing. **Memory and Cognition, 7,** 247-252

FOLKARD, S. (1980) A note on 'Time of day effects in schoolchildrens' immediate and delayed recall of meaningful material' - the influence of the importance of the information tested. **British Journal of Psychology, 71,** 95-97

FOLKARD, S. (1982) Circadian rhythms and human memory. In: F.M. Brown and R.C. Graeber (eds) **Rhythmic Aspects of Behaviour.** Hillsdown, NJ: Lawrence Erlbaum Associates

FOLKARD, S. (1983) Diurnal variation in human performance. In: G.R.J. Hockey (ed.) **Stress and Fatigue in Human Performance.** Chichester: Wiley

FOLKARD, S., KNAUTH, P., MONK, T.H. and RUTENFRANZ, J. (1976) The effect of memory load on the circadian variation in performance efficiency under a rapidly rotating shift system. **Ergonomics, 19,** 479-488

FOLKARD, S. and MONK, T.H. (1979) Time of day and processing strategy in free recall. **Quarterly Journal of Experimental Psychology, 31,** 461-475

FOLKARD, S. and MONK, T.H. (1980) Circadian rhythms in human memory. **British Journal of Psychology, 71,** 295-307

FOLKARD, S. and MONK, T.H. (1982) Circadian rhythms in performance - one or more oscillators? In: R. Sinz and M.R. Rosenzweig (eds) **Psychophysiology 1980.** Jena (GDR): VEB Gustav Fischer Verlag/Amsterdam: Elsevier Biomedical Press

FOLKARD, S., MONK, T.H., BRADBURY, R. and ROSENTHALL, J. (1977) Time of day effects in schoolchildrens' immediate and delayed recall of meaningful material. **British Journal of Psychology, 68,** 45-50

FOLKARD, S., WEVER, R.A., WILDGRUBER, C.M. (1983) Multi-oscillatory control of circadian rhythms in human performance **Nature, 305,** 223-226

FORT, A. and MILLS, J.N. (1976) Der Einfluss der Tageszeit und des vorhergehenden Schlaf-Wach-Musters auf die Leistungsfahigkeit unmittelbar nach dem Aufstehen. In: G. Hildebrandt (ed.) **Biologische Rhythmen and Arbeit.** Springer-Verlag

FREEMAN, G.L. (1948) **The Energetics of Human Behaviour.** Ithica, NY: Cornell University Press

FREEMAN, G.L. and HOVLAND, C.I. (1934) Diurnal variations in performance and other related physiological processes. **Psychological Bulletin, 31,** 777-799

FROBERG, J.E. (1979) Performance in tasks differing in memory load and its relationship with habitual activity phase and body temperature. **FOA Rapport C52002-H6.** Stockholm

GATES, A.I. (1916a) Diurnal variations in memory and association. **University of California Publications in Psychology, 1,** 323-344

GATES, A.I. (1916b) Variations in efficiency during the day, together with practice effects, sex differences, and correlations. **University of California Publications in Psychology, 2,** 1-156

GUNTER, B., JARRETT, J. and FURNHAM, A. (in press) Time of day effects on immediate memory for television news. **Human Factors**

HARTLEY, L.R. and SHIRLEY, E. (1976) Color-name interference at different times of day. **Journal of Applied Psychology, 61(1),** 119-122

HASHER, L. and ZACKS, R.T. (1979) Automatic and effortful processes in memory. **Journal of Experimental Psychology: General, 108,** 356-388

HITCH, G.J. (1980) Developing the concept of working memory. In: G. Claxton (ed.) **Cognitive Psychology: New Directions.** London: Routledge and Kegan Paul

HOCKEY, G.R.J., DAVIES, S. and GRAY, M.M. (1972) Forgetting as a function of sleep at different times of day. **Quarterly Journal of Experimental Psychology, 24,** 386-393

HOLLOWAY, P.J. (1967) The effect of lecture time on learning. **British Journal of Educational Psychology, 36,** 255-258

HORNE, J.A. and OSTBERG, O. (1976) A self-assessment questionnaire to determine morningness-eveningness in human circadian rhythms. **International Journal of Chronobiology, 4,** 97-190

HUGHES, D.G. and FOLKARD, S. (1976) Adaptation to an 8-hour shift in living routine by members of a socially isolated community. **Nature, 264,** 432-434

KERKHOF, G.A. (In press) Inter-individual differences in the human circadian systems. A review. **Biological Psychology**

KLEIN, K.E., HERRMAN, R., KUKLINSKI, P. and WEGMANN, H.M. (1977) Circadian performance rhythms: experimental studies in air operations. In: R.R. Mackie (ed.) **Vigilance: Theory, Operational Performance and Physiological Correlates.** London: Plenum Press

KLEIN, K.E., WEGMANN, H.M. and HUNT, B.I. (1972) Desynchronization of body temperature and performance circadian rhythm as a result of outgoing and homegoing transmeridian flights. **Aerospace Medicine, 43,** 119-132

KLEINSMITH, L.J. and KAPLAN, S. (1963) Paired associate learning as a function of arousal and interpolated interval. **Journal of Experimental Psychology, 65,** 190-193

KLEITMAN, N. (2nd edn, 1963) **Sleep and Wakefulness.** Chicago: Chicago University Press

LAIRD, D.A. (1925) Relative performance of college students as conditioned by time of day and day of week. **Journal of Experimental Psychology, 8,** 50-63

LOEB, M., HOLDING, D.H. and BAKER, M.A. (1982) Noise stress and circadian arousal in self-paced computation. **Motivation and Emotion, 6,** 43-48

MILLAR, K., STYLES, C.B. and WASTELL, D.C. (1980) Time of day and retrieval from long-term memory. **British Journal of Psychology, 71,** 407-414

MINORS, D.S. and WATERHOUSE, J.M. (1981) **Circadian Rhythms and the Human.** Bristol: J. Wright and Sons

MONK, T. (1982) The arousal model of time of day effects in human performance efficiency. **Chronobiologia, 9,** 49-54

MONK, T., ADAM, M.N., CONRAD, M.C. and FOLKARD, S. (1980) Time of day effects in the study of meaningful material. Unpublished manuscript, MRC Perceptual and Cognitive Performance Unit, University of Sussex

MONK, T.H. and LENG, V.C. (1982) Time of day effects in simple repetitive tasks: some possible mechanisms. **Acta Psychologica, 51,** 207-221

MONK, T.H. and FOLKARD, S. (1983) Circadian rhythms and shiftwork. In: G.R.J. Hockey (ed.) **Stress and Fatigue in Human Performance.** Chichester: Wiley

MONK, T.H., KNAUTH, P., FOLKARD, S. and RUTENFRANZ, J. (1978) Memory-based performance measures in studies of shiftwork. **Ergonomics, 21,** 819-826

MONK, T.H., LENG, V.C., FOLKARD, S. and WEITZMAN, E.D. (1982) Circadian rhythms in subjective alertness and core body temperature. **Chronobiologia, 10,** 49-55

MONK, T.H., WEITZMAN, E.D., FOOKSON, J.E., MOLINE, M.L., KRONAUER, R.E. and GANDER, P.H. (1983) Task variables determine which biological clock controls circadian rhythms in human performance. **Nature, 304,** 543-545

MOORE-EDE, M.C., SULZMAN, F.M. and FULLER, C.A. (1982) **The Clocks That Time Us: Physiology of the Circadian Timing System.** Cambridge, Mass: Harvard University Press

PALMER, J.D. (1976) **An Introduction to Biological Rhythms.** New York: Academic Press

PATKAI, P. (1970) Diurnal differences between habitual morning workers and evening workers in some psychological and physiological functions. **Reports from the Psychological Laboratories No. 311.** Stockholm: University of Stockholm

PATKAI, P. (1971) The diurnal rhythm of adrenalin secretion in subjects with different working habits. **Acta Physiologica Scandinavia, 81,** 30-34

POSNER, M.I. and SNYDER, C.R.R. (1975) Attention and cognitive control. In: R.I. Solso (ed.) **Information Processing and Cognition: The Loyola Symposium.** Hillsdale, NJ: Lawrence Erlbaum Assoc.

REVELLE, W., HUMPHREYS, M.S., SIMON, L. and GILLILAND, K. (1980) The interactive effect of personality, time of day, and caffeine: a test of the arousal model. **Journal of Experimental Psychology: General, 109(1),** 1-31

RUNDUS, D. (1971) Analysis of rehearsal processes in free recall. **Journal of Experimental Psychology, 89,** 63-77

RUTENFRANZ, J., ASCHOFF, J. and MANN, H. (1972) The effects of a cumulative sleep deficit, duration of preceding sleep period and body temperature on multiple choice reaction time. In: W.P. Colquhoun (ed) **Aspects of Human Efficiency: Diurnal Rhythm and Loss of Sleep.** London: English Universities Press

SHIFFRIN, R.M. and SCHNEIDER, W. (1977) Controlled and automatic human information processing: II. Perceptual learning, automatic attending, and a general theory. **Psychological Review, 84,** 127-190

TILLEY, A. and WARREN, P. (1983) Retrieval from semantic memory at different times of day. **Journal of Experimental Psychology, 9,** 718-724

TILLEY, A. and WARREN, P. (in press) Retrieval from semantic memory during a night without sleep. **Quarterly Journal of Experimental Psychology**

WEVER, R.A. (1979) **The Circadian System of Man: Results of Experiments under Temporal Isolation.** New York: Springer-Verlag

WEVER, R.A. (1982) Behavioural aspects of circadian rhythmicity. In: F.M. Brown and R.C. Graeber (eds) **Rhythmic Aspects of Behaviour.** London: Lawrence Erlbaum Associates

WEVER, R.A. (1983) Fractional desynchronization of human circadian rhythms. **Pflugers Archiv, 396,** 128-137

WEVER, R.A. (in press) Man in temporal isolation: basic principles of the circadian system. In: S. Folkard and T. Monk (eds) **Hours of Work: Temporal Factors in Work Scheduling.** London: Wiley

WINCH, W.H. (1911) Mental fatigue in day school children as measured by arithmetic reasoning. **British Journal of Psychology,** 315-341

COMPUTATIONAL VISION

M.J. Morgan

The visual system has evolved to give us information about the outside world, using the radiation reflected from the surface of objects into the eye. Optical information is useful in many ways: it allows us to walk over uneven terrain, to negotiate obstacles, to recognize food and predators, to jump across streams, to reach out and grasp objects, and so on. Given that these capacities have evolved under the pressure of natural selection, it is not surprising that observers agree in their perception of most scenes, even though many different interpretations are theoretically possible. Evidently, visual perception is a rule-governed process and its rules are shared by most, probably all, human beings, though as Kant put it 'not necessarily by every living thing'. Vision could not be rule-governed unless there were regularities in the world for it to exploit. The task of discovering these regularities and the rules which the visual system bases upon them is the essence of the computational approach to vision (Marr, 1982).

In the broad sense, computational vision is the study of any system that interprets images, including the visual system. An imaging device, such as the eye or a television camera, projects rays of light onto a bounded, two-dimensional surface. Such an image can be completely described as a spatially varying light-intensity function. (It may also vary over time.) The computational problem is to derive from this image a symbolic description of the three dimensional scene of which the image is a projection. This problem is an extremely difficult one, because there are very few direct one-to-one relationships between scenes and their images. Figure 1, for example, could theoretically represent an infinite variety of three-dimensional scenes, only one of which is the arrangement of four blocks which presumably the reader first perceives. Nor is the problem confined to the fact that the image is a flat projection of a three-dimensional scene: almost any property of objects in the scene involves the same ambiguity. For example, if the points in the image arising from one surface are more intense than those from a different surface, is this because the surfaces are different in reflectance, because they are differently illuminated, or because of their geometry (Marr, 1982, p.41)?

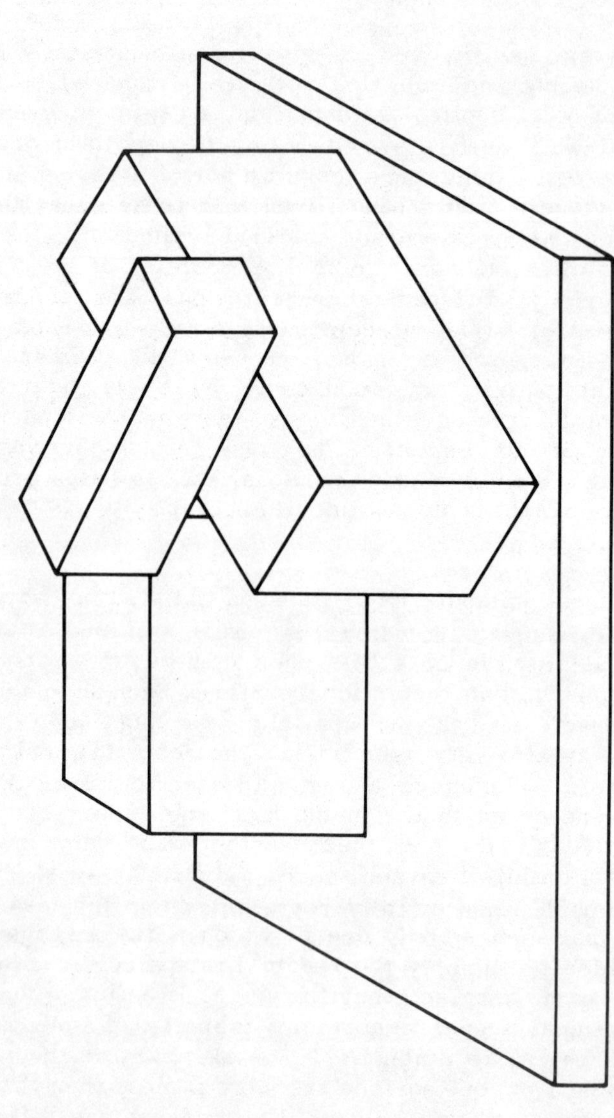

Figure 1. A two-dimensional image such as this could correspond to an infinite variety of objects or wires in a three-dimensional scene. Nothwithstanding this theoretical ambiguity, most human observers immediately interpret such images as representing solid objects. To understand how images can be interpreted as scenes is the goal of computational vision.

The role of inference in perception

It has been a commonplace since at least the late seventeenth century that vision requires interpretation of the retinal image. Locke spoke of 'judgements' in relation to the size-distance invariance problem. Berkeley so doubted that a three-dimensional scene could be obtained from a flat projection that he referred the whole problem away from vision to touch and movement. In the nineteenth century, Helmholtz propounded the theory of unconscious inference, which proposes that the visual system works backwards from the image to infer the objects that would have caused the image. Like the earlier Empiricists, Helmholtz believed that many of the rules used by the visual system to accomplish this feat were learned from experience, including the whole of Euclidean geometry. In recent years, R.L. Gregory has systematically advocated the view that visual perceptions are 'hypotheses' about reality.

Basic to the empiricist theory of perception was the belief that we have to learn rules for interpreting images. These rules could then be employed to make the 'best guess' about particular images. An analogous view in Artificial Intelligence saw perception as necessarily involving downward-flowing knowledge about likely objects in the scene. Similar views about the need for 'top-down' processing were held about language comprehension and speech perception. It was doubted whether low-level descriptions of the input could provide anything useful unless they were tested against pre-existing high level descriptions of known objects. An alternative view that has come to influence much recent work in computational vision is that many of the rules neded to interpret images can be embodied in the early stages of analysis, without reference to known 'objects'. The distinction between 'low' and 'high' level processes is evidently one of degree, but what we understand by a low level process in this context is one that precedes any attempted identification of familiar objects or states-of-affairs.

In empiricist theories the appeal to image interpretation was linked to the claim that perception is learned. This linking has no logical basis, and is no longer a feature of current computational theories. The interpretation of images, as we shall see, does not necessarily involve anything like traditional, sequential, logical deductions, and certainly not learned inferences (Hinton, 1980).

Pattern recognition and its limitations

A traditional concern of psychologists, and a pressing practical concern of industrial robot designers, is that of 'pattern recognition', which can be defined as the ability to classify a large number of possible images into a small number of categories. Animal psychologists investigated the ability of rats, goldfish, octopuses and primates to discriminate between simple two-dimensional patterns like circles, rectangles and diamonds (Sutherland, 1959, 1968). One of the main problems in pattern recognition has been seen as the need to recognize simple shapes independently of their position, size and angle of rotation in the image plane. Each different shape, independently of these attributes, must give rise to an internal representation that is sufficient to distinguish it from other shapes. The number of potential inputs is infinite, but the required number of outputs is very small, corresponding to the number of discriminations required. Therefore, the central problem of pattern recognition is that of removing redundant information from the image. It does not matter what kind of internal representation is chosen, so long as it does the job of distinguishing between shapes. For example, the amplitude spectrum of the two-dimensional Fourier transform of a shape does not change with the shape's position (this affects only phase information), and is therefore potentially useful for 'recognizing' shapes independently of their exact position.

This is only one of many simple algorithms that have been proposed for distinguishing simple geometrical shapes in high conrast images. For a recent example see the OLREC of Moss, Robinson and Poppelbaum (1983), which transfers the shape to polar co-ordinates, calculates the radial and circular profiles separately, and then matches to internal numerical templates.

Useful though the machine approach may be for practical purposes, it has its limitations in helping us to understand vision. There are infinitely many specialized algorithms that will reduce image redundancy in a parochial context: but what general principles emerge? A major difficulty here is that 'object recognition' is a comparatively specialized function of visual systems. The idea that all we require from vision is a distinct code corresponding to each of a variety of external 'objects' can lead us to contemplate quite arbitrary internal representations, such as the Fourier transform. But the actual functions of vision are much wider than such a preoccupation with objects would suggest (running through woods; building a sandcastle; interpreting a dance). What use would a Fourier transform be in deciding whether the opposite bank of a stream was suitable for a landing platform? Of course, an arbitrary transform of the image might be a useful preliminary to later analysis, but in itself it is not obviously more useful than the original intensity values. So instead of regarding the visual system as an 'object recognizer' we should perhaps be posing a completely different set of problems. Examples of current interest are as follows:

* what parts of the image belong to the same surface?

* what is the angle of a given surface to the viewer?

* does a particular intensity change in the image correspond to a reflectance change or an illumination change in the scene?

* what bits of the scene are moving together and in which direction?

The syntactic approach to pattern description

The aim of the syntactic as opposed to the 'recognition' approach is to produce structural descriptions of the input, rather than simply assigning it to a category (Sutherland, 1968; Oatley, 1978; McArthur, 1982; Rosenfeld and Kak, 1982, Volume 2, Chapter 12). An early example was Guzman's program (cf. McArthur, 1984), which did not deal with images as such, but with symbolic propositional descriptions about a 'block world' consisting of line drawings of simple polyhedra. The aim of the program was to decide which regions in a scene like Figure 1 belonged to the same physical object. To accomplish this, the program concentrated on local regions in the picture where two or more lines met (junctions) and was given a knowledge base concerned with the possible interpretations of each possible junction. For example, an 'arrow' type of junction is consistent with the joining of two surfaces belonging to the same object, while a 'T' junction arises from occlusion of one object by another. The key step in the program was to work out the possible interpretations of each kind of junction on a purely local basis, and then reduce the number of possibilities further by more global analysis. An obvious constraint is that the same surface cannot belong to two different objects. Moreover, the likelihood of two regions belonging to the same object is increased if this is a possible description arising from several junctions. The number of labelling possibilities is thus reduced by interactions between initially independent and local descriptions, and this process is continued until the number of possible scene descriptions can be reduced no further.

Although Guzman's program was concerned with a highly artificial 'block world', and not with real images, it illustrated an important general procedure. Purely local descriptions can be given to the image initially, which will generally result in a large set of possible labellings. But by placing constraints on possible combinations of labellings in separate parts of the image, the possibilities can be reduced. A later program by Waltz (1975) permitted line drawings with shadows, which greatly expanded the number of initial labelling possibilities, but which could reduce them, often to a unique solution, by a very simple 'filtering' algorithm. Lines were labelled '+' (convex) or '-' (concave) depending on whether the two adjoining surfaces were like a roof or like the inside corner of a room. An immediate constraint is that when three lines meet they must all be '-' or all be '+'. This reduced the number of initial labelling possibilities. Constraints involving more than one junction were then applied to reduce labelling possibilities still further: the co-occurrence principle required that a line labelled '+' at one junction could not be '-' at another. Applied several times in succession, this meant that the labelling possibilities at one junction could affect even those to which they were not directly connected. The scheme is thus:

(1) Assign possible descriptions to local regions of the image, for example lines at junctions;

(2) Reduce labelling possibilities by exploiting some physical constraint;

(3) Iterate, until a unique solution is reached.

When there are only two labelling possibilities for each line, the above procedure is termed 'binary constraint checking'. Rosenfeld and Kak give an example for the Necker cube which results in two possible interpretations, as in human vision. The cube (Figure 2) has twc kinds of vertices: 'A' vertices (a,b,c,f,g,h) and 'Y' vertices (d,e). Three constraints can be imposed on lines meeting at such vertices:

(1) All the lines at a 'Y' vertex are either all convex or all concave;

(2) At an 'A' vertex the outer two lines are both occluding (they represent an intersection with a hidden surface) and the included line is either convex (Case 1) or concave (Case 2);

(3) If a line is Case 1 from one of its ends it is Case 1 from the other.

From these constraints it follows immediately that ab, bf, fh, hg, gc and ca are occluding and db, dc, dh, ea, ef, eg are either convex or concave. Now suppose that one of the ambiguous lines, say dc, is convex. It is left as an exercise to the reader to show by applying the three constraints that a unique interpretation results, and that assuming dc to be concave results in another unique interpretation. These are the only two interpretations consistent with the constraints. So if a single choice is made, the effects of this choice propagate over the image, with an unambiguous result.

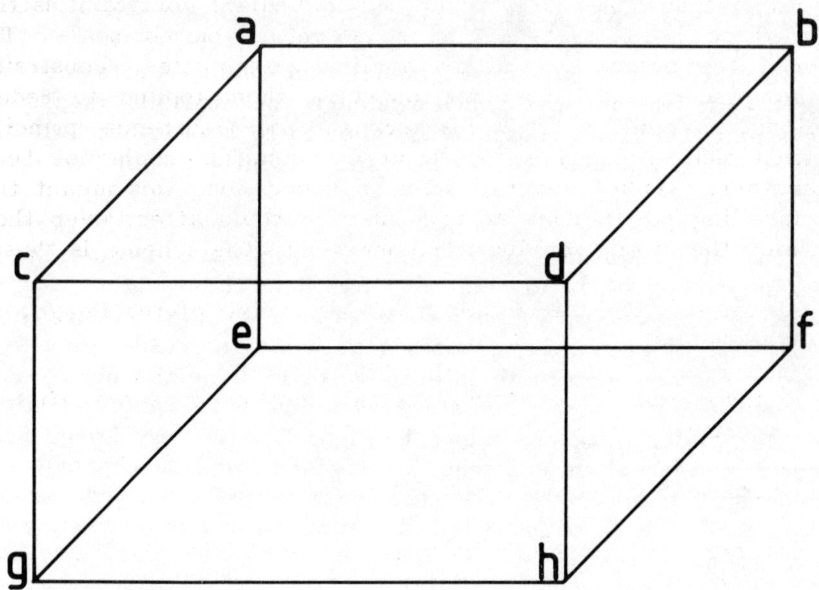

Figure 2. The Necker cube is ambiguous because each of its lines can be interpreted as the join between two surfaces viewed either from the inside (concave boundary) or outside (convex boundary). Making very simple physical assumptions, however, the number of possible solutions can be reduced to just two. (From Rosenfeld and Kak, 1982.)

Parallel, co-operative processes in vision

The kind of computational model we have been considering consists of a set of rules that represent constraints on possible scenes, and the whole procedure can therefore be called 'constraint satisfaction'. The term 'co-operative process' is also used, and the method of propagating constraints by iteration is referred to as a 'relaxation process' because of its resemblance to certain methods in numerical analysis (Davis and Rosenfeld, 1981). An interesting feature of this approach is that it lends itself readily to a parallel computational process. The conventional digital computer has a single central processor in which stored data, including the program, are processed sequentially. Many of the processes involved in image analysis are highly time consuming when carried out in this way. There is no reason to think that the visual system acts in this cumbersome fashion, and a realization of this difference between conventional computing methods and visual perception was perhaps at the back of J.J. Gibson's rejection of this whole computational metaphor (cf. Hinton, 1980). But there is an alternative computational model, in which operations are initially carried out quite independently by spatially distributed processors, which are subsequently allowed to interact according to rules that implement the 'constraints' which a solution must satisfy.

The rapidly reducing unit cost of hardware is making it increasingly possible to embody parallel image processing in specialized networks, which work rapidly in real time. Duff's (1983) CLIP image processor uses a network of parallel processors that can be programmed to interact with their neighbours so as to carry out filtering and other standard image processing operations: examples of its work are shown in Figure 7. As Very Large Scale Integration technology continues to advance, we can expect to see increasingly complicated computations carried out by parallel networks of this kind (see Ballard, Hinton, and Sejnowski, 1983, for a recent review).

As far as we know from physiological and anatomical studies of the visual system, its 'architecture' (Hubel and Wiesel, 1977) is much better suited to parallel, neighbourhood computations than to serial processing. Projections from the retina to the cortex maintain the neighbourhood relations of the retina, an arrangement which has been thought mysterious on the grounds that perception is not a 'picture in the head', but which finds a ready interpretation if further analysis of the image depends upon locally restricted interactions (Cowey, 1979). In the cortex itself, Hubel and Wiesel (1977) describe an apparently modular structure, in which small areas of cortex, 'hypercolumns', perform an analysis of orientation for separate parts of the image. According to Hubel and Wiesel: 'We end up, then, with a view of the cortex as containing a thousand small machines of more or less identical structure'. For further discussions of the role of parallel processing in vision, see Barlow (1981) and Ballard, Hinton and Sejnowski (1983).

Limitations of block-world analysis

The analysis of block worlds has suggested several generally important principles, but its limitations are obvious. These programs take as input highly symbolic descriptions of the image, which it is presumably the function of early visual processing to provide. The results succeed only in telling us which surfaces belong to which objects: they tell us nothing about the orientation of these surfaces or their properties, such as reflectance. The more recent trend in computational vision (Brady, 1981) has been to work with real images, despite their many difficulties, and to concentrate on specific 'modular' problems rather than attempting to produce whole descriptions of the scene.

An early example was Horn's work (Horn, 1975, cf. Ikeuchi and Horn, 1981) on the problem of recovering surface orientation from shading in an image. It is obvious that when there is a localized source of illumination, such as the sun, the intensity of surfaces will be affected by their orientation. The problem is to extract this information without being confused by changes in the properties of the surfaces themselves; that is, their reflectance. By a theoretical analysis, Horn formulated the problem as a non-linear first-order partial differential equation in two unknowns. Surprisingly, this could be solved if a very simple assumption was made about the physical surface: that its orientation varies smoothly over space. Thus, if you move a small amount over the image and note the new intensity, you can compute the new orientation. The best solution to the problem overall is the one that produces the smoothest changes over space. Ikeuchi and Horn (1981) discuss the precise definition of surface smoothness in detail. A fuller understanding of Horn's work depends upon the concepts of gradient space and the reflectance map, which are clearly explained by Marr (1982).

The theory of computational theory

From the above examples, we see that an important first step in a computational approach is to identify a clear goal of the computation, which makes explicit the desired information, and the problems to be overcome in obtaining it. Marr and Poggio (1976) and Marr (1982) call this step the formation of a 'computational theory.' A computational theory could apply either to a particular task, such as the recovery of surface orientation from shading, or to the understanding of a device such as the visual system, which is already carrying out the task. Indeed, the central claim of the computational approach to vision is that the most profitable way to understand a vastly complicated device like the visual system is precisely to identify its tasks, and then to form computational theories of them. Such theories will be at a level of generality that applies to any information processing device, and can thus be tested on a universal machine. Marr and Poggio distinguish three levels at which the visual system could be understood.

At the top level is the computational theory, which begins by specifying the exact goal of the computational task. A wrong or inexact formulation of the problem at this stage will vitiate the whole enterprise. Consider, for example, the perception of brightness. It might be thought that the aim of brightness computation is to describe the amount of light reaching the eye from a particular surface in the scene. But this would be incorrect, and would lead to bafflement when it was found that different surfaces can have the same intensity in the image, and yet be seen as different, and can also be perceived as the same when their image intensities are different. The many experiments on 'lightness constancy' (Kaufman, 1974, Chapter 5) suggest that the goal of brightness computation is not at all to describe image intensities, but rather the surface reflectance properties of objects in the scene. This is entirely sensible, given that the function of vision is to provide us with information about the world, not about our retinal images. So the computational problem for brightness may be stated along the following lines:

> Obtain the reflectance of surfaces in scene from the image intensity values, distinguishing image intensity changes due to reflectance from those due to illumination.

The second aim of a computational theory is to identify the physical assumptions or 'constraints' that will make the computation tractable. We met examples of constraints in dealing with block worlds. Brightness can provide another example. Changes in surface reflectance tend to take place relatively rapidly in the image at the boundaries between surfaces, while changes due to illumination are more gradual. This suggests that we might be able to separate the two types of effect by isolating image changes that take place at different scales. Land and McCann (1971), Horn (1975) and Marr (1974) proposed computational theories of this kind. Obviously, the spatial scale constraint will not be infallible. Some reflectance changes occur gradually, and some sharp changes in image intensity are due to illumination changes (sharp shadows). But the visual system is not infallible in these circumstances either, and it is instructive to compare its errors with those of a program implementing the computational theory.

Algorithms and implementations

The computational theory is a level of description that makes no reference to the particular method that will be used to ensure that a program extracts the desired information. The next stage according to the Marr-Poggio account is to look for a particular solution (algorithm) which exploits the constraints postulated in the computational theory. We saw examples in the block world of methods for propagating constraints across the image by rules for neighbourhood interaction. Here we shall once again consider brightness as an example. Figure 3 shows the hypothetical 'luminance profile' across an image. A luminance profile is simply a graph of the intensity values (vertical axis) at each point in the image as we move along a straight line (horizontal axis) in that image. For example, we could plot the intensity values along a single scan line of a TV image. The top line in Figure 3 shows a luminance profile in which three sharp changes in intensity, corresponding to the edges of objects, are superimposed on a gradual change in intensity across the whole profile, due to a gradient of illumination. The question is, how best to extract the sharp changes from the gradual ones due to illumination? A simple method is shown in the second and third lines of the figure. First, the image is slightly blurred, and then differentiated twice: this gives the profile shown in the middle line, and it will be seen that the illumination gradient has been eliminated. Finally (bottom line) the profile is integrated to fill in the regions between intensity discontinuities (Horn, 1974) and the different reflectance regions in the image are thereby revealed.

The mechanistic level of explanation ('hardware')

So far, we have said nothing about possible mechanisms. The central claim of the computational approach to vision is that it is logically possible to have a level of understanding of the visual processes without an exact knowledge of their physiology. But a final understanding will obviously involve an account of the neural mechanisms. Once again taking as our example brightness, we can note that the centre-surround receptive field structure of retinal ganglion cells makes them suitable to carry out the parallel spatial operations envisaged by the differencing algorithm. The availability of particular hardware devices has an important influence upon the choice of algorithm (Poggio, 1983).

Although, in principle, any algorithm can be carried out by a general purpose machine, in practice, some algorithms will be impossibly slow and cumbersome unless suitable hardware is

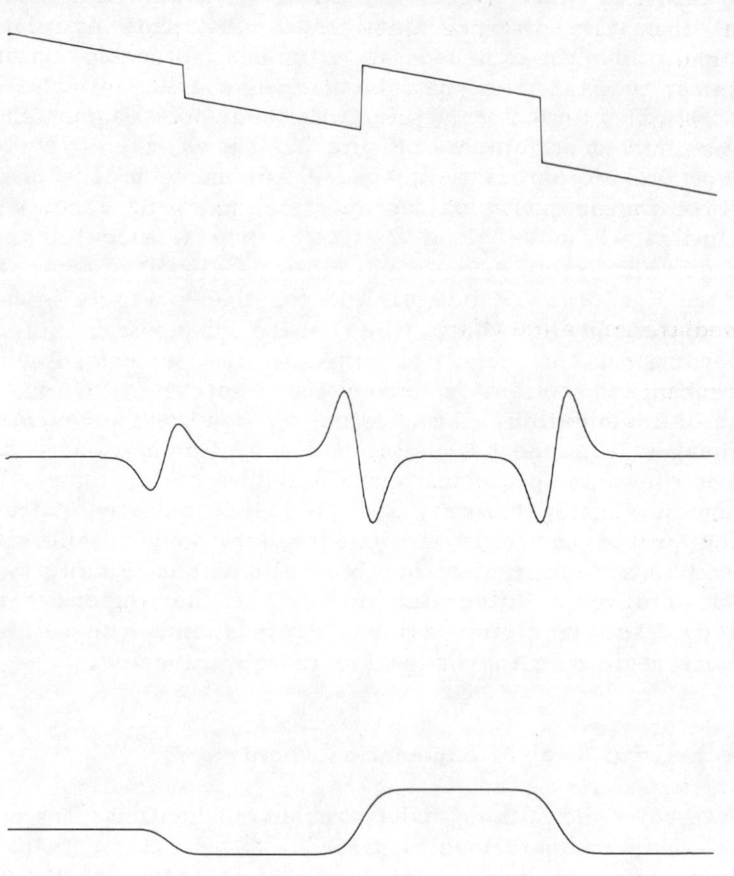

Figure 3. The top curve (a) plots the luminance profile across several sharp reflectance changes, superimposed upon which is a gradual decrease in illumination from left to right. In the middle curve (b) the profile has been filtered to remove the gradual illumination change. Finally, in (c) the filtered image has been thresholded to remove small absolute values, and integrated twice to display the reflectance changes in isolation from the more gradual illumination change. See text for further explanation.

available. The same point applies to the study of human vision. There is little point in postulating particular algorithms without taking into account the knowledge of mechanisms gleaned from physiology and psychophysics. To take just one example here, it is an old problem how we discriminate the direction of spatial offset of two abutting lines (vernier acuity) when the offset is much smaller than the distance between foveal photoreceptors. To understand this phenomenon at all, and to design particular algorithms, a vital first step is to realize that optical filtering of the retinal image removes spatial frequencies higher than the sampling limit of the receptor mosaic (Ditchburn, 1973; Barlow, 1979; Watt and Morgan, 1983). Without this knowledge, which is of a purely contingent physiological nature, theorizing is most likely to be futile.

Intermediate representations

Another characteristic of recent work in computational vision has been the emphasis on intermediate representations, such as Marr's 'Primal sketch' or Barrow and Tenenbaum's 'Intrinsic images'. Intermediate representations make certain kinds of information explicit, but fall short of a fully objective representation of the scene. Functionally, the reason for this approach is that it is easier to break a complex problem down into steps, rather than attempt to solve it in one go. Each step can then build upon the successes of the previous stages. This is a very familiar idea in logical problem solving, but it was a profound insight on David Marr's part to apply it to perceptual representation. What is the factual evidence for these intermediate representations in vision?

Marr points to the fact that we can interpret not only natural images, but also highly symbolic pictures, such as line drawings. A famous example is 'Attneave's cat' (Figure 4) in which points of maximum curvature on the animal's outline are joined together by straight lines. A seductive argument is that we can interpret these images because they correspond in at least some respects to an intermediate representation. As Marr (1982) puts it in relation to his 'Primal sketch':

> A drawing of a scene adequately represents the scene, despite the very different grey level description to which it gives rise. It therefore seems reasonable to suppose that the artist's local symbols are in correspondence with natural symbols, that are computed out of the image during the normal course of its interpretation.

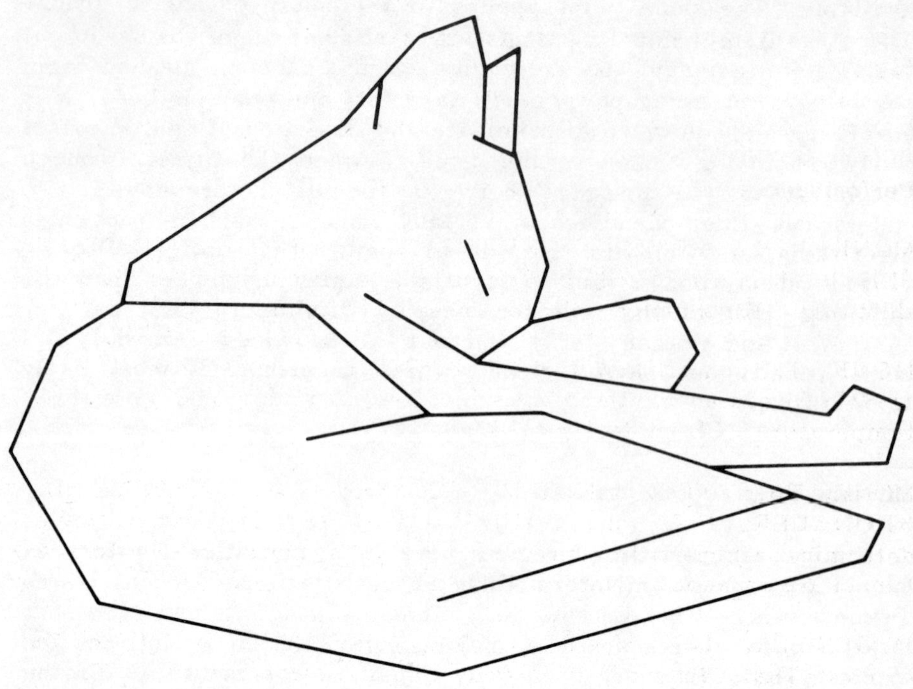

Figure 4. Attneave's cat: points of maximum curvature have been joined by straight lines. (From Kaufman, 1974.)

The main point of Marr's 'raw primal sketch' is to capture the important intensity changes in the image, corresponding to biologically significant boundaries in the world. The sketch is derived from zero-crossings in band-pass filters (explained below) and culminates in primitives called EDGES, BARS, BLOBS and TERMINATIONS, which have attributes of orientation, contrast, length, width and position. Even though this is only an intermediate representation, Marr states that 'subjectively, you are aware of the primal sketch ...'

However, the raw primal sketch does not delineate regions of different texture, and has no descriptions of surface properties like orientation. The next stage in the hierarchy is the 'full primal sketch', which combines elements (tokens) from the raw sketch into groupings. Texture regions are thereby delineated, but not surface orientation or depth. In the next stage, which Marr calls the 'two-and-a-half-dimension' sketch, surfaces become labelled in order to show their orientation relative to the viewer.

The information for orientation and depth can arise from numerous independent sources which are combined at this stage:

binocular disparity;
motion parallax;
texture and shading;
and surface-contours (Stevens, 1981).

The two-and-a-half-dimensional image, which resembles Barrow and Tenenbaum's 'intrinsic image' can be symbolically represented by a 'needle map', which shows local surface orientation relative to the viewer by arrows pointing in the surface normal direction (Figure 5). This is still a viewer-centred description of the object and describes visible surfaces only. The next stage is to construct object-centred descriptions in which the relation of object parts to one another and to axes of object symmetry is made explicit. Perhaps the best way to appreciate the distinction between viewer- and object-centred descriptions is to think about Shepard's 'mental rotation' task, in which the viewer has to decide whether two shapes of different angular orientation in the picture plane are 'same' or 'mirror images'. To do this, the shapes have to be first described in an object-centred co-ordinate frame, and as Hinton and Parsons (1981) point out, the construction of this description from the original viewer-centred framework may be what takes up the time in 'mental rotation'.

Before we go on to consider some specific computational problems in more detail, some critical examination of the philosophy behind intermediate representations is in order.

Marr argues that because we can interpret line drawings so readily, they must correspond to some natural code. Plausible though the reasoning may sound, it needs careful examination. If we have a system that represents X as Y, it by no means follows that it will represent Y as Y. If the function of the 'Primal sketch' is to produce a line drawing, the same process applied to a line drawing might produce nonsense. Marr's argument ignores the possible role of learning and convention in our interpretation of cartoons and line drawings. As long ago as the sixteenth century the Port-Royal logicians made a distinction between 'natural' and 'conventional' symbols, using a portrait of Caesar as an example of the first, and the representation of Victory by a laurel wreath for the latter. Marr's case is that cartoons correspond to natural symbols, but there is no compelling evidence for this, and some evidence against. Like the representation of K-K4 for a particular move in chess, cartoons and other line drawings may involve conventional symbols.

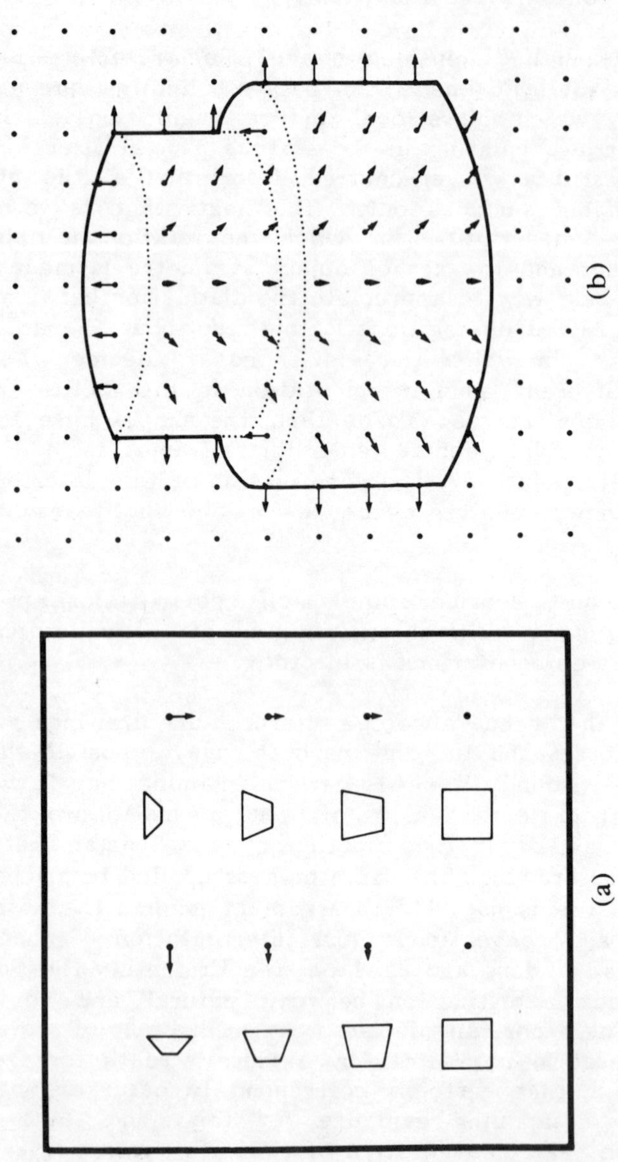

Figure 5. Illustration of the two-and-a-half dimension sketch. The dots with arrows symbolically represent the orientation of the surface relative to the viewer. (From D. Marr 'Vision', copyright 1982 by W.H. Freeman & Co. Adapted from Marr and Nishihara, 1978.)

EXAMPLES OF COMPUTATIONAL VISION

The following examples are chosen to give something of the flavour of computational vision, following the framework of Marr (1982) and Marr and Poggio (1977). We emphasize the search for the physical assumptions which make image interpretation possible, and comment on algorithms and hardware when it is relevant. The reader is warned, first, that the examples are arbitrarily chosen from a large field, and second, that this rapidly changing area is bound to be controversial. Few, if any, of the solutions discussed below are likely to survive in detail for very long, but one hopes that the general approach will be more durable. Above all, computational theories should be computable: that is, expressed with enough precision to be programmed on a universal machine. If applied to human vision, they should be psychophysically testable.

Finding boundaries (edges) in images

A necessary first step in image analysis must be to identify and localize intensity changes in the image corresponding to important boundaries in the scene. Unfortunately, this task is far from simple. Recall that an image itself consists of a space-varying light intensity function. A boundary or edge in the scene must be detected by some change in this function over space. But what magnitude and shape of change should we look for? Binford (1981) described the following problems which had to be faced:

* boundary finders missed low contrast edges;
* they gave masses of spurious boundaries in the presence of shading;
* they gave poor estimates of locations and angles of boundaries;
* they were largely unable to find texture boundaries;
* they had poor resolution for thin features and at junctions;
* they required extensive computation;
* they were not effective with diffuse or defocused boundaries.

Most attempts to solve these problems have used some form of spatial frequency filtering. Changes in light intensity over the image occur at many different rates, varying from the slow changes of gradual shading to the rapid changes of a fine texture. It will help to think of this graphically. In Figure 6 it is obvious that there is a general slow drift, superimposed upon which are changes at a higher rate. The aim of filtering is to isolate these changes at different scales. Slow changes can be isolated by smoothing, in which each point is replaced by the average of points in its

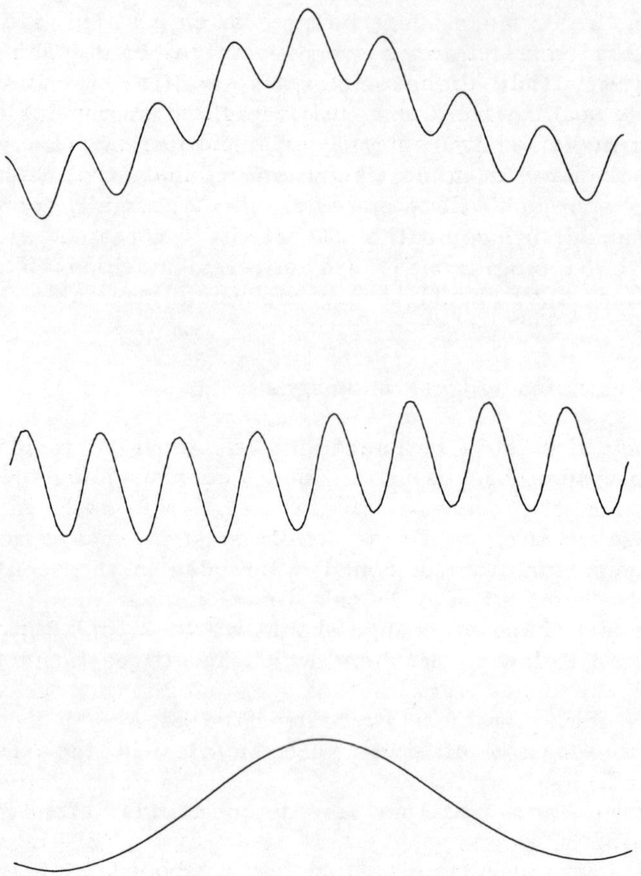

Figure 6. The graph in (a) shows changes at two different rates: a slowly changing bump with a more rapid oscillation superimposed. In (b) the bump has been removed by differentiation, while in (c) the more rapid oscillation has been removed by smoothing. Differentiation and smoothing are two important techniques in image processing.

neighbourhood; technically, something enhances low spatial frequencies and removes high frequencies. The opposite process is differentiation, which replaces points in the image by their differences from neighbourhood points: this enhances abrupt changes and removes slow changes.

The idea is readily extended to two dimensions by replacing points with averages or differences of points in a two-dimensional surrounding area. Examples are seen in Figure 7, in which filtering has been accomplished by replacing each picture element or 'pixel' in the original image by some weighted combination of its own and surrounding pixel values. The numbers in the boxes below each image show the weights applied to each pixel. A series of weighting values such as these is referred to as a 'neighbourhood operator' (Duff, 1983) or 'mask'. For example, in the 'light smoothing' case each pixel is replaced by the average of its own value, given a weight of 4 and the values of the surrounding pixels given weights of 1. The Laplacian (differentiating) operator on the other hand, replaces each pixel with the weighted sum of its own value (weighted -4) and the surrounding values, each rated unity. After this operator has been applied, a pixel will have a non-zero value only if the rate of change in the image was itself changing: thus the Laplacian effectively differentiates the image twice, and emphasizes high spatial frequencies in the image.

It is important to realize that in the filtering operation, the operator is applied to every pixel in the image in parallel: in other words, the image must be thought of as being processed by a large set of overlapping 3 x 3 masks, each centred on one pixel. This is the digital equivalent of convolution, in which each point of a function is replaced by the sum of a series of multiplications between the values of that function and those of a second function (in this case, the mask) centred at that point. Filtering by this method can easily be implemented as a parallel computational process, in which the same operation is carried out simultaneously on each point in the image. It is evident that this parallel process is much faster than applying the same operation to each pixel in turn.

There is now considerable evidence (reviewed by Robson, 1983) that the early stages of visual processing involve a variety of local spatial frequency filters, sensitive to different rates of intensity change in the image. These filters could correspond to receptive fields of different size at various stages of the visual pathways. A receptive field can be thought of as a special kind of local operator or filter, which weights different regions by means of excitation and inhibition. In the concentric centre-surround

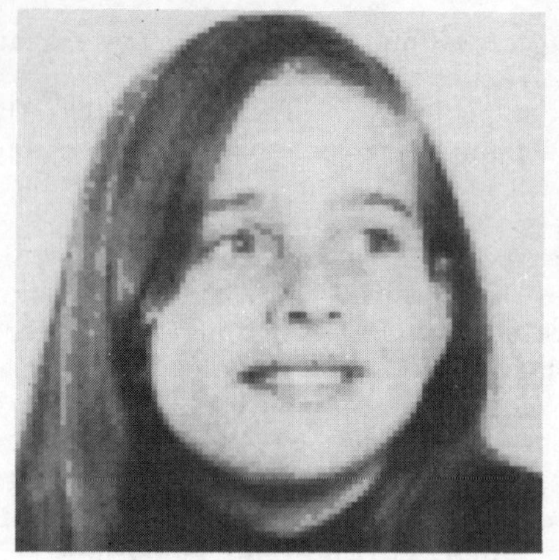

(a) Original

(b) Smoothed

$$\begin{matrix} 1 & 1 & 1 \\ 1 & 1 & 1 \\ 1 & 1 & 1 \end{matrix}$$

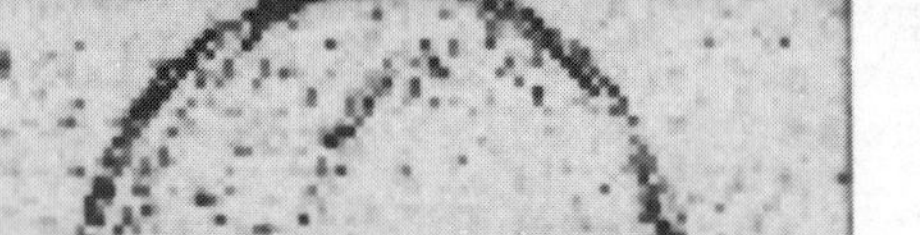

(c) Laplacian

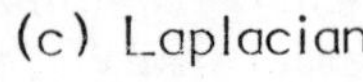

$$\begin{matrix} 0 & 1 & 0 \\ 1 & -4 & 1 \\ 0 & 1 & 0 \end{matrix}$$

type, the centre is oppositely weighted from the surround, so that the unit responds only to changes across its field, reminiscent of the Laplacian operator. We can think of an early 'neural image' (Robson, 1983) resulting from the convolution between the retinal image intensity function, and the receptive field weighting function. Examples of convolutions between a step edge and centre-surround operators of various sizes are shown in Figure 8. The top line shows the luminance profile corresponding to a single sharp boundary in the image. If this boundary fell across a set of cells with receptive fields of the antagonostic centre-surround type, and if we then plotted the activity of these cells across space as a 'neural profile', then we should see patterns such as those in Figure 8. The wider patterns would result from large receptive fields, and the narrow response (bottom) from a smaller field. Note that the cells actually on the step itself do not respond at all, and neither do those sufficiently remote from the step.

How would such a multiple-scale description of the image assist in identifying and localizing important intensity changes? A first question is what feature of filtered profiles such as those in Figure 8 might be useful in localizing an intensity change. Marr and Poggio (1979) made the precise suggestion that the important feature is the 'zero crossing' where the filtered output changes sign. One advantage of this feature is that it corresponds to the exact position of a sharp edge, no matter how much the image of that edge is blurred (and there is always some degree of blurring in the retinal image because of aberrations and diffraction). The next, and crucial question is how the results of different spatial frequency filters should be combined. We can regard this indeed as the fundamental computational question:

> Given that changes in the image can be described at a variety of different scales, how can these descriptions be best combined so as to identify intensity changes in the image that correspond to important boundaries in the scene?

Figure 7. *Images (b) and (c) have been derived from the original (a) by smoothing or differentiation techniques, similar to those illustrated more simply in Figure 6. In each of the processed images, every point (pixel) has been replaced by a weighted combination of the lightness values in a neighbouring set of points in the original image. The weights are shown in the 'masks' at the side of each image. For smoothing the weights are all positive. For differentiation the Laplacian mask is used, which calculates differences between points and their neighbours. (With permission of Professor Michael J.B. Duff, University College, London.)*

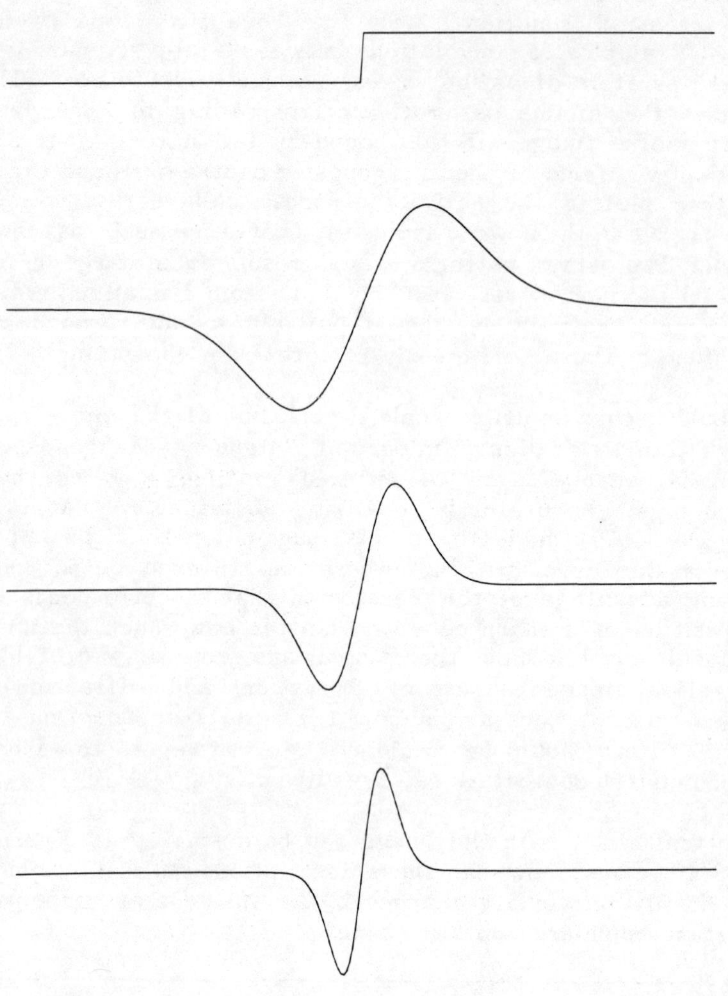

Figure 8. The figure illustrates the response of three different filters of increasing size to a step change in the image. Note that the point at which the filter output crosses zero corresponds to the position of the unfiltered edge, independently of the filter size. It has been proposed that such 'zero crossings' in the output of physiological filters are important in the detection of luminance discontinuities. For further explanation see the text.

Note that the single edge in Figure 8 gives rise to spatially coincident zero-crossings in filters of different size. This is because the edge is a broad-band stimulus in spatial frequency terms. On the other hand, rapid spatial changes in intensity due to noise in the transduction process, or gradual changes of illumination, will not produce equivalent zero-crossings in different filters. Marr and Hildreth (1980) suggested that this could be exploited in the form of a constraint they call the 'spatial coincidence assumption'.

> If a zero-crossing segment is present in a set of independent (filters) over a contiguous range of sizes, and the segment has the same position and orientation within each (filter), then the set of such zero-crossing segments indicates the presence of an intensity change in the image that is due to a single physical phenomenon (a change in reflectance, illumination, depth or surface orientation). (Marr, 1982)

So the theory here is to make a comparison between analysis at different scales the basis for identifying important boundaries in the image. In Marr's theory, the primitives identified at this stage form the basis for the raw primal sketch. The specific algorithm proposed looks for coincidence of zero-crossings in the outputs of a particular kind of filter (the Laplacian of a Gaussian). This scheme seems to work well in practice with quite complicated images, but its psychophysical and physiological status is less clear. Robson (1983) argues that retinal filters fail to conform to the Laplacian model. The use of non-oriented filters, rather than receptive fields of the elongated 'bar detector' type, is controversial, and although Marr and Hildreth (1980) advance arguments in favour of non-oriented filters, they seem to be ignoring a useful constraint in images: the tendency of significant boundaries to be continuous over regions. Finally, attempts to test the zero-crossing model psychophysically, although providing some evidence in favour (Watt and Morgan, 1983) have also turned up contrary evidence (Mayhew and Frisby, 1981). For example, Morgan et al. (1984) have shown that there is an apparent movement of an edge when its blur is suddenly changed: this should not happen on the zero-crossing model, unless there is a nonlinearity preceding the filter.

The measurement of motion

The available evidence suggests that movement can occur at several different levels of image description (Anstis, 1980; Braddick, 1980). At the highest level perceived motion can occur between objects that are defined only by textural differences from the surround, while in other cases, motion detection must logically precede shape detection, since common motion of elements is the only evidence for the shape (Braddick, 1974). In the latter case, motion measurement seems to be initially a local process, since there is an upper limit to the displacements that can be detected, a limit that presumably depends upon the receptive field sizes of cortical motion detectors.

Local measurement gives rise to the 'aperture problem' (Marr and Ullman, 1981), which is illustrated in Figure 9. Whatever the true velocity of the moving object, local measurement can only determine the component at right angles to the edge. The velocity component parallel to the edge is locally undetectable. Thus local measurements around the contour of a moving shape yield a set of vectors, each orthogonal to the local contour orientation. Evidently these vectors give information about the movement of the shape as a whole, and the computational problem is to derive the true movement from the local measures making the fewest and most plausible assumptions. Each local vector must be replaced by a new vector representing the true motion of that part of the image in space. There are many possible solutions, and the problem is to constrain them, if possible to a unique solution. Horn and Schunck (1981) suggested finding the velocity field that varies least across the image. Intuitively, this means that points close together in space are not flying off in different directions, although points further apart may be. The constraint appealed to here is that the real world consists of solid objects whose surfaces are generally smooth compared to their distance from the viewer (Hildreth, 1983). A smooth curve in motion generates a smoothly varying velocity field.

Hildreth (1983) and Ullman and Hildreth (1983) have applied the smoothness constraint to a number of cases, and shown that applied to points along the figure boundary it is capable of extracting the true velocity field (see Figure 10). More remarkably, the scheme seems to predict well-known errors in the perception of motion by human observers. A nearly circular ellipse rotating around its centre appears to stand still while its contour pulsates and exactly the same is found in Hildreth's (1983) computation of the least-varying velocity field (Figure 11).

Maximizing the smoothness of the velocity field, because it depends upon comparisons between neighbouring points in the image, lends itself well to solution by a co-operative algorithm. Once again, we see that the way in which the visual system maintains neighbourhood relations in its anatomical projection may be significant for the underlying computational tasks that it faces.

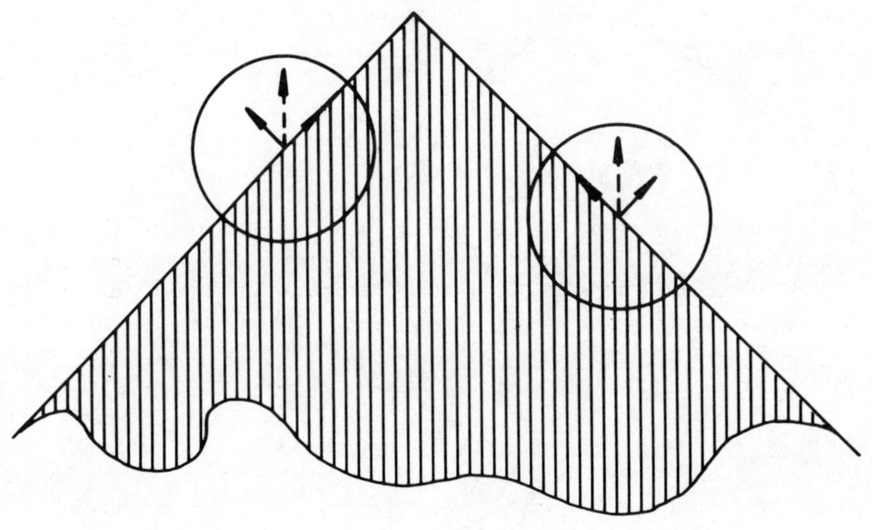

Figure 9. The 'aperture problem' in motion detection. Although the shaded object is actually moving in the direction of the dotted arrow, within the circular local apertures such movement cannot be discriminated from motion at right angles to the contour. To determine the true direction of motion, the vector component at right angles to the contour must also be determined, but it cannot be extracted within a single aperture. Only by combining the measures from several apertures can the true direction of motion be determined. (cf. Marr, 1982, p.166.)

Binocular stereopsis

This has become a highly technical subject and we can do no more than touch on some of the main themes.

Because the left and right eyes look at the three dimensional world from slightly different vantage points, their images are not identical, and the visual system makes use of the small differences (disparities) to discern relative distances of objects from the observer. As the reader can verify by looking up through the branches of a leafy tree, first with one eye open and then with two, binocular information is very potent in giving us the

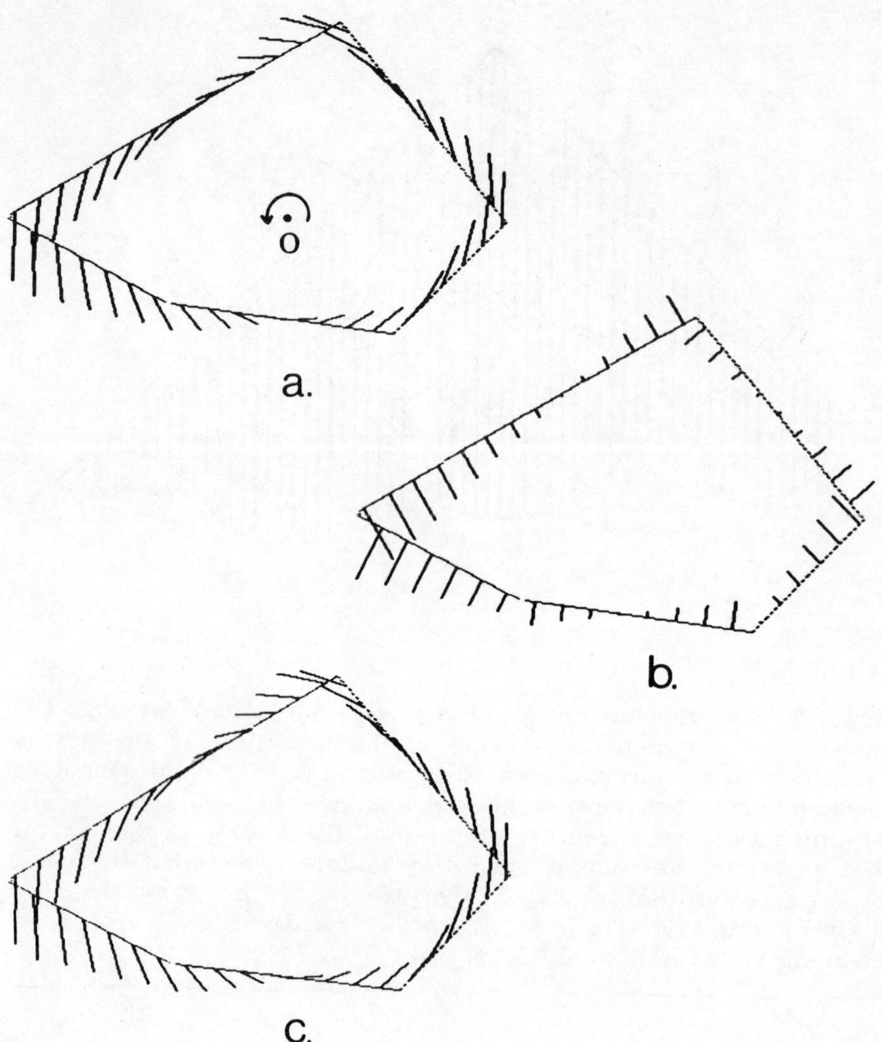

Figure 10. The three figures show how the movement of a rotating polygon is determined by Hildreth's (1983) method. (a) shows the true velocity field for the object, each line representing the local movement of the contour, (b) shows a set of local measurements each of which can determine only the velocity component at right angles to the contour (see the 'aperture problem', Figure 9). Finally, (c) shows the computed velocity field of least variation, which in this case corresponds quite closely to the true velocity field. (From E. Hildreth (1984) 'The Measurment of Visual Motion', MIT Press. Reproduced by permission of the author and the MIT Press.)

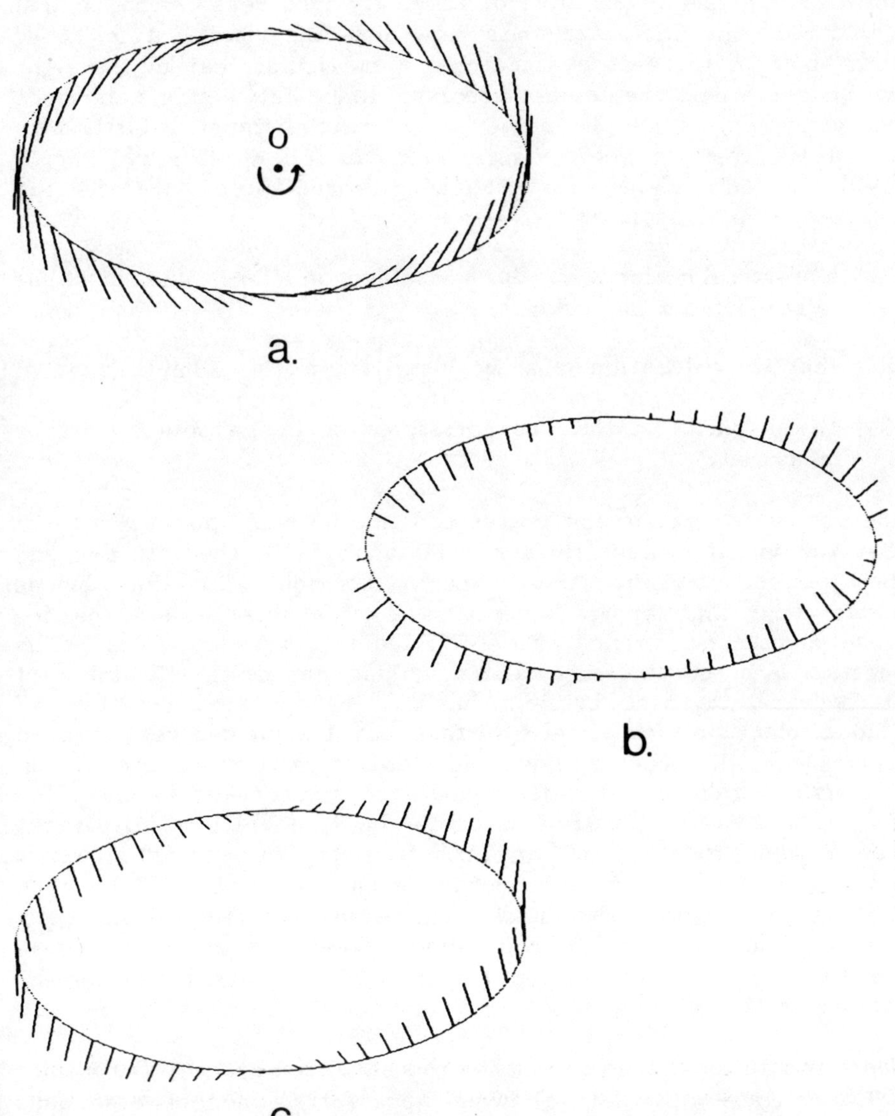

Figure 11. Rotating ellipse. As in Figure 10, (a) shows the true velocity field, (b) the results of local measurement and (c) the computed velocity field of least variation. In this case, the computed result is incorrect: instead of rotating, the ellipse appears to pulsate. Human observers experience a similar illusion. (From Hildreth, 1984.; reproduced by permission of the author and the MIT Press.)

impression of 'solid vision' - the literal meaning of 'stereopsis'. However, this same example of the leafy tree reveals the central problem of binocular stereopsis: how does the visal system 'know' which leaf in the left eye matches a particular leaf in the right eye image? Unless the correct **correspondence** between left and right eye image points can be achieved, correct distance relationships cannot be inferred. More exactly, we can follow Marr and Poggio (1979) in identifying the following three steps (S) in the measurement of a disparity:

(S1) a particular location on a surface in the scene must be selected from one image;

(S2) that same location must be identified in the other image;

(S3) the disparity in the two corresponding image points must be measured.

The obvious answer to the 'correspondence problem' may seem to be that the visual system finds a certain shape in the left eye and then searches for the same shape in the right. But this obvious answer begs the important question: what exactly is a 'shape' for these purposes? A branch, a twig, a leaf, or a part of a leaf? This question is posed in a particularly striking way by the Random Dot Stereogram, invented by Bela Julesz. One eye sees a pattern of random black dots on a white surface, as if paint had been sprayed from a can; the other eye sees an identical pattern except that in a certain region all the dots are shifted horizontally to one side. To the observer, this region containing the shifted (disparate) dots appears to stand out in depth from the background. Thus it appears that a correct correspondence can be established between the two sets of dots, but since each pattern viewed in isolation is strictly random, it is far from evident what 'shapes' the two eyes can be fusing. If each dot is a shape, what identifies its correct partner in the other eye?

The computational theory of stereopsis advanced by Marr and Poggio (1976) began with the following apparently innocent assertions about the physical world:

(a) a given point on a physical surface has a unique position in space at any one time;
(b) matter is cohesive, it is separated into objects, and the surfaces of objects are generally smooth.

Applying these assumptions to the case of the stereogram, Marr and Poggio derived the following three rules:

1. **Compatibility:** the eyes match only same-coloured dots. (The same physical object has a similar colour in the two eyes.)

2. **Uniqueness:** the matching process is one-to-one, not one-to-many. (A single object does not give rise to more than one image in each eye. Unfortunately, several objects can give rise to one image, so this rule is fallible.)

3. **Continuity:** the disparity of the matches varies smoothly almost everywhere over the image. (This is the depth analogy to the motion smoothness constraint, discussed earlier.)

Note that this computational theory does not tell us directly how to solve the correspondence problem. To do that we need an algorithm, and to drive home the point that there is a logical distinction between the computational theory and the algorithm, Marr (1982) describes two quite different algorithms for solving random dot stereograms. The first (Marr and Poggio, 1976) uses a co-operative method, as originally suggested by Julesz himself in his 'dipole' theory, designed to suppress matches in which neighbouring dots have different depth values, and to enhance matches where neighbours are similar. A network of notional 'processors' corresponding to every conceivable match of each left eye dot with each right eye dot is initially loaded so that each processor has a '1' if there is a possible match there, and a '0' if not. (Note the similarity to the original labellings in Waltz's filtering algorithm.) Each processor then interacts with its neighbours according to the co-operative rules; some possible matches are thereby eliminated, and others are strengthened. The process is iterated until a stable solution is reached. Examples showing the successful operation of this method are illustrated in Marr (1982).

A quite different kind of idea was put forward by Marr and Poggio (1979), starting from the observation that the correspondence problem would be a lot easier to solve if we could confine the search for possible matches to a small region about each dot. Unfortunately, this is not immediately helpful, because disparities can be easily detected even when they are many dot diameters in size, so that the region to be searched will still contain several candidate dots. Suppose however that we could in some way effectively 'blur' the pattern, thereby removing the individual detail of the dots, and replacing them with a smaller number of fuzzy 'clumps'. The centres of these clumps are necessarily separated by at least the clump diameter, so if we now confine our search for partner clumps to a region of approximately twice the clump size, we shall find no problem in making unique matches.

Of course the idea of blurring here is only an optical metaphor, but in reality the process could be carried out neurally by different spatial frequency tuned filters, of the kind we considered earlier in relation to edge detection. When Marr and Poggio put forward this theory, Julesz and Miller (1975) had already shown that human stereoscopic vision could use independent spatial frequency tuned filters: in other words, that stereopsis could occur independently at different spatial scales, ranging from coarse to fine. Julesz and Miller added masking noise of controlled spatial frequency content to bandpass filtered random dot stereograms. They found that stereopsis was unaffected provided that the noise was far enough away in frequency (to be precise, two octaves) from the stereoscopic image. Frisby and Mayhew (1980) obtained confirming evidence from their 'rivalrous texture stereograms'.

Marr and Poggio therefore proposed the following. First, the image is examined at a coarse spatial scale (low spatial frequencies, large 'clumps'); the search for partners is confined to an area similar to the clump size, and since this size is large, big disparities can be detected without the problem of ambiguous matches. However, the penalty for using coarse filtering is that we lose fine spatial detail: what we now need is to examine the image more finely. To do this, Marr and Poggio propose that the results of the first coarse analysis are used to guide a **vergence eye movement,** which has the effect of bringing the disparate parts of the image into closer spatial registration. The size of the search area for matches can now be reduced without the fear of missing real disparities, and the image an therefore be analysed on a correspondingly finer scale. Such a 'coarse to fine' algorithm is particularly satisfying, because it suggests one functional reason for independent spatial frequency channels in the visual system. Unfortunately, although the method seems to work well enough in theory, there is some evidence against its involvement in human stereopsis.

Mowforth, Mayhew and Frisby (1981) found that large disparities could elicit appropriate vergence movements even in narrow-band filtered stereograms containing high spatial frequencies. Their result underscores the point that however elegant and plausible a a particular algorithm might be, it need not bear any resemblance to the methods used by the visual system. Beautiful algorithms can be murdered by ugly little psychophysical facts.

GENERAL READING

Frisby's 'Seeing' is a very well illustrated introduction to the computational approach for the general reader. David Marr's posthumously published 'Vision' is a useful introduction to his technical papers. Volume 17 of the journal 'Artificial Intelligence' is devoted to papers on computer vision. A recent symposium on 'Physical and Biological Processing of Images' by Braddick and Sleigh features papers on psychophysics, physiology and image processing. Rosenfeld and Kak's classic 'Digital Picture Processing' has recently appeared in a new two edition volume. Gonzalez and Wintz's 'Digital Image Processing' provides a particularly clear account of Fourier methods.

REFERENCES

ANSTIS, S.M. (1980) The perception of apparent movement. **Philosophical Transactions of the Royal Society of London, B290,** 153-168

BALLARD, D.H., HINTON, G.E. and SEJNOWSKI, T.J. (1983) Parallel visual computation. **Nature, 306,** 21-26

BARLOW, H.B. (1979) Reconstructing the visual image in space and time. **Nature, 279,** 189-191

BARLOW, H.B. (1981) Critical limiting factors in the design of the eye and visual cortex. The Ferrier Lecture, 1980. **Proceedings of the Royal Society of London, B212,** 1-34

BINFORD, T.O. (1981) Inferring surfaces from images. **Artificial Intelligence, 17,** 205-244

BRADDICK, O.J. (1974) A short-range process in apparent motion. **Vision Research, 14,** 519-527

BRADDICK, O.J. (1980) Low-level and high-level processes in apparent motion. **Philosophical Transactions of the Royal Society of London, B290,** 137-151

BRADDICK, O.J. and SLEIGH, A.C. (1983) **Physical and Biological Processing of Images.** New York: Springer-Verlag

BRADY, M. (1981) The changing shape of computer vision. **Artificial Intelligence, 17,** 1-15

COWEY, A. (1979) Cortical maps and visual perception. **Quarterly Journal of Experimental Psychology, 31,** 1-18

DAVIS, L.S. and ROSENFELD, A. (1981) Co-operating processes for low-level vision: a survey. **Artificial Intelligence, 17,** 245-263

DITCHBURN, R.W. (1973) **Eye Movements and Visual Perception.** Oxford: Clarendon Press

DUFF, M.J.B. (1983) Neighbourhood operators. In: O.J. Braddick and A.C. Sleigh (eds) **Physical and Biological Processing of Images.** New York: Springer-Verlag

FRISBY, J.P. (1979) **Seeing.** Oxford: Oxford University Press

FRISBY, J.P. and MAYHEW, J.E.W.)1980) Spatial frequency tuned channels: implications for structure and function from psychophysical and computational studies of stereopsis. **Philosophical Transactions of the Royal Society of London, B290,** 95-116

GONZALEZ, R.C. and WINTZ, P. (1977) **Digital Image Processing.** Reading, Mass: Addison-Wesley

HILDRETH, E. (1984) **The Measurement of Visual Motion.** Cambridge, Mass: MIT Press

HINTON, G.E. (1980) Inferring the meaning of direct perception. **Behavioral and Brain Sciences, 3,** 387-388

HINTON, G.E. and PARSONS, L.M. (1981) Frames of reference and mental imagery. In: J. Long and A. Baddeley (eds) **Attention and Performance IX.** Hillsdale, NJ: Lawrence Erlbaum

HORN, B.K.P. (1975) Obtaining shape from shading information. In: P.H. Winston (ed.) **The Psychology of Computer Vision.** New York: McGraw Hill

HORN, B.K.P. and SCHUNK, B.G. (1981) Determining optical flow. **Artificial Intelligence, 17,** 185-203

HUBEL, D. and Wiesel, T.N. (1977) Functional architecture of macaque monkey visual cortex. **Proceedings of the Royal Society of London, B198,** 1-59

IKEUCHI, J. and HORN, B.K.P. (1981) Numerical shape from shading and occluding boundaries. **Artificial Intelligence, 17,** 141-184

JULESZ, B. and Miller, J. (1975) Independent spatial-frequency-tuned channels in binocular fusion and rivalry. **Perception, 4,** 125-143

LAND, E.H. and McCANN, J.J. (1971) Lightness and retinex theory. **Journal of the Optical Society of America, 61,** 1-11

McARTHUR, D.J. (1982) Computer vision and perceptual psychology. **Psyhological Bulletin, 92,** 283-309

MARR D. (1974) The computation of lightness by the primate retina. **Vision Research, 14,** 1377-1388

MARR, D. (1982) **Vision.** San Francisco: Freeman

MARR, D. and HILDRETH, E. (1980) A theory of edge detection. **Proceedings of the Royal Society of London, B207,** 187- 217

MARR, D. and POGGIO, T. (1976) Co-operative computation of stereo disparity. **Science, 194,** 283-287

MARR, D. and POGGIO, T. (1977) From understanding computation to understanding neural circuitry. **Neurosciences Research Progress Bulletin, 15,** 470-488

MARR, D. and POGGIO, T. (1979) A computational theory of human stereo vision. **Proceedings of the Royal Society of London, B204,** 301-328

MARR, D. and ULLMAN, S. (1981) Directional selectivity and its use in early visual processing. **Proceedings of the Royal Society of London, B211,** 151-180

MAYHEW, J.E.W. and FRISBY, J.P. 81981) Psychophysical and computational studies towards a theory of human stereopsis. **Artificial Intelligence, 17,** 349-385

MORGAN, M.J., MATHER, G., MOULDEN, B. and WATT, R.J. (1984) Intense-response nonlinearities and the theory of edge localization. **Vision Research, 24,** 713-719

MOSS, R.M. ROBINSON C.M. and POPPELBAUM, W.J. (1983) On-line recognition (OLREC): a novel approach to visual pattern recognition. **Pattern Recognition, 16,** 535-550

MOWFORTH, P. MAYHEW, J.E.W. and FRISBY J.P. (1981) Vergence eye movements made in response to spatial-frequency-filtered random dot stereograms. **Perception, 10,** 299-304

OATLEY, K. (1978) **Perceptions and Representations.** London: Methuen

POGGIO, T. (1983) Visual algorithms. In: O.J. Braddick and A.C. Sleigh (eds) **Physical and Biological Processing of Images.** New York: Springer-Verlag

ROBSON, J.G. (1983) Frequency domain visual processing. In: O.J. Braddick and A.C. Sleigh (eds) **Physical and Biological Processing of Images.** New York: Springer-Verlag

ROSENFELD and KAK, A.C. (1982) **Digital Picture Processing.** (2 volumes). New York: Academic Press

STEVENS, K.A. (1981) The visual interpretation of surface contours. **Artificial Intelligence, 17,** 47-73

SUTHERLAND, N.S. (1959) Visual discrimination of shape by octopus: circles and squares, circles and triangles. **Quarterly Journal of Experimental Psychology, 11,** 24-32

SUTHERLAND, N.S. (1968) Outline of a theory of visual pattern recognition in animals and man. **Proceedings of the Royal Society of London, B171,** 291-397

ULLMAN, S. and HILDRETH, E.C. (1983) The measurement of visual motion. In: O.J. Braddick and A.C. Sleigh (eds) **Physical and Biological Processing of Images.** New York: Springer-Verlag

WALTZ, (1975) Generating semantic descriptions from drawings of scenes with shadows. In: P.H. Winston (ed.) **The Psychology of Computer Vision.** New York: McGraw Hill

WATT, R.J. and MORGAN, M.J. (1983) Mechanisms responsible for the assessment of visual location: theory and evidence. **Vision Research, 23,** 97-109

DRUGS AND HUMAN INFORMATION PROCESSING

D.M. Warburton and K. Wesnes

This chapter will discuss research that has identified some of the mechanisms that control information processing in the brain. Information processing is conceptualized as a flow of neurally-coded data through the brain systems which, through a series of transformations, results in complex psychological events like perception, thinking and memory. The mammalian brain has evolved as an organ for processing complex information: the billions of neurones in the brain are not randomly connected but are organized as neural networks (Warburton, 1975). The input of information to these networks comes from sensory receptors and intero-receptors distributed throughout the body. This neurally coded information is integrated with information which is already in the network to determine behaviour.

We have deliberately chosen to use the concepts of information processing to emphasize the relation between these events. We believe that parts of information processing models can be mapped onto the body of data on transmitter systems and neural information processing. This mapping involves the co-ordination of the concepts of cognitive psychology with those of the neurochemistry of behaviour to produce mechanism hypotheses of information processing (Warburton, 1983a).

It is believed that some of the processes that are involved in this information flow are limited in capacity with respect to the amount of information that they can handle at any one time. It is the thesis of this paper that some of the cholinergic and noradrenergic systems in the brain are involved in the control of this information processing capacity and thus the efficiency of information processing. The evidence for this hypothesis has come from studies in which cholinergic and noradrenergic drugs have been used as tools to investigate the processes of information processing. The first process that we will consider is attention and cholinergic drugs.

ATTENTION AND CHOLINERGIC DRUGS

Some of the first evidence for the involvement of the transmitter substance **acetylcholine** in information processing came from studies of soldiers who were given **atropine** during tests of agents to protect against nerve gases. The nerve gases poison by producing massive increases of acetylcholine in the synapses of cholinergic neurones in the body, while atropine blocks cholinergic synapses. When given atropine, the soldiers reported difficulty in concentrating and a shortened attention span (Ketchum et al., 1973). They could answer simple questions (Ostfeld, Machne and Unna, 1960) but could not understand complex conversations and carry out instructions (Ketchum et al., 1973). These data suggest that atropine impairs control over the information that is processed and the information that is ignored.

In experimental studies of this phenomenon, atropine produced more errors on the Stroop test (Callaway and Band, 1958), in which subjects name the print colour of a colour word printed in a different colour (for example, the word RED printed in BLUE), because the drug increased the distraction from the conflicting semantic information. Drugged subjects also had difficulty in filtering out irrelevant parts of the design in the embedded figures test (Callaway and Band, 1958). In contrast, drugged subjects discovered new methods of solving problems faster than the control group in a series of problems of how to obtain a given volume of water with three different measures.

Callaway and Band (1958) hypothesized that atropine produced 'broadened attention', which they defined as an increase in the influence of peripheral information which is removed from the central focus of attention by space, time, or by differences of meaning. However, improved performance on some tasks could be explained in terms of atropine broadening the attention, a process which is beneficial for performance in some situations.

This hypothesis was tested further by examining the effects of **scopolamine,** another cholinergic blocker, on a 60-minute visual vigilance task (Wesnes and Warburton, 1983a). Vigilance performance was analysed using signal detection theory, which yields two parameters - stimulus sensitivity and response bias. The stimulus sensitivity parameter is changed by factors affecting information input like attention, while the response bias parameter is sensitive to factors affecting response output, like motivation. It was found that there were changes in stimulus sensitivity which were not accompanied by any change of response bias. These results demonstrated unequivocally that cholinergic blockade modified behaviour by modifying the stimulus input but not by changing motivation or motor control of response output. **Methscopolamine,** which does not get into the brain but acts on cholinergic neurones in the rest of the body, had no effect on either stimulus sensitivity or response bias, showing that only cholinergic mechanisms in the brain were involved in these effects.

A second scopolamine experiment determined the effects of cholinergic blockade on the efficiency of rapid visual information processing performance (Wesnes and Warburton, 1984a). The task involved the detection of sequences of three consecutive odd or even digits from a series of digits presented visually at the rate of 100 per minute for 20 minutes, a test of sustained attention. In order to control for the peripheral actions of scopolamine, the effects of methscopolamine were again measured. On the basis of the reduction in stimulus sensitivity produced by scopolamine in a vigilance task we predicted that the drug would lower the efficiency of task performance. This prediction was confirmed; following scopolamine, correct detections were significantly lower over the 20-minute period whereas no decrement was observed with methscopolamine.

Many compounds which increase cholinergic function are extremely dangerous, like the nerve gases. One cholinergic compound that can be administered to people is **nicotine.** Nicotine acts on cholinergic neurones and releases acetylcholine at the cortex. If smokers inhale, as over 80 per cent of smokers do, then over 95 per cent of the nicotine in the smoke is absorbed by the lungs. In a study of smoking and visual vigilance (Weanes and Warburton, 1978), groups of deprived smokers, smokers who were allowed to smoke, and non-smokers performed the 80-minute task. Both non-smokers and deprived smokers showed a marked decrement in detections, whereas the smoking group maintained their initial level of concentration over the session.

In a similar experiment with nicotine tablets (Wesnes, Warburton and Matz, 1983), nicotine tablets helped reduce the vigilance decrement in non-smokers, light smokers and heavy smokers. For all three types of subject, nicotine significantly prevented the decrement in stimulus sensitivity which occurred over time in the non-drug condition. It had no effect on response bias which gave no evidence of changes in any response output system. Once again there was only evidence for a change in an information input system.

In other studies (Wesnes and Warburton, 1983b, 1984b) we investigated the effects of smoking on the performance of a rapid visual information processing task. Smoking improved both the speed and accuracy of performance above rested baseline levels, the greatest improvement occurring with the highest nicotine delivery cigarette. Performance deteriorated over time after not smoking as well as after smoking a nicotine-free cigarette. Thus nicotine from cigarettes does not simply restore information processing performance to pre-smoking levels, but actually improves performance above these levels for the session as a whole. In another experiment a similar design was used to study the effects of nicotine tablets. Nicotine helped prevent both the decline in detections and the increase in reaction time which occurred over time in the non-drug condition.

These findings indicate that scopolamine and nicotine with opposite effects on central cholinergic pathways produce opposite effects on performance. A further experiment determined whether these two drugs are antagonistic in their effects on the efficiency of the performance of the rapid visual information processing task and the Stroop test (Wesnes and Revell, 1984). Subjects received both nicotine and scopolamine and testing was carried out over a longer time period and Stroop testing was introduced at the end of the session. Nicotine completely counteracted the decrement in performance produced by scopolamine on both the rapid information processing task and the Stroop test.

In conclusion, these experiments provide evidence that cholinergic pathways are involved in human information processing. The cholinergic stimulation produced by nicotine increased processing efficiency while the cholinergic blockade produced by atropine and scopolamine decreased efficiency. These data are consistent with the hypothesis that cholinergic pathways in the brain determine the efficiency of information processing. It seems that a brain cholinergic system is involved in a mechanism responsible for selecting the relevant information which determines appropriate behaviour from the total information input, the processes of attention.

ACETYLCHOLINE AND INFORMATION PROCESSING CAPACITY

It has been argued that attention is the allocation of the available 'mental effort' to particular aspects of information processing (Kahneman, 1973). An elaboration of this idea was made by Norman and Bobrow (1975) who suggested that attention is the direction of processing resources to the various potential sources of information input. Both of these approaches consider that the available resources can be flexibly allocated to various stages of processing as well as among different concurrent sources of information. However, processing capacity is limited and these limitations are revealed when the individual attempts to process more information than the available resources permit.

Different mental activities impose different demands on the limited capacity. When capacity does not meet the demands, poor performance would be expected. According to Kahneman's model, an activity can fail, either because there is not enough total capacity to meet its demands or because resources are not allocated to it. The impairment is non-specific, and depends only on the performance-resource needs of these processes. If an increase in the amount of processing resources can result in more efficient performance, then performance on that task is said to be 'resource limited' (Norman and Bobrow, 1975) and impairment can only be observed when a process is operating within its resource-limited region.

Kahneman (1973) suggested that efficient processing depends on both a specific information input and a non-specific sensory input which he called 'effort' or 'capacity'. Many neural structures receive inputs of information and each structure can be 'activated' by an input from the non-specific, limited resources. He pointed out that physiological arousal and effort co-vary which suggests that they could be related and that both arousal and capacity increase or decrease with the changing demands of mental activity. Kahneman was not specific about the type of arousal that was involved. It could be behavioural arousal, autonomic arousal or electrocortical arousal and these are sometimes dissociated.

Psychophysiological studies have revealed that behavioural efficiency is correlated with the type of electrical activity at the cortex (Lindsley, 1952). Cortical desynchronization (beta activity) is correlated with a state of full alertness and concentration in the person while slower, more synchronized cortical activity (alpha activity) is correlated with relaxed wakefullness. In a study of EEG and human attention, Groll (1966) found parallel decreases in the percentage of correct detections and the average EEG frequency over the session as the activity became more synchronized. She discovered that the average frequency immediately before a missed target was slower than before a detected target. The latency of responses for detected targets was negatively correlated with the EEG frequencies in the one-second intervals preceding the targets. This study is just one of many that show that the efficiency of attentional performance is directly related to electrocortical arousal, rather than other types of arousal.

Electrocortical arousal is controlled by cholinergic pathways from the reticular formation (Domino, Yamamoto and Dren, 1968). This relationship is supported by the electrocortical effects of the drugs that have been used in the behavioural studies that we have cited already. For example, nicotine injections increase human electrocortical arousal (see review in Edwards and Warburton, 1983), whereas atropine and scopolamine decrease electrocortical arousal (Ostfeld and Aruguette, 1962). On the basis of their studies of the distribution of cholinergic pathways in the central nervous system, Shute and Lewis (1967) proposed that cholinergic pathways from the mesencephalic reticular region to the sensory cortices form the anatomical basis of the electrocortical arousal system.

Thus, variations in information processing can be seen as the outcome of changes in activity in the ascending cholinergic pathways to the cortex that converge on the cortical sensory neurones. This activity is seen as alterations in acetylcholine release and changes in electrocortical arousal. The release of acetylocholine at the cortex increases the size of the potentials and thus improves the probability of their being distinguished from the background cortical activity (Warburton, 1981).

Capacity theories (Kahneman, 1973; Norman and Bobrow, 1975) assume that the total amount of effort which can be deployed at any time is limited. Thus two key aspects of this conceptualization are the person's evaluation of demand on the limited capacity and their effort allocation policy which will be based on the demand and on the arousal level. A person can allocate processing resources in many different ways, concentrating sometimes on some aspect of the sensory input through the sensory organs, sometimes on processing of internally-generated information, sometimes on integrating information from different sources, and sometimes on preparing for an action. Moreover, the processing system is working to combine all sources of information at its disposal into a unified, understandable picture.

Resource allocation can result from either the nature of the input, a 'bottom-up' data-driven sequence of processing or from internal hypotheses, a 'top-down', conceptually-driven sequence of processing (Rabbitt, 1981). Evidence for variations in allocation of the resources of the cholinergic information processing system have come from a study by Andersson and Hockey (1977). They examined selection of information in a task in which subjects were asked to remember the words in presentation order, that is, the words and their order were relevant but location was irrelevant. There were no differences between the nicotine and no nicotine groups for the percentage of words that were recalled in the correct order, or for the percentage of words that were recalled correctly regardless of word order. The most interesting finding was that position on the screen was recalled significantly less well with nicotine.

In a second test in which subjects were asked to remember words, word order and location as well, the groups did not differ significantly in their recall although there was a trend for location to be recalled better after nicotine than when deprived. This study suggests that nicotine can enable more selective processing of information but only of information that is thought to be irrelevant by the subjects. In other words, nicotine is not acting via a passive processing system but is making resources available for active allocation by a 'top-down' system.

Conclusion

In summary, the evidence in the previous section supports the hypothesis that cholinergic blocking drugs modify a cortical mechanism that is involved in information processing. This mechanism is an interaction between the sensory input in all modalities and the amount of cortical desynchronization. Desynchronization is produced by a cholinergic pathway ascending from the mesencephalic reticular region. We believe this system is mediating the resources that are allocated to different tasks and so the capacity for processing information.

MEMORY AND THE CHOLINERGIC SYSTEM

If a cholinergic pathway to the cortex is important in controlling the information processing resources, then we can ask if this system is important in other cognitive activities, like memory. As before, the major compounds that have been used in these studies have been cholinergic blocking agents, atropine and scopolamine, and drugs which activate the cholinergic pathways, physostigmine and nicotine. There are major reviews of the literature on the relation between the cholinergic system and learning and memory in humans (for example, Drachman and Sahakian, 1979; Squire and Davis, 1981), and only some representative studies will be presented here.

A problem of many learning and memory studies is that it cannot be concluded that the drug has modified the learning process unless subsidiary studies have ruled out alterations in sensory processing, motivation or motor output. In addition, they give no evidence about the stage in memory that the drug has modified. It could be information input, information storage or retrieval. One procedure that can help with this problem is a state dependent design. In a state dependent design, one group of subjects learns after a drug dose (D) while a second group learns without the drug

(ND). For the recall test both groups are divided, one half of the drug group are tested with the drug (DD), the other half with no drug (D-ND), while half of the group which had no drug at learning are given no drug (ND-ND) and half are given a dose of the drug (ND-D).

A state dependency design enables the psychologist to test three sets of hypotheses: an information input change, a change in information storage processes, and a change in retrieval. If the drug is modifying input then we would expect the same recall scores when the learning and recall conditions were the same (D-D = ND-ND) and better than when the conditions were switched (D-ND = ND-D). If a drug is only changing storage, then the two groups that had the drug at the time of learning will have similar recall scores (D-ND = D-D) but be different from those who had no drug (ND-ND = ND-D). A retrieval change will result in similar scores for the groups which received the drug at the time of recall (D-D = ND-D) and similar scores for those with no drug at recall (D-ND = ND-ND).

State dependent learning with nicotine has been investigated in several studies. For example, in a recognition study, smokers who had been deprived of cigarettes since the previous night were given a nicotine cigarette or nothing immediately before serial presentation of a set of Chinese characters (Warburton, Wesnes and Shergold, 1982). Subjects who smoked prior to learning had significantly better recognition scores than the subjects who did not smoke. There was no effect of nicotine on recall performance. A significant interaction term indicated that changing the drug state from learning to recall interfered with recognition indicating an information input change, as one would expect from the earlier section on attention, because the drug would be altering the processing of information.

A second experiment examined the effect of a dose of nicotine on both short-term and long-term memory to investigate these effects on both input and storage further. After a nicotine or non-drug tablet, smoker subjects listened to a list of words and then did successive subtraction for one minute to prevent rehearsal before a free recall test was given. One hour later, they were given either nicotine or non-drug tablets, depending on their group, and asked to recall as many of the words as they could in another 10-minute free recall test. The short-term recall data revealed a very significant superiority of the nicotine group over the non-drug group. Long-term recall was also significantly better when subjects had taken nicotine prior to learning but not when taken prior to recall. The very significant interaction term again gave evidence for an information input effect of nicotine and showed that nicotine was facilitating the input of information to storage and also had an effect on storage but no effect on retrieval.

Further evidence for this hypothesis has come from work with other cholinergic drugs. Drachman and Leavitt (1974) injected young adults with **scopolamine** or **physostigmine.** While immediate memory was not modified significantly, storage of new information was significantly impaired by scopolamine, both for ordered recall of digits and for free recall of word lists. Retrieval by category, a test presumed to depend on intactness of both the retrieval mechanisms and long-term memory stores, showed mild impairment. Interpretation of this test was made difficult, however, by the lapses in attention of the subjects, who would often retrieve items from other categories in the middle of an otherwise adequate performance. Physostigmine did not produce any significant memory or cognitive effects although some subjects performed marginally better.

In a study of Drachman and Sahakian (1979), groups of normal volunteers were given scopolamine, methscopolamine or either 1.0 mg or 2.0 mg of physostigmine. A battery of memory tests was used to examine the drug effects on immediate memory, memory storage in terms of free recall, and ordered recall and retrieval from long-term storage. After scopolamine, immediate memory span was unimpaired but the ability of subjects to store new information, both for serial order of digits and for free recall of words, was severely disrupted. In addition, retrieval from long-term memory was significantly impaired after scopolamine. Those subjects who received methscopolamine were not significantly worse on any memory measure in comparison with undrugged subjects. Normal subjects receiving a low dose of physostigmine performed slightly better, and those receiving a higher dose of physostigmine slightly worse than normal controls, but these differences were not statistically significant.

The effects of scopolamine and its interaction with physostigmine on human memory were also studied by Mewaldt and Ghoneim (1979); scopolamine did not impair retrieval processes but impaired immediate recall of information. As the recall tasks were thought to exceed the capacity of short-term storage and retrieval was not affected by the drug then the memory deficit results from an interference with information storage. They found that scopolamine impairs the transfer of information from the short-term to the long-term store, but does not interfere with the retrieval of information. Physostigmine antagonized most of the memory impairment produced by scopolamine. Thus, the amnesic action of scopolamine and its blockade by physostigmine suggests a cholinergic mechanism in the encoding of new information into long-term storage.

An important study was done recently to investigate scopolamine's effects on specific categories of encoding operations (Frith et al., 1984). They examined the drug's action on the phonemic, semantic and imaginal mnemonic representation. These three types are believed to be implicated in the storage of information both about the occurrence of individual items of information and about the order of presentation of the information (Craik and Lockhart, 1972). In order to do this, they compared the use of imaginal and verbal encoding by examining the retention of concrete and abstract material, and the use of phonemic and semantic encoding by comparing the effects of phonemic and semantic similarity upon immediate serial recall. The use of a serial-recall task provided the opportunity to study the retention of both item information and order information.

Recall with scopolamine was impaired, irrespective of whether an item-recall scoring criterion or an ordered-recall scoring criterion was used. This suggests that the major locus of their amnesic effects was in the encoding of information concerning the occurrence of individual words, rather than information concerning the order of their occurrence. However, the amnesic effects of scopolamine could not be definitively attributed to impairment of specific categories of encoding operations.

This drug produced similar deficits on concrete and abstract words in terms both of ordered recall and of item recall and did not reduce the superiority of the retention of concrete material which was found in the non-drug condition. Superior retention of concrete words is believed to be the result of using mental imagery as a means of encoding strategy for long-term storage (Richardson, 1980). Consequently, it must be concluded that the drug does not disrupt this form of mnemonic encoding.

In terms of ordered recall, scopolamine produced deficits on phonemically confusable, semantically related, and unrelated words. The drug did not reduce the magnitude of the phonemic similarity effect. The phonemic similarity effect is thought to be due to the use of phonemic encoding as a means of representing serial-order information. It must therefore be concluded that scopolamine does not appear to disrupt this sort of phonemic encoding either.

Scopolamine produced impaired performance in terms of item recall on lists of unrelated words, but this impairment was reduced when the words to be remembered were phonemically or semantically related to one another. This suggests that the drug disrupted the encoding operations normally employed to represent item information in human memory, but that the subjects could compensate for this deficit by attending to the phonemic or semantic properties of the material when this basis of mnemonic organization was clearly suggested by the structure of the lists to be learned.

Mewaldt and Ghoneim (1979) had found that scopolamine disrupted performance at both early and middle serial positions. Frith and his colleagues also found a significant effect of scopolamine on the shape of serial-position curve and the nature of intrusion errors. Scoring for either ordered recall or item recall, scopolamine appeared to affect items at both early and middle serial positions. Unfortunately, their theoretical implications are unclear. The primary source of intrusion errors under scopolamine appeared to be items related in some way to the current list. Earlier research with the drug has not considered intrusion errors, even though these errors provide important information on the encoding operations being used. The results of this analysis suggest that scopolamine disrupts intrinsic cues relating to phonemic and semantic properties of the items themselves. This suggestion, although tentative, is important for theories of the function of the cholinergic system and long-term storage.

These results suggest that the memory impairment produced by cholinergic blockers, like scopolamine, is due to a temporary, biochemical 'lesion' of cholinergic neurones. Increasing activity with a small dose of physostigmine in the cholinergic neurones improved memory slightly. Thus we would expect that dosing subjects with physostigmine after scopolamine would reverse the effects of the latter. This prediction was confirmed and subjects treated with physostigmine showed a significant improvement in information storage.

A test of the information storage hypothesis can also be made by post-training administration of the drug. Use of this procedure means that the drug cannot have affected information input nor information retrieval. Any differences in the recall test between the drug and no drug groups can only be ascribed to a drug effect on the brain mechanisms that are involved in information storage.

To our knowledge, no human studies have investigated the effects of post-training doses of cholinergic drugs on information storage and the only work has been done with animals. In rats, post-trial injections of physostigmine were given after training in a spatial maze (Stratton and Petrinovich, 1963). Lower doses facilitated learning and as the neuropharmacological effects are gone long before the next day, the only effects on the next day's performance could have been by an action on the information storage processes. In another study, Squire (1969) injected rats with physostigmine before the first trial or at different times after learning alternation. When a treatment preceded or immediately followed Trial One, physostigmine increased this probability. If the drug followed Trial One by more than 15 minutes, then the probability of alternation was unaffected.

The results of Stratton and Petrinovich and of Squire suggest that a cholinergic mechanism is involved in memory storage but is only acting for a short time after acquisition. Pre-trial injections have a clear effect but post-trial injections are only effective immediately after training. These data can be interpreted as evidence of a cholinergic system mediating some aspect of the storage process.

Animal studies have given some ideas about the nature of cholinergic involvement in information storage. This research studied the action of 'significant' events on electrocortical activity. Marczynski (1969) observed that reward of a hungry cat with milk produced cortical synchronization, termed post-reinforcement synchronization, and positive steady potential shift in the same region which depended on the appropriateness of the reward, the reward contingent positive variation (RCPV). The RCPV was not specific to food intake reward, but could be obtained by perineal stimulation in the oestrous cat and rat and positively reinforcing electrical stimulation of the lateral hypothalamus. It was also elicited by aversive electrical shock to the skin and aversive hypothalamic stimulation. If a neutral stimulus was paired with a positive or negative reinforcing stimulus then the previously neutral stimulus elicited the steady potential shift which showed that a conditioned stimulus had the same effect (Rowland et al., 1967). Thus these electrical changes at the cortex were elicited by 'significant' events for the animal.

The occurrence of these events results in an enhancement of any evoked potentials presented at this moment, regardless of whether they are from 'relevant' stimuli or not (Marczynski, 1971). Stimuli presented without reward produced poorly-developed evoked potentials. In other words, we have a mechanism which enhances and prolongs evoked potentials that occur in temporal conjunction with the reinforcing stimulus. Significantly, Marczynski (1971) found that scopolamine and atropine blocked the post-reinforcement synchronization. Thus there is a cholinergic mechanism that is activated immediately after significant events which enhances the size of any sensory evoked potentials at the cortex. This would meet the specifications of a mechanism that initiates information storage.

MEMORY AND NORADRENALIN

As we saw from the last studies, the cholinergic mechanism for information storage can be activated by rewarding electrical stimulation of the lateral hypothalamus. Studies of the precise neural pathways which mediate reward have been studied by the technique of electrical self-stimulation of the brain. The studies of Huang and Routtenberg (1971) have suggested that the pathways have their origins around the locus coeruleus in the pons, and Crow (1972a,b) obtained self-stimulation responding from electrode sites close to the locus coeruleus. Histochemical staining (Ungerstedt, 1971) has demonstrated that there is a dorsal noradrenalin pathway which has its cell bodies in the locus coeruleus and ascends in the medial forebrain bundle. The dorsal noradrenalin pathway innervates practically all areas of the brain but especially the cerebral cortex, cerebellar cortex and the hippocampus.

Crow (1972b) points out that there is an association between the dorsal noradrenalin pathways from the locus coeruleus and the central connections of gustation which may mediate the reinforcing effects of gustatory stimulation and that association would explain the similar effects of food and electrical self-stimulation on the RCPV. Related to this hypothesis, Crow (1968) suggested that it is the projection of the dorsal noradrenalin fibres to the neocortex which initiates the plastic changes that are involved in learning.

This suggestion was similar to one made by Kety (1970) who postulated that the cortical release of noradrenalin might provide additional excitation to sensory cells that had recently been fired by an input of information. At the sensory cortex many cells will be active during processing of a sensory input and all these will be affected by the reinforcement mechanism. With a number of repetitions of this process the random activity in the synapses would be averaged out and the essential adaptive connections would be formed.

Most tests of this hypothesis in people have been made using drugs that increase activity in noradrenalin systems in the brain, like the **amphetamines.** The amphetamines both potentiate the release of and interfere with the re-uptake of noradrenalin and dopamine. Although amphetamines have been widely studied in animals for their effect on learning and memory (Hunter et al., 1977), the results of human experiments have been mixed.

Short-term memory was tested by Talland and Quarton (1965) using a running digit span test. Eight strings of single digits were presented auditorily to subjects. These strings consisted of lists of 8 to 20 numbers. The end of a string was indicated by a soft buzzer sound, and the subjects were instructed to recall the last five items of a string in the correct order. The test was given first with items spoken every second and then every four seconds. The subjects believed that two components determine the running digit span; one involves shifts of attention as the input changes, the other its organization, rehearsal, and other strategies by which the information is stored and made available for recall. No differences from the no drug condition were found with methamphetamine. In other words, the running memory span is determined by the capacity to shift attention and by the effective application of appropriate strategies of short-term information storage. These were not altered by an amphetamine.

The effects of a related compound, **methamphetamine,** on short-term memory in people were investigated by Crow and Bursill (1970). Subjects memorized sets of seven digits presented to them through headphones. After intervals of from 1 to 32 seconds they were asked to recall the digit series. The test was thus one of the subjects' capacity to register sensory information and to retain it in short-term storage. There was no evidence that the drug affected retention. A second experiment was designed to find out if the result could be explained by the subjects' rehearsing. In order to prevent rehearsal, the subjects had to do another task in the interval before recall. However, there was again no evidence for potentiation of short-term memory processes by methamphetamine.

In the same study in which he tested the effectiveness of physostigmine in reversing the scopolamine-induced memory loss, Drachman (1977) also studied the effects of amphetamines alone on free recall as well as its potency in reversing the effects of scopolamine. In untreated subjects, d-amphetamine, however, produced a small but significant improvement on the performance without affecting memory. Thus, again there was no evidence that amphetamine in human subjects improved memory. Although physostigmine significantly improved both memory storage and cognitive performance, d-amphetamine produced no significant improvements.

Mewaldt and Ghoneim (1979) also studied the effects of methamphetamine with 70 people who learned and recalled a series of word lists. Methamphetamine produced a small improvement of delayed recall of words, little effect on immediate recall and no significant influence on retrieval of information. This pattern of findings suggests that the drug is enhancing processes that are occurring after the input of information because methamphetamine had a larger effect in delayed recall than immediate recall. In contrast to the study of Drachman (1977), Mewaldt and Ghonheim (1979) did find that methamphetamine antagonized most of the memory impairment changes produced by scopolamine, although antagonism of scopolamine-impaired performance on the immediate recall test did not reach statistical significance. There are several possible reasons for the difference between the two sets of results. In addition to using different tests, Mewaldt and Ghonheim think that if Drachman had used a smaller dose of scopolamine and a larger dose of amphetamine (more than two to three times the dose he used) his results would have been different.

The other piece of evidence that supports the involvement of noradrenalin in human memory comes from a study with adrenergic blockers. Hypertension can be treated with drugs that can reduce the function of adrenergic neurones and two of these are **methyldopa** and **propranolol hydrochloride.** Clinical reports mention 'forgetfulness' occurring in patients taking these compounds. This phenomenon has been investigated in the laboratory (Solomon et al., 1983). The possible effect of hypertension on memory was controlled for with two control groups, one of hypertensive patients being treated with a non-adrenergic drug and the other, non-hypertensive patients taking an adrenergic drug. Subjects were read two brief paragraphs and were asked immediately after each paragraph to repeat it word for word. Then they were shown geometric designs of increasing complexity for 10 seconds and asked to draw them from memory. After an interval of approximately 20 minutes, the subjects again were asked to recall the paragraphs and to draw the designs.

There was severely-impaired verbal memory in both hypertensive and non-hypertensive subjects taking methyldopa or propranolol as compared with controls. The hypertensives were next divided into two groups. The first group consisted of patients who acknowledged increased forgetfulness and absentmindedness. The second sub-group of patients categorically denied any awareness of a memory problem. The performance on both the verbal and visual tests were similarly impaired whether or not patients were aware of their deficit.

Confirmation of the role of noradrenalin in information storage has been obtained from studies in which noradenergic drugs have been injected after learning. However, no human studies seem to have been done and we must rely on animal research for some clues. In a typical animal study, injections of amphetamine were given up to 30 minutes before, immediately before, immediately after, and up to 30 minutes after three trials of an appetitive visual discrimination (Krivanek and McGaugh, 1969). The performance of mice on the following day was facilitated by the dose given immediately after training. We have described amphetamine as a compound that potentiates noradrenergic function, but it also has the same effect on the activity of dopamine neurones. Thus the data only suggest that either noradrenalin or dopamine is involved in the process of information storage.

Resolution of this question has come from an experiment using diethyldithiocarbamate (McGaugh et al., 1975). Analysis of noradrenalin was decreased at this time while dopamine is significantly increased by diethyldithiocarbamate. Mice were given one trial passive avoidance training and injections of diethyldithiocarbamate either 30 minutes before, immediately after or two hours later. Retention of the passive avoidance was impaired by the drug dose preceding training and by a dose up to 60 minutes after training. These data indicate a specific noradrenergic involvement and it is certain that dopaminergic effects can be ruled out. Persuasive support for this idea has come from a study by Stein, Belluzzi and Wise (1975) in which they injected diethyldithiocarbamate prior to the training and impaired retention, but found that intraventricular injections of noradrenalin protected against the drug's amnesic effects.

In conclusion, this research on post-acquistion doses of noradrenergic drugs gives convincing evidence for the role of noradrenalin in consolidation, but the human data suggest that it is not involved in short-term memory.

NEURAL MECHANISMS OF CONSOLIDATION

Consolidation refers to the changes in the nature of the memory trace which make it relatively insensitive to external interference. The evidence for a period of memory fixation is strong. In hospitals, retrograde amnesia can occur after concussion and periods of up to 30 minutes or more of amnesia can occur after severe brain injury. It is important for the theory of consolidation that patients examined just after the injury may give information which later on is completely lost (Russell and Newcombe, 1966). These observations suggest that there is labile, short-term storage as well as a more permanent form of storage.

From this evidence, we can make the following hypotheses about information storage. A 'significant' event activates a noradrenergic pathway which inhibits electrocortical arousal at the cortex for a brief time. As we pointed out earlier in our discussion of attention, and elsewhere (Warburton, 1975, 1981), cortical desynchronization enables selection of stimuli in the environment by masking the smaller evoked potentials with desynchronized activity. However, when the reinforcement pathway inhibits the desynchronization, all evoked potentials at the cortex are enhanced. The magnitude of the evoked potential initiates the change in the characteristics of the cortical cells, that is, consolidation. After a single presentation of a reinforcing stimulus, the evoked potentials of many stimuli would be enhanced. With successive presentations of the reinforcing stimulus, the activity from randomly occurring stimuli would be averaged out. As a result, only the patterns of activity which occurred constantly in contiguity with the reinforcing stimulus which inhibited electrocortical activity, will be consolidated.

The most commonly-held belief about the neurochemical nature of information storage is that it results from a change in protein synthesis. Research which has supported this view has come from animal experiments and will not be discussed here. It is covered comprehensively in Warburton (1975) and in outline in Warburton (1983b). Changes in protein synthesis could be in the nature of increases in transmitter synthesizing enzymes which would increase the presynaptic stores of transmitter, making more available for release at each synapse. Another possibility is the development of new synaptic connections by protein synthesis. The outcome of both of these changes would be enhanced synaptic transmission.

In summary, there seem to be at least two forms of information storage. One form of storage is initiated by the input of information. It is shorter term, labile and can be enhanced and weakened by cholinergic drug treatments which act on the pathways which control electrocortical arousal. The second form of storage is also initiated at the same time as the labile storage, or shortly thereafter, and gradually becomes more resistant to any form of disruption over a period of an hour. Its establishment seems to depend on the activity of a noradrenergic pathway. This second type of storage involves a permanent change in protein.

CONSOLIDATON IN COGNITIVE TERMS

Traditionally in psychology memory has been separated into short-term memory storage and long-term memory storage. Short-term memory serves as a temporary holding place for newly-arrived information before material is transferred to a long-term memory store and, in people, this occurs by the process of rehearsal. This model fits with the neurochemical evidence for the long-term store being the outcome of protein synthesis.

However, these multi-store models are now considered as too simple. Craik and Lockart (1972) pointed out that sensory information can only be interpreted by comparing it with information in long-term storage. For example, reading requires an interaction between sensory information and information in long-term memory. Thus, information in short-term memory has already been processed by using information in long-term memory. Craik and Lockart think of memory as a continuum of analysis from the results of sensory analyses in short-term memory which results from semantic associative processes.

They believe that the strength of the memory trace arises from perceptual processing and that its persistence is a function of depth of analysis, so that deeper levels of analysis are associated with more elaborate, longer lasting, and stronger traces (Craik and Lockart, 1972). Short-term memory is thus a transitional stage between the receipt of information and initial interpretation and its final structuring into the long-term memory. Rehearsal is a process of organization (Norman, 1976) and provides time for further depth of processing to take place. Unless further processing does occur, the information will not leave any long lasting trace. This conception of a series of hierarchy of processing stages is often referred to as 'depth of processing' where greater 'depth' implies a greater degree of analysis.

As efficient information retrieval requires that relationships be found between the newly-arrived information and what a person already knows (Norman, 1976), retrieval will be improved by elaborate encoding. This elaborate encoding results from new associations and new relations which are formed between the newly presented material and information currently stored in long-term storage. It seems possible from the evidence that has already been discussed that the noradrenalin pathways to the cortex enable this elaborative consolidation of new information to occur. Support for this hypothesis comes from a study of amphetamine given to hyperactive and normal children, in which the drug was found to improve semantic processing, organization in recall, and free retrieval of information (Weingartner et al., 1980). It follows from this idea that any impairment of either the cholinergic or noradrenergic systems will result in memory impairment and that our discussion of the treatment of memory disorders will be focused on drugs that act on cholinergic and noradrenergic neurochemical systems.

TREATMENT OF MEMORY DISORDERS

As health care improves, the world is going to face an epidemic of senile dementia as the average age of the population increases. One of the most dramatic changes in cognitive function associated with senile dementia is memory impairment, especially the acquisition of new information. In many respects, senile dementia seems to be an exaggeration of the normal neurochemical processes of ageing, with Alzheimer's Disease as its most extreme form, although there are some differences (Rossor et al., 1984). It is significant that in senile dementia, there is a reduction in the levels of noradrenalin and acetylcholine at the cortex and hippocampus as well as the enzymes that are involved in their metabolism. It is a current working hypothesis that some types of senile dementia are a consequence of the failure of cholinergic and noradrenergic systems in the brain (Crow et al., 1982).

It follows from this hypothesis that a drug which would enhance one or both of these systems would reverse the cognitive deficits including the memory deficit. Consequently, extensive research has been devoted to the study of the nature of neurochemical changes of ageing and to discovering drugs which may ameliorate the psychological disabilities that result from the changes. Unfortunately, there are relatively few compounds available for treating cognitive problems in the elderly. However, as we have described, our understanding of the neurochemical processes which mediate normal cognitive functions is increasing.

Some clinical trials have been made to enhance memory in the elderly by giving them daily supplements of choline, from which acetylcholine is synthesized. In general, however, the choline has not led to a significant improvement of memory (for example, Davis et al., 1979, 1980) and clinicians are now dubious about the general usefulness of choline treatment (see Drachman and Sahakian, 1979; Ferris et al., 1979; Davis et al., 1980).

Earlier, we discussed the effects of physostigmine on scopolamine-induced memory loss. Subjects treated with physostigmine showed a significant improvement in both memory storage and cognitive performance. If the scopolamine loss is due to a temporary, biochemical 'lesion' of cholinergic neurones and senile dementia is due in part to pathological damage to cholinergic neurones, then restoring synaptic transmission within the cholinergic system should improve senile dementia.

In order to test this hypothesis, Drachman and Sahakian (1980) carried out a preliminary study in which a group of normal, aged volunteers were given a small dose of physostigmine. Memory and cognitive functions were compared with a set of untreated, aged subjects and a trend toward improvement was seen in the experimental group for each of the cognitive measures tested, particularly in memory storage. However, the variance in this population was too large for statistical significance with only 13 subjects in each group. Other studies have improved memory with lower doses of physostigmine, but the dose is crucial (Davis et al., 1976).

The problem with physostigmine treatment is that there is evidence of a wide range of individual sensitivities to the drug. Another difficulty of treatment of memory dysfunction with drugs that increase cholinergic activity, is the narrow range of therapeutic efficiency of most of them. In addition, memory loss can result from many illnesses, such as infection, depression, decreased cerebral blood flow as well as decreased cholinergic function in the brain. From what we have said earlier, there could be a selective loss of noradrenergic neurones. Thus we can only expect that a sub-sample of demented individuals will show marked improvement with cholinergic agonists. It might be possible to predict from some biochemical 'marker' from the body fluids, for example, cerebrospinal fluid, which patients may be treated successfully with cholinergic agonists.

In the absence of such a marker, a better approach may be to use compounds that have a broad spectrum of action on cholinergic and noradrenergic pathways. One compound which has these properties is **RU 24722** which releases noradrenalin at the cortex, acetylcholine in the hippocampus, and in addition acts on protein synthesis. We have found that doses of RU 24722 in young, normal volunteers produced highly significant improvements in verbal recall at 0, 4 and 8 hours after dosing. There was a trend for an improvement in recognition memory. In contrast, there was no evidence for any changes in attentional performance, as assessed by the rapid visual information processing test or the Stroop test. If RU 24722 is capable of improving performance in the absence of cognitive impairment then it should be effective in improving memory in the elderly. It remains to be seen whether the drug will enter clinical use, but this drug gives some idea of the sort of compound that should be useful.

Before concluding this chapter, we should point out that use of drug therapy does not preclude the use of other forms of therapy. We have already described some of the cognitive processes that occur during consolidation. Cherkin and Riege (1983) have advocated a multi-modal approach to therapy of senile amnesias and we would endorse this opinion. They suggest using behavioural methods to improve cognitive performance in the elderly as well as drug therapy. Some behavioural methods do seem to improve cognitive performance in dementia. Training in verbal strategies and concept identification has been effective in immediate tests and in tests over six months and one year. Practice in inductive reasoning, category organization, imagery, and association has improved memory performance relative to controls. Thus, the elderly do respond to training and can modify their mnemonic techniques, although training has not always generalized to similar tasks or to day-to-day living. Consequently, it is essential to design a programme based on the patient's strengths and to match the cognitive therapy strategies to the patient's needs and abilities.

Acknowledgements

We thank Ms C. Ayres, Dr T.J. Crow, Dr V. Hamilton, Dr J.L. McGaugh, Dr R. Pigache, Dr D.S. Segal and Ms A.Walters for their help with this chapter.

REFERENCES

ANDERSSON, K. and HOCKEY, G.R. (1977) Effects of cigarette smoking on learning and retention. **Psychopharmacologia, 41,** 1-15

CALLAWAY, E. and BAND, I. (1958) Some psychopharmacological effects of atropine. **Archives of Neurology and Psychiatry, 79,** 91-102

CHERKIN, A. and RIEGE, W.H. (1983) Multimodal approach to pharmacotherapy of senile amnesias. In: J. Cervos-Navarro and H.I. Sarkander (eds) **Brain Aging: Neuropathlogy and Neuropharmacology. (Aging, 21, 415-435).** New York: Raven Press

CRAIK, F.I.M. and LOCKART, R.S. (1972) Levels of processing: a framework for memory research. **Journal of Verbal Learning and Verbal Behavior, 11,** 671-676

CROW, T.J. (1968) Cortical synapses and reinforcement. **Nature, 219,** 245-246

CROW, T.J. (1972a) A map of the rat mesencephalon for electrical self-stimulation. **Brain Research, 36,** 265-73

CROW, T.J. (1972b) Catecholamine-containing neurones and electrical self-stimulation. 1. A review of some data. **Psychological Medicine, 2,** 414-421

CROW, T.J. (1977) A general lamine hypothesis. **Neuroscience Program Bulletin, 15,** 195-205

CROW, T.J. and BURSILL, A.E. (1970) An investigation into the effects of methamphetamine on short-term memory in man. In: E. Costa and S. Garattini (eds) **Amphetamines and Related Compounds,** 889-896. New York: Raven Press

CROW, T.J., CROSS, A.J., GROVE-WHITE, I.G. and ROSS, D.G. (1982) Central neurotransmitters, memory and dementia. In: D. Wheatley (ed.) **Psychopharmacology of Old Age.** Oxford: OUP

DAVIS, K.L., HOLLISTER, L.E., OVERALL, J., JOHNSON, A. and TRAIN, K. (1976) Physostigmine: effects on cognition and affect in normal subjects. **Psychopharmacology, 51,** 23-27

DAVIS, K.L., MOHS, R.C., TINKLENBERG, J.R., HOLLISTER, L.E., YESAVAGE, J.A. and KOPELL, B.S. (1979) The treatment of memory deficits in the aged with choline chloride. In: K.L. Davis and P.A.Berger (eds) **Brain Acetylcholine and Neuropsychatric Disease,** 253-262. New York: Plenum Press

DAVIS, K.L., MOHS, R.C., TINKLENBERG, J.R., HOLLISTER, L.E., PFEFFERBAUM, A. and KOPELL, B.S. (1980) Cholinomimetics and memory. The effect of choline chloride. **Archives of Neurology, 37,** 49-52

DOMINO, E.F., YAMAMOTO, K. and DREN, A.T. (1968) Role of cholinergic mechanisms in states of wakefulness and sleep. **Progress in Brain Research, 28,** 113-133

DRACHMAN, D.A. (1977) Memory and cognitive function in man: Does the cholinergic system have a specific role? **Neurology, 27,** 783-790

DRACHMAN, D.A. and LEAVITT, (1974) Human memory and the cholinergic system: a relationship to aging? **Archives of Neurology, 30,** 113-121

DRACHMAN, D.A. and SAHAKIAN, B. (1979) Effects of cholinergic agents on human learning and memory. In: A. Barbeau, J.H. Growdon, and R.J. Wurtman (eds) **Nutrition and the Brain.** New York: Raven Press

DRACHMAN, D.A. and SAHAKIAN, B.J. (1980) Memory and cognitive function in the elderly. A preliminary trial of physostigmine. **Archives of Neurology, 37,** 674-675

EDWARDS, J.A. and WARBURTON, D.M. (1983) Smoking, nicotine and electrocortical activity. **Pharmacology and Therapeutics, 19,** 147-164

FERRIS, S.H., SATHANANTHAN, G., REISMAN, B. and GERSHON, S. (1979) Long-term choline treatment of memory-impaired elderly patients. **Science, 205,** 1039-1040

FRITH, C.D., RICHARDSON, J.T.E., SAMUEL, M., CROW, T.J. and McKENNA, P.J. (1984) The effects of intravenous diazepam and hyoscine upon human memory. **Quarterly Journal of Experimental Psychology, 36a,** 133-144

GHONEIM, M.H. and MEWALT, S.P. (1975) Effects of diazepam and scopolamine on storage, retrieval and organizational processes in memory. **Psychopharmacologia, 44,** 257-262

GROLL, E. (1966) Zentralnervose und periphere Akitivierrungsvariablen bei Vigilanzleistungen (Central nervous sysem and peripheral activation variables during vigilance performance). **Zeitschrift fur Experimentelle und Angewandte Psychologie, 13,** 248-264

HUANG, Y.H. and ROUTTENBERG, A. (1971) Lateral hypothalamic self-stimulation pathways. **Physiology and Behavior, 7,** 419-432

HUNTER, B., ZORNETZER, S.F., JARVIK, M.E. and McGAUGH, J.L. (1977) Modulation of learning and memory. In: L.L. Iversen, S.D. Iversen, and S.H. Snyder (eds) **Handbook of Psychopharmacology.** New York: Plenum Press

KAHNEMAN, D. (1973) **Attention and Effort.** Englewood Cliffs, NJ: Prentice-Hall

KETCHUM, J.S., SIDELL, F.R., CROWELL, E.B., AGHAJANIAN, G.K. and HAINES, A.H. (1973) Atropine, scopolamine and ditran: comparative pharmacology and antagonists in man. **Psychopharmacologia, 28,** 121-145

KETY, S.S. (1970) The biogenic amines in the central nervous system: their possible roles in arousal, attention and learning. In: F.O. Schmitt (ed.) **Neurosciences: Second Study Program.** 324-336. New York: Rockefeller University Press

KRIVANEK, J. and McGAUGH, J.L. (1969) Facilitatory effects of pre-and post-trial 1-amphetamine administration of discrimination learning in mice. **Agents and Actions, 1,** 36-42

LINDSLEY, D.B. (1952) Psychological phenomenon and the electroencephalogram. **Electroencephalography and Clinical Neurophysiology, 4,** 443-448

MARCZYNSKI, T.J. (1969) Postreinforcement synchronization and the cholinergic system. **Federation Proceedings, 28,** 132-134

MARCZYNSKI, T.J. (1971) Cholinergic mechanism determines the occurrence of reward contingent positive variation (RCPV) in cat. **Brain Research, 28,** 71-83

McGAUGH, J.L., GOLD, P.E., VAN BUSKIRK, R. and HAYCOCK, J. (1975) Modulating influences of hormones and catecholamines on memory storage. In: W.H. Gispen, Th. B. van Wimersma Griedanus, B. Bohus and D. de Wied (eds) **Progress in Brain Research.** Amsterdam: Elsevier

MEWALDT, S.P. and GHONEIM, M.M. (1979) The effects and interactions of scopolamine, physostigmine and methamphetamine on human memory. **Pharmacology, Biochemistry and Behavior, 10,** 205- 210

NORMAN, D.A. (1976) **Memory and Attention.** New York: Wiley

NORMAN, D.A. and BOBROW, D.G. (1975) On data-limited and resource-limited processes. **Cognitive Psychology, 7,** 44-64

OSTFELD, A.M. and ARUGUETTE, A. (1962) Central nervous system effects of hyoscine in man. **Journal of Pharmacology and Experimental Therapeutics, 137,** 133-139

OSTFELD, A.M., MACHNE, X. and UNNA, K.R. (1960) The effects of atropine on the electroencephalogram and behaviour in man. **Journal of Pharmacology and Experimental Therapeutics, 128,** 265-272

PLUM, F. (1979) Dementia, an approaching epidemic. **Nature, 279,** 372-373

RABBITT, P. (1979) Current paradigms and models in human information processing. In: V. Hamilton and D.M. Warburton (eds) **Human Stress and Cognition: An Information Processing Approach.** London: Wiley

RICHARDSON, J.T.E. (1980) **Mental Imagery and Human Memory.** London: Macmillan

ROSSOR, M.N., IVERSEN, L.L., REYNOLDS, G.P., MOUNTJOY, C.Q. and ROTH, M. (1984) Neurochemical characteristics of early and late onset types of Alzheimer's disease. **British Medical Journal, 288,** 961-964

ROWLAND, V., BRADLEY, H., SCHOOL, P. and DEUTSCHMAN, D. (1967) Cortical steady-potential shifts in conditioning. **Conditioned Reflex, 2,** 3-22

RUSSELL, W.R. and NEWCOMBE, F. (1966) Contribution from clinical neurology. In: D. Richter (ed.) **Aspects of Learning and Memory.** New York: Basic Books

SHUTE, C.C.D. and LEWIS, P.R. (1967) The ascending cholinergic reticular system: neocortical, olfactory and subcortical projections. **Brain, 90,** 497-520

SOLOMON, F., HOTCHKISS, E., SARAVAY, S.M., BAYER, C., RAMSAY, P. and BLUM, R.S. (1983) Impairment of memory function by antihypertensive medication. **Archives of General Psychiatry, 40,** 1109-1112

SQUIRE, L.R. (1969) Effects of pretrial and post-trial administrationof cholinergic and anticholinergic drugs on spontaneous alternation. **Journal of Comparative and Physiological Psychology, 69,** 69-75

SQUIRE, L.R. and DAVIS, H.P. (1981) The pharmacology of memory: a neurobiological perspective. **Annual Review of Pharmacology and Toxicology, 22,** 323-356

STEIN, L., BELLUZZI, J.D. and WISE, C.D. (1975) Memory enhancement by central administration of norepinephrine. **Brain Research, 84,** 329-335

STRATTON, L.O. and PETRINOVICH, L. (1963) Post-trial injections of an anticholinesterase drug and maze learning in two strains of rats. **Psychopharmacologia, 5,** 47-54

TALLAND, G.A. and QUARTON, G.C. (1965) The effects of methamphetamine and pentobarbital on the running memory span. **Psychopharmacologia, 7,** 379-382

UNGERSTEDT, U. (1971) Stereotaxic mapping of the monoamine pathways in the rat brain. **Acta Physiologica Scandinavica Supplement, 367,** 1-48

WARBURTON, D.M. (1975) **Brain, Behaviour and Drugs.** London: Wiley

WARBURTON, D.M. (1981) Neurochemical bases of behaviour. **British Medical Journal, 37,** 121-126

WARBURTON, D.M. (1983a) Extrapolation in the neurochemistry of behaviour. In: G. Davey (ed.) **Animal Models and Human Behaviour.** London: Wiley

WARBURTON, D.M. (1983b) Towards a neurochemical theory of learning and memory. In: A. Gale and J.A. Edwards (eds) **Physiological Correlates of Human Behaviour.** London: Academic Press

WARBURTON, D.M., WESNES, K. and SHERGOLD, K. (1982) Facilitation of learning and state dependency with nicotine. **Proceedings of the Thirteenth Collegium Internationale Neuropsychopharmacologium Congress**

WEINGARTNER, H., RAPOPORT, J.L., BUCHSBAUM, M.S., BUNNEY, W.E., EBERT, M.H., MIKKELSEN, E.J. and CAINE, E.D. (1980) Cognitive processes in normal and hyperactive children and their response to amphetamine treatment. **Journal of Abnormal Psychology, 89,** 25-37

WESNES, K. and REVELL, A.D. (1984) The separate and combined effects of scopolomine and nicotine on human information processing. **Psychopharmacology**

WESNES, K. and WARBURTON, D.M. (1978) The effect of cigarette smoking and nicotine tablets upon human attention. In: R.E. Thornton (ed.) **Smoking Behaviour: Physiological and Psychological Influences.** London: Churchill-Livingstone

WESNES, K. and WARBURTON, D.M. (1983a) Effects of scopolamine on stimulus sensitivity and response bias in a visual vigilance task. **Neuropsychobiology, 9,** 154-157

WESNES, K. and WARBURTON, D.M. (1983b) The effects of smoking on rapid information processing performance. **Neuropsychobiology, 9,** 223-229

WESNES, K. and WARBURTON, D.M. (1984a) Effects of scopolamine and nicotine on human rapid information processing performance. **Psychopharmacology, 82,** 147-150

WESNES, K. and WARBURTON, D.M. (1984b) The effects of cigarettes of varying yield on rapid information processing performance. **Psychopharmacology, 82,** 338-342

WESNES, K., WARBURTON, D.M. and MATZ, B. (1983) The effects of nicotine on stimulus sensitivity and response bias in a visual vigilance task. **Neuropsychobiology, 9,** 41-44

THE RELATION BETWEEN LANGUAGE AND THOUGHT IN YOUNG CHILDREN

George Butterworth

When asked for his views on the relationship of thought to language, Noam Chomsky replied that this was a question that he could not answer (Reiber, 1983). To ask about the relationship between the development of language and of thought may be to assume that they are mutually exclusive abilities. As a result, we may overlook the possibility that language may be regarded as one aspect of cognition and language development as one component of a developing cognitive system. From this perspective we may suppose not only that thought will have its influence on language but also that the acquisition of language will have an influence on thought. Furthermore, if there is any truth in Chomsky's idea that the capacity for language so readily displayed by humans is a reflection of a species-typical cognitive system (Chomsky, 1980), then may we expect to observe not only cognitive precursors to language but also linguistic determinants of thought as they develop?

Campbell (1979) has suggested that the best advice one might offer a student intent on pursuing the question of the relation between language and thought is 'Danger - Keep Off'. There is an enormous quantity of research that has a bearing on the question yet very little coherent theory exists to link work in the many areas of cognitive functioning that might be considered components of language such as emotional expression, auditory and visual perception, phonology and concept formation. There are major problems even with the definition of language itself; for example, although American Sign Language (ASL) is generally accepted as a language, it is uncertain whether it should be so regarded when it is taught to apes (see, for example, Sebeok and Umiker-Sebeok, 1980).

Rather than enter into such controversies a simple-minded approach will be adopted here. It will be assumed that the general contrast on the one hand between language as communication by means of spoken symbols and thought on the other hand, as reflective, mental activity will suffice to carry the preliminary distinctions necessary. Considered in this simple-minded way it is possible to ask:

whether thought has its origins in language;

whether thought is a form of speech for self;

whether language without thought is possible; and,

whether basic cognitive operations can develop in the absence of language.

In this chapter, two classical accounts of the developmental relationships between language and thought will be contrasted. These are the accounts put forward by the Swiss psychologist Jean Piaget (1926) and the Soviet psychologist Lev Vygotsky (1962).* Then, some contemporary evidence from developmental psychology will be reviewed. This will concentrate on the period towards the end of infancy and the early years of childhood, when the beginnings of both thought and language can be seen to emerge.

PART 1. CLASSICAL THEORIES OF THE RELATION BETWEEN LANGUAGE AND THOUGHT IN YOUNG CHILDREN: PIAGET AND VYGOTSKY

Piaget's theory

Piaget (1926) asserted that language provides food for thought but that it cannot create thought. Thinking, considered as mental operations upon concepts, has its developmental roots in the sensori-motor activities of babies and is not founded upon language. Four major sources of evidence led Piaget to conclude that mental operations are primary in development and themselves give structure to language. Sinclair (1982) provides a detailed exposition and defence of Piaget's position:

1. The crux of Piaget's argument rests on his studies of infant development (Piaget, 1951, 1953, 1954), for he argues that the fundamental precursors of thought can be observed in the infant's behaviour long before the child utters its first words. Thus, the capacity for language cannot give rise to thought. On the contrary, Piaget argues that certain elementary forms of thought, such as the possession of the concept of object

---

* *Vygotsky's important book, 'Thought and Language' was first published in 1934, in Russian; all references to it in this chapter are to the first English translation, 1962.*

permanence, are a necessary condition for language acquisition. The concept that objects have names may be seen as a natural outgrowth of more elementary forms of knowledge about objects. (The concept of object permanence encompasses the belief that objects have their own unique identity, a type of knowledge that would seem intimately linked to naming. See Butterworth, 1981, for a review of Piaget's theory on this topic and also Moore and Meltzoff, 1978.) The general view, then, is that cognitive development occurring during infancy is a necessary (but not sufficient) condition for language acquisition. This formulation is not unique to Piaget. It has been adopted by many contemporary theorists concerned to explain the origins of language (see, for example, Cromer, 1974).

2. A second source of evidence against the identical nature of language and thought comes from Piaget's theory of symbolic development (Piaget, 1951). Spoken language emerges almost simultaneously with four other behaviour patterns at the end of infancy: deferred imitation, symbolic play, evocative memory and mental imagery. Piaget therefore argues that the important changes in cognitive processes that give rise to language are much more extensive than is apparent if the focus is restricted to speech. The first words are just one consequence of acquiring the 'semiotic function', best understood as the ability to reason in terms of symbols. According to Piaget, spoken language emerges at the end of the sensori-motor period because it depends upon mental representation, which in turn derives from 'internalized' imitation of objects and events. It therefore has many qualities in common with the other activities, such as play, in which objects may be made to stand as symbols for other objects and which can be observed in early childhood. These similarities are taken as additional evidence that language has its roots in more general cognitive processes.

3. Further evidence concerning the relation between language and thought comes from studies of reasoning in young children. Possession of language does not prevent the child from making errors typical of his or her stage of intellectual development. The pre-school child uses words which, to the adult mind, incorporate mental operations such as quantifiers (that is, words referring to number, volume, weight or any aspect of quantity), comparatives (for example, more, less), yet this does not prevent errors in conservation tasks and other difficulties with logical reasoning problems (which Piaget has extensively demonstrated). Hence, Piaget argues that the words comprising the language are themselves being defined and redefined in terms of the child's level of mental development. Logically equivalent

evidence, in terms of its importance for the debate on language and thought, comes from research showing that children born deaf nevertheless pass through broadly the same stages in cognitive development as those who can hear and speak (Furth, 1966), demonstrating that thought can develop even in the absence of speech.

4. One of Piaget's main sources of evidence on the relation between language and thought in young children comes from his studies of 'egocentric speech' (Piaget, 1926). Egocentric speech is defined as monologue (where the child talks with no apparent audience), collective monologue (talking aloud to the self but with other people present) and repetition or playing with words. Piaget found that roughly 50 per cent of the speech of pre-school children did not result in any effective communication with others. In fact, the concept of egocentrism is often misunderstood so it is perhaps as well to point out that the pre-school child in Piaget's view clearly intends to communicate with others but often fails because he or she lacks the intellectual operations necessary to reciprocate appropriately in verbal exchanges (see Butterworth, 1980, for a discussion of the concept of egocentrism).

In summary, Piaget insists that language depends upon intellectual operations for its development. Unlike Chomsky, Piaget is not arguing that language is a cognitive process in its own right; rather he places language in the position of a 'figurative' content of thought, a kind of 'substance' upon which the mind can operate.

Vygotsky's theory

Vygotsky (1962) has much in common with Piaget in his analysis of the relation between language and thought, as well as some points of profound disagreement. He shares in common with Piaget the genetic method of enquiry, that is, the analysis of complex cognitive processes by studying how they develop. He agrees that thought and speech spring from different developmental roots, pointing out that many primates have relatively advanced intellectual abilities but that nevertheless, they lack speech. A pre-linguistic phase can be observed in the evolution of thought - chimpanzees clearly can solve problems requiring thought, yet they do not speak - and a pre-intellectual phase can be observed in the evolution of speech (since parrots can imitate speech yet they have only limited intellectual abilities by comparison to man and the primates). Man's particular achievement is to combine these capacities to give rise to spoken language. In young children, the separate roots of thought and speech can also be observed. The evidence comes from experiments on intellectual development in babies before the emergence of speech. Evidence for the separate origins of language comes from the presumed precursors such as infants' babbling, the very early reactions of the baby to the human voice, early communicative gestures and social responsiveness before there is any evidence of thought. Around the age of two, these separate developmental streams are said to merge with the child's realization that each thing has its own name. The child discovers the symbolic function of words and, from then on, speech begins to serve the intellect - thoughts begin to be spoken.

At this point, Vygotsky's theory diverges from Piaget's. For Vygotsky, verbal thought marks a point of contact, a potentially indivisible basic unit where language and thought unite. To be sure, verbal thought is not the only type of thought available to the human race. However, through its analysis and especially through an understanding of how word meanings are acquired by children, the specifically verbal aspects of thought can be established. For Vygotsky, unlike Piaget, verbal thought is one area of cognition where language is not subordinate to thought but co-equal with it.

The primary function of speech is communication, and communication has its roots in social relations. Hence, according to Vygotsky, verbal thought is the outcome of a prolonged developmental process in which the child transfers initially overt speech, which serves a social function and is of social origin, inwards to the mental plane. On its way 'inwards', thought and language passes through an egocentric stage, in which thoughts are spoken aloud (or equally one might say speech is loud thought). However, Vygotsky emphatically denies that egocentric speech is not yet social. On the contrary, he asserts that since language is rooted in social relations, the direction of development is from social to private speech (rather than from private to socialized, as Piaget argued). Typically, this transition from overt speech, to speech for self, to inner speech is complete by about eight years of age.

The first words the child acquires are global and undifferentiated. In a sense, they carry an excess of meaning because they represent not only the specific referent intended by the adult but also many other aspects of the context in which the utterance is made and the behaviours that co-occur with the speech of the adult. These global (syncretic) characteristics are also typical of thought in young children. However, Vygotsky argues that Piaget overestimates the extent to which the pre-school child's thought is illogical. When circumstances are favourable, the child will demonstrate an aptitude for logical reasoning that is necessarily undetected by Piaget in his rather abstract tests of the child's cognition and language.

This brief historical sketch of the two major positions on the relationship between language and thought in young children has raised many issues concerning the origins of these human capacities, the nature of egocentrism, the acquisition of word meaning, the relation between word meaning and verbal thought, and the nature of the interiorization of language and its relation to logical reasoning. These are complicated problems that have by no means been solved in the half century that has elapsed since Piaget and Vygotsky sketched out the broad terms of the debate. Nevertheless, some of these issues can now be explored in relation to the contemporary literature, to establish how they have become clarified in relation to the experimental evidence.

PART 2: RECENT RESEARCH ON THE RELATION BETWEEN LANGUAGE AND THOUGHT IN YOUNG CHILDREN

It is beyond the scope of this chapter to attempt to reconcile all the points of disagreement between Piaget and Vygotsky. The approach will be to tackle two of the general issues involved, namely: (1) whether there is any evidence for intellectual underpinnings to language in infant development, as Piaget maintained; (2) whether language can influence thought in young children and thereby act as a system for the self regulation of behaviour, as Vygotsky argued.

A great deal of research has been carried out in the various branches of developmental psychology that are relevant to this discussion. Clearly it is impossible to do justice to all of them in a short space and it has proved necessary to be highly selective in the material to be incorporated. Some relevant research will be found in previously published 'Psychology Surveys' (Harris, 1979; Martlew, 1979; McShane, 1980) and so will not be duplicated here. The reader wishing for a more extensive review will find an extremely useful account of theory and research into early language acquisition in Goodwin (1980).

Intellectual development and the acquisition of language: pre-requisites for communication

It is obvious that newborn babies neither speak nor think, yet both thought and language must have their origins in the capacities of the neonate to gain information about the world and to store and make use of the knowledge acquired. A very brief discussion of the starting point for human communicative development may be useful in gaining an understanding of how thought and language eventually inter-relate.

The origins of language have often been traced to systems of pre-verbal communication. Goodwin (1980), for example, has suggested that the following constitute the minimum set of cognitive and behavioural pre-requisites:

(a) Intersubjectivity. Infants must recognize others as con-specifics with whom they may interact and communicate.

(b) There must be some means of coordinating activity between the infant and adult participants and there must be some means of regulating 'turn taking' in the communication process.

(c) There must exist an adequate repertoire of communicative acts at the non-verbal level to control the joint activity of the participants.

(d) There must be coordinated attention to objects in the environment if infant and caretaker are to agree on the topic which is at the focus of their joint activity.

It is clear that these pre-requisites place heavy demands on what is required by way of perceptual and communicative abilities in the young infant, even before there is any question of spoken language.

In recent years, there has been increasing recognition of the perceptual and social sophistication of the neonate and it is quite possible that the minimum conditions Goodwin describes may actually be satisfied in the innate repertoire. For example, newborn babies are particularly sensitive to the rhythmic properties of speech (Condon and Sander, 1974) and will move in synchrony with patterned sounds. They will imitate mouth and tongue movements and hand movements (Meltzoff, 1982; Vinter, 1983) and there appears to be rudimentary turn taking and joint attention in various social activities (Trevarthen, 1982; Scaife and Bruner, 1975). The origins of language may therefore lie in various aspects of the interaction between parents and babies (see Bullowa, 1979; Golinkoff, 1983).

Also, great emphasis has been placed on the skills of adults in regulating their social interaction with infants in ways that make comprehension easier for the child (for example, Collis and

Schaffer, 1975). However, it is necessary to remember that although various abilities may be general pre-requisites for communication (and some of them may therefore apply to species other than humans) the specific problem here is to determine whether changes in the child's intellectual abilities occurring through cognitive development give rise to communication by means of spoken language. Although knowledge of the innate repertoire of infants is useful in showing where development originates, it does not really help in pinpointing the cognitive changes that may support the emergence of speech. Furthermore, it should not be forgotten that however sophisticated or rudimentary the infant's abilities, they are supplemented and supported by adults; the adult's cognitive abilities ensure the success of early communication. Bruner (1983) has given the adult's role of 'scaffolding' the child's language development the acronym 'LASS' - language acquisition support structure. He did this to emphasize the complementarity of the social structure with any innate abilities that may comprise Chomsky's 'LAD' - language acquisition device. Early communication, for example, smiling or other non-verbal signals, may therefore serve to maintain social interaction. But from the baby's point of view any communication that occurs may simply be an inadvertent consequence of the infant-adult interaction. Such a system of shared meanings may be characterized as 'protocommunication': it may precede communication proper, but it does not in and of itself comprise a language.

Cognitive development prior to the emergence of language

As well as coming into possession of an adequate repertoire of words and acquiring detailed knowledge of the environment to help in interpreting the meaning of utterances, the infant must acquire concepts about objects, means of classifying those objects and an understanding of the relationships that people and things may enter into with the environment if meaningful speech is to develop. Even when the first words have been acquired, once speech departs from the immediate 'here and now', further intellectual development involving memory and representation may be necessary. The ability to refer to objects that are not immediately present ('displacement of reference') involves objects or events common to the represented experiences of speaker and hearer and a conventional, symbolic means of communication to allow the topic of a conversation to go beyond the constraints of the immediate context.

Golinkoff (1983) offers a useful (if gross) distinction between an early kind of communicative competence that can be observed in the first six months of life, and a more sophisticated form of instrumental communication that can be observed in babies towards the end of the first year. Instrumental communication may be one of the cognitive precursors of language that arise in the course of the child's own cognitive development. It can be observed once infants begin to use pre-verbal communication intentionally to influence others to carry out their wishes, as for instance when the fourteen-month-old baby vocalizes to catch the mother's attention and then points to the object it desires. Even though the infant may not immediately succeed in conveying what it means to the mother, it will persevere until the message is understood. In fact, the child's failed messages are particularly revealing of communicative intent, since the child will often reject the mother's interpretation of its behaviour.

It is clearly something in the intellectual development of the infant (rather than the adult simply attributing communicative intent to the child) that gives rise to the qualitative difference between the interactional communication of the young baby and intentional communication. Even though there is little evidence of any relationship between object concept development and language acquisition (Corrigan, 1979), Piaget may still have been correct to emphasize the more general influence of changes in the child's abilities that give rise to intentional control of manual and articulatory gestures and which may underpin the instrumental use of language.

This example of an intellectual precursor to spoken language (that is, the intentional use of signals) also raises the centrally important topic of reference and its role in language acquisition.

Put at its simplest, reference concerns how one individual may indicate to another, an object for their joint attention. How an infant understands reference is important in unravelling the relation between thought and language in young children because the language that the infant hears must become an object of its own thought before it can become an instrument of thought. Reference enables a connection to be established between words and things. In the example above, given by Golinkoff, the infant points with its finger at the object it desires and even though it does not immediately succeed in fulfilling its intention of obtaining the object, it does eventually do so. Is there any relation between such pre-linguistic forms of referring and the redirection of attention by linguistic means?

Bruner (1983) discusses the emergence of reference in detail. The earliest form that can be observed consists in joint visual attention to an interesting object; when the mother turns to look at an object that catches her attention, her infant, even as young as two months, will turn and look in the same direction, as if aware of a potentially interesting sight at the terminus of their joint direction of gaze. This most primitive mechanism can also be observed in other species; for example, the leader of a herd of gazelle will signal danger by looking in a particular direction, whereupon the remainder of the herd will dash off in the opposite direction. Although evidence from other species shows that regulating joint visual attention is not a particularly linguistic process (since it occurs in species that never acquire language), it may nevertheless serve a linguistic function for humans.

Detailed studies of joint visual attention between infants and their mothers has revealed that 'looking where someone else is looking' is governed by three progressively more sophisticated cognitive mechanisms that emerge sequentially in the first 18 months of life (Butterworth and Cochran, 1980; Butterworth and Jarrett, 1980).

The first mechanism, which governs joint visual attention up to about 9 months, consists in the infant looking in the same direction as the mother and selecting an object for attention which is intrinsically attractive. That is, the communication between mother and infant depends to some extent on the fact that the infant is distractible, both by the mother's change of attention and by the intrinsic properties of objects in the world.

This mechanism is superseded somewhere between 9 and 12 months by a much more precise 'geometric' process, whereby the infant can determine which of two objects the mother is looking at even when the objects themselves are identical. This process has been called 'geometric' because it seems to involve extrapolating an invisible line along the mother's line of gaze to the target, using the angular displacement of the mother's head as the cue. Acquiring this ability coincides with the ability to comprehend the mother's manual pointing.

In a third phase of development between 12 and 18 months, the infant extends its comprehension of looking and pointing to areas outside its own immediate visual field. Now, if the mother looks or points behind the baby, the infant will understand the reference to a hidden object and search for the object singled out by the mother By the time the infant has entered the second year of life it is well able to comprehend the meaning of indexicals, words such as 'where' or 'what', which the mother will use extensively when presenting objects to the baby in teaching the names of things (see Bruner, 1983).

Clearly, this aspect of language acquisition has its roots not only in primitive forms of intersubjectivity such as joint visual attention, but also it develops by incorporating the primitive form into later-appearing control systems. Cognitive development extends the infant's comprehension of looking and pointing. Intellectual development therefore enters both into the intentional production of communicative gestures by the infant and into the comprehension by the infant of the referential behaviour of others before speech has been acquired.

Other examples of cognitive development in infancy that seem intimately related to the production (as well as the comprehension) of language have been described by Langer (1983) and Sugarman (1983). Langer has published an extensive series of analyses of changes in the cognitive abilities of babies that occur between 6 and 18 months. He argues that conceptual development in infancy takes two forms:

(a) changes in the ways in which the baby can relate 'parts' and 'wholes', and

(b) changes in the way babies construct relations between means and ends.

The former series of developments ensures that by 18 months the infant has the ability to unite as many as four single objects into composite structures, which themselves can be reunited into recompositions, involving substitution, exchange or replacement of components.

Parallel developments occur in means-ends relations so that by 18 months there is systematic variation of means and ends in the child's exploration of causality. For example, babies come to understand very well the relationships between physical events such as pushing a ball and movement, and blocking its path of movement and stopping. Langer suggests that the infant has already developed a very extensive repertoire of logical abilities that can now be applied to symbols. Clearly, the intellectual abilities Langer describes may serve a useful purpose in the comprehension and production of language, most obviously in the mastery of grammatical distinctions such as actor, agent and object and in the substitution of words within a basic syntactic framework.

The implication of Langer's analysis is that the symbolic function of which Piaget speaks, constitutes a separate branch of the cognitive system, to which intellectual operations may be applied. His work shows that there certainly exists a rich intellectual foundation at the end of infancy upon which symbol acquisition may build.

To take one classic example (from Stern, 1924) some names may be acquired in infancy by a kind of part-whole analysis. Names such as 'woof-woof' for a dog may commonly occur because the child will use a part of the object (in this case the auditory 'part') to stand for the whole. The developments in part-whole analysis revealed by Langer may therefore be helpful in unravelling the mystery of where symbols come from. In fact, a good case can be made that early words such as these are not yet symbols. On a strict definition, a symbol enables meaning to be shared through intentional signification because the members of a community have arbitrarily assigned the symbol a particular meaning. The use of 'woof-woof' for a dog may be better thought of as an index; the word stands for something else but not in the arbitrary and conventional way that is typical of most symbols. (Kaye, 1982, offers a very helpful discussion of the subtle distinction between gesture, index, sign and symbol and of the long apprenticeship in human systems of communication that will lead to the true use of symbols.)

Although the evidence suggests that there are aspects of intellectual development in infancy that may be implicated in the acquisition of language, it is not the case that the developing logical abilities which Langer describes are all that is required for meaningful speech to emerge. Harris (1982) has argued that what determines the timetable for language acquisition, that is, when certain concepts will be expressed verbally, may not be the emergence of thought per se but the ease with which the child's ideas can be mapped into the particular language of the community to which the child belongs. Language acquisition not only proceeds from the 'inside' out through the progressive development of processes fundamental to thought. It also involves contact with the culture and movement from the 'outside' in.

Linguistic aspects of thought and the regulatory functions of language in young children

Having examined the evidence for an effect of the development of thinking upon language the discussion will now turn to the opposite side of the problem: whether an effect can be observed of language acquisition upon thought. There are at least two broad areas in which the influence of language on thought may be demonstrated in young children. The first concerns linguistic categorization and its effects on thought; the second concerns the child's ability to use language (and verbal thought) to monitor his or her own behaviour in an active, 'overseeing' fashion. The latter area of research in contemporary psychology has become known as a part of the study of 'metacognition'; the verbal regulation of behaviour through the internalization of speech is a topic that is particularly important in Soviet psychology (Luria and Yudovitch, 1956).

Effects of language on categorization: the Whorfian hypothesis

Evidence that language may influence thought is very much scarcer than evidence for the influence of thought upon language. That such an influence may indeed exist is known as the Whorfian hypothesis, after Benjamin Lee Whorf (1897-1941) who suggested that conceptual categorization of reality may, at least in part, be determined by the structure of the native language (Whorf, 1956).

Sugarman (1983) has performed a similar study of the child's early classifications of objects to that of Langer. She also showed that the child by two and a half years has consistent ways of grouping objects that enable categorical links to be made between quite distinct things. However, she uses the data to point to the influence of language on thought with an example in which a child groups a square with a triangular block because 'it would make a good house'. Her work illustrates a reciprocal influence of language on thought; not only does classification allow entry into the language, but language itself may lead to particular ways of classifying things.

Another way to discover the effect of language on thought is through the study of bilingual children. Children brought up simultaneously to speak two languages offer a natural control for the effects of cognition upon language, since whatever their stage of intellectual development in the Piagetian sense, this is presumably a factor common to both languages.

There are examples of bilingual children who make errors on Piagetian tasks when they are questioned in one language and yet they do not make errors on the same task when questioned in their other language. These phenomena are observed in class inclusion problems, problems of quantifying and situations where relational judgements such as 'more than' or 'less than' are involved. The most parsimonious explanation is that some languages express these concepts in a more complicated way than others, that is, it is the structure of the language itself that influences the child's thought. Effects such as these have been found for bilingual Turkish-English children, and in comparisons between Spanish and

English children who are at the same Piagetian stage of cognitive development. They depend upon differences in the ways in which words in particular languages express particular meanings and seem related to contextual cues and aspects of reference derived from social interaction with the adult (Donaldson and Balfour, 1968; Donaldson, 1982). Where languages encode reality in idiosyncratic fashion, an influence of language on thought can be observed (see Slobin, 1973).

The verbal regulation of behaviour. One of the most intriguing aspects of Vygotsky's theory is his suggestion that egocentric speech in children reflects a transition from the social use of language in interpersonal behaviour to 'inner speech' for the self. Vygotsky argued that between three and seven years of age the child's egocentric speech differentiates away from social speech. Vocalization drops out (although it will return if the child is faced with unexpected difficulties) and the child begins to 'think in words' instead of pronouncing them.

According to Vygotsky, inner speech is more than speech without sound: it develops a structure all of its own. Since it is speech for self, it possesses its own peculiar syntax; it becomes condensed, it omits the subject while preserving the predicate of the sentence, it uses many fewer words, and there is a preponderance of 'sense' over meaning. Inner speech only slowly becomes transformed into verbal thought, it is not simply a matter of suppressing vocalization.

The main tests of Vygotsky's theory were carried out by his student A.R. Luria (Luria and Yudovitch, 1956). Luria proposed that there are three main stages in the acquisition of verbal control over behaviour. He carried out simple experiments in which the child had to make a manual response of squeezing a rubber bulb whenever a light signal came on. His results led him to conclude that from 18 months to three years verbal control resides in the social relations with adults; their commands can initiate actions, but they fail to inhibit actions in the child. Between three and five years verbal control still lies mainly with adults but the child's actions may now be inhibited by their commands.

This stage is a transitional one and Luria shows that children can activate motor responses for themselves if they verbalize aloud. For example, the child is taught to say 'go' on seeing the light signal and this helps in making an appropriate motor response. However, action is not yet regulated by the meaning of the word. Rather it is simply activated or energized by the self-initiated command; the child cannot inhibit behaviour through its own speech.

The motor response is as much activated when the child says 'stop' on seeing the light signal as when the child says 'go'.

Transfer from control by the impulsive effect of language to control based on word meaning is said to occur around four and a half years and is shown through the child's ability to use language to inhibit or activate behaviour in a variety of simple tasks. Verbal control occurs first in overt form (egocentric speech) and eventually becomes covert (verbal thought) at about seven years. Luria's experiments are controversial and there have been a number of failures to replicate his results by American researchers (Bloor, 1977, discusses these studies).

It is often argued that there are logical problems with the theory of verbal regulation of behaviour. For example, in order to affect the listener, speech must be understood in terms of its meaning. Since meaning depends on knowledge which the listener already possesses, it is difficult to see how inner speech can serve to tell the listener something that is not already known. Furthermore, if language regulates behaviour, what regulates the behaviour called language?

Wozniak (1975) and Bloor (1977) rescue the theory from this infinite regress by suggesting that speech for self acts as a feedback system at phonetic, syntactic and semantic levels. Considered as a feedback process, speech can embody information about the success (or failure) of acts which themselves arise from complex inter-coordination of systems and in that way, it can contribute to self-regulation.

Karmiloff-Smith (1984) has suggested another metacognitive function for speech (and verbal thought). It may serve as a superordinate means of re-representing other types of stored experience, for example, spatial or kinaesthetic memory, so that the single, common code provided by language may aid in the inter-coordination of aspects of experience.

Contemporary psychology therefore offers some support for Vygotsky's theory of the verbal regulation of behaviour. It is a theory that has become easier to understand as cybernetic systems, which also exercise control through feedback, have become more common.

CONCLUSION

This chapter has progressed through a very large number of issues with the aid of a simple-minded dichotomy between language and thought. It should be clear by now that a better characterization of their relations is to be found with Chomsky's insight that language is one aspect of cognition and, as such, there is a reciprocal influence between language and thought which can be observed in development. Both Piaget and Vygotsky had legitimate perspectives on the problem. The Piagetian point that receives the greatest empirical support from research with babies is that there is a relationship between the development of intentional communication and the acquisition of speech. The Vygotskian point can also be made that there is a discontinuity between sensori-motor and representational intelligence that may be a consequence of the development of symbolism. Speech enables the transmission of culture through the symbolic medium of language. The spoken (and written) word connects the individual with the accumulated knowledge of society and it is through cultural media such as these that the further education of the young child's thought will proceed.

REFERENCES

BLOOR, D. (1977) The regulatory function of language. An analysis and contribution to the current controversy over Soviet theory. In: J. Morton and J.C. Marshall (eds) **Psycholinguistics Series 1. Developmental and Pathological.** London: Paul Elek

BRUNER, J.S. (1983) **Child's Talk: Learning to Use Language.** Oxford: OUP

BULLOWA, M. (1979) **Before Speech: The Beginnings of Interpersonal Communication.** Cambridge: CUP

BUTTERWORTH, G.E. (1980) A discussion of some issues raised by Piaget's concept of childhood egocentrism. In: M.V. Cox (ed.) **Are Young Children Egocentric?** London: Batsford

BUTTERWORTH, G.E. (1981) Object permanence and identity in Piaget's theory of infant cognition. In: G.E. Butterworth (ed.) **Infancy and Epistemology.** Brighton: Harvester

BUTTERWORTH, G.E. and COCHRAN, E. (1980) Towards a mechanism of joint visual attention in human infancy. **International Journal of Behavioral Development, 3,** 253-272

BUTTERWORTH, G.E. and JARRETT, N. (1980) The geometry of preverbal communication. Paper presented at a meeting of the Developmental Psychology Section of The BPS, Edinburgh

CAMPBELL, R.N. (1979) Cognitive development and child language. In: P. Fletcher and M. Garman (eds) **Language Acquisition: Studies in First Language Development.** London and New York: CUP

CHOMSKY, N. (1980) **Rules and Representations.** Oxford: Blackwell

CONDON, W.S. and SANDER, L.W. (1974) Neonate movement is synchronized with adult speech: interactional participation and language acquisition. **Science, 183,** 99-101

COLLIS, G. and SCHAFFER, H.R. (1975) Synchronization of visual attention in mother infant pairs. **Journal of Child Psychology and Psychiatry, 4,** 315-320

CORRIGAN, R. (1979) Cognitive correlates of language: differential criteria yield differential results. **Child Development, 50,** 617-631

CROMER, R.F. (1974) The development of language: the cognition hypothesis. In: B.M. Foss (ed.) **New Perspectives in Child Development.** London: Penguin Education

DONALDSON, M. (1982) Conservation, what is the question? **British Journal of Psychology, 73,** 199-207

DONALDSON, M. and BALFOUR, G. (1968) Less is more: a study of language comprehension in children. **British Journal of Psychology, 59,** 461-471

FURTH, N. (1963) **Thinking Without Language.** New York: Free Press

GOLINKOFF, R.M. **The Transition From Prelinguistic to Linguistic Communication.** Hillsdale, NJ: Lawrence Erlbaum

GOODWIN, R. (1980) Two decades of research into early language acquisition. In: J. Sants (ed.) **Developmental Psychology and Society.** London: Macmillan

HARRIS, P.L. (1979) Perception and cognition in infancy. In: K. Connolly (ed.) **Psychology Survey No. 2.** London: George Allen and Unwin

HARRIS, P.L. (1982) Cognitive prerequisites to language? **British Journal of Psychology, 73,** 187-195

KARMILOFF-SMITH, A. (1984) Children's problem solving. In: M.E. Lamb, A.L. Brown and B. Rogoff (eds) **Advances in Developmental Psychology, Volume 3.** Hillsdale, NJ: Lawrence Erlbaum

KAYE, K. (1982) **The Mental and Social Life of Babies: How Parents Create Persons.** Brighton: Harvester

LANGER, J. (1983) Concept and symbol formation by infants. In: S. Wapner and B. Kaplan (eds) **Towards a Holistic Developmental Psychology.** Hillsdale, NJ: Lawrence Erlbaum Associates

LURIA, A.R. and YUDOVITCH, F. (1956) **Speech and the Development of Mental Processes in the Child.** London: Penguin

MARTLEW, M. (1979) Young children's capacity to communicate. In: K. Connolly (ed.) **Psychology Survey No. 2.** London: George Allen and Unwin

McSHANE, J. (1980) Early communication and the beginnings of language development. In: M. Jeeves (ed.) **Psychology Survey No. 3.** London: George Allen and Unwin

MELTZOFF, A.N. (1982) Imitation, intermodal coordination and representation in early infancy. In: G.E. Butterworth (ed.) **Infancy and Epistemology.** Brighton: Harvester

MOORE, M.K. and MELTZOFF, A.N. (1978) Object permanence, imitation and language development in infancy: toward a neoPiagetian perspective on communicative and cognitive development In: F.D. Minifie and L.L. Lloyd (eds) **Communicative and Cognitive Abilities - Early Behavioural Assessment.** Baltimore: University Park Press

PIAGET, J. (1926) **The Language and Thought of the Child.** London: Routledge and Kegan Paul. Paperback edition 1960

PIAGET, J. (1951) **Play, Dreams and Imitation in Childhood.** London: Routledge and Kegan Paul

PIAGET, J. (1953) **The Origins of Intelligence in the Child.** London: Routledge and Kegan Paul

PIAGET, J. (1954) **The Construction of Reality in the Child.** London: Routledge and Kegan Paul

REIBER, R.W. (1983) **Dialogues on the Psychology of Language and Thought.** New York: Plenum

SCAIFE, M. and BRUNER, J.S. (1975) The capacity for joint visual attention in the infant. **Nature, 253,** 265

SEBEOK, T.A. and UMIKER-SEBEOK, J. (1980) **Speaking of Apes.** New York: Plenum

SINCLAIR, H. (1982) Piaget on language: a perspective. In: S. Modgil and C. Modgil (eds) **Jean Piaget: Consensus and Controversy.** London: Holt, Rinehart and Winston

SLOBIN, D. (1973) Cognitive pre-requisites for the development of grammar. In: C.A. Ferguson and D. Slobin (eds) **Studies of Child Language Development.** New York: Holt, Rinehart and Winston

STERN, W. (1924) **Psychology of Early Childhood up to the Sixth Year of Age.** London: George Allen and Unwin

SUGARMAN, S. (1983) **Children's Early Thought: Developments in Classification.** Cambridge: CUP

TREVARTHEN, C. (1982) The primary motives for cooperative understanding. In: G.E. Butterworth and P.H. Light (eds) **Social Cognition Studies of the Development of Understanding.** Brighton: Harvester

VINTER, A. (1983) **Imitation, representation, et mouvement dans les premiers mois de la vie.** Unpublished These de Docteur en Psychologie, University of Geneva

VYGOTSKY, L.S. (1962) **Thought and Language.** Cambridge, Mass.: MIT Press. First published 1934

WHORF, B.L. (1956) **Language, Thought and Reality.** Cambridge, Mass: MIT Press

WOZNIAK, R. (1975) Speech for self as a multiply reafferent human action system. In: K. Riegel and J. Markham (eds) **The Developing Individual in a Changing World.** The Hague: Mouton

PERSONALITY DIMENSIONS: AN OVERVIEW OF MODERN TRAIT PSYCHOLOGY

Chris Brand

Psychology is one - perhaps a rather central one - of various more or less systematic approaches to human nature. By 'systematic approach' we understand that psychology is not, like history, concerned in the last analysis to provide an exhaustive account of how people have, up till now, thought, felt, and lived their lives; nor is it, like literature, concerned especially with the most fluent and imaginative constructions of human experience and insight. Of course, all bio-social scientists - from geneticists and biologists through to sociologists and social anthropologists - ignore history and literature at their peril. Nevertheless, the chosen task of the scientist is that of bringing some kind of demonstrable and simplifying (yet not over-simplifying) order to the rich diversity of the human condition.

Such systematization is achieved in two ways. First, the bio-social scientist will typically have a favourite explanatory concept - the gene, the cell, social class, kinship or culture, which will be tested out for such understanding as it may yield. Secondly, the scientist will have evolved methods by which the hypothetical influences of such potentially explanatory factors can be established or falsified: there will be at least some professional consensus as to what counts as evidence for the influence on people of, say, sex-linked genes or polygamy.

Seen in this light, psychology must sometimes seem a failed subject, whose practitioners might do well to seek solace in history, literature, theology or benevolence at the earliest opportunity. For what is the psychologist's 'key concept' that is to unlock any decent number of important mysteries? It is clearly no longer the conditioned reflex, which today plays but a small part even in psychologists' understandings of the rat; nor is it the enduringly inaccessible Unconscious and its still untestable ways. Nor can it be - at least as yet - the infinite number of black boxes of software and hardware to which modern cognitive psychlogists make casual - if inventive - appeal as it suits them. Again, what are the agreed methods by which psychologists explore phenomena and trace them to any identifiable source? (Indeed, some may cruelly ask: What are the very phenomena themselves? in days when the humblest attempts at description of people are apparently regarded by some psychologists themselves as grotesque and elitist acts of 'labelling'.) Psychologists undertake all kinds of studies, to be sure; but there are few areas of psychology in which straightforward scientific hard work by established methods is guaranteed to yield definite answers to the problems which first prompted their enquiries. Naturally, with hope, faith, perseverance and empathy, the psychologist may make progress in curing a case of writer's cramp or offering an ingenious explanation of the moon illusion; but success is emphatically not guaranteed - as the large number of unpublished theses testify - and, meanwhile, the parsnips are buttered by taxpayers, whose expectations (that psychologists can 'psycho-analyse' them) run way ahead of psychology's achievements. Countless surveys of compulsive gamblers and alcoholics bring no relief to them or their families; there is still, despite donkeys' years of labour, no agreed explanation of the serial position curve in short-term memory that is one of psychology's best known and most iron laws; and modern developmental psychologists still do not know why children get brighter as they grow older.

By contrast with the sorry spectacle that confronts us across vast tracts of territory that psychology has claimed as its own, there are some areas in which steady empirical progress is routinely made and in which explanations of a kind can be had for the asking. Two of these are the fields of psychometry and psychogenetics and they share a concern with what are the major broad ways (or dimensions) in which people differ. For the psychometrician, who asks 'What truly goes with what so as to make any talk of "measurement" possible?', and the psychogeneticist, who asks 'Are there any important long-term effects of genetic or environmental differences between people?', have a clear, shared interest in the delineation of the major dimensions of human variability.

Such enquirers could, of course, go their own separate ways: the psychometric psychologist could labour alone to establish whether 'fidgeting' or 'achievement motivation' were, on the surface of it, measurable traits having diverse manifestations; and the psychogeneticist could, if he cared, conduct twin-studies into the heritability of blinking or success as a concert violinist. But the psychometrician would feel happier if his 'trait' of fidgeting turned out to have an identifiable basis in demonstrable genetic or environmental differences between people; and the psychogeneticist would be more interested in establishing the heritability (whether it was 0 per cent or 100 per cent) of a broad trait of 'fidgeting' than of some particular example of that hypothetical genre.

The two disciplines of psychometry and psychogenetics do, of course, in their concerns with continuously distributed variables and their inter-correlation, pre-date the arrival of such twentieth-century forms of psychology as behaviourism, psycho-analysis, information-processing analyses, Piagetianism and so forth. They go back to Charles Spearman and indeed to Sir Francis Galton. For Spearman first spelled out the factor-analytic method of identifying statistical dimensions of co-variation; while, before him (in 1876), Galton had indicated how human differences might be traced to their genetic or environmental origins by means of asking whether identical twins were more similar to each other than were fraternal twins. In the 1970s, following the loss of behaviourism as the flagship for scientific psychology, the 'trait psychology' that had come increasingly to rest on these pillars of factor analysis and twin study was brought under sustained attack from social psychologists, who envisaged human beings as chameleon-like creatures governed by their 'situations' or by the 'labels' that other people occasionally chose to hang around their necks. However, although such theorists provided affecting reminders that we all enjoy a lot of freedom (not least to respond to others' ideas about us) and that some of us (especially people of a more emotional disposition) rejoice in such freedom to the point of marked inconsistency in our behaviour, it remained clear that there were many remarkable and general consistencies in the behaviour of most people, suggesting that we are steered across diverse 'situations' by underlying continuities of personality that have defied the methodologically inadequate attempts of situationists to get round them (for example, Furnham and Jaspers, 1983). Today, even the often-dismissed trait of 'leadership' is found to have cross-situational continuity (Kenny and Zaccaro, 1983) and Table I shows the approximate long-term reliabilities and the probable heritablities of a number of dimensions that have been investigated by differential psychologists in the recent past. (Several recent studies of the continuity of personality have even impressed some of trait psychology's gloomier critics (Rorer and Widiger, 1983).) In most cases the dimensions submitted to such laborious enquiry are those that have repeatedly appeared as worthy of study because of their frequent appearance in factor-analytic work; and in each case it is clear that there is substantial individual continuity over time - a continuity that might be partly (though not wholly) explained by reference to genetic factors (Eysenck, 1976; Olweus, 1980; Matthews et al., 1981; Bouchard and McGue, 1981; Yule, Gold and Busch, 1982; Torgersen, 1983; Conley, 1984).

Are the psychogeneticist's methods - the twin studies, adoption studies, studies of natural in-breeding and so forth - adequate to the purpose of telling us a trait's degree of genetic or

Table 1. Current empirically-based estimates of the long-term reliability and the heritability of personality dimensions when conventionally assessed (see text for references to sources)

DIMENSION	TEST - RE-TEST CORRELATION OVER 10 YEARS	PROPORTION OF VARIANCE DUE TO GENETIC FACTORS (h2/B)
General Intelligence[1]	.80	.60
Neuroticism,[2] Anxiety vs Stability, Adjustment, Composure	.50	.50
Extraversion,[3] Exvia vs Introversion	.70	.60
Independence[4] 'Promethean Will' vs Subduedness	.70	no estimate available
Conservatism,[5] Conventionality, 'Anal personality' vs Liberalism, Permissiveness of social attitudes	no estimate available	.60
Tender-mindedness,[6] Social interest Altruism, Empathy vs Tough-mindedness, Machiavellianism, Psychoticism	no estimate available	.70
Various personality[7] traits (e.g. Aggression, Achievement motivation)	.50	.45

environmental determination? This is one of the major current technical questions about the enterprise of discovering the origins and reality of dimensions of personality, albeit one that is of less dramatic importance when it is considered: (i) that the psychogeneticist only applies to human personality the same techniques that allow us presently to say that human height is more heritable than weight; and (ii) that current psychogenetic results only provide rather general testimony as to the involvement of genetic factors in personality differences rather than allowing the development of differentiated accounts of each of them.

More problematic altogether is the question: 'How do we know, irrespective of knowledge of their origins, what are the major dimensions of personality?'. Could it be, after all, that any major aspects of personality variation might have been missed by such giants of factor-analytic psychology as Cattell, Guilford and Eysenck? And, come to think of it, what exactly is such a 'dimension' in the first place?

If he were obliged to specify the 'basics' of his enterprise, the researcher of personality dimensions would hope to answer along the following lines.

> I listed, from dictionaries and 'Roget's Thesaurus', all the concepts available in the English language (at least in modern usage) for discriminating between people: the vocabulary of such a widely used language can be regarded as a treasure-trove of hypotheses as to meaningful human differences. I ignored subjective terms of crude commendation or abuse ('lovable',

---

Notes to Table 1

(1) Recent h2/B estimates range from 40% to 70%. Confirmation of a substantial h2/B for I.Q. is expected from T.J. Bouchard's study of separated MZ twins at the University of Minnesota. 40-year reliability is about .70.

(2) 40-year reliability is about .35.

(3) Some well-conducted studies report 10-year reliabilities as low as .30.

(4) The main hypotheses are still that sex-linked genes and hormone-levels (at critical periods) cause differences in this dimension (see Thomas, 1983).

(5) Few studies are available so far.

(6) Estimates of h2/B for Psychoticism have sometimes been as high as 100%.

(7) Several major American studies were completed in the late-1970s (see e.g. Conley, 1984).

'crotchety'); and I assimilated synonyms to words that were relatively widely used (thus dropping 'forthright' for 'frank'). I had people rate people whom they knew for the hundreds of terms that still remained. I observed much co-variation amongst their ratings - rated 'dominance' correlated fairly well with rated 'argumentativeness' - these correlations being higher when the raters knew their acquaintances especially well. I called these packages 'traits' and named them by common sense ('competitiveness', 'assertiveness') while also offering technical names ('Parmia', 'Neuroticism') to indicate their strictly technical origins which might require everyday usage of terms to be set aside in understanding them. I observed that correlations remained amongst such traits (for example, between 'cynicism', 'manipulativeness' and 'realism') and thus I arrived at broader (or second-order) dimensions (for example, 'Extraversion', or 'Exvia', which arose because dominance, liveliness, impulsiveness, risk-taking, jocularity and affiliative tendencies tended to some extent to go together).

I tried to write specific items for questionnaires that might tap these traits and dimensions in the self-reports of respondents; I tried to test people for mental abilities and behavioural choices that might be related; I looked for further correlates in physique, non-verbal behaviour, psychophysiological functioning, drug susceptibility, occupation, opinionation, psychopathology and so on. Some of my variables continued to correlate with each other and thus to further define the dimensions of personality that I had first observed in ratings of acquaintances. So there seem to be various major dimensions of personality variation - and I am checking that the same patterns of co-variation occur in Uganda and Japan. So far, studies indicate that at least some of the 'dimensions' have similar heritabilities in men and women and in different cultures: so these would seem strong candidates as basic, biologically provided dimensions of personality; and some of them consistently discriminate the sexes and various ethnic groups over the years, regardless of emancipation and decolonization, so as to suggest that such (relatively slight) group differences may themselves have some biological basis. What stands out overall, however, is the enormous variability (even of people from similar and politically equalized socio-cultural environments) and the systematic expression of such variability in apparently meaningful and recognizably dimensional ways - whether under capitalism or communism or in the Third World.

Such, at least, would be the answer of Cattell (for example, Cattell and Kline, 1977), whose measures have, since 1940, been through all these stages of being tried out - and especially through the important first stage of derivation from the full body of discerning possibilities that are bequeathed to us in the English language. Naturally, the dimensions of variation that are at first discovered in people's ratings of each other might be held to reflect nothing but the workings of the eye of the beholder and to be nothing but mere dimensions of subjective meaning; and it is probable that Osgood's three broad, widely-applicable dimensions of semantic connotation (see Figure 1) bear some correspondence to Cattell's personality dimensions.

But the co-variation of ratings that yields such dimensions is greater when real known individuals are rated than when raters merely express their ideas as to which characteristics tend to go together in virtual strangers (Norman and Goldberg, 1966); and, in any case, even Cattell's major 'second order' dimensions are more numerous than Osgood's. In so far as there is a consensus about how people differ, it is arguable that the consensus is a response to, rather than an imposition upon, reality: findings of biological bases and correlates for the dimensions must reinforce such argument. To be sure, some psychologists (for example, Goldberg, 1981) would like to avoid any evaluatively loaded descriptions of people. They have, however, yet to show how the descriptive elements of important terms like 'wise', 'reliable', and 'intelligent' - qualities of which we can hardly have enough - can be separated from their equally strong evaluative connotations.

Certainly, if we decline the strategies of ignoring value-laden dimensions of human difference, a considerable accord becomes visible between the dimensions that emerge in the systematic study of how English personality descriptors work and the broad dimensions that have repeatedly appealed, under various guises, to students of personality. Anticipating what follows, two of these are evaluative while being at the same time fully descriptive: one is the dimension of general intelligence (g) and its many correlates in educational level, fluency, analyticity, capacity for moral reflection, sensitivity to social and aesthetic experience, and organizational abilities; the other is that of neuroticism (n) with its correlates of moodiness, depression, apprehensiveness, irritability, suspicion and fatigue. The other four are distinguishable aspects of Osgood's very broad descriptive dimensions of Potency and Activity: the first two, of will (w) and affection (a), both appear to allow contrasts along the traditionally 'masculine versus feminine' lines of Osgood's Potency dimension. The second two, of energy (e) and conscience (c), both allow contrasts along the lines of Osgood's Activity. It will be suggested that these six broad, independent, objectively measurable dimensions - reflecting perhaps relatively cognitive and

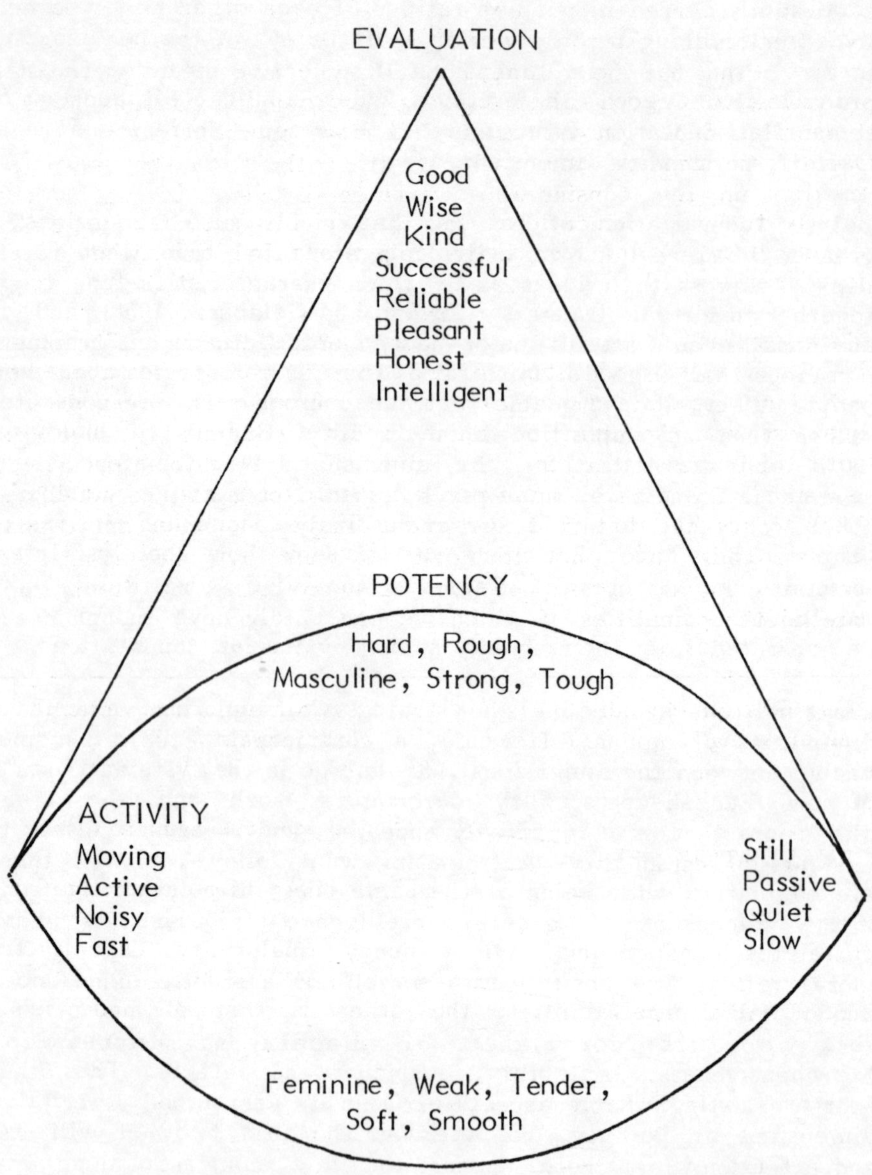

Figure 1. A conical representation of Osgood's three major dimensions of meaning (see for example, Warr and Knapper, 1968), showing adjectives that specially tend to define them.

emotional instantiations of Osgood's three dimensions of meaning (see Figure 2) are sufficient to embrace most of the distinctions that personality researchers currently register, although many familiar personality traits ('sensation-seeking', 'field-independence', 'authoritarianism'/'learned helplessness', 'locus of control' and so forth) achieve a special status by drawing on variance from two or more of these dimensions at the same time. In particular, it has proved harder than many psychologists would have wished to measure personality traits without at the same time picking up the considerable variance between people in their intellectual and educational levels. We will therefore begin our examination of the six major dimensions by looking at general intelligence itself.

That general intelligence (g) is a major dimension of variation in human abilities is still, after some 60 years of (occasionally reluctant) psychometric testimony, a controversial claim in some quarters; and the claim is still more hotly contested when coupled with the suggestion that g is substantially heritable and that it is causal to a person's achieved social status in mature adulthood. Thus to suggest that it is, yet more largely, a major determinant of personality and that it tends to endow its possessors with positive, highly valued qualities of many kinds may seem quite beyond the pale.

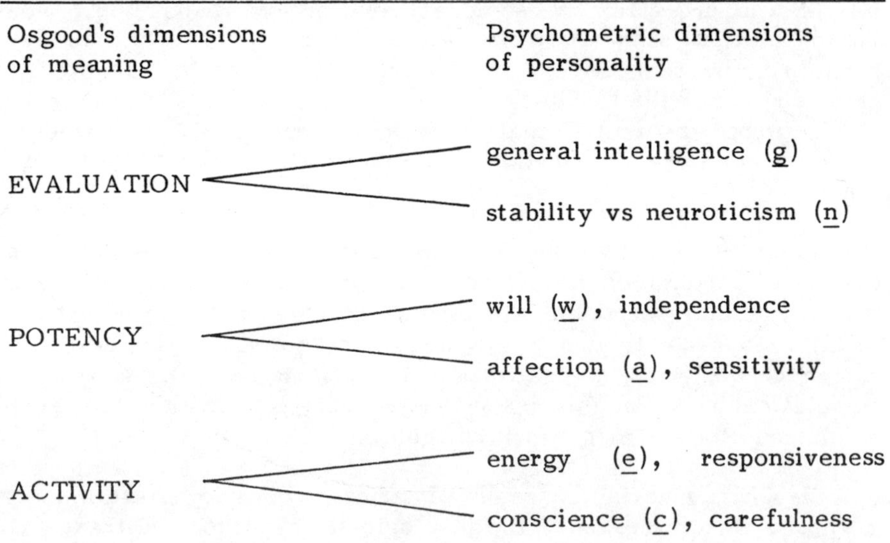

Figure 2. Six putative dimensions of pesonality represented as aspects of Osgood's dimensions of meaning.

Intriguingly, disbelief in the importance of 'innate general cognitive ability' is not, as many disbelievers like to think, a prerogative of the political wings of left or right to which they may belong. While modern left-wingers may believe that a person's final attainments in many fields reflect his or her family's degree of 'advantage' (especially financial), right-wingers like to think that attainment is a result of the 'hard work' and 'self-discipline' that are themselves held to result from good moral training. Both outlooks envisage that the provision of specific types of education is crucial to every form of intellectual and moral development. Both thus suppose that there will be a trade-off such that the more educational time is spent in cultivating some of the potentials of a child, the less the child's other abilities will flourish. Thus, out of a proper respect for gifted all-rounders of the past, supporters of these political outlooks favour 'generalist' educational curricula so that children will develop the desirable 'well-rounded personalities'.

This is a happy vision of human development, at least in its recognition of the importance of 'all-roundedness'. Amazingly, given that pupils in its pedagogic thrall today are deprived of the opportunity to become positively excellent by training in any one subject until an advanced age, there is not one shred of decent evidence for its basic empirical postulate. Simply, it is not the case, through childhood and adolescence or even in adulthood, that people who are strong in some abilities are correspondingly weak (by population standards) in others. This is counter-intuitive, certainly, in that we all feel that one more day devoted to chemistry or William Golding is one day less for physics or Iris Murdoch; but the fact is that, even at university, students who are good at one subject that they study tend also to be better at the others.

The same is true within degree-subjects: students' beliefs that they are better at 'developmental' or 'differential' psychology than at 'social' or 'clinical' psychology are not borne out by results. Indeed, though it is irreverent to state the truths of human co-variation in egalitarian days, it is only the substantial correlation between abilities in these areas that makes the award of classed Honours degrees justifiable.

If so much is true in the realm of strictly educational attainments - where, to some extent, the ideologically hypothesized trade-offs are simply bound to occur - how much more is it true in the realm of the mental abilities that it is not the precise aim of the educator to inculcate! Not only are mental abilities not opposed to each other in the general population but, despite the fondest beliefs and most assiduous test-constructing efforts of many psychologists of the past, mental abilities are not even independent of each other: rather, they have much in common. Table 2 shows the correlations with g that are found in the general population for abilities which are conceptually distinguishable and which are naively envisaged to be independent by many people whose convenient beliefs that 'we all have our strengths and weaknesses' would be greatly disturbed if they could be troubled to look at the facts. In a similar way, most mental abilities develop in parallel throughout childhood and many of them decline together after 40 years of age - or earlier under the influence of alcohol-abuse.

Table 2. Mental tests and their correlations with (that is, loadings on) the factor of general intelligence (g)

NAME OF SCALE	NATURE OF SCALE	CORRELATION WITH g
Information	General knowledge	.76
Digit span	Testee repeats digit-strings	.57
Vocabulary	Rough idea of word-meanings	.81
Arithmetic	Elementary mental arithmetic (timed)	.71
Comprehension	Understanding common rules, practices	.74
Similarities	Finding similarities between objects, ideas	.74
Picture completion	Detecting missing part in picture	.66
Picture arrangement	Re-arrange cartoon pieces to right order	.60
Block design	Use blocks to copy 2-dimensional pattern	.71
Digit symbol	Copy symbols (going with digits) at speed	.57
Object assembly	Jig-saw puzzles	.60

Note: The table shows the mean loadings for each test across ages 16 to 74 for the American standardization sample of the WAIS, 1981. The g factor here is extracted as a first, unrotated factor in a hierarchical factor analysis; it thus assumes its full strength, accounting for 47 per cent of test-score variation across the 11 sub-tests of the WAIS. (Source: Blaha and Wallbrown, 1982.)

Just why such positive co-variation occurs has long perplexed psychologists: the lack of any secure understanding of what g really 'is' has meant that the dictum of the appropriately named genius E.G. Boring (1923) that 'intelligence is what the tests test' has yet to be superseded. Lately, new evidence has appeared to suggest that g is strongly associated, at least across most of its normal range in the general population, with speed and efficiency of the processing of extremely simple types of information. Thus g has proved to be correlated at around .70 with choice reaction times to lights, with inspection times for visual, auditory and kinaesthetic stimulation, and even with average evoked cortical potentials recorded from the brains of people who are not engaged in a decision-making task at all (Eysenck, 1982; Haier et al., 1983; Brand, 1984; Fraser, 1984; Nettelbeck, in press). It is possible that relatively intelligent subjects in these experiments use special strategies for handling these trivial problems (for example, Nettelbeck, 1982; Rabbitt, 1984), but it is hard to see how the full extent of a person's all-round intellectual advantage on standard tests could come to be so well reflected in such ephemera if special strategies alone were responsible. It seems more likely that good basic information-processing abilities help their possessors to build up, over the course of development, a wide range of superiorities at many particular tasks, with the result that such particular tasks then inter-correlate to yield the psychometric dimension of g.

Note 1.
Nettelbeck (1982) concluded from his own data that Inspection Times 'did not give reliable evidence of a strong association' with IQ in non-retarded groups. Brand (1984) agrees that 'for subjects of above IQ 100, correlations of around -0.25 have been typical', but notes that Nettelbeck's studies have involved few subjects in the IQ range 86-100, and that the Inspection Times (for light-emitting-diode displays) of a bimodal distribution of young men having IQs around 115 and 90 yielded a fully significant difference in the predicted direction ($r = -0.51$; $p < .02$, two-tailed). Brand (1984) concludes that 'probably there is a linear relation between IT and IQ up to about IQ 110, but little relation beyond that point', and Nettelbeck (1984, personal communication) has indicated that he accepts Brand's paper as a reasonable summary of available evidence. Donald Sharp (personal communication) has recently found tachistoscopic IT to correlate at -0.50 ($p < .01$) with Raven's Progressive Matrices in an unselected sample of 15-year-old comprehensive-schoolchildren in Aberdeen; and that correlation would be still higher if the subjects who achieved specially low ITs (probably by means of special strategies) were excluded.

Interestingly, the new 'mental speed' tasks suggest that *g* is particularly involved with 'taking in' perceptual information rather than with the rapid executing of any particular decisional or motoric performances: perhaps psychologists would have come to understand *g* earlier if they had considered that, in English, the term intelligence has particular reference to information gathering (as in its classic military usage) rather than to the final use of such information, which is often distorted by features of motivation and temperament.

Whatever may be the 'basis' of individual differences in *g* - and the psychogenetic evidence as to the substantial heritability of *g* must further suggest that this basis is partly biological -the breadth of *g*'s correlations is itself such as to defy attempts to understand it by reference to tricks or strategies that merely make some people 'good at IQ tests'. Table 3 shows some of the correlations that *g*-measures have been found to yield, with important 'specific' abilities, traits and attainments that psychologists have attempted to measure. Lest such correlations be thought somehow artifactual, reflecting a priori features of psychometric measures, it may be observed that ratings by 165 Irish schoolteachers of 500 pupils have recently been found to yield one major factorial dimension which was highly loaded by 'Keenness to get on', 'Enquiring mind', 'Concentration', 'Achievement tendencies' and 'Intelligence', and which had further loadings of about .50 for such superficially disparate variables as 'Common sense', 'Originality', 'Independence', 'Self-confidence', 'Appreciation of beauty' and 'Sensitivity' (Greaney and Kellaghan, 1984). Such is the enormous range of *g*'s correlations with valued human characteristics, especially across the normal and lower ranges of IQ and mental age, that the former endeavours of psychometricians and the present-day efforts of 'cognitive' psychologists to associate *g* especially with reasoning or decision-making can be recognized as far too narrow. Indeed, given normal modern access in the West to schooling and television, a person's vocabulary will typically serve as an excellent measure of *g*. To answer a vocabulary test requires very little conspicuous mental effort at all; but it does require an exposure to the world in conjunction, over time, with an ability to apprehend it.

To some extent people must specialize in the course of their development; such specialization is, in empirical reality, much less conspicuous than the general co-variation of vocabulary items and the overall correlation of vocabulary in turn with many other measured abilities. So strong is the correlation of vocabulary with general intelligence that vocabulary items are indeed learned in a strictly predictable sequence as children grow up (Gilhooly and

Table 3. Correlations between general intelligence and measures of personality and attainment

Broad category of personality measure	Examples and notes	Approximate correlation	r*
STABILITY vs NEUROTICISM, ANXIETY	Nunn, 1974 (Normal elderly)	.31	
	Jensen, 1980; Baron, 1982 (Reviews)	.30	.30
	Johnson et al. 1983 (Survey of parents and their children)	.26	
	(Anorexia nervosa sufferers are the only highly intelligent unstable group, having a mean I.Q. of 120		
FLUENCY, CREATIVITY	Hargreaves and Bolton, 1972 (Children)	.45	
	Willerman, 1979; Jensen, 1980; Baron, 1982 (Reviews)	.40	.40
	Fontana et al., 1983 (Polytechnic students)	.35	
	(Fluency typically correlates positively with extraversion)		
INDEPEND-ENCE, INITIATIVE	Minton and Schneider, 1980 (Reviewing Witkin's 'field-independence')	.55	
	Johnson et al. (1983)		
	Cattell's 'M' scale: wilfulness	.35	.40
	Masculinity (amongst females)	.25	
	Jensen, 1980 (Review)		
	Leadership (when emergent rather than elected)	.30	
	Achievement motivation	.30	
MORAL DEVEL-OPMENT, CONSCIENTIOUS-NESS	Austin, 1975 (Interpersonal Maturity)	.41	
	Eisenberg-Berg, 1979 (Prosocial moral reasoning in boys)	.57	
	Messer, 1976 (Non-impulsiveness)	.30	
	Jensen, 1980 (Review)		.30
	Motoric restraint	.40	
	Non-delinquency	.45	
	Gargiulo, 1984 (Prosocial reasoning correlated with Mental Age)	.35	
	(Self-ratings of conventional conscient-iousness correlate negatively with IQ and Mental Age, partly because of falsification.)		

TENDER-MINDEDNESS SOCIAL INTEREST	Argyle, 1975 (Altruism found to be correlated with social intelligence)	.35	
	Eysenck and Eysenck, 1976 (Review)		
	Non-Psychoticism in students	.20	
	Non-Psychoticism in abnormal offenders	.44	.30
	Brand, 1981 (Review) Humanitarianism correlated with verbal intelligence)	.40	
	Johnstone, 1983 (Trust vs defensive-ness)	.25	
EDUCATIONAL, OCCUPATIONAL and RECREATIONAL ATTAINMENTS	Humphreys, 1981 (Piagetian measures correlated with I.Q. and education)	.88	
	Jensen, 1980 (Review)		
	Musical talent	.35	
	Occupational success (within typical occupations)	.35	
	Heim et al. 1977 (Breadth and depth of a wide range of interests)	.60	.50
	Waller, 1971 (Upwards mobility, between generations)	.40	
	Touhey, 1973 (Upwards vs downward intergenerational mobility	.60	
	Lynn et al. 1983		
	Public exams in adolescence	.64	

r* = Estimate of approximate correlation in general population

Gilhooly, 1980): items that are hard for adults are those that are only learned at an advanced age by children. Although we rightly feel that we could quite easily learn new words - and many other 'tricks' that would improve our intelligence-test scores - the fact seems to be that our general capacity to assimilate information rises naturally to a peak at about 16 years of age, remains on something of a plateau till late middle age, and then declines markedly (while leaving us with many of our attainments or investments) as old age sets in.

Whether we need to differ from each other as much as we do in intelligence is undoubtedly the largest social-scientific and socio-biological problem for our insistently egalitarian age. Intellectual differences clearly provide the foundation of the modern hierarchies of status, power, wealth, influence, and leadership. It must be doubted whether the feelings of respect and admiration that enable and enhance much of our social intercourse would be so commonly experienced amongst us if individual differences in g were greatly reduced by the selective application of Headstart programmes and intelligence-boosting drugs only to people who would otherwise be of less than superior intelligence. On the other hand, pending advances in socio-biological understanding, there would seem to be no conclusive reason for a society to tolerate, let alone insist upon, such differences once it possessed the power to control them. At present we can blame our personal limitations upon relatively bad luck in a genetic and environmental lottery; by contrast, a society in which people of lower levels of g blamed their parents, their parents' genetic counsellors or their nursery nurses would seem barely sustainable. Clearly, a viable society must aim to revere people's own use of such talents as they have rather than reward only the talents themselves or their rather predictable expressions; yet, historically, this moral enterprise has been the business of religion rather than of civil society as we know it. The easy way out of such moral problems is to deny or play down the existence of lasting individual differences in g, and such a denial is made the more possible by our present-day habits of mixing and mating chiefly with people of similar intelligence to ourselves. Such a repressive stratagem is not, however, open to the serious student of human nature, as the empirical strength of the g dimension continues to indicate.

The second most important type of co-variation in the observed and self-reported lives of people is that which yields the dimension of neuroticism (n). Although this dimension appears under many names in the writings of personality theorists - 'anxiety' and 'emotionality', for example, as opposed to 'adjustment' and 'self-esteem' - it is readily recognizable by its loadings for self-reports of moodiness and insecurity and by its more particular correlates in fearfulness, depression, over-sensitivity, distractibility and irritability. It accounts for some 50 per cent of individual variation in self-reported psychopathology (for example, Gotlib, 1984). At the low-*n* end of the dimension, people report themselves as calm, unflappable, and resilient and may appear to be positively sluggish and under-motivated. High levels of *n* are found in most psychiatric patients, while low levels seem to be characteristic of aircraft pilots, doctors and bomb-disposal officers, whose work requires a high tolerance for stress. Although most neurotic people would like to be less anxious, *n* actually shows a slight positive correlation with success in higher education.

Although *n* is a broad, important and universally recognized dimension of personality, a person's level of *n* will typically fluctuate somewhat over time. Thus, while *g*'s year-to-year reliability is about .99 (judging by its stability over many years), that of *n* is only .98 (Conley, 1984). Such changes may reflect the impact of life-events and stressors - though probably to a smaller extent than psychologists of the 1970s used to suppose (Gurney and Taylor, 1981; Cooke and Hole, 1983). However, somewhat paradoxically, *n* must certainly - in so far as it consists in a person's degree of variability (M.W. Eysenck, 1977), cross-situational inconsistency (Campus, 1974; Ashton and Warr, 1976) and moodiness (Howarth and Schokman-Gates, 1981) - show 'unreliability' as a person becomes more generally settled and consistent with maturation. Another inconsistency is that a person's level of *n* may be unclear even to quite close friends, for it takes time and opportunity to see people in various situations if one is to work out how variable they are. Some express attempts have been made to measure *n* as a state-of-mood rather than as a lasting trait: this does not solve the problem posed by *n*'s intrinsic nature, for 'state' and 'trait' measure of anxiety generally appear to correlate at about .60 (for example, Kirkcaldy, 1984, where *n* correlated significantly with each of ten separate mood-state indices such as tiredness, depression, over-sensitivity and lack of concentration). People who are high-*n*, when studied over time, simply experience more frequent and less agreeable changes of mood.

Note 2.
The year-to-year reliability of a trait is an estimate of one-year reliability derived from the trait's stability over a number of years. Thus if IQ has (as it seems to have) a 40-year stability of about .70, this could have come about by IQ having year-to-year reliability of .99: for $.99^{40} = .68$.

In what, then, can *n* itself consist in terms of psychological mechanisms and processes? One possibility is that, as some workers once envisaged for *g*, there are important interactions among hypothetical 'components' of *n* that serve to yield its final psychometric unity. Thus it could be that experiencing depression might make a person more anxious or irritable, and it is certainly remarkable how such unpleasant emotional experiences co-vary amongst the psychiatrically ill, where one would expect lower correlations because of 'restriction of range' effects (Foulds and Bedford, 1976). Another hint of complex determinants of *n* is that *n*-factors are less clear-cut amongst brighter, better-educated, field-independent people (Leff, 1973; Parkes, 1981): apparently, higher cognitive abilities allow people a differentiated experience of, for example, depression without concomitant anxiety, irritability, fatigue and so on. Certainly there is reason from modern studies to suppose that high levels of *n* place extra demands on cognitive resources. At least amongst people of relatively modest intelligence, high *n* has been found to be accompanied by reports of many everyday cognitive failures such as forgetfulness (Hogg, 1983; Deary, 1984). Laboratory testing suggests that high-*n* subjects find it difficult to do two things at once (M.W. Eysenck, op.cit.), as if dual tasks placed undue strain upon their already over-taxed cognitive resources.

Such dynamic possibilities may one day be spelled out more fully; meanwhile there is at least one relatively simply story that unites historical understandings of *n* with modern evidence of the involvement of cognitive overload.

Classically, such workers as Eysenck (for example, 1979) and Gray (for example, 1981) have stressed the tendency of anxious subjects to condition well and to extinguish poorly: indeed, the failure of extinction might almost be thought definitional to the problems of the clinically neurotic, and such failure is particularly marked for passive avoidance learning in which a person maintains and even strengthens habits of thought and action that may once have had the function of avoiding punishment or frustrative non-reward. Notoriously, the neurotic individual finds it hard to accommodate or adjust to new realities even when the need to do so has been cognitively assimilated. What happens is possibly that the neurotic learns everything and forgets nothing: while the low-*n* person rewrites his mental programs and re-arranges his sub-routines to dispose of former habits of reaction, the high-*n* subject merely adds conflicting possibilities to existing programs and has then to call repeatedly on higher-level processing to decide between alternatives. An example of such a difference presents itself in the area of memory: most of us, playing Kim's Game, tend to recall what we have seen in clusters - grouping together the animals, table-cutlery, the items having to do with smoking and so on; by contrast, though high-*n* subjects have as good recall as low-*n* subjects, their order of recall is more idiosyncratic and unclustered (Mueller, 1976; Deary, 1984). It is as if the memory task had been handled by assimilation alone and without much immediate accommodation or re-arrangement. This phenomenon might itself be partially understood in terms of a more general theory of long-term learning (Crick and Mitchison, 1983), which holds that we 'learn' everything that happens to us each day but that dream sleep serves to eliminate material that is not readily connected with the consolidated body of our knowledge: it may be that high-*n* individuals, who commonly suffer sleep disturbance, can retain relatively disconnected material, albeit at the expense of constant daily vigilance in sorting useful from useless memories. (It certainly bears consideration that the two familiar anti-anxiolytic drugs Valium and alcohol sometimes have the impressive effect of preventing retention of everyday events that occur while the user is under their influence. Of course they do not interfere with the long-term memories that the user has consolidated over the years.)

Whatever may be the basis of the high-*n* person's rigidities, conflicts and variabilities as he lurches - sometimes out of reach of cognitive control - between one set of behavioural stratagems and another, it must be observed that the worst effects of high *n* are phenomenological rather than behavioural. The high-*n* person certainly reports that he is less than resolute, conscientious, affectionate and energetic: he feels that he has not 'got his act together'. Yet such characterological virtues are not so much diminished in the high-*n* person as they are idiosyncratically expressed: obstinacy, obsessionality, hyper-sensitivity and agitation may be experienced and admitted even when their more highly valued counterparts are denied. Whatever else it is, neuroticism is at least a scrambling device that permits idiosyncracy, unresolved conflict and richness of experience to persist: such idiosyncracy is a valuable human variation, even if we would not wish it to characterize airline pilots.

As we look for co-variation beyond that which yields *g* and *n*, it must be at once admitted that there is - at least by the demanding standards of expert psychometricians - little official, acknowledged consensus among factorial psychologists at present (for example, Kline and Barratt, 1983). Eysenck's Extraversion (versus Introversion) - involving a person's degree of sociability, liveliness and impulsivity - would certainly be a strong candidate for the status of a third major dimension of personality, and it correlates with Osgood-style ratings of Activity (Gray, 1973); however, its unity has been disputed (for example, Guilford, 1977), its psychological basis is still conjectural, despite thousands of experimental studies (Eysenck, 1981; Bowyer, Humphreys and Revelle, 1983), and other dimensions such as 'sensation-seeking' (Zuckerman, 1983) have lately been put forward as alternatives to it. The weaknesses of this putative dimension of Extraversion are in fact instructive as to problems that arise for many other dimensions that have been envisaged from time to time. It is easy to see what Eysenck was originally driving at as he formulated his concept of Extraversion: it was Osgood's dimension of Activity, to the positive end of which dimension Eysenck contrasted the behavioural inhibition and restraint of the introvert. Yet 'activity' and 'restraint' - not to mention creative fluency and articulate conscientiousness - can hardly be considered, let alone measured, without acknowledging the influence of g and n. Thus good intelligence will endow a person with capacities for social skill, leadership and wit that will make for sociability. Yet, at the same time, g will militate against the more unreasonable expressions of sheer impulse: so g will make for apparent extraversion in some ways and for apparent introversion in others.

The influence of n is similar: although n and extraversion are broadly independent of each other, n correlates negatively with measured sociability and positively with self-reported impulsiveness. To imagine that a person's behaviour and his reporting of it can escape the influences of g and n is to fly wilfully in the face of the facts: if there are any pure differences in 'activity' or 'extraversion' between people, we will only see them clearly amongst the people of similar levels of g and n. Probably there are such differences - consisting perhaps in differential preferences for speed versus accuracy, or in some of the many differences in 'arousal' that have been mooted as distinguishing extraverted and introverted university students in laboratory tasks. But it is not surprising that such contrasts have not emerged clearly through the normally superimposed individual differences in g and n: only when factorial psychologists fully extract such variance before rotating their axes will the rest of the structure of personality beome clear (cf. Jensen, 1980).

If perceived differences along the lines of Activity can barely emerge as a unitary dimension of 'extraversion', Osgood's Potency dimension - with its masculine versus feminine contrasts - has at least as hard a struggle to appear as a unitary dimension of 'tough-mindedness'. There are many measures - such as Eysenck and Eysenck's (1976) 'psychoticism' and Witkin's 'field-independence'

(Witkin, Goodenough and Oltman, 1979) - that yield sex differences of more than half a standard deviation; none of them begins to escape the influences of g and n. Thus Eysenck's Psychoticism (involving hostile, cynical and extremely impious ideas) is correlated negatively with g and positively with n, while Witkin's field-independence has a high positive correlation with g in the general population, and a negative correlation with n. Psychoticism thus reflects the unacceptable face of masculinity, while field-independence reflects its more positive (though still far from obliging) features. This position is paralleled in more direct attempts to measure sex-linked interests, for it turns out that masculine and feminine interests are by no means negatively correlated since high-g people are relatively strong in both of them. Of course, there is probably some kind of 'tough-mindedness' dimension which specially embeds the sex difference: notoriously, males tend to be more exploitative in their preferences for sexual activities that show scant regard for others' wishes and interests, while females tend to be more eager to enjoy affectionate relationships. Yet this sort of difference is largely overshadowed in its expression by g and n. A serious possibility is that there are omnipresent differences between people in whether they attend narrowly to (self-)selected aspects of reality or whether they are more broadly attentive; but since high-g subjects are better at most types of attention, and since high-n subjects attend idiosyncraticaly, individual differences in selectivity versus breadth of attention are necessarily hard to trace.

Whether for such reasons or otherwise, it comes about that factorial searches for co-variation seem most commonly to yield not simple equivalents of Osgood's Potency and Activity but rather four dimensions that arguably reflect the development that people show (or claim) of the virtues associated with both Activity and Restraint and with both Potency and Sensitivity. To use the more obvious names that the English language makes available, these might be called dimensions of energy (e), conscience (or at least conventional conscientiousness) (c), will (w) and affection (a). The important empirical finding, regardless of nomenclature, is that four independent dimensions other than g and n quite commonly emerge from large-scale researches into personality (see

---

Note to Table 4.
Capitals are used for titles of the authors' dimensions as named by them. In some cases the authors' factor-numbers are given for reference purposes. The lower case is used to indicate test-components that load the putative dimensions - (as a prefix) indicates that reversed keying is required.

Table 4. Dimensions of personality (other than g and n) which appear in modern factorial studies and test-batteries

Brand (see text)			
ENERGY (e)	WILL (w)	CONSCIENCE (c)	AFFECTION (a)
Cattell and Kline			
EXVIA	INDEPENDENCE	GOOD BREEDING	PATHEMIA
Surgency	Self-sufficiency	Superego	Tendermindedness
Boldness	Dominance	Self-control	Trust
Affiliation	Radicalism	'Anality'	Affiliation
Eysenck			
EXTRAVERSION		CONSERVATISM	TENDERMINDEDNESS
Sociable		'LIE' SCALE	-PSYCHOTICISM
Lively		-Impulsiveness	
Guilford			
SOCIAL ACTIVITY		INTROVERSION	-Paranoid disposition
Sociability		Restraint	Co-operative
General Activity		Reflectiveness	
Ascendance			
Comrey Personality Scales			
SOCIAL EXTRA-VERSION	MASCULINITY (vs EMPATHY)	ORDERLINESS, CONFORMITY	EMPATHY, TRUST
ACTIVITY			

California Personality Inventory			
SOCIAL EXTRA-VERSION	INDEPENDENT THOUGHT	CONVENTIONALITY	SENSITIVITY
Jackson Personality Research Form			
ASCENDANCE	INDEPENDENCE	INFANTILE CONTROL	AESTHETIC-INTELLECTUAL ORIENTATION
Edwards Personal Preference Schedule			
Exhibition (Dominance)	Autonomy Aggression -Abasement	Order Deference Endurance (= persistence)	Nurturance Affiliation (-Achievement)
Grygier's Dynamic Personality Inventory			
Phallic Scales (= excitement seeking)	Oral Aggression Initiative	Anal Scales (= liking for order)	Oral dependence Feminine interests
Howarth, 1976 (2)			
(2) SURGENCY Energetic Cheerful Talkative	(3) Independent, Strong-willed, Analytical (4) Self-contained	(5) SUPEREGO Responsible Conventional Conscientious	(1) CONSIDERATION CO-OPERATIVE Other-oriented Tender-hearted
Forbes, 1980 (1)			
(1) EXTRA-VERSION Sociability Dominance, Optimism	(4) SELFISH-NESS (-Empathy)	(5) ORDERLINESS (6) CONFORMITY	(2) CYNICISM Accept others Trust

Table 4, continued

Rushton and Chrisjohn, 1981			
EXTRAVERSION	TOUGH	HARD WORK	OPEN-NESS TO
Sociable	AUTONOMY	Achievement	EXPERIENCE
Affiliative	(-Succorance	Order	Sentience
Exhibitionistic	-Abasement	Endurance, Play	Understanding
	-Nurturance)		
Ormerod and Billing, 1982			
CLASSIC	NON-CLASSIC	CONSCIENTIOUS	TENDERMINDEDNESS
EXTRAVERSION	EXTRAVERSION	CAREFUL	Submissive
Zestful	Self-	-EXPEDIENT	
Surgent	sufficient	Superego	
Adventuresome	Aloof	Self-control	
	Individualistic		
Kline and Cooper, 1983			
EXTRAVERSION	MASCULINE	OBSESSIONALITY	-MACHIAVELLIANISM
Surgent	DOMINANCE	Fascism	Anti-hedonistic
Adventuresome	Suspicious	Militarism	Tender-minded
	Coarse	Superego	-Psychoticism
	Radical	Anality, Self-	
		control, -Psychoticism	
Nowlis Mood-Adjective Checklist (e.g. Johnstone and Hackman, 1977)			
Lively	Confident	Alert	Affectionate
Depressed	-Fearful	-Fatigued	-Hostile
		-Casual	

(Table 4). It may be that some contrasts of a two-dimensional kind could be envisaged, as in Figure 3, but it is only realistic to say that in the absence of explicit attempts to allow g and n to be responsible for all the variance that is due to them, four independent dimensions of variation are what the 'state of the art' requires. This independence may offer a certain moral encouragement: it implies that the efforts that people may make to be (say) recognizably more conscientious or more affectionate need not enjoy success only at the expense of exuberance or initiative.

The grouping together of differently titled dimensions from diverse sources in Table 4 risks being too ambitious in its implication of underlying agreements between different factorial researchers, in its setting to one side of the personal inconsistencies (not all of them disagreeable) arising from n and of the personal achievements that reflect g, and in the relatively small number of dimensions that is suggested. About the first two of these doubts it can only be hoped that they might be resolved by research that tested more expressly what is presented here as an integrative, six-dimensional hypothesis. As to whether six is the right number of dimensions, let it merely be said that few theorists would want to go much lower at present and that any who want to allow a larger number might begin by looking at Cattell's suggestion that there are eight such dimensions and asking whether Cattell's extra two (of 'discreetness versus coarseness' and 'subjectivity versus practicality') find more of an echo in

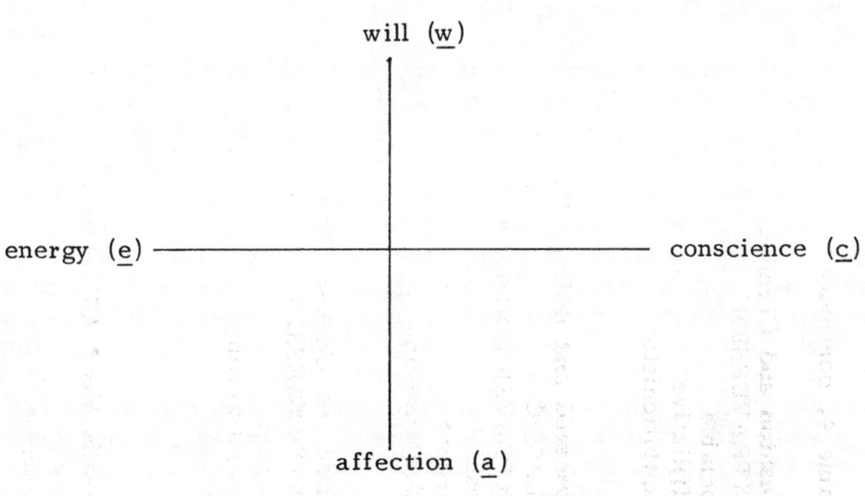

Figure 3. Tendencies to opposition (negative correlation) that sometimes appear amongst four dimensions of personality.

others' researches than the present writer has been able to detect. 'Practicality' has certainly appeared a promising dimension in recent work on the cross-situational consistency of personality (Kenrick and Stringfield, 1980).

Greater, however, may be the surprise at the small role that has apparently been found in Table 4 for dimensions of moral and political attitudes that have often - for example, in the case of conservatism versus liberalism - seemed to provide substantial and meaningful distinctions between people. Let it therefore be observed expressly that many of the discovered dimensions that have been listed under c and a in Table 4 do in fact possess at least a gentle moral and political flavour. For example, Kline and Cooper's c-type dimension involved high loadings for Cattell's intended measure of 'super-ego strength' and for measures of fascism and conservatism. Again, their a-type dimension chiefly defined by non-Machiavellianism - had a clear moralistic flavour, with high scorers rejecting relatively unloving and impersonal forms of sexual behaviour. Indeed, the general lack of any clear-cut empirical opposition in many published reports between e and c and between w and a may itself partly reflect:

1. The fact that c and a are more attitudinal - involving beliefs and values - while e and w express more of temperament and purely personal preference;
2. The likelihood that some people - especially those who are high in n - show rather modest consistency between aspirations and behaviour (Lauterbach, 1975; Lobel, 1982).

None of this is to imply that any special virtue attaches to a person's being high in such agreeably named dimensions as c and a. The very fact that c, as it typically emerges, has strongly conservative connotations and that high-a tends to be something of a female prerogative can appropriately serve to cast doubt on any such simple idea. Yet, if a low level of conventional conscientiousness is not of itself a cause for worry, its combination in a person with a high level of e may give us cause to wish that such a person had at least a reasonably high level of g and perhaps a long-term level of n that allowed a few inconsistencies with such a general picture of carefree spontaneity. Again, we might see the hostility and cynicism of low-a as something of a menace if the initiative and independent-mindedness of high-w were combined with it. Our moral aspiration for ourselves and our neighbours is probably that there will at least be a reasonable and intelligent balancing of the qualities around the circle of Figure 3. Interestingly, it can be argued that major conventional forms of political endeavour in Western democracies do indeed tend to offer such 'dynamic compromises' - with socialists offering to use the power and authority of the state strictly in assistance of kindly and liberal ends, while political conservatives promise to allow the initiatives of entrepreneurs to do their varied creative works within morally acceptable limits as traditionally conceived (see Brand, 1985).

In short, then, the claim made in this review of dimensions of personality is that there are some six broad dimensions of human variation that repeatedly present themselves to psychologists. Two of these - *g* and *n* - are universally recognized; the other four - *e*, *w*, *c* and *a* - still attract varying nomenclature and theoretical disputation as to their true psychological bases, and it is possible to see negative tensions between them that sometimes allow them to appear and to be rendered very broadly as dimensions of Activity (*e* versus *c*) and Potency (*w* versus *a*).

All these six dimensions (but most commonly *g*, *n*, and *e*) have been subjected to repeated psychogenetic enquiry and have appeared to an important degree to be heritable (for example, Eysenck, 1976; Tysoe, 1983). But, to the social scientist, the most surprising feature of the last 30 years' work is the failure to find any clear environmental determination of any of them, despite their having been widely conjectured to be under an important degree of environmental influence from socialization procedures. Particularly striking in this regard has been the evidence that dimensions other than *g* show considerable within-family variance (Rose, 1981), whereas most social-environmental theories of personality are obliged to predict a substantial similarity between siblings because of their shared environment, if not also for genetic reasons. Genetic explanations fare more easily in the face of such phenomena, since even siblings share, on average, only 50 per cent of their genes in common; yet such explanations themselves are clearly insufficient to account for all true personality variance even when the inadequacy of psychometric assessments is borne in mind. It has thus to be seriously considered that personality differences reflect an important element of individual free choice over the course of development. Cynics might call this source of variance 'luck', and pious bio-social scientists would invoke 'complex interaction effects', but the fact is that no known causal processes have been identified to the satisfaction of scientific observers, whose deterministic optimism has known no bounds other than those of the taxpayer's pocket. The sheer scale of the failure to fully identify 'bases' and 'causes' and 'functions' of human personality differences should not be underestimated as an exercise in falsification of the favourite environmentalistic ideas of psychologists of the past.

Matters might have been otherwise if all students of personality had forged ahead more systematically with the manageable task of discovering the major dimensions of personality rather than riding their individualistic hobby-horses off into the gloaming. All too often, the neglect of g which is intrinsic to such caprice culminates finally in a profound pessimism that 'there is never going to be a really impressive theory in personality or social psychology' (Loevinger and Knoll, 1983). As we have seen, there is in principle plenty to agree about: most notably that the dimension of g has many ramifications in the field of personality - it even predicts a person's 'values' better than do most conventional 'personality traits' (Rim, 1984). Yet there is an important advantage in personality theorists having 'done their own thing' through years of behaviourism, psychoanalysis and social environmentalism: by the very diversity and eclecticism of their endeavours, the unities that they have continually managed to register are the more impressive. Nobody can accuse them of wilfully neglecting a catholic recognition of human differences, and the tendency of their efforts to yield a six-dimensional space-albeit one within which g and n are properly to be considered as of predominant yet still insufficiently recognized importance - is all the more impressive for that minimally disciplined exercise of imagination.

REFERENCES

ARGYLE, M. (1975) **Report to the Social Science Research Council, UK**

ASHTON, S. and WARR, P. (1976) Drivers' use of seat belts as a function of attitude and anxiety. **British Journal of Social and Clinical Psychology, 15(3),** 261-266

AUSTIN, R.L. (1975) Construct validity of I-level classification. **Criminal Justice and Behaviour, 2(2),** 113-129

BARON, J. (1982) Personality and intelligence. In: R.J. Sternberg (ed.) **A Handbook of Human Intelligence.** Cambridge: CUP

BLAHA, J. and WALLBROWN, F.H. (1982) Hierarchical factor structure of the WAIS-Revised. **Journal of Consulting and Clinical Psychology, 50(5),** 652-660

BORING, E.G. (1923) Intelligence as the test tests it. **New Republic, 35,** 35-37

BOUCHARD, T.J. and McGUE, M. (1981) Familial studies of intelligence: a review. **Science, 212(4498),** 1055-1059

BOWYER, P.A., HUMPHREYS, M.S. and REVELLE, W. (1983) Arousal and recognition memory: the effects of impulsivity, caffeine and time on task. **Personality and Individual Differences, 4(1),** 41-50

BRAND, C.R. (1981) Personality and political attitudes. In: R. Lynn (ed.) **Dimensions of Personality.** Oxford: Pergamon

BRAND, C.R. (1984) Intelligence and inspection time: an ontogenetic relationship? In: C.J. Turner (ed.) **The Biology of Human Intelligence.** London: Eugenics Society

BRAND, C.R. (in press) The psychological bases of political attitudes and interests. In: S. Modgil and C. Modgil (eds) **Hans Eysenck: Consensus and Controversy.** Sussex: Falmer

CAMPUS, N. (1974) Transitional consistency as a dimension of personality. **Journal of Personality and Social Psychology, 29,** 593-600

CATTELL, R.B. and KLINE, P. (1977) **The Scientific Analysis of Personality and Motivation.** New York: Academic Press

CONLEY, J.J. (1984) The hierarchy of consistency: a review and model of longitudinal findings on adult individual differences in intelligence, personality and self-opinion. **Personality and Individual Differences, 5(1),** 11-26

COOKE, D.J. and HOLE, D.J. (1983) The aetiological importance of stressful life events. **British Journal of Psychiatry, 143,** 397-400

CRICK, F. and MITCHISON, G. (1983) The function of dream sleep. **Nature, 304,** 111-114

DEARY, A.V.A.H. (1984) **The Neurotic Memory: A Study of its Task-Oriented Relevance and Efficiency.** Edinburgh University Psychology Department: Final Honours Thesis

EISENBERG-BERG, N. (1979) Relationship of prosocial moral reasoning to altruism, political liberalism and intelligence. **Developmental Psychology, 15(1),** 87-89

EYSENCK, H.J. (1976) Genetic factors in personality development. In: A.R. Kaplan (ed.) **Human Behaviour Genetics.** Springfield, Illinois: C.C. Thomas

EYSENCK, H.J. (1979) The conditioning model of neurosis. **The Behavioural and Brain Sciences, 2(2),** 155-200

EYSENCK, H.J. (ed.) (1981) **A Model for Personality.** Berlin: Springer-Verlag

EYSENCK, H.J. (ed.) (1982) **A Model for Intelligence.** Berlin: Springer-Verlag

EYSENCK, H.J. and EYSENCK, S.B.G. (1976) **Psychoticism as a Dimension of Personality.** London: Hodder and Stoughton

EYSENCK, M.W. (1977) **Human Memory: Theory, Research and Individual Differences.** Oxford: Pergamon

FONTANA, D., LOTWICK, G., SIMON, A. and WARD, L.O. (1983) A factor analysis of critical, convergent and divergent thinking tests in a group of male polytechnic students. **Personality and Individual Differences, 4(6),** 687-688

FORBES, A.R. (1980) In search of psychoticism: some conclusions revisited. **Personality and Individual Differences, 1(4),** 335-340

FOULDS, G.A. and BEDFORD, A. (1976) The relationship between anxiety-depression and the neuroses. **British Journal of Psychiatry, 128,** 166-168

FRASER, I.C. (1984) **The Psychophysiological Measurement of Adult Intelligence.** Edinburgh University Psychology Department: Final Honours Thesis

FURNHAM, A. and JASPERS, J. (1983) The evidence for interactionism in psychology. A critical analysis of the situation - response inventories. **Personality and Individual Differences, 4(6),** 627-644

GARGIULO, R.M. (1984) Cognitive style and moral judgement in mentally handicapped and non-handicapped children of equal mental age. **British Journal of Developmental Psychology, 2(1),** 83-89

GILHOOLY, K.J. and GILHOOLY, M.L.M. (1980) The validity of age-of-acquisition ratings. **British Journal of Psychology, 71(1),** 105-110

GOLDBERG, L.R. (1981) From Ace to Zombie: some explorations in the language of personality. In: C.D. Spielberger and J.N. Butcher (eds) **Advances in Personality Assessment, Volume 1.** Hillsdale, NJ: Lawrence Erlbaum

GOTLIB, I.H. (1984) Depression and general psychopathology in university students. **Journal of Abnormal Psychology, 93(1),** 19-30

GRAY, J.A. (1981) The psychophysiology of anxiety. In: R. Lynn (ed.) **Dimensions of Personality.** Oxford: Pergamon

GRAY, J.E. (1973) Dimensions of personality and meaning in self-ratings of personality. **British Journal of Social and Clinical Psychology, 12(3),** 319-322

GREANEY, V. and KELLAGHAN, T. (1984) **Equality of Opportunity in Irish Schools.** Dublin: The Educational Company of Ireland

GUILFORD, J.P. (1977) Will the real factor of extraversion-introversion please stand up? - a reply to Eysenck. **Psychological Bulletin, 84(3),** 412-416

GURNEY, R. and TAYLOR, K. (1981) Research on unemployment: defects, neglect and prospects. **Bulletin of The British Psychological Society, 34,** 349-352

HAIER, R.J., ROBINSON, D.L., BRADEN, W. and WILLIAMS, D. (1983) Electrical potentials of the cerebral cortex and psychometric intelligence. **Personality and Individual Differences, 4(6),** 591-600

HARGREAVES, D.J. and BOLTON, N. (1972) Selecting creativity tests for use in research. **British Journal of Psychology, 63(3),** 451-462

HEIM, A.W., UNWIN, S.M. and WATTS, K.P. (1977) An investigation into disordered adolescents by means of the Brook Reaction Test. **British Journal of Social and Clinical Psychology, 16(3),** 253-268

HOGG, L.I. (1983) **The Psychological Correlates of Ageing.** Edinburgh University Psychology Department: Final Honours Thesis

HOWARTH, E. (1976) Were Cattell's 'personality sphere' factors correctly identified in the first instance? **British Journal of Psychology, 67(2),** 213-230

HOWARTH, E. and SCHOKMAN-GATES, Kar-La (1981) Self-report multiple mood instruments. **British Journal of Psychology, 72(4),** 421-442

HUMPHREYS, L.G. (1981) The primary mental ability. In: M.P. Friedman, J.P. Das and N. O'Connor (eds) **Intelligence and Learning.** New York: Plenum

JENSEN, A.R. (1980) **Bias in Mental Testing.** London: Methuen

JOHNSTON, M. and HACKMANN, A. (1977) Cross-validation and response sets in repeated use of mood questionnaires. **British Journal of Social and Clinical Psychology, 16(3),** 235-240

JOHNSON, R.C., NAGOSHI, C.T., AHERN, F.M. and WILSON, J.R. (1983) Correlations of measures of personality and of intelligence within and across generations. **Personality and Individual Differences, 4(3),** 331-338

KENNY, D.A. and ZACCARO, S.J. (1983) An estimate of variance due to traits in leadership. **Journal of Applied Psychology, 68(4),** 678-685

KENRICK, D.T. and STRINGFIELD, D.O. (1980) Personality traits and the eye of the beholder. **Psychological Review, 87(1),** 88-104

KIRKCALDY, B.D. (1984) The interrelationship between state and trait variables. **Personality and Individual Differences, 5(2),** 141-150

KLINE, P. and BARRATT, P. (1983) The factors in personality questionnaires among normal subjects. **Advances in Behaviour Research and Therapy, 5,** 141-202

KLINE, P. and COOPER, C. (1983) A factor-analytic study of measures of Machiavellianism. **Personality and Individual Differences, 4(5),** 569-572

LAUTERBACH, W. (1975) Covariation of conflict and mood in depression. **British Journal of Social and Clinical Psychology, 14(1),** 49-53

LEFF, J.P. (1973) Culture and the differentiation of emotional states. **British Journal of Psychiatry, 123(574),** 299-306

LOBEL, T.E. (1982) Personality variables and cognitive inconsistency. **Personality and Individual Differences, 3(3),** 333-334

LOEVINGER, J. and KNOLL, E. (1983) Personality: stages, traits and the self. **Annual Review of Psychology, 34,** 195-222

LYNN, R., HAMPSON, S.L. and MAGEE, M. (1983) Determinants of educational achievement at 16+: intelligence, personality, home background and school. **Personality and Individual Differences, 4(5),** 473-482

MATTHEWS, K.A., BATSON, C.D., HORN, J. and ROSENHAN, R.H. (1981) 'Principles in his nature which interest him in the fortune of others ...': the heritability of empathic conern for others. **Journal of Personality, 49(3),** 237-247

MESSER, S.B. (1976) Reflection - impulsivity: a review. **Psychological Bulletin, 83,** 1026-1052

MINTON, H.L. and SCHNEIDER, F.W. (1980) **Differential Psychology.** Monterey CA: Brooks/Cole

MUELLER, J.H. (1976) Anxiety and cue utilization in human learning and memory. In: M. Zuckerman and C.D. Spielberger (eds) **Emotions and Anxiety: New Concepts, Methods and Applications.** Potomac, Maryland: Lawrence Erlbaum

NETTELBECK, T. (1982) Inspection time: an index for intelligence? **Quarterly Journal of Experimental Psychology, 34A,** 299-312

NETTELBECK, T. (in press) Inspection time and mild mental retardation. **International Review of Research in Mental Retardation**

NORMAN, W.T. and GOLDBERG, L.R. (1966) Raters, ratees and randomness in personality structure. **Journal of Personality and Social Psychology, 4(6),** 681-691

NUNN, C., BERGMANN, K., BRITTON, P.G., FOSTER, E.M., HALL, E.H. and KAY, D.W.K. (1974) Intelligence and neurosis in old age. **British Journal of Psychiatry, 124,** 446-452

OLWEUS, D. (1980) The consistency issue in personality psychology revisited - with special reference to aggression. **British Journal of Social and Clinical Psychology, 19(4),** 377-390

ORMEROD, M.B. and BILLING, K. (1982) A six orthogonal factor model of adolescent personality derived from the HSPQ. **Personality and Individual Differences, 3(2),** 107-118

PARKES, K.R. (1981) Field dependence and the differentiation of affective states. **British Journal of Psychiatry, 139,** 52-58

RABBITT, P.M.R. (1984) IQ: decision times and motor skills in childhood and old age. **Bulletin of The British Psychological Society, 37,** A19

RIM, Y. (1984) Importance of values according to personality, intelligence and sex. **Personality and Individual Differences, 5(2),** 245-246

RORER, L.G. and WIDIGER, T.A. (1983) Personality structure and assessment. **Annual Review of Psychology, 34,** 431-463

ROSE, R.J. (1982) Separated twins: data and their limits. **Science, 215,** 959-960

RUSHTON, J. P. and CHRISJOHN, R.D. (1981) Extraversion, neuroticism, psychoticism and self-reported delinquency: evidence from eight separate samples. **Personality and Individual Differences, 2(1),** 11-20

THOMAS, H. (1983) Familial correlational analysis, sex differences, and the X-linked gene hypothesis. **Psychological Bulletin, 93(3),** 427-440

TORGERSEN, S. (1983) Genetic factors in anxiety disorders. **Archives of General Psychiatry, 40,** 1085-1092

TOUHEY, J.C. (1973) Intelligence, Machiavellianism and social mobility. **British Journal of Social and Clinical Psychology, 12(1),** 34-37

TYSOE, M. (1983) Do you inherit your personality? **New Society, 65(1078),** 49-51

WALLER, J.H. (1971) Achievement and social mobility: relationships among IQ score, education and occupation in two generations. **Social Biology, 18,** 252-259

WARR, P.B. and KNAPPER, C. (1968) **The Perception of People and Events.** London: Wiley

WILLERMAN, L. (1979) **The Psychology of Individual and Group Differences.** San Francisco: W.H. Freeman

WITKIN, H.A., GOODENOUGH, D.R. and OLTMAN, P.K. (1979) Psychological differentiation: current status. **Journal of Personality and Social Psychology, 37(7),** 1127-1145

YULE, W., GOLD, R.D. and BUSCH, C. (1982) Long-term predictive validity of the WPPSI: an 11-year follow-up study. **Personality and Individual Differences, 3(1),** 65-72

ZUCKERMAN, M. (1983) **Biological Bases of Sensation Seeking, Impulsivity and Arousal.** Hillsdale, NJ: Lawrence Erlbaum

CORE CONCEPTS IN ATTRIBUTION THEORY

Charles Antaki

Attribution theory is one of experimental social psychology's most popular areas of research. Although it sounds as if it is one theory, it is, as many commentators have pointed out, actually more like a set of mini-theories clustering around a central proposition. That proposition is the entirely reasonable and understandable claim that 'people's perception of the causes of an event affects what they do and how they feel'. Two kinds of attribution theory have developed around this idea. The first is work on the cognitive mechanisms by which someone makes an attribution, and the second is work on what consequences that attribution has on his or her actions. Juliet might attribute a failed relationship to fate, while Romeo blames it on their parents; how has each made their judgement, and what effect does it have on their actions?

There are attribution theories which address both questions, and they tend to be rather separate from one another. Kelley (1978) and Kelley and Michela (1980) make the point that the attribution literature falls into two broad camps. Although the division is not totally rigid, it is a useful one to make in surveying the literature, so I shall be referring to attribution process theory when I mean cognitive attribution theory about what might be happening inside the lovers' heads, and behavioural attribution theory for theories about how the products of those cognitive processes lead them to fulfil their tragic destiny. These aren't quite the terms that Kelley and Michela use, but I have avoided their terms because they can be a little confusing.

Attribution theory in the general sense of interest in people's causal attributions has been very popular with both practitioners and consumers of social psychology. Reference to attributions can now be found in such diverse fields of study as organizational management, international conflict, penology, and mental health. Its promise is to uncover the way in which we, as ordinary men and women, act as scientists in tracking down the causes of behaviour; it promises to treat ordinary people, in fact, as if they were psychologists.

I shall be concentrating on two things about attribution theory in this survey: what it tells us about how people cognitively process their judgements about the causes of behaviour, and what it tells us about the language in which people express those causes. These are two main themes in the attribution literature; for intelligent recent collections of papers on attribution in the widest sense, the reader is referred to Jaspars, Fincham and Hewstone (1983) and Hewstone (1983). For a short but integrated treatment of the entire field, Harvey and Weary (1981) is recommended, and for denser treatment the reader is referred to Kelley and Michela (1980).

How are attributions cognitively processed?

To attribute an event is to assign it to some cause or other. The favourite pair of causes in the attribution literature are 'internal' and 'external' causes - causes to do with the person, and causes to do with his or her situation. We shall be considering these at some length later on. The idea that people explained each other's actions in this way proved extremely popular in the mid-seventies, and a great deal of empirical work was done in what was loosely called 'attribution theory'. Figure 1 shows the rise in appearance of attribution entries in 'Psychological Abstracts' over the years 1973 to 1982, with attitude entries and interpersonal attraction entries for comparison.

The graph speaks for itself, but some translation is necessary. Not all the work the attribution curve represents tells us about attribution processes: many of the entries represent what Kelley (1978) calls attribution-based research. Here attributions were used as easily manipulated (or measured) variables affecting (or recording) people's perceptions of miscellaneous social phenomena. Intuitive predictions were made of how social behaviour would be perceived, given the experimenters' independent manipulation of its apparent cause, or given their manipulation of some information about its history, circumstances, or consequences. It was found that (for example) students would be less put off exams if they thought a previous failure was attributable to something 'external' (like luck, or a strict marker), or that travellers on the New York underground would refrain from helping someone in distress if they attributed its cause 'internally' (say, to the distressed person being irresponsibly drunk). A lot of work was done with people's perceptions of the participants in social issues like, for example, rape, where it was found that, in some circumstances, people attributed some degree of blame to the victim even though the rapist was clearly the physical assailant. We shall see in a moment how psychologists have tried to identify the mental rules people

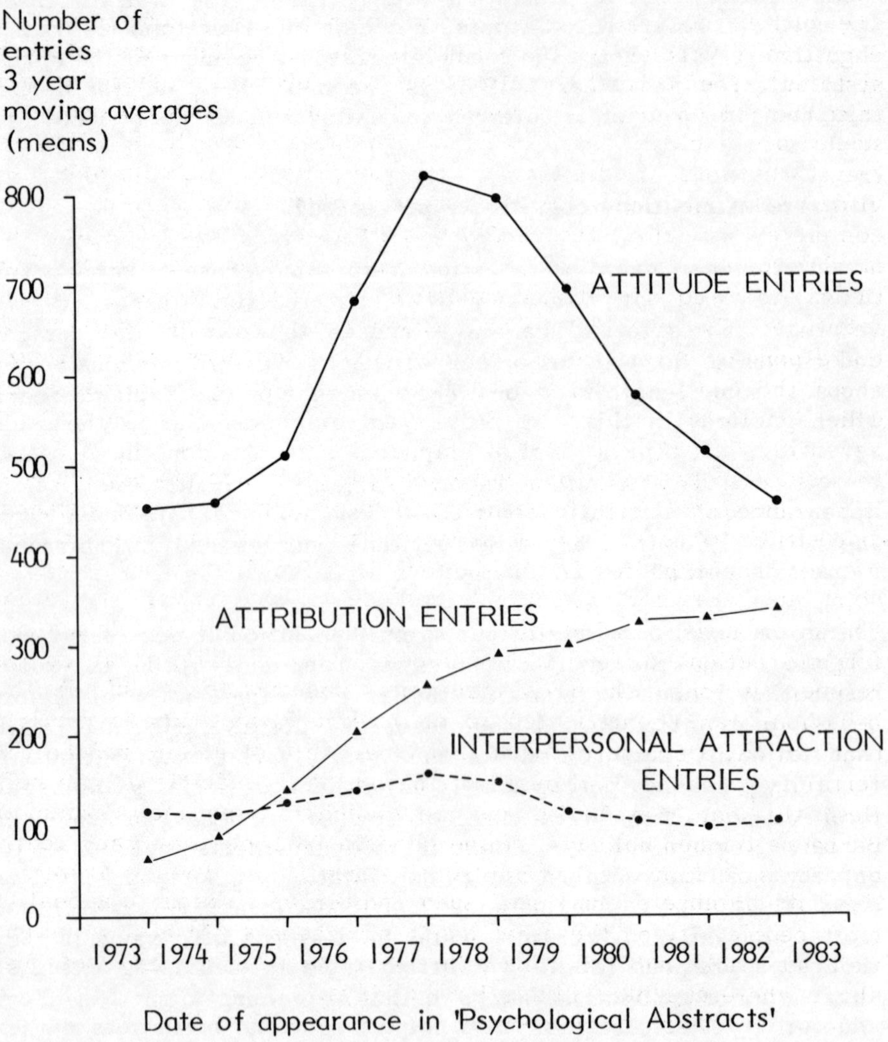
Number of
entries
3 year
moving averages
(means)
800
700
600
500
400
300
200
100
0
ATTITUDE ENTRIES
ATTRIBUTION ENTRIES
INTERPERSONAL ATTRACTION
ENTRIES
1973 1974 1975 1976 1977 1978 1979 1980 1981 1982 1983
Date of appearance in 'Psychological Abstracts'

Figure 1.

use when they make attributions like this, and how those mental rules are actually put into operation cognitively.

A word on terminology may be useful to some readers here. Modern cognitive psychology goes out of its way to try and describe mental functions and mental faculties in terms of systematic machinery. The current machine analogy is the computer, so the systems that cognitive psychologists use as their source models are software systems. The typical cognitive process involves something like this: the person accepts some kind of information (say, the visual scene of a clock face) which then goes through a series of transformations inside his or her head (say, transforming the visual data into semantic information about 'time') which, when complete, will allow the person to perform some operation that he or she couldn't do before (say, telling you what time it is). The things that do the transformation are the processes, or the software. The two classic attribution theories (Jones and Davis's correspondent inference model and Kelley's co-variance model) are about the goals the software has to reach and the information on which it works.

In Jones and Davis's (1965) correspondent inference model, the goal is for an explainer to attribute someone's actions to and personal disposition. This can be achieved if a certain series of criteria is met. The explainer has to believe that Smith knows what she is doing and what her actions will produce. If she forwent one other course of action, and if the consequences between the chosen and forgone actions differ in one unique respect, and if that unique respect is one which is generally undesirable, then Smith's behaviour can be attributed to an internal disposition to perform that action. Departures from this ideal state of affairs reduce the certainty of a dispositional attribution. An example might help flesh this out. Say Smith has the choice of going to Albania or Barbados for her holidays. If she chooses Barbados, we can't really be very sure that she has any particularly strong feeling about it, since its promise of sun, sea, sand and servants seems to appeal to most people. If, on the other hand, she chooses Albania, we might well sit back and think it tells us a great deal, and not just about where she likes taking her holidays.

Jones and McGillis (1976) slightly elaborated the stage at which the undesirability of the consequences of the action are computed. In the new version, 'desirability' is replaced by the more neutral 'unexpectedness of the action', which is computed from our personal knowledge of Smith or, if it is unknown to us, from her general demographic characteristics. More recently, Giordano (1983) has elaborated the theory somewhat in a particular application to the understanding of deviant behaviour. Other than that, the model is as it was in 1965, telling us about the psycho-logical steps involved in coming to a dispositional attribution.

Kelley's co-variance model (Kelley, 1972a) is more catholic than Jones and Davis's in that it is applicable not only to actions which need to have some element of choice, but also to experiences which might be involuntary. The goal of the explainer here is to discover which or who among a range of possible 'causers' of an event is the real cause. The explainer's job is to compute whether Smith's history of association with the event is any better (co-varies more reliably) than any other candidate's. Let's say Smith interrupts a lecturer in mid-flow to ask him to speak up a little. Why? It may, obviously, be because he was mumbling but what would we think if we were told that Smith was prone to do this kind of thing (she has what Kelley calls 'high consistency'), that no-one else ever asked the lecturer to speak up (there is 'low consensus') and that Smith interrupted every lecturer she ever heard (this particular lecturer isn't special - he has 'low distinctiveness')? As Kelley said, the more the candidate shows an association with the class of event over its several examples in time, venue and particular manifestation, then she attracts an internal attribution for its production (in our example, it's clearly something to do with Smith, although, teasingly, we don't know what). Often, of course, we have no idea about what someone's done before or elsewhere, but in cases like that, we have to rely on previous experience, which is stored as packages of information and rules of thumb, or what Kelley calls schemata (Kelley, 1972b).

Before we look at what the two models tell us about cognitive process, let us see how they have fared since their original statements. Figure 2 shows that the two theories have held up remarkably well in their citations, though both are experiencing a drop now that the attribution literature has established its own momentum. Of the two, posterity has been kinder to the co-variance model than to the correspondent inference model.

Quite why the co-variance theory has fared better is not obvious. One human, if not strictly rational, reason is hinted at by Kelley (1978): his theory was built around the analysis of variance, a notion immediately graspable by his fellow experimental social psychologists, and one representable in a neat and heuristic 'ANOVA cube' diagram. Jones and Davis's model, by contrast, was wordy, had implication rules and necessary conditions - anathema to easy operationalization and experimentation.

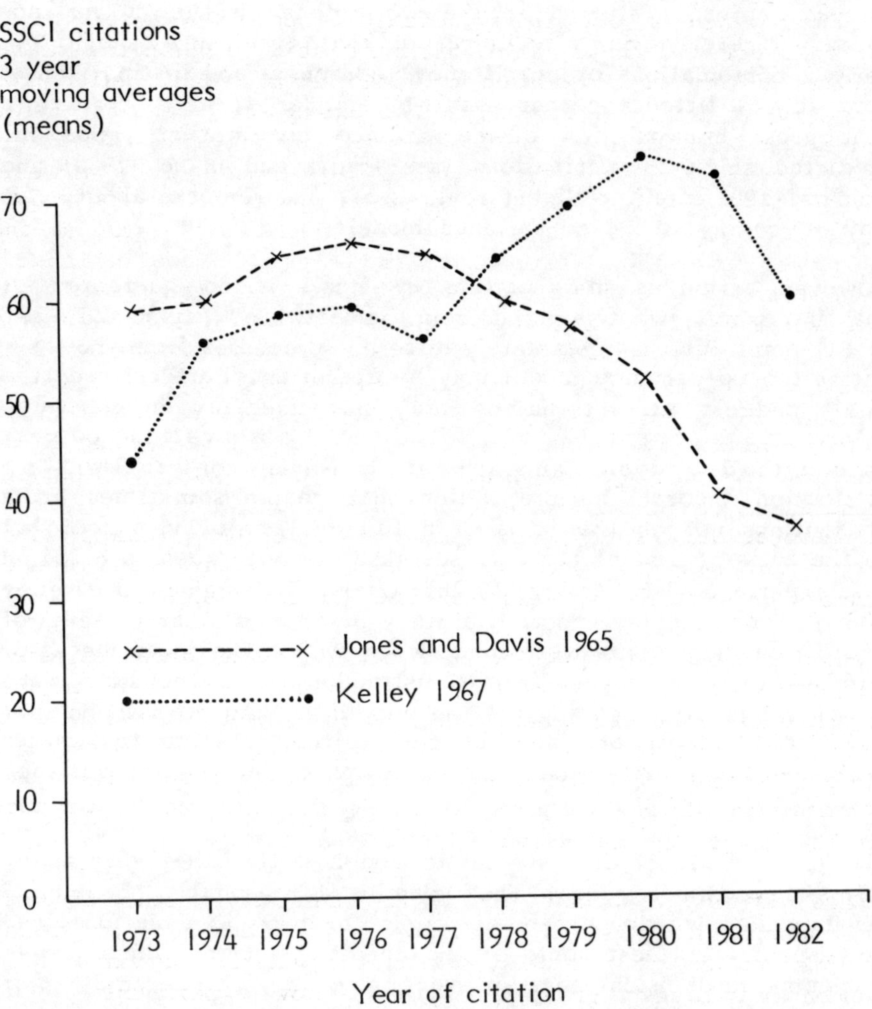
SSCI citations
3 year
moving averages
(means)
70
60
50
40
30
20
10
0
Jones and Davis 1965
Kelley 1967
1973
1974
1975
1976
1977
1978
1979
1980
1981
1982
Year of citation

Figure 2.

In spite of these apparent differences, what both models do, and do very well, is to give a formalized idea of what rules people must be using in making attributions. They don't specify just how those rules are carried out in cognitive software, and that is where current developments are at their most exciting in the attribution-process literature.

The search for how the mental rules which the classic attribution models represent started in the work done on the co-variance theory. There is quite a literature that tests how people use various combinations of consistency, consensus and distinctiveness (see above) fitted together, and, by and large, most work finds that gross manipulation of co-variance information yields the predicted shifts in attributions (see Pruitt and Insko (1980) and Jaspars (1983) for intelligent reviews of, and remarks about, this way of looking at the co-variance model).

However, stimulus manipulation by itself is no guarantee of charting exactly what is going on in the software. Taylor and Fiske (1981) point out that completely different processes from those set out in the co-variance model may be operating. Furthermore, the 'real' process of attribution may not use any co-variance information. Support for this latter observation comes, paradoxically, from another of Kelley's contributions to attribution theory: the proposition that people sometimes make attributions not on the basis of a full analysis of variance, but on the basis of part of the data set eked out with guesses based on past experience (see Kelley, 1972b). Orvis, Cunningham and Kelley (1975), for example, reported a study in which similar patterns of attribution judgements were made when two of the three pieces of information were dropped from the stimulus set as when they were present. Such findings suggest the very intriguing proposition that the cognitive software may be quite different from the rather rational-looking detection that is implied in the co-variance model.

The great virtue of the two classic models is that they very nicely formalize common sense. They give us a reasonably economical language into which we can set people's ordinary explanations, and they specify at least some of the conditions under which people will come to decisions that an event is to do with one or other of the people involved. Using just the first principles of the classic attribution models, we could enquire into whether different people, or people under different conditions, differently use the kinds of information the models specify, and how important each type was. When an explainer says, for example, that Romeo and Juliet 'brought it on themselves', does he or she believe, as the correspondent inference theory suggests, that the lovers knew the results of their actions, chose to press on with them, and positively looked forward to their resolution? Does he or she believe (as the co-variance model suggests) that what the lovers did would be done by few other people, and that the lovers were always doing things of this sort? The two classic models give the framework for this kind of enquiry, and several research possibilities may well suggest themselves to readers.

We need, though, to look elsewhere for the cognitive processes underlying how those judgements are made. The system has to be described in other terms and mapped with techniques different from manipulation of the co-variance information. One of the most promising lines in attribution theory is work done by borrowing ideas and procedures from mainstream cognitive psychology.

Cognitive mechanisms

A good example of the shift towards process models borrowed from cognitive psychology is the reaction to the finding that, of the three kinds of co-variance information involved in the computation, consensus information seemed to be less used that the other two. That is to say, if people knew that Mary liked heavy metal bands, they tended to think that this was something rather peculiar to her. This kind of belief in personal causation, or the location of people's behaviour 'in' themselves (sometimes called the 'fundamental attribution error', as we shall see below) is quite resistant to information about how many other people share the same tastes; people tended not to be very impressed when they heard that Mary wasn't the only one who liked heavy metal bands - they'd still think that it told them a good deal about Mary. Rationally, of course, the more one knows that many others share a reaction to a stimulus, the less one ought to be certain that any one person's reaction to it means something queer about them.

As the boundaries of this effect were studied, reasons were sought for the failure of the purely rational co-variance computation to predict judgements. Kassin (1979) and Borgida and Brekke (1981) reviewed the evidence and report that where consensus information is statistical and sample-based, it has impact really only if it is particularly strong, salient, easily translatable, representative of the criterion population, and causally relevant. In this case, it suggests, as was indeed first noted by Nisbett and Borgida (1975), that people are insensitive to base rates when making predictions about a particular person - a cognitive-process deficit identified by Kahneman and Tversky (1973). The base rate fallacy is an intriguing one, suggesting as it does that people are rather poor at dealing with dry, merely statistical information, for reasons of cognitive limitations on the ease with which they can call to mind living examples of what the statistical information is trying to tell them. Ross (1977) gives a nice example of this. A man is thinking of buying a certain make of car - say a Safetyfirst Special - and reads up all about it in the car magazines. All reports say it is superbly reliable, and the performance of thousands of Specials is reported to be excellent. The day before his appointment at the local Safetyfirst dealer he goes to a party and is told a dreadful story by someone there; apparently, their car had always given them trouble, and last week on the motorway it just blew up. To his chagrin, he discovers that it was a Safetyfirst. So impressed is he by the vividness of the case, that he immediately cancels his order and buys a Machodream Roadster instead.

Now we know that this one extra incident adds a negligible fraction of information to the thousands of cases that are reported in the tests, and that the odds are still magnificently in favour of the Special's reliability; yet it is very powerful in ordinary thinking. In attributional terms, it may be something like this that accounts for people's comparative lack of rationality when using consensus information and, as we shall soon see, it might explain why different people might give conflicting explanations for the same event.

The search for the reason for the limited impact of consensus information joins the literature on encoding, representation and retrieval functions involved in attribution. As Ostrom (1981) points out, attributions considered as products of the cognitive system are no different in kind from any other product, and are as well served by an information processing paradigm as any other cognitive judgement. Taylor and Fiske (1981) look over the growing literature and tie its many methods to the nature of the process being examined. Some of the methods are superficially similar to the stimulus-manipulation procedures of classical attribution theory in that they interfere with the presentation with the input in some way. Three notable methods are:

prior priming of related or unrelated information (Higgins, Rholes and Jones, 1977);
giving biasing information before or after presentation to probe encoding and retrieval biases (Rothbart, Evans and Fulero, 1979);
overloading the system to prevent some channels being used (Taylor et al., 1979).

These do resemble the stimulus-manipulation methods, but the point to note is that these procedures alter the process characteristics of the stimuli, and not their information along such classic dimensions as the desirability of the consequences of the performer's actions, his or her association with the event, and so on.

Other procedures from the cognitive stable record process characteristics of the subject's behaviour rather than manipulate characterstics of the information presented to him or her. The duration of visual scanning can be measured (for example, McArthur and Post, 1977), as can the quantity and sequencing of recall, (for example, Fiske, Kenny and Taylor, 1979) and the time taken on task (for example, Markus, 1977).

A procedure reviewed by Taylor and Fiske (1981) which might at first sight be thought particularly exotic is computer modelling of the decision process involved in coming to a causal judgement. In fact the classic models themselves are rather like decision procedures set out in prose, and the Jones and Davis model lends itself particularly well to being represented as a flow chart (some readers might like to try this, using the information on p.215).

However, Taylor and Fiske warn that fitting behavioural data into such models risks the danger inherent in any correlational study, and students of cognitive psychology may well be reminded of similar worries over the methods used in probing the way in which knowledge is represented in long-term memory.

Taylor and Fiske (1981) concentrate on mainstream cognitive psychology procedures to the comparative exclusion of procedures on the boundaries of social and cognitive work. Since their review, it is possible to identify an exciting growth of interest in what might loosely be called 'representation structure' work and, more familiarly, the cognitive-heuristic domain. In the former, researchers have been interested in discovering a number of characteristics of how attributions, or attribution-related judgements, are cognitively represented. For example, there is some work showing how such judgements tend to persevere in the face of other evidence, or because of a strong starting hypothesis (Tetlock, 1983, Hansen, 1980; Anderson, Lepper and Ross, 1980; Anderson, 1983a). Work is also done on how attributions and related judgements are influenced by such things as the availability of rival explanations (Reyes, Thomson and Bower, 1980; Anderson, 1983b); how they are influenced by the impact of the unexpected (Clary and Tesser, 1983; Lalljee, Watson and White, 1982), or the inertia of the expected (Kulik, 1983; Nesdale, 1983).

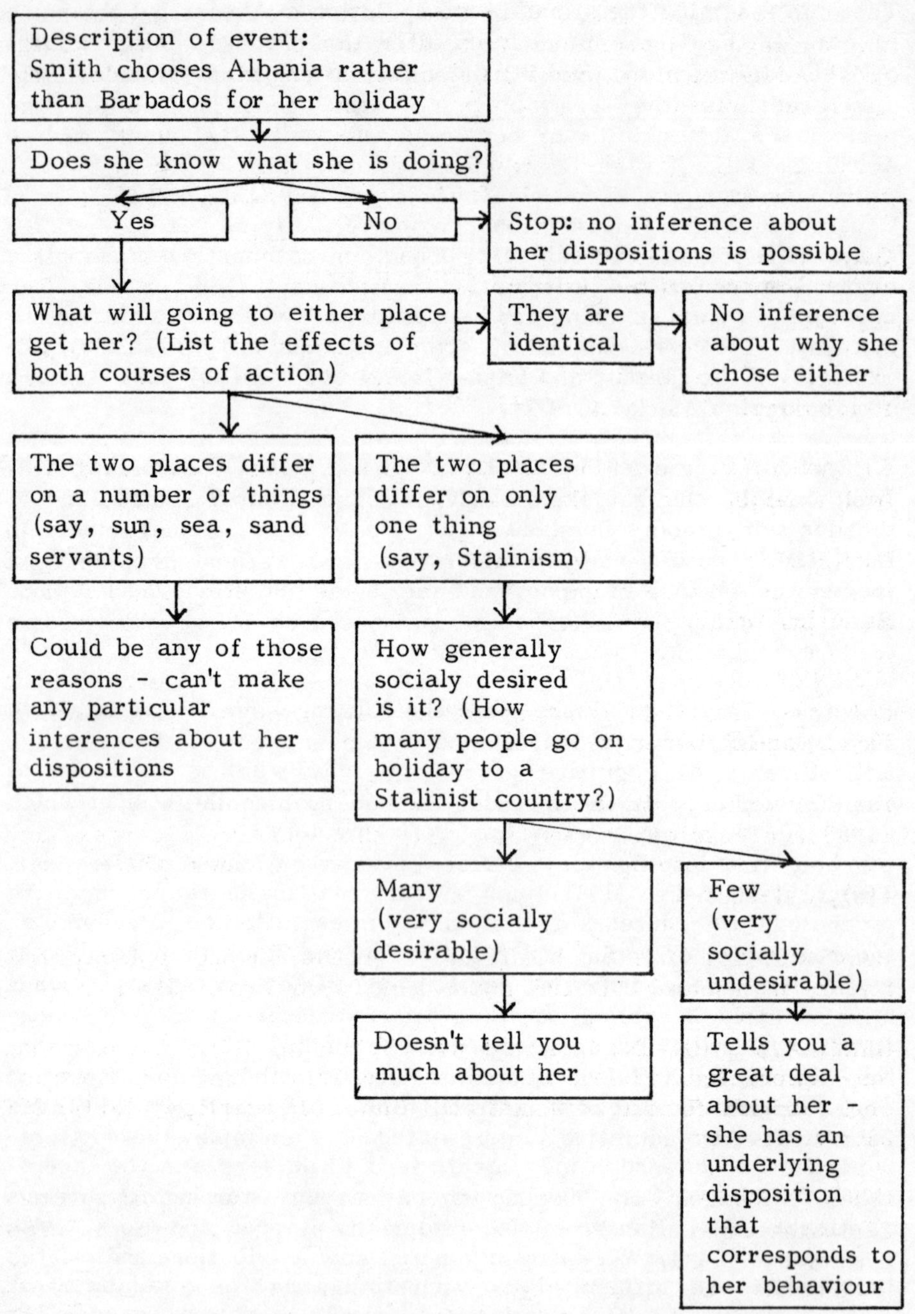

Figure 3. The correspondent inference model as a decision tree.

A great deal is now known about the degree of bias and rule-of-thumb thinking in social judgements; in the cognitive-heuristic avenue of research, Nisbett and Ross (1980) is the required reading and the interested reader will also find the collection of readings in Kahneman, Slovic and Tversky (1982) very useful.

The way of thinking about attribution processes described above seems to set up a contradiction between the rationality of the classic attribution models and the picture of biased and faulty mechanisms drawn for us by cognitively oriented psychologists. This is a contradiction only if we think that the pictures are meant to represent the same creature - that is to say, if we imagine that the classic models are models of process. As we saw above, the classic models are better seen as descriptions of stimuli-response patterns whose internal workings are to be modelled in another language. Once this is said, it seems reasonable to say that they are complementary enterprises, the one describing (rational) information and the other identifing its (possibly irrational, and certainly a-rational) cognitive modes of processing.

The actor-observer difference

One particular phenomenon of great interest in ordinary explanation has attracted some specific considerations about cognitive processes. This is Jones and Nisbett's (1972) classic observation that the performers of an action tend to attribute the action to external causes, while their audience tend to attribute it to the performers' dispositions.

The psychology of the processes which cause this difference is fascinating, and their identification is of obvious significance to our everyday understanding of each ȯthers' actions. First stages in work under the heading 'actor-observer differences' have been, rather like the attribution field in general, valuable principally in demonstrating the effect at work, and have been rather a-theoretical. Examples of such attribution-based, rather than attribution-process, work include demonstrations of the actor-observer differences among students' perceptions of themselves and their friends. Nisbett et al. (1973), for example, reported that students attribute their own choices of university course, or friends at university, to facts about the university or their friends - but they think that other students' choices of friends and courses reflects something about them. Why might there be such a difference in explaining one's own and others' actions?

Jones and Nisbett (1972) had three theories for the effect. One was straightforward - that the performer simply knows more about the event, so has more of the sort of information that rationally results in an external attribution. This has been neglected by attribution workers (bar Monson and Snyder, 1977), presumably because it is so obvious that it does not require any empirical validation. The second, much more interesting theory is that the actor forms the figure against the ground for the observer, but, for the actor, the salient percept is the environment. Causation, taking the theories of Michotte (1946) and Heider (1944), is attributed to what is salient: hence the actor-observer difference. Very few strict experimental tests of this Gestalt proposition have been performed, and its status is tantalisingly equivocal. The third of the theories has been energetically taken up from a rather vague formulation in Jones and Nisbett's original statement, and that is that the information available to the actor and the observer is differently processed. Some writers take this to be just a restatement of the Gestalt principle. Others though develop the idea that there's something in the way that actors and observers use the historical and current information available to them differently as a consequence of the cognitive heuristics we saw above. Ross (1977), for example, sets the difference down to what he calls the 'fundamental attribution error', which is the error of being overgenerous in attributing behaviour to people's dispositions; according to Ross, everyone is guilty of this underestimation of situational causes. The fundamental attribution error in turn is due to actors being more prone than observers to the error of 'false consensus' - believing that what they themselves do or feel is quite common ('I like fish-and-chips - but everyone does, don't they?'). The reason why actors are more prone to this is that when they have to guess at how many other people would do something (dine on fish-and-chips, say), what they do is retrieve their memories of how often they've seen it done. How many they can conjure up determines how common a choice they think it is, and, since they can conjure up a good many, they tend to think it's a common choice. The final link in the chain is that since it's a common choice and other people like it too, the actor thinks that the 'cause' of his behaviour must be 'external' - something to do with the food, and not something peculiar about him or her.

Take another example: suppose that someone is accounting for her belief in a nuclear defence policy. She claims that this is only rational, and, after all, the silent majority of people in this county agree. In other words, she attributes her belief to the persuasive nature of the policies, as warranted by the evidence that other people find it persuasive too (she might say, for example, that so many million people can't be wrong). According to the cognitive account, what happens is that when she thinks how many other people share her feelings, she finds it much easier to call to mind positive examples of pro-nuclear attitudes, since she has these well established in her own mind. The advantages of nuclear defence and the disadvantages of its non-nuclear alternative are salient and vivid, making them more available for retrieval from memory, so (for purely cognitive reasons) her estimation is biased. She then goes ahead and deduces that if pro-nuclear sentiment is so common, then it can't be anything special about her that accounts for this particular example of it; so she gives an external attribution for actions. If we asked a group of observers, however, to explain her actions, some of them might find it difficult to call to mind any positive examples of a belief in nuclear defence, so they would tend to attribute her behaviour internally, to something informative about her.

Ross's account is an ingenious retelling of the cognitive stories buried in the classic attribution models, and falls nicely into line with the cognitive-heuristic work done on the processes that might mediate them. At the moment, we don't know whether it's right or not; like the other explanations of the Jones and Nisbett observations, there have been few direct and unequivocal tests of the theory. In fact, most of the energy in the area has gone not into theories about the cause of the actor-observer difference, but into examination into whether the phenomenon is a reliable one.

Here Watson's review (Watson, 1982) is indispensable. He reviews all the evidence for the full actor-observer set of propositions, which, he notes, is more than the basic observation that actors make more external attributions than observers do. The full set of propositions is that actors make more external than internal attributions, that observers make more internal than external attributions, and that actors make more external, and fewer internal attributions than observers do. He finds that if there is a general main effect, it exists between internal and external attributions, the former being more favoured by both actors and observers. Where the difference between the two emerges is in the interaction. In further work, he finds that this is principally due to actors and observers differing in how much they use external attributions. Internal attribution stays much the same for both people. This finding is consistent with Ross's observation that there is the 'fundamental attribution error' of overestimating dispositional causation at the expense of situational causation, so his explanation of the actor-observer difference might be right. Future work will tell.

Process in behavioural attribution theories

Behavioural attribution theories are those that make a link between what someone thinks is the cause of an event and how they then feel or act. They are unlike the classic attribution models in two ways: they are fairly agnostic about what information the person works on to make his or her judgement, and they usually focus on people's explanations of their own behaviour. The two best known behavioural attribution theories apply to people's feelings about achievements (like tests and exams), and to people's feelings about bad events in their lives. Weiner's theory of attribution-mediated achievement behaviour (Weiner et al., 1972; Weiner, 1979) is predicated on the fairly straightforward premise that people's attributions for their successes and failures affect their future performance. Someone who attributes failure to something long-standing about themselves tends to think less happily about future tests than someone who can put it down to some temporary problem. Abramson, Seligman and Teasdale's (1978) behavioural attribution theory is similarly predicated on a straightforward idea - that people who attribute bad things to themselves will feel depressed.

Both theories are obviously useful and, by now, have had some empirical support. The interested reader is referred to recent reviews of Weiner's theory in Weiner (1979) and of Abramson et al.'s theory in Peterson (1982). We should note in passing that both are called 'cognitive' theories, but in applied contexts 'cognitive' is a word often used to distinguish between a theory which has some regard for mental events and a purely behavioural theory. The word alerts us that theorists are talking about intrapsychic processes, but warn us that these will be specified only at the logical-entailment level; that is to say, what is psycho-logically necessary for the brain to process before it comes to the judgement, or before the judgement has its predicted effect. The software details won't be specified.

What is logically entailed in both models is a contingent judgement that the event under discussion is to do with one set of causes or another: the axis around which all attribution theory revolves is the dimension of ordinary explanation which sets causes 'within the person' at one end and 'outside the person' at the other. We now turn, in the final section, to this most familiar feature of attribution theory.

Is ordinary explanation causal?

It is a hallmark of attribution theory, of whatever sort, that it claims, implicitly or explicitly, that people's explanations of events are causal. That is to say, that if I look up from the page and see you reading these words, I will explain your behaviour as being caused by something; say, in this case, having to read up for an essay. You might think that the first thing that psychologists interested in attribution did was to survey ordinary language empirically to see what attributions people actually used. In fact, this surveying did not happen for many years into attribution theory. The reason for that was the plausibility of the a priori description of ordinary attributions that was given by Heider (1958), the acknowledged father of attribution theory. Heider was at some pains to give a rounded picture of ordinary explanation, but the most durable of his contributions to attribution theory has been his division of ordinary causal attribution into two: attribution of the action to something to do with the performer (an 'internal', 'dispositional' or 'personal' attribution), and something to do with his or her situation (a 'situational' or 'external' attribution). This dimension (often referred to as the 'locus of causality dimension') is used as a dependent measure or an independent variable throughout the attributional literature.

Internal-external attributions in rating scales

The avoidance of direct surveying of ordinary explanations and an immediate rush to formalize Heider's bilateral division of ordinary explanation has had to be paid for by much missing of the point in the concerns over the definitions of attributions. Interestingly, the early concerns were not how to identify attributions in ordinary talk, but rather how to devise reliable rating scales on which subjects could be asked to respond (their willingness to use attributions being taken for granted). Soon it was noted that there were discrepancies in the supposedly psychometric properties of the rating scales used (for example, that scales measuring internal attribution did not necessarily correlate negatively with those measuring external attribution, as theoretically they were supposed to do). The early attribution studies asked subjects to explain the behaviour at issue by indicating, on a rating scale, to what degree it was due, at one end of the scale, to a dispositon of the actor's, and at the other, a feature of the environment. Refinements of the technique were to leave off specific examples of what the experimenter thought were such causes (for example, Storms, 1973) and leave it up to the subject. Later refinements were to separate the two scales (Solomon, 1978).

It was also noted that there was wide variation in the terms used to anchor the ends of the scales. Early studies used intuitive representations of personal and situational attributions, and, though when specified in methods sections these were often convincing, shades of meaning were inevitably different, and comparison of different results across studies was made more complex. Compare, for example, Storms' (1973) question:

> Personal characteristics about yourself ... how important were your personality, trait, character, personal style, attitudes, mood and so on in causing you to behave the way you did? (Storms, 1973, p.168)

with McArthur's more laconic 'something to do with the person?' (McArthur, 1972).

Later work moved towards the less detailed specification of questions, but the question of what shades of meaning subjects themselves saw in the questions made it, and still makes it, a matter of interpretation what a subject means when he or she ticks one end of a scale. It has been well noted by Newcombe and Rutter (1982 a,b) that a huge variety of different explanatory constructs fall under each heading. To make a mark on the 'internal' end of the rating scale could mean anything from attributing the action to a passing whim, to a longstanding policy decision, and to make a mark at the other end could mean anything from saying the actor had a gun pointing at her head, to a claim that he was momentarily distracted by a bee. The width of the categories does not perhaps matter in most attribution-based work (which tests - or records - the effect of rather gross explanations), but is important in theoretical statements of the response end of the stimulus-response pattern the classic models describe.

Probably the most important aspect of ordinary explanation left unaddressed by the rush to internal-external categories in attribution theory is the individual's choice in describing the event which is then attributed to a causal candidate. The explanation of Romeo and Juliet's behaviour depends, of course, on how we choose to describe it. If we say, remembering vaguely something we read about it once, that it's (really) just a display of petty bourgeois morality, then what we shall say in explaining its various parts will be rather different from (and altogether less grand than) what we should say if we stuck to the safe reading of it as the working out of tragic fate.

There is some work in and around attribution theory that examines how the 'same' event can be interpreted in different ways by different people (a phenomenon long known to social psychologists and, of course, everyone else). A good example is the work of Duncan (1976), in which people had the opportunity of categorizing a videotaped ambiguous event (a black or white man apparently 'shoving' another man) before attributing it to a cause. Taking this extra measurement of what people were doing revealed that they would so describe the event as to predispose a certain way of attributing it. When the man doing the 'shoving' was white, the behaviour tended not to be described as shoving, but when he was black, it was. Theoretically, there isn't a lot of attention paid in attribution theory to this very interesting stage of the process of ordinary explanation, although Newston (1976) is working towards a theory of the perception of behaviour units, and Wilder and Cooper (1980), among others, note the problem of description in their discussion of the effect of categorization on judgement. Antaki and Fielding (1981) recommend the examination of descriptions as explanations, and Hewstone (1983) charts the attention paid to linguistic labelling in attribution theory since Kanouse (1972). Greatest attention, though, is paid to the descriptive stage of explanation outside attribution theory and outside social psychology (see, for example, Gilbert and Abell, 1983).

This is not to say that there is no mileage in the idea of taking the first stage of describing the event for granted, and proceeding with looking at what people atribute it to. Many things in social life do have fairly fixed labels or names. When the experimenter presents his or her subjects with an event to explain what the experimenter has described, we are obliged to remember that this does mimic at least some occasions in social life. Once we have presented subjects with events to explain, then, again, we need to remember that many occasions in social life are indeed explained using the fairly crude explanations that attributions represent. And such explanations may not be crude: as Totman (1982) points out, legal, philosophical and moral reasoning depend on just that kind of distinction (more subtly expressed, perhaps, than internal and external causation). In court cases, guilt can hinge on proving that the defendant was or was not fully in control of his or her actions; to do that, the prosecution has to convince the jury that the defendant knew what he or she was doing, intended to do it, could have done otherwise, and was not temporarily insane - in other words, the barrister has to persuade the jury to make a strong, subtle and damning internal attribution.

Attribution theorists' confidence in causes as exhaustive concepts in ordinary explanation has, until the very recent past, tended to make the theory rather narrower than it might otherwise have been. A certain widening is currently visible, however, and attribution work is moving broadly to encompass the ideas of other ways of thinking about ordinary explanation (for a source of such alternatives, see Antaki, 1981). Attribution theory is expanding, and it is also developing. As it widens its conception of ordinary explanation, and addresses the question of cognitive process, it will have more and more to tell about the way in which we understand each others' behaviour - and our own.

REFERENCES

ABRAMSON, L.Y., SELIGMAN, M.E.P. and TEASDALE, J.D. (1978) Learned helplessness in humans: critique and reformulation. **Journal of Abnormal Psychology, 87,** 49-74

ANDERSON, C.A. (1983a) Inoculation and counterexplanation: debiasing techniques in the perseverance of social theories. **Social Cognition, 1,** 126-139

ANDERSON, C.A. (1983b) Abstract and concrete data in the perseverance of social theories: when weak data lead to unshakeable beliefs. **Journal of Experimental Social Psychology, 19,** 93-108

ANDERSON, C.A., LEPPER, M.R. and ROSS, L. (1980) Perseverance of social theories: the role of explanation in the persistence of discredited information. **Journal of Personality and Social Psychology, 39,** 1037-1049

ANTAKI, C. (ed.) (1981) **The Psychology of Ordinary Explanations of Social Behaviour.** London/NY: Academic Press

ANTAKI, C. and FIELDING, G.F. (1981) Research into ordinary explanation. In: C. Antaki (ed.) **The Psychology of Ordinary Explanations of Social Behaviour.** London/NY: Academic Press

BORGIDA, E. and BREKKE, N. (1981) The base rate fallacy in attribution and prediction. In: J.H. Harvey, W.J. Ickes and R.F. Kidd (eds) **New Directions in Attribution Research, Volume 3.** New Jersey: Erlbaum

CLARY, E.G. and TESSER, A. (1983) Reactions to unexpected events: the naive scientist and interpretative activity. **Personality and Social Psychology Bulletin, 9,** 609-620

DUNCAN, B. (1976) Differential social perception and attribution of intergroup violence: testing the lower level of stereotyping of blacks. **Journal of Personality and Social Psychology, 34,** 590-598

FISKE, S.E., KENNY, D.A. and TAYLOR, S.T. (1979) Structural models for the mediation of salience effects on attribution. Unpublished MS, Carnegie-Mellon University

GILBERT, G.N. and ABELL, P. (1983) **Accounts and Action.** Aldershot, Hants: Gower

GIORDANO, P. (1983) Sanctioning the high-status deviant: an attributional analysis. **Social Psychology Quarterly, 46,** 329-342

HANSEN, R.D. (1980) Commonsense attribution. **Journal of Personality and Social Psychology, 39,** 976-1009

HARVEY, J.H. and WEARY, G. (1981) **Perspectives on Attribution Processes.** Dubuque: Wm. Brown

HEIDER, F. (1944) Social perception and phenomenal causality. **Psychological Review, 51,** 358-374

HEIDER, F. (1958) **The Psychology of Interpersonal Relations.** New York: Wiley

HIGGINS. E.T., RHOLES, W.S. and JONES, C.R. (1977) Category accessibility and impression formation. **Journal of Experimental Social Psychology, 13,** 141-154

HEWSTONE, M. (ed.) (1983) **Attribution Theory: Social and Functional Extensions.** Oxford: Basil Blackwell

JASPARS, J. (1983) The process of causal attribution in common sense. In: M. Hewstone (ed.) **Attribution Theory: Social and Functional Extensions.** Oxford: Basil Blackwell

JASPARS, J., FINCHAM, F. and HEWSTONE, M. (eds) (1983) **Attribution Theory and Research: Conceptual Developmental and Social Dimensions.** London/New York: Academic Press

JONES, E.E. and DAVIS, K.E. (1965) From acts to dispositions: the attribution process in person perception. In: L. Berkowitz (ed.) **Advances in Experimental Social Psychology, Volume 2.** New York: Academic Press

JONES, E.E. and MCGILLIS, D. (1976) Correspondent inferences and the attribution cube: a comparative reappraisal. In: J.H. Harvey, W.J. Ickes and R.F. Kidd (eds) **New Directions in Attribution Research, Volume 1.** Hillsdale, N.J.: Erlbaum Associates

JONES, E.E. and NISBETT, R.E. (1972) The actor and the observer: divergent perceptions of the causes of behavior. In: E.E. Jones, et al. (eds) **Attribution: Perceiving the Causes of Behaviour.** Morristown, N.J.: General Learning Press

KAHNEMAN, D. and TVERSKY, A. (1973) On the psychology of prediction. **Psychological Review, 80,** 237-251

KAHNEMAN, D., SLOVIC, P. and TVERSKY, A. (1982) **Judgement Under Uncertainty: Heuristics and Biasses.** New York: CUP

KANOUSE, D. (1972) Language, labelling and attributions theory. In: E.E. Jones, D.E. Kanouse, H.H. Kelley, R.E. Nisbett, S. Valins and B. Weiner (eds) **Attribution: Perceiving the Causes of Behavior.** Morristown, N.J.: General Learning Press

KASSIN, S.M. (1979) Consensus information, prediction and causal attribution: a review of the literature and issues. **Journal of Personality and Social Psychology, 37,** 1966-1981

KELLEY, H.H. (1972a) Attributions in social interaction. In: E.E. Jones, D.E. Kanouse, H.H. Kelley, R.E. Nisbett, S. Valins, and B. Weiner (eds) **Attribution: Perceiving the Causes of Behavior.** Morristown, N.J.: General Learning Press

KELLEY, H.H. (1972b) Causal schemata and the attribution proces. In: E.E. Jones, D.E. Kanouse, H.H. Kelley, R.E. Nisbett, S. Valins, and B. Weiner (eds) **Attribution: Perceiving the Causes of Behavior.** Morristown, N.J.: General Learning Press

KELLEY, H.H. (1978) Conversations with E.E. Jones. In: J.H. Harvey, W.J. Ickes and R.F. Kidd (eds) **New Directions in Attribution Research, Volume 2.** New Jersey: Erlbaum

KELLEY, H.H. and MICHELA, J.L. (1980) Attribution theory and research. **Annual Review of Psychology, 31,** 457-501

KILIK, J. (1983) Confirmatory attribution and the perpetuation of social beliefs. **Journal of Personality and Social Psychology, 44,** 1171-1181

LALLJEE, M., WATSON, M. and WHITE, P. (1982) Explanations, attributions and the social context of unexpected behaviour. **European Journal of Social Psychology, 12,** 17-29

McARTHUR, L.A. (1972) The how and what of why: some determinants and consequences of causal attribution. **Journal of Personality and Social Psychology, 22,** 171-193

McARTHUR, L. and POST, D. (1977) Figural emphasis and person perception. **Journal of Experimental Social Psychology, 13,** 100-110

MARKUS, H. (1977) Self schemas in processing information about the self. **Journal of Personality and Social Psychology, 35,** 63-78

MICHOTTE, A.E. (1946) **La Perception de la Causalité** (Translated as 'The Perception of Causality'. New York: Basic Books, 1963.)

MONSON, T.C., and SNYDER, M. (1977) Actors, observers, and the attribution process: toward a reconceptualization. **Journal of Experimental Social Psychology,** 89-111.

NESDALE, A. (1983) Effects of person and situation expectation on explanation and seeking and causal attributions. **British Journal of Social Psychology, 22,** 93-99

NEWCOMBE, R. and RUTTER, D. (1982a) Ten reasons why ANOVA theory and research fail to explain attribution processes. 1: conceptual problems. **Current Psychological Reviews, 2,** 95-108

NEWCOMBE, R. and RUTTER, D. (1982b) Ten reasons why ANOVA theory and research fail to explain attribution processes. 2: methological problems. **Current Psychological Reviews, 2,** 153-170

NEWSTON, D. (1976) Foundation of attribution: the unit of perception of ongoing behaviour. In: J.H. Harvey, W.J. Ickes and R.F. Kidd (eds) **New Directions in Attribution Research, Volume 3.** New Jersey: Erlbaum

NISBETT, R.E. and BORGIDA, E. (1975) Attribution and the psychology of prediction. **Journal of Personality and Social Psychology, 32,** 932-943

NISBETT, R.E., CAPUTO, C., LEGANT, P., and MARACEK, J. (1973) Behavior as seen by the actor and as seen by the observer. **Journal of Personality and Social Psychology, 27,** 154-164

NISBETT, R.E. and ROSS, L. (1980) **Human Inference: Strategies and Shortcomings of Social Judgement.** New Jersey: Prentice-Hall.

ORVIS, B.R., CUNNINGHAM, J.D., and KELLEY, H.H. (1975) A closer examination of causal inferences: the roles of consensus distinctiveness and consistency information. **Journal of Personality and Social Psychology, 32,** 605-616

OSTROM, T.M. (1981) Attribution theory: whence and whither. In: J.H. Harvey, W.J. Ickes and R.F. Kidd (eds) **New Directions in Attribution Research, Volume 3.** New Jersey: Erlbaum

PETERSON, C. (1982) Learned helplessness and attributional interventions in depression. In: C. Antaki and C. Brewin (eds) **Attributions and Psychological Change.** London and New York: Academic Press

PRUITT, D.J. and INSKO, C.A. (1980) Extension of the Kelley attribution model: the role of comparison-object consensus, target-object consensus, distinctiveness and consistency. **Journal of Personality and Social Psychology,** 39-58

REYES, R.M., THOMPSON, W.C., BOWER, G.H. (1980) Judgemental biases resulting from differing availabilities of arguments. **Journal of Personality and Social Psychology, 39,** 2-12

ROSS, L. (1977) The intuitive psychologist and his shortcomings: distortions in the attribution process. In: L. Berkowitz (ed.) **Advances in Experimental Social Psychology, Volume 10.** New York: Academic Press

ROTHBART, M., EVANS, M. and FULERO, S. (1979) Recall for confirming events: memory processes and the maintenance of social stereotyping. **Journal of Experimental Social Psychology, 15,** 343-355

SOLOMON, S. (1978) Measuring dispositional and situational attributions. **Personality and Social Psychology Bulletin, 4,** 589-594

STORMS, M.D. (1973) Videotape and the attribution proces: reversing actors' and observers' point of view. **Journal of Personality and Social Psychology, 27,** 165-175

TAYLOR, S.E., CROCKER , J., FISKE, S.T., SPRINZEN, M. and WINKLER, J. (1979) The gereralizability of salience effects. **Journal of Personality and Social Psychology, 37,** 357-368

TAYLOR, S.E. and FISKE, S.T. (1981) Getting inside the head: methodologies for process analysis in attribution and social cognition. In: J.H. Harvey, W.J. Ickes and R.F. Kidd (eds) **New Directions in Attribution Research, Vol. 3.** New Jersey: Erlbaum

TETLOCK, P.E. (1983) Accountability and the perseverence of first impressions. **Social Psychology Quarterly, 46,** 285-292

TOTMAN, R. (1982) Philosophicl foundations of attribution therapies. In: C. Antaki and C. Brewin (eds) **Attribution and Psychological Change.** London/New York: Academic Press.

WATSON, D. (1982) The actor and the observer: how are their perceptions of causality divergent? **Psychological Bulletin, 92,** 682-700

WEINER, B. (1979) A theory of motivation for some classroom experiences. **Journal of Educational Psychology, 71,** 3-25

WEINER, B., FREIZE, I., KUKLA, A., REED, L., REST, S. and ROSENBAUM, R.M. (1972) Perceiving the causes of success and failure. In: E.E. Jones, D.E. Kanouse, H.H. Kelley, R.E. Nisbett, S.Valins and B. Weiner (eds) **Attribution: Perceiving the Causes of Behavior.** Morristown, N.J.: General Learning Press

WILDER, D.A. and COOPER, W.E. (1981) Categorisation into groups: consequences for social perception and attribution. In: J.H. Harvey, W.J. Ickes and R.F. Kidd (eds) **New Directions in Attribution Research, Volume 3.** New Jersey: Erlbaum

POLITICAL IDEOLOGY

Michael Billig

An excuse is needed for introducing the concept of ideology into a social-psychological discussion, for not only is the concept one of the most troublesome in the social sciences, but it is also one which most social psychologists find they can happily do without. Although typically social psychologists will talk about 'attitudes' rather than 'ideologies', there are important differences between the two concepts; in fact some important issues in the social psychology of political belief, and indeed in social-psychological theory generally, will be overlooked if attention is always paid to attitudes rather than to ideologies.

Although there have been many competing definitions for both concepts, a broad distinction between attitude and ideology can be drawn. Unlike an ideology, an attitude refers to a single unit of thought, belief or feeling. For example, Eiser (1980) mentions that we all have a rough idea of what an attitude is:

> To say that someone has an attitude towards some object, issue or person is a shorthand way of saying that he has certain feelings of like, or dislike, approval or disapproval, attraction or repulsion, trust or distrust, and so on. (p. 17)

The point is not whether attitudes are based on feelings, or on tendencies to behave, but that they relate to 'some object, issue or person'. In this sense, one can have an attitude towards the Common Market, or towards the Prime Minister or any other political issue or figure. Nor need attitudes be confined to political topics, but people will have attitudes about a vast array of different matters.

When public opinion surveyors ask members of the public whether they believe the death penalty should be restored (often requiring them to choose one from a limited range of options, such as 'yes', 'no', 'don't know'), or whether the government is to blame for unemployment, they are seeking to discover the public's attitudes to these issues (for examples of such questions, see the large compendium published by Gallup, 1976). However, a question about the desirability or otherwise of capital punishment does not of itself reveal the respondent's ideology, for an ideology is something more than an attitude. An ideology refers to a pattern of attitudes, and in this sense attitudes towards individual topics or people might form components of an overall ideology. To use a psychological metaphor, one might say that the attitudes resemble individual stimuli, such as the dots or lines in a picture, but the ideology is equivalent to the Gestalt or general pattern, which can give meaning to the individual elements.

Several problems are immediately raised by the notion of ideology as a pattern of attitudes. One might ask how such patterns should be recognized, what is the nature of the pattern and whether all attitudes can be said to form parts of wider patterns or ideologies. Any attempt to answer these questions would lead directly into some of the most difficult and contentious issues in the social sciences, where there are deep divisions of opinion about the nature of ideology (for example, Lichtheim, 1965; Gable, 1974; Seliger, 1976, 1977). In order to skirt around some of the more difficult theoretical issues involved in these debates, and in order to concentrate on a limited number of problems with social-psychological implications, a distinction between three concepts of ideology will be made:

* Social concept

* Individual concept

* Political concept.

Social concept

The social concept seeks to locate the patterns of ideas or beliefs, which might comprise an ideology, in the structure of society. Thus, an ideology represents the patterns of attitudes which a social class or a social group might possess. The classic formulation of the social concept of ideology was that advanced by Marx and Engels, especially in 'The German Ideology'. Here, Marx and Engels put forward the important notion that 'the ideas of the ruling class are in every epoch the ruling ideas' (1970 edn, p.64; for discussion of Marx's various theories of ideology, see Larrain, 1979, 1983). This was clearly a social concept of ideology, for Marx and Engels were arguing that in order to understand why certain ideas might be held in a particular society at a particular time, one must relate those ideas to the power structure of that society; therefore, the pattern of ideas embodied in an ideology would be related to the pattern of power within that society.

Although Marx and Engels may have been amongst the first thinkers to use 'ideology' in this way, the social concept is by no means confined to a Marxist, or even generally left-wing position. For example, Karl Mannheim in 'Ideology and Utopia' specifically sought to develop Marx and Engels' theory of ideology by removing it from their political theory. Whereas Marx and Engels had attempted to analyse the ideologies of their time with a view to refuting and overcoming such ideologies, Mannheim sought, at least initially, a science of ideology; this would provide an 'objective description of the structural differences in minds operating in different social settings' (1960 edn, p.51). Mannheim still retained the basic premise of Marx and Engels that:

> We refer to the ideology of an age or of a concrete historico-social group, for example, of a class, when we are concerned with the characteristics and composition of the total structure of this epoch or of this group. (pp.49-50)

In other words, an ideology refers to that pattern of attitudes and thoughts which can be associated with a particular group within a society or to the pattern of the society as a whole.

Although this social concept of ideology has been used principally within sociology, and particularly by specialists in the sociology of knowledge, similar ideas are becoming increasingly important within social psychology. This is particularly true of a development within European social psychology which is concentrating upon the study of 'social representations' (see, for example, Doise, 1978, 1982; Farr and Moscovici, 1984; Herzlich, 1972; Moscovici, 1981, 1982). There is a very close similarity between the notion of 'social representation', as used by social psychologists, and the social concept of ideology. The term 'social representations', like ideology, refers to patterns of attitudes which likewise are to be understood in terms of the structures and functions of groups. Thus, Moscovici has argued that 'social representations have their own properties, which can only be discovered by studying their relations with social groups' (Moscovici, 1982, p.135). The similarity between this social-psychological concept of representations and Mannheim's notion of ideology has been noted by Farr (1978), who suggests that these notions could provide a link between social psychology and other social sciences.

All in all, the social concept of ideology, or the concept of social representations, locates the patterning of attitudes in the existence of social groups; according to this conception, when one is talking about an ideology, one is talking about an ideology of a particular group, for example, the ideology of a class, political party or profession, etc. From an empirical point of view, it would then be helpful if there were a way of categorizing simply the different sorts of patterns which might be found in different sorts of groups. One way of making such a categorization has been to look at the values which an ideology is said to express.

Some of the most significant work in the social psychology of values has been conducted by Milton Rokeach (for example, Rokeach, 1968 and 1973). According to Rokeach, values provide the basic patterns to the attitudes of individuals and groups; whereas people may have thousands of attitudes, there are only a small number of basic values, and a knowledge of the basic values within a society will allow one to predict the attitudes prevalent in that society. Thus Rokeach (1979a) wrote that:

> Human values are conceptualized as consisting of a relatively small number of core ideas or cognitions present in every society about desirable end-states of existence and desirable modes of behaviour instrumental to their attainment that are capable of being organized to form different priorities. (p.49)

In Rokeach's theory, ideologies can be categorized according to the differing importance they attach to basic values. Although one might argue about which are the basic values, Rokeach in his **Value Survey** has concentrated upon 18 'terminal values' (or desirable end states) and 18 'instrumental values' (or desirable ways of attaining end-states). Examples of 'terminal values' are 'happiness', 'wisdom', 'sense of accomplishment' and examples of instrumental values are 'honest', 'clean', 'courageous'. Even if all these values are positively esteemed in most ideologies, nevertheless, according to Rokeach's theory, ideologies differ crucially in the relative importance placed on such values, and this, Rokeach argues, constitutes the very basis of ideology.

As regards political ideologies, Rokeach (1973) has proposed a **Two-Value Model,** which concentrates on the terminal values for 'freedom' and 'equality'. The model asserts that communism, fascism, socialism and conservatism should be distinguished in terms of these two values: socialism values both highly, conservatism values only freedom highly, communism only equality, whilst fascism values neither highly. He has also reported a content analysis of key texts expressing these four ideological positions, and he interprets this analysis as supporting the main assumptions of the Two-Value Model (Rokeach, 1973). Certainly, in Rokeach's analysis of Hitler's 'Mein Kampf' there was little evidence of a high value for either equality or freedom, but when other fascist texts have been selected for content analysis a different patterning of values has been found (for example, White, 1949; Eckhardt, 1968; Billig, 1978).

Rokeach's work on values has been very suggestive, especially since it provides an elegant and economical model of ideology, as well as a simple means of measuring values by the Value Survey. His book 'The Nature of Human Values' contains many interesting data, particularly on the patterns of values held by different sections of American society. Similarly, Searing (1978 and 1979) has reported a unique study of the values held by British Members of Parliament, using an adaptation and extension of Rokeach's method. However, it would appear that ideologies are too complex to be reduced to two basic values. For example, Billig and Cochrane (1979), and Cochrane, Billig and Hogg (1979a,b) looked at the values of activists and supporters of the Labour, Conservative, Communist and National Front parties in Britain (see also Ellerman, 1983). Although the activists of these four parties could be distinguished by their valuation of 'equality', in a way broadly compatible with Rokeach's model, the value of 'freedom' was rated highly by the activists of all persuasions. Even the activists from the fascist party, the National Front, rated this value highly. Although the fascists might use 'freedom' as a value, nevertheless this value, or political symbol, may contain different meanings when used by this group, from its use by, for example, Conservative or Labour supporters (Rokeach, 1979b). As such it may be necessary to look beyond the value itself, in order to uncover the various meanings which the value-symbol might contain. This implies that there might not be a simple relation between an ideology, its expressed values and its social context. Therefore, unravelling the meanings of an ideology, or social representation, and relating them to group and social structure remains a difficult, and indeed major, task for social psychologists investigating ideology from a social perspective.

Individual concept

In contrast to the social concept of ideology, there is an individual concept, which has been particularly used by psychologists rather than sociologists. Moscovici (1982), in stressing the 'collective character' of social representations, commented that they 'are incapable of accounting for individual differences, but only for differences between groups' (p.129). An individual approach to ideology, on the other hand, looks primarily at the various patterns of attitudes to be found in individuals, rather than groups, and seeks to discover what it might be about certain individuals which leads them to adopt different patterns of attitudes from other individuals. This approach has been particularly attractive to personality theorists, who claim that individuals of different personalities and motivations will be drawn towards different patterns of social attitudes.

There have been many studies which have attempted to relate the patterning of political attitudes to underlying personality factors. For example, the classic study 'The Authoritarian Personality', by Adorno, Frenkel-Brunswik, Levinson and Sanford (1950), related racial prejudice and far-right political ideas to an underlying personality variable of authoritarianism. Similarly, McClosky (1958) suggested that Americans with conservative attitudes, particularly with respect to issues of foreign policy, were less trusting in their personal lives than politically-liberal Americans, and Wilson (1973) also argues that conservative attitudes act as a defence against personal weaknesses. Similarly, there have been attempts to explain left-wing political views in terms of personality factors. For example, in the wake of the anti-Vietnamese war demonstrations, which took place in the United States during the late 1960s, there were a number of studies commenting upon the psychological motivations of the protestors. Investigators such as Keniston (1968 and 1971), Fishkin, Keniston and MacKinnon (1973) and Flacks (1967) saw the protesters as possessing non-neurotic and well-integrated personalities; in particular, they argued that the politics of the protesters were related to a developed sense of morality. More recently, a less flattering personal portrait of the protesters has been drawn; Rothman and Lichter (1978, 1980) concentrate on such factors as narcissism, self-assertiveness and a lack of concern for interpersonal warmth (see also Gold, Christie and Friedman (1976) for an analysis which concentrates on social factors rather than personality ones).

In all such studies there is a focus upon ideology rather than on attitudes as such. The investigators are not so much interested in attitudes towards a single issue, as in the way the individual views the world in general. For example, Adorno et al. (1950) and Wilson (1973) suggest that there is a whole constellation of attitudes which comprise far-right and conservative thinking; those who support the death penalty will be likely to defend conventional sexual morality and religious ideas, to be racially prejudiced and generally chauvinistic, as well as being hostile to modern art and to informal styles of behaviour and dress. As such, conservatism is seen as a pattern of various different attitudes, some overtly political and some relating to general cultural issues, and these researchers seek to explain this pattern, or ideology, in terms of underlying patterns of personality. This general approach has been particularly popular amongst psycho-analytic theorists, who see the consciously held attitudes as being an expression of unconsciously repressed weaknesses (for a recent discussion of unconscious motivations lying behind racial attitudes in contemporary Britain, see Sherwood, 1980). In this way, it is argued that psychological factors hold together the different strands of an ideology and provide a hidden meaning behind all the different attitudes.

Political concept

This concept of ideology is used in a specific, and more restricted way than the social or individual concepts. Both the individual and the social concepts of ideology assume that there are meaningful patterns of attitudes; in the one case, the meaning is to be sought within the individual's psyche and in the other case the meaning is derived from the group. However, there is also the problem of what constitutes a pattern of attitudes; does any constellation of beliefs, either at an individual or a group level, constitute an ideology, or are there certain patterns which should be called ideological and which should accordingly be distinguished from non-ideological patterns? For instance, a pattern of attitudes which encompasses views about the desirability of strict sexual morality, harsher sentences for criminals, lower welfare payments for the unemployed and heavier state spending on military armaments can be identified as a conservative pattern of attitudes, whilst the opposite of such attitudes can be thought of as a liberal or socialist pattern. However, it would be harder to pin an ideological label to a pattern which involved agreement with sexual morality and harsher sentencing, but rejected the other two positions. The difficulty of finding a readily available label itself suggests that not all patterns might constitute a political ideology, but, if this is so, one might ask whether there are any intrinsic differences between the patternings of attitudes which can be called ideological and those which are non-ideological.

It is just these considerations which have led some social scientists to use the term 'ideology' to describe only those patterns of attitudes which are tightly structured and this forms the basis of the political concept of 'ideology'. For example, Raymond Aron has written that 'an ideology presupposes an apparently systematic formalization of facts, interpretations, desires and predictions' (1977, p.309). This implies that the person who possesses an ideology has some sort of overall political theory integrating individual attitudes. The typical image of such an ideology is that of Marxism, which provides the believer with a whole framework, or an internal logic, for interpreting the world. The Marxist, possessed of such a framework, does not work out his or her position on each issue in isolation, but refers each issue to the ideology of the class struggle. Marxism is not the only way of looking at the world which, on this definition, would be called ideological, but, as Lane (1962) suggested, 'a Jesuit's outlook' or even 'a Benthamite-Adam Smith liberalism' can be seen as consituting 'a well thought-out "completed" ideology, with the connective links between one area of thought and another pushed through and bolted down, anchored to absolute value' (Lane, 1962, p.464).

In the social sciences there has been much debate about the 'correct' uses of the concept of 'ideology'. For example, some, but by no means all, defenders of the social concept claim that all thought is ideological because it can be related to wider social patterns. They go on then to claim that the 'political concept' is misconceived because it implies that some thinking is 'non-ideological', whereas according to the social concept of ideology all thinking is ideological. This would imply that the political concept of ideology is an illegitimate use of the word 'ideology'. However, for present purposes it is not necessary to stipulate what are legitimate and illegitimate uses of the word, so long as the different senses of the social and political concepts are not forgotten. If one bears in mind that they describe different sorts of phenomena, then confusion can be minimized, whilst certain empirical issues about the structure of attitudes and the relation between this structure and social context are examined.

IDEOLOGY AND CONTEMPORARY ATTITUDES

From a social-psychological point of view, the political concept of ideology is particularly useful, because it suggests a distinction between two broad patterns of thinking about the world. On the one hand there is ideological thought, which possesses a tight internal logic: for the ideological thinker, the relation between attitudes and basic principles rather resembles the relation between hypotheses and axioms in a formal scientific theory. On the other hand, there is a more fluid and looser way of thinking about the world: here the attitudes resemble collections of hypotheses derived from a jumble of different experiments and theoretical hunches, without being systematically integrated into an over-arching theory. Where there is such a lack of systematization, it is possible that an individual might possess contrary hypotheses or attitudes, whereas a more systematic or ideological way of thinking will seek to resolve all internal contradictions (Billig, 1982).

One can ask whether in contemporary Western society the beliefs of most people fit the ideological or non-ideological pattern of thinking; in other words, one is asking whether Western states fit Shils's (1968) definition of an 'ideological state' as one which is 'characterized by a high degree of integration among the elements of the culture' (p.75). A social-psychological perspective on this wide and important question can be provided by considering one of the central components of attribution theory (see Antaki, this volume): attribution theorists distinguish between explanations for social events which are personal and those which are situational. Although most of the work conducted by attribution theorists has concerned explanations for non-political everyday events, it is possible to view political ideologies in terms of whether they offer situational or personal explanations for major social phenomena. For example, a thorough-going conservative (in the Benthamite-Adam Smith mould, mentioned by Lane) might possess an ideology which viewed society principally in terms of individual actions and motivations; thus, poverty would be given a personal explanation, it being suggested that the poor are poor because they are lazy and that the rich are rich because they work hard. On the other hand, a Marxist might offer a situational explanation of the social world, where the 'system' or social structure is blamed for poverty, not the characteristics of the poor themselves (see Billig, 1982, Chapter eight, for a discussion of ideology in terms of attribution theory).

There have been a number of studies to suggest that different sections of Western society tend to either the situational or individual explanations of poverty. For example, in different studies conducted in the United States, Australia and Great Britain, it has been found that the young, the supporters of liberal/left political parties and the less affluent on average tend to favour situational explanations of poverty more than do the old, the more right-wing and the more affluent (for example, Feagin, 1972; Feather, 1974; Furnham, 1982, 1983). Thus, one might say that these groups possess different social representations of poverty. However, the results of these studies should not be taken as indicating that there is a strong ideological division in modern society between those who adopt a rigorously individualist perspective on the world and those who have an equally rigorous situationalist perspective. In the main, such studies have looked for the statistically significant differences in the responses given to questionnaire items by different social groups. Whilst it is true that there might be differences between the groups, it nevertheless is possible that there may also be important similarities. For example, Nilson (1981) specifically looked at both the possible similarities and differences; she found that the majority of her American respondents agreed with both individualist and situational explanations of poverty. Whilst some respondents (especially the religiously conservative, the old and those from the South) were more prone to give personal explanations, nevertheless situational explanations were also used. According to Nilson, the dominant response of her respondents was a 'hybrid' one, which accepted that there was institutional discrimination against the poor, but also accepted that the poor, when offered opportunities, could do something about their situation. Because of this ambivalence, Nilson concluded that her results 'provide an excellent illustration of the lack of ideology and ideological cleavage in America' (p.545).

There is similar evidence from studies which have used in-depth interviews of a small number of respondents, rather than employing formal questionnaires for large numbers of respondents. The advantage of in-depth interviews is that they can reveal more information about the complex ways people might think about the world in general and one can explore the meaning of their various attitudes, instead of judging them consistent or inconsistent on the basis of agreement or disagreement with a limited number of formal questions. The disadvantage of the in-depth interview is that it is often difficult to know whether the small sample of interviewees is representative of the population at large, and accordingly whether the patterns of attitudes found in the small sample are indicative of the patterns to be found in the society at large.

Lane's (1962) pioneering study of twelve working-class Americans showed how rich insights can be gained by sensitive in-depth interviewing. Not only was he able to construct convincing portraits of each individual, thereby showing how deep-seated personal motivations became subtly intertwined with general political attitudes, but Lane was also attentive to the general patterns of thinking shared by most of his respondents. In this sense his study was concerned with both the individual and social concepts of ideology, not to mention their complex interrelations. Lane's study revealed the extent to which ordinary people think deeply about, and are genuinely perplexed by, the social world in which they live. He stressed that his respondents did not have simple ways of categorizing the world, but often combined both personal and situational explanations. For example, most of his inteviewees used personal explanations to criticize the motivations of the unemployed poor living off welfare subsidies, whilst at the same time using a situational perspective when describing how the social system prevented equal opportunities for all. (Sennett and Cobb (1977) found similar patterns of attitudes in their interviews of working-men, as did Willis (1978) and Griffin (in press) at least in more attenuated forms, in their respective studies of working-class adolescents.) Lane stressed that such contrary themes in the thinking of ordinary people should not be considered as contradictions in any simple sense:

> The premises of much of our thought, of the thinking of one mind, is contradictory; but very often what seems contradictory is not more so than the 'contradiction' between gravity and levitation of a balloon - opposing tendencies seeking a balance. (Lane, 1962)

Such an image of the contradictory themes in contemporary political thinking lies at the root of the provocative thesis of Murray Edelman (1964, 1977), who argues that most people have at their disposal two contradictory ways of thinking about politics. On the one hand there are the arguments (or social representations) which blame the poor for their lack of ambition or moral fibre, and indeed which praise those who escape poverty by dint of hard work and sterling character. On the other hand there is the pattern of argument which sees the poor as oppressed victims of an unjust system. According to Edelman (1977), much modern political discourse consists of shifts from one to the other of this 'pair of opposing political myths'. Edelman claims that both myths are readily available within the culture and the existence of such 'multiple realities has profound, if non-obvious, consequences for politics', because 'it encourages both the powerful and the powerless to accept their situations while permitting both to express their abhorrence of poverty and their dedication to reform' (Edelman, 1977, p.142). Edelman's analysis implies that the pair of contradictory myths are not separated into two separate political ideologies, but they become intertwined in complex, non-ideological patterns. Similarly, Tomkins (1966) has suggested that 'middle-of-the-road' political positions combine both left-wing and right-wing attitudes: for recent applications of Tomkins' ideas about the social psychology of ideology, see Loye (1977), Stone (in press).

Edelman's arguments can be interpreted as offering criticism against any simple social-psychological theory of consistency. Festinger's book 'A Theory of Cognitive Dissonance' (1957) provides the most famous example of such a consistency theory. Festinger suggested that people have a basic motivation to reduce inconsistency in their thoughts. If someone has two cognitions which are perceived to be inconsistent, then that person will experience an uncomfortable state of dissonance and will be motivated to change one or other of the inconsistent cognitions. Despite the intuitive appeal of this simple theory of cognitive dissonance, social psychologists have nevertheless found difficulty in producing conclusive evidence that there is a general motivation to reduce dissonance (for example, McGuire, 1969). Edelman's work suggests that far from inconsistency being a state which people wish to avoid, it may describe something general in modern society. Thus, people, according to Edelman, possess the capacity for making two apparently inconsistent sorts of argument about poverty. The individualistic themes do not contradict the situational ones in a way which leads to people becoming either wholly individualistic or wholly situational. Instead of the contradiction producing a psychologically unsatisfactory state, it is, according to Edelman, psychologically reassuring, and thereby in the long run politically conservative.

It is possible to go further and interpret Edelman's arguments as evidence that there is no overall ideology (using the term in the political, not the social, sense) in modern Western societies. Certainly a distinction can be drawn between communist societies and contemporary capitalist ones in this regard. In communist countries, such as the Soviet Union, there is an official ideology, that of Marxist-Leninism, promulgated and interpreted by the Communist party. Working from basic principles, the appointed ideologists formulate the official positions on the many issues of the day. There is no direct parallel of this process in the West, and indeed it is arguable whether there is a single ideology of capitalism which is comparable to the ideology of Marxist-Leninism. It might be thought that the ideology of capitalism would be built upon the principle that there should be uncluttered competition, and that individuals should be allowed to pursue their interests without restriction - a theory, for example, enumerated in Adam Smith's classic work on the principles of capitalism 'An Inquiry into the Nature and Causes of the Wealth of Nations' first published in 1776. Certainly the individualistic explanations of poverty, described by Edelman, are in accord with such a philosophy of individual self-reliance. However, as Edelman argues and as the evidence from the attribution studies suggests, this individualism is only one theme in the way people think about the world; the theme of individualism is typically 'balanced' by an opposing theme of situational explanations (if one can use the word 'balance' differently from consistency theorists: see Billig (1982) for a discussion of these two contrasting senses of 'balance').

In addition, the contrast between the individual and the situational explanations could be said to match a complexity in the structure of Western society. Present day capitalism is not based upon a simple competition between individual entrepreneurs, each doggedly pursuing their own economic interests, in a way which Adam

Smith believed to be the ideal economic arrangement. Instead of such individual competition, today there are large monopolies and public companies, and, moreover, the state intervenes in the economy to a degree which would have horrified Smith and which horrifies his monetarist admirers of our time. In contemporary capitalism the state possesses the complex role of facilitating competition between industrial businesses, as well as providing welfare for the victims of this competition, such as the unemployed. Thus both competition and welfare co-exist, in an economic arrangement which combines the principles of individualism and corporate organization.

In such conditions, there may be no systematic overall ideology; the contrary themes, or social representations, of 'competition' and 'caring', of 'individual responsibility' and 'social injustice', etc., may not be integrated into a rigid, internally consistent pattern of thought. For example, Abercrombie and Turner (1978) have argued that:

> the so-called 'dominant ideology' of late capitalism is ... at best an uneven and uneasy amalgam of assumptions about private property and about the importance of state intervention in economic life. (p.163)

This same diagnosis of the attitudes prevalent in modern Western society has been made by both left-wing and right-wing social scientists; thus, from the conservative right, theorists like Bell (1976), Hayek (1949) and Crozier (1975) have stressed the lack of an overall political ideology in the West just as much as Marxist thinkers like Mandel (1975) and Marcuse (1968) have done (although alternative analyses can be found in Althusser, 1971; Miliband, 1973; Parkin, 1967). From a social-psychological perspective this implies that in Western societies one should look for complexity in the social representations which people hold about the political world. One might say that the contradictions of the society will be reproduced directly in the minds of most of those who live in the society.

This can be illustrated by considering racial attitudes. Western societies contain both democratic institutions as well as structures which permit economic and social discrimination against immigrant minorities. In such societies one would not expect most people's thinking about race to be dominated by theories of blood differences between Aryans and non-Aryans. Such ideologies of race, which suggest that there are unbridgeable differences between groups, conflict with the norms of democratic societies, where equality before the law is stressed. On the other hand, in societies where there is institutional racism, whether in terms of immigation laws which discriminate against certain groups, or discriminatory police practices or whatever, one would not expect that the public's attitudes would represent a position of consistent tolerance. Instead, one finds that public opinion on race reflects the contrary trends of both tolerance and prejudice. Doctrines, or ideologies, of racial purity are confined to a small minority, whereas the majority will have both prejudiced and tolerant themes in their thinking on race. For example, people are likely to say 'I'm not prejudiced but ...', before complaining about the 'problems' of immigrants and immigration; in so doing, such a person is expressing the norm of tolerance and recognizing that one should not be predjuced, whilst at the same time transgressing that norm. (See Van Dijk (1982), Cochrane and Billig (1984), Dummett (1973) for examples of the complex and ambivalent ways the majority population talks about minorities in contemporary society.)

Detailed examination of the ways people balance, reconcile or juggle the contradictory themes contained in common social representations might necessitate a shift in the direction of social-psychological research from quantitative techniques to qualitative ones. Traditional quantitative research has sought statistically signficant differences between the coded responses of different groups of respondents, who typically have answered formal questionnaires. In this sort of research there is frequently, but not inevitably, a tendency to divide respondents into distinct groups, such as the prejudiced/tolerant, the personal attributors/situational attributors, etc.; in this way the complexities of the 'tolerant' person's prejudices, or the 'prejudiced' person's tolerances become overlooked. On the other hand, a qualitative approach would not, at least initially, be seeking to translate the verbal responses of respondents into numerical data. Instead, a qualitative approach would look directly at the complex and ambivalent ways ordinary people talk and think about politics. Here the emphasis would be upon uncovering the subtle meanings of political discourse, in order to unpack the contradictory meanings which are condensed into familiar political symbols (Bennett, 1980; Edelman, 1964; Graber, 1976). Methodologically, such an approach might resemble those qualitative studies undertaken by 'ethogenists' or 'symbolic interactionists' (for general discussions of this issue, see, for example, Billig, 1977; Harré, 1980; Harré and Secord, 1972; Kroger, 1982).

IDEOLOGY AND PERSONALITY

If the majority of people in contemporary Western society do not possess political ideologies, in the sense of having systematized belief-systems, then there is nevertheless the social-psychological problem of accounting for the minority who do possess such ideologies. Often this problem is viewed as the problem of explaining the attractions of political extremism, for it can be argued that such ideologies are to be found on the extremes of politics, rather than in the non-ideological centre of contemporary politics. For example, on the far left there is the ideology of Marxist-Leninism, which seeks to explain political history in terms of the theory of class struggle and the inevitable triumph of the working-class. On the extreme right there is a different ideology: most fascist and far-right groups hold an ideology which asserts that politics should be explained in terms of the actions of a small group of evil conspirators (typically thought to be Jews, Freemasons or Jewish freemasons) who are seeking to dominate the world (for discussions of the history of this ideology, see, for example, Cohn, 1967; Holmes, 1979; Roberts, 1974). Both Marxist-Leninism and the conspiracy theory are ideologies, in the political sense of the concept, for both possess their own respective fundamental assumptions and rules of internal logic, which enable the believer to derive particular attitudes. In addition, on the far right and left are to be found professional ideologists who are experts in the logic of their ideologies, and can thereby formulate the ideologically correct 'party line' on the issues of the day.

One very influential line of research within psychology has asked the question whether people of a particular personality are attracted to systematized ideologies. This has led to a search to identify an 'ideological' type of personality, which would characterize people who have inner needs to hold systematized beliefs. As such, this line of research has sought to explain the attractions of political ideologies in terms of individual motivations and particularly in terms of personality weaknesses or deficiencies.

Authoritarianism and ideology

The classic work in the psychology of political ideology is 'The Authoritarian Personality' published in 1950 by Adorno, Frenkel-Brunswik, Levinson and Sanford. It was not so much that the ideas of this book were especially novel; the theory of 'The Authoritarian Pesonality' contains ideas similar to those which Wilhelm Reich had expounded in his 'The Mass Psychology of Fascism', written shortly after Hitler had come to power in Germany in 1933, and also to those which Erich Fromm had published in his 'Fear of Freedom' during the Second World War. All three books were addressed to the question whether there is a particular type of person, who, because of their personality, is attracted towards fascism, and all three argued that there is indeed such a 'fascist personality'. What, however, distinguishes 'The Authoritarian Personality' is the sheer scope of the empirical research conducted by Adorno and his co-workers. Nearly two thousand respondents, mainly living in California, completed a series of questionnaires designed to measure a variety of attitudes, such as those towards Jews, Blacks, foreigners, politics, etc. There were also in-depth interviews with large numbers of the most prejudiced and least prejudiced respondents, and the interviewers probed the childhood experiences and the unfulfilled hopes of these respondents in detail. Lastly there was the formulation of the famous **F Scale;** this was a questionnaire designed to measure those personality characteristics which Adorno and his co-workers believed to constitute the core of the fascist personality.

Adorno et al. argued that there was a syndrome of factors underlying the psychology of fascism. The person who was anti-semitic was also likely to be racist and generally prejudiced against foreigners. Similarly, such a person would have a strict sense of what constituted proper and improper sorts of behaviour, and would be hostile to all those who transgressed this strict code of behaviour. Above all, the prejudiced, potential fascist would have a rigid sense of hierarchy, believing that some individuals and groups occupied superior positions, whilst others should be confined to an inferior status. Adorno et al., following Reich and Fromm, formulated an ingenious psychological theory to account for such a syndrome. They hypothesized that the fascist, or authoritarian, had been raised by parents of a similar personality. These authoritarian parents had demanded complete obedience from their offspring, and in consequence the children had learned never to criticize their parents. In fact the children would grow up believing, at least consciously, that their parents were well-nigh perfect, and in the in-depth interviews many of the authoritarian respondents talked in exaggeratedly idealized tones about their parents. However, Adorno et al. argued that such respondents has repressed all negative feelings against their harsh and disciplinarian parents. These negative feelings would then be deflected onto other targets, such as minority groups. This split bewteen the outwardly admitted positive feelings and the repressed negative feelings towards the parents lay at the root of a basic split in the psyche of the authoritarian. According to the theory of 'The Authoritarian Personality', it gave rise to a general style of thinking, in which the authoritarian needs to divide the world up into absolute categories and is 'intolerant of ambiguity'. Thus, the authoritarian was said to think that there were certain people or groups who were absolutely good, and others which were the epitome of all evil. Above all, there was a need to worship heroes, just as much as there was a need to 'scapegoat' inferiors; the authoritarian, then, would accept uncritically whatever the admired figures said. Unable to formulate views on individual issues, but needing to accept the wisdom of an admired authority, such a person falls prey to what Adorno called 'ticket thinking' (see also Horkheimer and Adorno's 'Dialectic of Enlightenment' (1973) for an earlier formulation of the idea of ticket thinking). In this way, the need for 'tickets', which would prescribe what is the 'correct' line to take on all manner of issues, formed the psychological basis of ideology. As such, the authoritarian should be attracted to ideological systems which remove all ambiguity from the world by providing clearly identifiable heroes and villains and by suggesting clear-cut explanations of complex events.

Like most innovative pieces of research, the work of Adorno et al. has attracted much controversy. From the start there were methodological criticisms of the ways in which they conducted their research (for example, Christie and Jahoda, 1954; Kirscht and Dillehay, 1967; see also Sanford, 1973, for a defence of the original work). In particular, a number of critics focused upon alleged technical deficiencies of the F Scale, and have produced other scales designed to measure the personality variable of authoritarianism (for example, Altemeyer, 1981; Lederer, 1982; Warr et al., 1967). Other investigators have argued that the sort of authoritarianism described by Adorno et al. is not so much a product of personality factors as of social conditions (for example, Brown, 1965; Baker, 1976; Gabbennesch, 1972; Lipset, 1960; Stewart and Hoult, 1959). Such critics have argued that it is low socio-economic status and lack of education, and not family processes, which produce authoritarianism and the rigidly restricted outlook of authoritarians.

Of interest here is the possibility that authoritarianism might predict who will join or support fascist movements and be attracted to the ideology of fascism. Unfortunately it is difficult to assess the efficacy of the F Scale as a predictor of fascist membership. Although Adorno et al. claimed that the scale was assessing the personality of the 'potential fascist', it should be emphasized that their high scoring respondents were not themselves members or supporters of fascist parties; Adorno et al. were claiming that these were just the sort of people who would become fascist supporters were the political climate to change and fascism become a popular mass movement. Such an argument must necessarily remain conjectural until there is such a political change; only then could one test whether it is the authoritarians who would flock to the fascist standard, looking for the strong anti-democratic leadership which appeals to their inner needs.

Nevertheless, there are certain indications that it might be too simple to equate psychological authoritarianism with support for fascism. Evidence from the rise of Nazism in Germany in the 1930s suggests that many different types of people, with differing personal motivations, were attracted to fascism. In a revealing study, the Polish sociologist Abel organized a competition for Nazi party members to write an essay on the topic of why they joined the party. The essays, published in 'Why Hitler Came to Power' (Abel, 1938), reveal that authoritarianism appears to be only one of a multitude of factors, and this led Abel (1945) to argue against offering explanations of the rise of fascism in terms of any simple personality constellation (see also Koonz, 1976, and Merkl, 1975, for interesting re-analyses of Abel's unique data). Abel argued that psychologists should not forget that many people supported the Nazis in Germany because they believed that Hitler would set the economy back on its feet and that this sort of support does not need to be explained in terms of a deep-seated psychological motivation for an authoritarian father-figure. On the other hand, detailed psychiatric investigations of some of the leading Nazis captured by the Allies after the war suggest that a number had disturbed personality patterns, suggesting extreme states of authoritarianism (see, for example, Dicks, 1972; Gilbert, 1948; Fromm, 1974).

Investigations of small fascist groups, which exist on the margins of today's political scene, also reveal that it is too simple to equate support for fascism with authoritarianism. For example, Billig (1978) and Billig and Cochrane (1981), looking at the National Front in Britain, argue that this fascist party recruits not just authoritarians, but also violent individuals, who show a different psychological pattern from the classic authoritarian. Whereas the authoritarians seek some sort of brittle control over their impulses, the hooligan element in fascist movements often rejoices in a lack of control and shows distinctly anti-authoritarian tendencies.

It might be argued that the authoritarians will be attracted to the ideological aspects of fascism, whereas the violent individuals will be attracted by the promise of direction action which fascism offers. Such an argument would then link authoritarianism to the 'ticket thinking' aspects of fascism, rather than to fascist support per se. Direct evidence on this issue is hard to come by, as those few studies which have administered the F Scale to actual members of fascist parties (for example, Eysenck and Coulter, 1972;

see below) have tended to treat their fascist respondents as a homogeneous group, rather than distinguishing between those who may be complete believers in the ideology of their group and those who have not incoporated the ideology into their thinking. Suggestive evidence comes from studies of the John Birch Society in the United States. The JBS is not a fascist party and in fact it is not a political party in the strict sense of the term. It is a society which seeks to promote an extreme right-wing ideological interpretation of the world in terms of a global communist conspiracy; its founder Robert Welch even thought that the right-wing President of the United States, Dwight Eisenhower, was a conscious communist agent (Stone, 1974). Because the Society exists only to promote this view, all its supporters are aware of the ideology; this is not necessarily true of a fascist party, which might mount anti-immigrant campaigns and attract supporters ignorant of the party's ideology of conspiracy. Studies of John Birch Society members have not shown them to be overwhelmingly authoritarian or to be suffering from any particular psychological disturbance (for example, Elms, 1969, 1970; Rohter, 1969). As such, there are reasons for thinking that factors, other than authoritarianism, may contribute to the possession of such an extreme right-wing ideology as the conspiracy theory of politics.

Dogmatism and ideology

A number of critics have argued that 'The Authoritarian Personality' only measured one sort of authoritarianism and that, by concentrating upon the potential fascist, Adorno et al. ignored the possibility of authoritarianism of the left. This criticism was forcibly argued by Shils (1954), who suggested that the extreme left and the extreme right were similar 'in many very striking respects'. In particular, he argued that the authoritarianism which Adorno et al. located in fascist support had its parallel on the extreme left, where left-wing positions would be defended in an authoritarian way. However, according to Shils, the F Scale had only measured right-wing authoritarianism and what was needed was an approach which would be sensitive to other sorts of authoritarian thinking.

Milton Rokeach aimed to provide such an approach in 'The Open and Closed Mind' (1960). His basic theory was similar to that of 'The Authoritarian Personality', in that he related the growth of closed-minded ticket-thinking to conflicts and worries in early childhood. He argued that closed-minded, dogmatic individuals feel threatened by ambiguity and therefore they need to experience the world in simplified and well-structured terms. He argued that his Dogmatism

Scale provided an advance over the F Scale of Adorno et al. in that the Dogmatism Scale measured dogmatism per se, rather than a particular form of dogmatism. In consequence, dogmatism was intended to represent ideological thought, for it was the dogmatists who were presumed to need the intellectual security of a well-ordered ideology. As a result, one of the predictions of the theory of dogmatism was that communists and fascists should both score highly on the Dogmatism Scale. Rokeach (1960) tested a small sample of British communists and claimed that their scores on the Dogmatism Scale were higher than the scores of Labour, Liberal and Conservative supporters. However, on some items of the scale they scored less highly than the 'moderates', whilst on other items they were more dogmatic and their overall mean scores were more dogmatic. There is some evidence that the items on the Dogmatism Scale may not be free of political content, so that left-wingers are likely to agree with some items and right-wingers with other items on the basis of their political beliefs rather than on the basis of a presumed dogmatic style of thinking (Parrott and Brown, 1972); moreover, it has been argued that those items which differentiated the communists from the 'moderates' were in the main items which contained political content (see Billig, 1982, Chapter six). If this is so, then the case for considering communists to be dogmatic is weakened.

The claim that communists share a similar personality disposition to fascists has also been made by Hans Eysenck (for example, Eysenck, 1954; Eysenck and Wilson, 1978). Instead of talking about dogmatism, Eysenck claims that both fascists and communists are equally 'tough-minded' and that 'tough-mindedness' constitutes the basis of a predisposition to ideological thought. The key study for Eysenck's theory was one conducted by Coulter (1953) and described in Eysenck (1954) and Eysenck and Coulter (1972). However, Eysenck's reports of this study and his scales for assessing tough-mindedness have been severely criticized on theoretical and methodological grounds (for example, Billig, 1979, 1981; Christie, 1956a,b; Hanley and Rokeach, 1956; Rokeach and Hanley, 1956). Although Eysenck (1956a,b) made an attempt to reply to some of the serious accusations made against his research, the position today remains basically the same as it was when Brown (1965) made his judicious review of the controversy, coming down on the side of Eysenck's critics. The unresolved difficulties with Eysenck's work, as well as Rokeach's inconclusive data on the dogmatism of communists, has led Stone (1980) to argue recently that the idea of left-wing authoritarianism is a 'myth' for which adequate psychological evidence is lacking (see also Stone, in press).

Michael Billig

SOCIAL APPROACHES TO POLITICAL IDEOLOGY

The hypothesis that people are attracted towards political groups with extreme ideologies because they personally need a clear belief-system is an attractive one because of its simplicity. However, in order to understand why people might be drawn to such ideologies, it is necessary to go beyond broad hypotheses about personal motivations; one needs to look in detail at the groups themselves and locate the ideology within the social context of the group. This entails adopting a more social approach than that typically taken by those concentrating on the dynamics of personality. By taking such an approach, it is possible to note similarities between the extreme left and the extreme right. Instead of suggesting that such similarities reflect common underlying psychological predispositions, it can be argued that some similarities arise from the common social situations of the extreme right and extreme left. Both extremes often find themselves in a position of trying to preserve an ideological tradition in a general climate which is inimical to that tradition, and at the same time they seek to attract supporters whose attitudes may reflect the general climate rather than the ideology of the group in question.

What this implies is that many who are drawn to the extremes of politics may not be initially aware of the ideology of the group to which they are attracted. Firstly, such people must experience some sort of disillusion with traditional politics, experiencing what has been called 'political alienation' (for example, Long, 1981, 1982). However, this disillusion may focus upon a few issues. For example, Lipset and Raab (1971), in their lengthy survey of the history of extreme right-wing political groups in the United States, argue for the importance of 'selective support', and claim that such right-wing groups, when they are able to attract mass support, do so on the basis of a few issues. Similarly, studies of the National Front in Britain suggest that support has derived from the party's publicised anti-immigration campaigns, and such support is gained in spite of, rather than because of, its ideology of a Jewish conspiracy (Husbands, 1983; Taylor, 1982). Almond's (1954) classic study based on interviews with over two hundred ex-members of the Communist party in the United States and Europe, and Newton's (1969) detailed study of the British Communist party reveal a similar pattern of issue support, rather than ideological commitment, on the far left (see also Denver and Bochel, 1973). Both Almond and Newton distinguish between a small inner core of ideologists, steeped in the intricacies of dialectical ideology, and the majority of ordinary members, whose general political thinking is more fragmented. Similarly, Billig (1978) interviewed members of the National Front and found that many, whilst not possessing the full ideology of conspiracy, were picking up bits and pieces of the ideology, by virtue of mixing in an environment where this ideological culture is being preserved.

At present little is known about which individuals, having entered an extreme group, are liable to develop the full ideological consciousness of their chosen group, and which are likely either to remain selective supporters or to drop out altogether. How members of such groups change their perceptions and interpretations of politics is an important question for social-psychological theory. Whereas attention in social psychology is turning towards the issue of 'conversion' (Moscovici, 1980), there is little work exploring the subtleties of change, by which people adopt new vocabularies and habits of explanation, and how the possession of new political symbols might affect attitudinal and ideological beliefs. Some of these issues have been raised in social psychology with respect to attitudes (for example, Eiser and Ross, 1977), but the problem here is to relate them to ideologies and the existence of social groups. In this respect, problems of ideological change and stability stretch beyond considering this or that individual's motivations, but raise fundamental questions about the ways group create and maintain their interpretations of the world: in other words they raise issues about the ways in which reality is socially constructed (Berger and Luckmann, 1967).

Acknowledgements

The author wishes to thank Lindsey Quin for her helpful comments.

REFERENCES

ABEL, T. (1938) **Why Hitler Came to Power.** New Jersey: Prentice Hall

ABEL, T. (1945) Is a psychiatric interpretation of the German enigma necessary? **American Sociological Review, 10,** 457-464

ABERCROMBIE, N. and TURNER, B.S. (1978) The dominant ideology thesis. **British Journal of Sociology, 29,** 149-170

ADORNO, T.W., FRENKEL-BRUNSWIK, E., LEVINSON, D.J. and SANFORD, R.N. (1950) **The Authoritarian Personality.** New York: Harper and Row

ALMOND, G.A. (1954) **The Appeals of Communism.** New Jersey: Princeton University Press

ALTEMEYER, R.A. (1981) **Right-Wing Authoritarianism.** Manitoba: University of Manitoba Press

ALTHUSSER, L. (1971) **Lenin and Philosophy and Other Essays.** London: New Left Books

ARON, R. (1977) **The Opium of the Intellectuals.** Westport: Greenwood Press

BAKER, T.L. (1976) The weakening of authoritarianism in black and white college students. **Sociology and Social Research, 60,** 440-460

BELL, D. (1976) **The Cultural Contradition of Capitalism.** London: Heinemann

BENNETT, W.L. (1980) The paradox of public discourse: a framework for the analysis of political accounts. **Journal of Politics, 42,** 792-817

BERGER, P.L. and LUCKMANN, T. (1967) **The Social Construction of Reality.** London: Allen Lane

BILLIG, M. (1977) The new social psychology and 'fascism'. **European Journal of Social Psychology, 7,** 393-432

BILLIG, M. (1978) **Fascists: A Social Psychological View of the National Front.** London: Academic Press

BILLIG, M. (1979) Eysenck's political psychology. **Patterns of Prejudice, 13(5),** 9-16

BILLIG, M. (1981) **L'Internationale Raciste: de la Psychologie à la 'Science' des Races.** Paris: Maspero

BILLIG, M. (1982) **Ideology and Social Psychology.** Oxford: Basil Blackwell

BILLIG, M. and COCHRANE, R. (1979) Values of political extremists and potential extremists: a discriminant analysis. **European Journal of Social Psychology, 9,** 205-222

BILLIG, M. and COCHRANE, R. (1981) The National Front and youth. **Patterns of Prejudice, 15(4),** 3-15

BROWN, R. (1965) **Social Psychology.** London: Collier Macmillan

CHRISTIE, R. (1956a) Eysenck's treatment of the personality of communists. **Psychological Bulletin, 53,** 411-430

CHRISTIE, R. (1956b) Some abuses of psychology. **Psychological Bulletin, 53,** 439-451

CHRISTIE, R. and JAHODA, M. (eds) (1954) **Studies in the Scope and Method of 'The Authoritarian Personality'.** Glencoe: Free Press

COCHRANE, R. and BILLIG, M. (1984) I'm not National Front, but ... **New Society, 68,** 255-258

COCHRANE, R., BILLIG, M. and HOGG, M. (1979a) Politics and values in Britain: a test of Rokeach's two-value model. **British Journal of Social and Clinical Psychology, 18,** 159-167

COCHRANE, R., BILLIG, M. and HOGG, M. (1979b) Values as correlates of political orientations. In: M. Rokeach (ed.) **Understanding Human Values.** New York: Free Press

COHN, N. (1967) **Warrant for Genocide.** London: Chatto/ Heinemann

COUTLER, T.T. (1953) An experimental and statistical study of the relationship between prejudice and certain personality types. Unpublished PhD thesis, University of London

CROZIER, M. (1975) Western Europe. In: M. Crozier, S.P. Huntington and J. Watanuki **The Crisis of Democracy.** New York: New York University Press

DENVER, D.T. and BOCHEL, J.M. (1973) The political socialization of activists in the British Communist Party. **British Journal of Political Science, 3,** 53-71

DICKS, H.V. (1972) **Licensed Mass Murder: a Socio-Psychological Study of Some SS Killers.** London: Chatto Heinemann

DOISE, W. (1978) Images, représentations, idéologies et expérimentation psychosociologique. **Social Science Information, 17,** 41-69

DOISE, W. (1982) **L'Explication en Psychologie Sociale.** Paris: Presses Universitaires de France

DUMMETT, A. (1973) **A Portrait of English Racism.** Harmondsworth: Penguin

ECKHARDT, W. (1968) The values of fascism. **Journal of Social Issues, 24,** 89-104

EDELMAN, M. (1964) **The Symbolic Uses of Politics.** Urbana: University of Illinois

EDELMAN, M. (1977) **Political Language: Words That Succeed and Policies That Fail.** New York: Academic Press

EISER, J.R. (1980) **Cognitive Social Psychology.** London: McGraw Hill

EISER, J.R. and ROSS, M. (1977) Partisan language, immediacy and attitude change. **European Journal of Social Psychology, 7,** 477-489

ELLERMAN, D.A. (1983) Radical social movement participation: a social psychological analysis. Unpublished PhD thesis, University of Bristol

ELMS, A.C. (1969) Psychological factors in right-wing extremism. In: R.A. Schoenberger (ed.) **The American Right-Wing.** New York: Holt, Rinehart and Winston

ELMS, A.C. (1970) Those little old ladies in tennis shoes are no nuttier than anyone else, it turns out. **Psychology Today, (Feb),** 27-59

EYSENCK, H.J. (1954) **The Psychology of Politics.** London: Routledge and Kegan Paul

EYSENCK, H.J. (1956a) The psychology of politics: a reply. **Psychological Bulletin, 53,** 177-182

EYSENCK, H.J. (1956b) The psychology of politics and the personality similarities between fascists and communists. **Psychological Bulletin, 53,** 431-438

EYSENCK, H.J. and COUTLER, T.T. (1972) The personality and attitudes of working-class British communists and fascists. **Journal of Social Psychology, 87,** 59-93

EYSENCK, H.J. and WILSON, G.D. (eds) (1978) **The Psychological Basis of Ideology.** Lancaster: MTP Press

FARR, R.M. (1978) On the varieties of social psychology: an essay on the relationships bewteen psychology and other social sciences. **Social Science Information, 17,** 503-525

FARR, R.M. and MOSCOVICI, S. (eds) (1984) **Social Representations.** Cambridge: CUP

FEAGIN, J.R. (1972) Poverty: we still believe that God helps those who help themselves. **Psychology Today, 6,** 101-129

FEATHER, N.T. (1974) Explanations of poverty in Australian and American samples: the person, society or fate? **Australian Journal of Psychology, 26,** 199-216

FESTINGER, L. (1957) **A Theory of Cognitive Dissonance.** New York: Row Peterson

FISHKIN, J., KENISTON, K. and MacKINNON, C. (1973) Moral reasoning and political ideology. **Journal of Personality and Social Psychology, 27,** 107-119

FLACKS, R. (1967) The liberated generation: an exploration of the roots of student unrest. **Journal of Social Issues, 23,** 35-61

FROMM, E. (1942) **Fear of Freedom.** London: Routledge and Kegan Paul

FROMM, E. (1974) **The Anatomy of Human Destructivess.** Harmondsworth: Penguin

FURNHAM, A. (1982) Why are the poor always with us? Explanations for poverty in Britain. **British Journal of Social Psychology, 21,** 311-322

FURNHAM, A. (1983) Attributions for affluence. **Personality and Individual Differences, 4,** 31-40

GABEL, J. (1974) **False Consciousness.** Oxford: Basil Blackwell

GABENNESCH, H. (1972) Authoritarianism as world view. **American Journal of Sociology, 77,** 857-875

GALLUP, G.H. (ed.) (1976) **The Gallup International Public Opinion Polls, Great Britain 1937-1975.** New York: Random House

GILBERT, G.M. (1948) Hermann Goering: amiable psychopath. **Journal of Abnormal and Social Psychology, 43,** 211-229

GOLD, A.R., CHRISTIE, R. and FRIEDMAN, L.N. (1976) **Fists and Flowers: A Social Psychological Interpretation of Student Dissent.** New York: Academic Press

GRABER, D.A. (1976) **Verbal Behavior and Politics.** Urbana: University of Illinois

GRIFFIN, C. (in press) **Typical Girls?** London: Routledge and Kegan Paul

HANLEY, C. and ROKEACH, M. (1956) Care and carelessness in psychology. **Psychological Bulletin, 53,** 183-186

HARRÉ, R. (1980) **Social Being.** Oxford: Basil Blackwell

HARRÉ, R. and SECORD, P.F. (1972) **The Explanation of Social Behaviour.** Oxford: Basil Blackwell

HAYEK, F.A. (1949) **Individualism and Economic Order.** London: Routledge and Kegan Paul

HERZLICH, C. (1972) La représentation sociale. In: S. Moscovici (ed.) **Introduction à la Psychologie Sociale.** Paris: Larousse

HOLMES, C. (1979) **Anti-Semitism in British Society, 1876-1939.** London: Edward Arnold

HORKHEIMER, M. and ADORNO, T.W. (1973) **Dialectic of Enlightenment.** London: Allen Lane

HUSBANDS, C.T. (1983) **Racial Exclusionism and the City: The Urban Support of the National Front.** London: George Allen and Unwin

KENISTON, K. (1968) **Young Radicals.** New York: Harcourt Brace Jovanovich

KENISTON, K. (1971) **Youth and Dissent.** New York: Harcourt Brace Jovanovich

KIRSCHT, J.P. and DILLEHAY, R.C. (1967) **Dimensions of Authoritarianism.** Kentucky: University of Kentucky Press

KOONZ, C. (1976) Nazi women before 1933: rebels against emancipation. **Social Science Quarterly, 56,** 553-563

KROGER, R.O. (1982) Explorations in ethogeny: with special reference to the rules of address. **American Psychologist, 37,** 810-820

LANE, R.E. (1962) **Political Ideology.** New York: Free Press

LARRAIN, J. (1979) **The Concept of Ideology.** London: Hutchinson

LARRAIN, J. (1983) Ideology. In: T.B. Bottomore (ed.) **A Dictionary of Marxist Thought.** Oxford: Basil Blackwell

LEDERER, G. (1982) Trends in authoritarianism: a study of adolescents in West Germany and the United States since 1945. **Journal of Cross-Cultural Psychology, 13,** 299-314

LICHTHEIM, G. (1965) The concept of ideology. **History and Theory, 4,** 164-195

LIPSET, S.M. (1960) **Political Man.** New Jersey: Doubleday

LIPSET, S.M. and RAAB, E. (1971) **The Politics of Unreason.** London: Heinemann

LONG, S. (1981) A psychopolitical theory of systemic disaffection. **Micropolitics, 1,** 395-420

LONG, S. (1982) Irrational political beliefs: a theory of systemic rejection. **International Journal of Political Education, 5,** 1-14

LOYE, D. (1977) **The Leadership Passion: A Psychology of Ideology.** San Francisco: Jossey Bass

MANDEL, E. (1975) **Late Capitalism.** London: Verso

MANNHEIM, K. (1960) **Ideology and Utopia.** London: Routledge and Kegan Paul

MARCUSE, H. (1968) **One Dimensional Man.** London: Sphere Books

MARX, K. and ENGELS, F. (1970) **The German Ideology.** London: Lawrence and Wishart

McCLOSKY, H. (1958) Conservatism and personality. **American Political Science Review, 52,** 27-45

McGUIRE, W.J. (1969) The nature of attitudes and attitude change. In: G. Lindzey and E. Aronson (eds) **Handbook of Social Psychology.** Reading, Mass.: Addison-Wesley

MERKL, P.H. (1975) **Political Violence under the Swastika.** Princeton: Princeton University Press

MILIBAND, R. (1973) **The State in Capitalist Society.** London: Quartet

MOSCOVICI, S. (1980) Toward a theory of conversion behavior. In: L. Berkowitz (ed.) **Advances in Experimental Social Psychology, Volume 13.** New York: Academic Press

MOSCOVICI, S. (1981) On social representation. In: J.P. Forgas (ed.) **Social Cognition.** London: Academic Press

MOSCOVICI, S. (1982) The coming era of representations. In: J.P. Codol and J.P. Leyens (eds) **Cognitive Analysis of Behaviour.** The Hague: Martinus Nijhoff

NEWTON, K. (1969) **The Sociology of British Communism.** London: Allen Lane

NILSON, L.B. (1981) Reconsidering ideological lines: beliefs about poverty in America. **Sociological Quarterly, 22,** 531-548

PARKIN, F. (1967) Working-class conservatives: a theory of political deviance. **British Journal of Sociology, 18,** 178-290

PARROTT, G. and BROWN, L. (1972) Political bias in the Rokeach Dogmatism Scale. **Psychological Reports, 30,** 805-806

REICH, W. (1975) **The Mass Psychology of Fascism.** Harmondsworth: Penguin

ROBERTS, J.M. (1974) **The Mythology of the Secret Societies.** St Albans: Paladin

ROHTER, I.S. (1969) Social and psychological determinants of radical rightism. In: R.A. Schoenberger (ed) **The American Right Wing.** New York: Holt, Rinehart and Winston

ROKEACH, M. (1960) **The Open and Closed Mind.** New York: Basic Books

ROKEACH, M. (1968) **Beliefs, Attitudes and Values: A Theory of Organization and Change.** San Francisco: Jossey-Bass

ROKEACH, M. (1973) **The Nature of Human Values.** New York: Free Press

ROKEACH, M. (1979a) From individual to institutional values: with special reference to the values of science. In: M. Rokeach (ed.) **Understanding Human Values.** New York: Free Press

ROKEACH, M. (1979b) The two-value model of political ideology and British politics. In: M. Rokeach (ed.) **Understanding Human Values.** New York: Free Press

ROKEACH, M. and HANLEY, C. (1956) Eysenck's tender-mindedness dimension: a critique. **Psychological Bulletin, 53,** 169-176

ROTHMAN, S. and LICHTER, S.R. (1978) The case of the student left. **Social Research, 45,** 535-609

ROTHMAN, S. and LICHTER, S.R. (1980) Personality and political dissent. **Journal of Political and Military Sociology, 8,** 198-204

SANFORD, N. (1973) Authoritarian personality in contemporary perspective. In: J.N. Knutson (ed.) **Handbook of Political Psychology.** San Francisco: Jossey-Bass

SEARING, D.D. (1978) Measuring politicians' values: administration and assessment of a ranking technique in the British House of Commons. **American Political Science Review, 72,** 65-79

SEARING, D.D. (1979) A study of values in the British House of Commons. In: M. Rokeach (ed.) **Understanding Human Values.** New York: Free Press

SELIGER, M. (1976) **Ideology and Politics.** London: George Allen and Unwin

SELIGER, M. (1977) **The Marxist Conception of Ideology.** Cambridge: CUP

SENNETT, R. and COBB, J. (1977) **The Hidden Injuries of Class.** Cambridge: CUP

SHERWOOD, R. (1980) **The Psychodynamics of Race.** Sussex: Harvester

SHILS, E.A. (1954) Authoritarianism: 'right' and 'left'. In: R. Christie and M. Jahoda (eds) **Studies in the Scope and Method of 'The Authoritarian Personality'.** Glencoe: Free Press

SHILS, E.A. (1968) Ideology: the concept and function of ideology. In: D. Sills (ed.) **International Encyclopedia of the Social Sciences.** New York: Macmillan

SMITH, A. (1911) **An Inquiry into the Nature and Causes of the Wealth of Nations.** London: Dent and Sons

STEWART, D. and HOULT, T. (1959) A social psychological theory of the authoritarian personality. **American Journal of Sociology, 65,** 274-279

STONE, B.S. (1974) The John Birch Society: a profile. **Journal of Politics, 36,** 184-197

STONE, W.F. (1980) The myth of left-wing authoritarianism. **Political Psychology, 2,** 3-19

STONE, W.F. (in press) Left and right in personality and ideology: an attempt at clarification. **Journal of Mind and Behavior**

TAYLOR, S. (1982) **The National Front in English Politics.** London: Macmillan

TOMKINS, S.S. (1966) Affect and the psychology of knowledge. In: S.S. Tomkins and C.E. Izard (eds) **Affect, Cognition and Personality.** London: Tavistock

van DIJK, T.A. (1982) Towards a model of ethnic prejudice in cognition and discourse. Working Paper No. 1, University of Amsterdam

WARR, P.B., FAUST, J. and HARRISON, G.J. (1967) A British ethnocentrism scale. **British Journal of Social and Clinical Psychology, 6,** 267-277

WHITE, R.K. (1949) Hitler, Roosevelt and the nature of war propaganda. **Journal of Abnormal and Social Psychology, 19,** 351-358

WILLIS, P. (1978) **Learning to Labour.** Farnborough: Saxon House

WILSON, G.D. (1973) **The Psychology of Conservatism.** London: Academic Press

PSYCHOLOGICAL AND SOCIAL STRESS

J. Michael Innes

In this chapter we shall examine some of the factors which have been posited to play a role in the induction in an individual person of a physiological state of stress, and consider some of the physical and mental consequences of that stress over the longer term.

THE STRESS REACTION

In common parlance the term stress is taken to mean several different things. It is used to refer to the feelings of a person who has a great deal to do, or little time in which to do it. It is also used to describe the conditions which evoke those feelings. So we have the term 'under a great deal of stress', which suggests that the 'stress' causes the reaction.

The varied intepretations of the term in lay conversation is to some degree shared by variation in definition within the scientific literature. Stress is an open-ended term and as such it has been given almost any intepretation that the research worker or reader has cared to put on it. Stress has been regarded as the reaction of an organism to a noxious event (Hinckle, 1973). The event which may evoke this reaction will be referred to as the stressor, to maintain a distinction between the response and the stimulus. A point to be borne in mind is that a stressor is a potential elicitor of stress, not a necessary one.

Early research on animals demonstrated that exposure to a wide range of noxious environmental stimuli, for example, heat, anaesthesia, or surgery, resulted in a characteristic three-stage response, which was termed the General Adaptation Syndrome (GAS). The first stage involved the release of catecholamines from the medulla of the adrenal gland. This primary stage can be called the alarm reaction; it is an alerting response by the organism to possible threat or physical injury. The production of catecholamines enables the mobilization of the energy resources stored in the body; there is a general stimulation of the organism to react quickly and effectively.

Stress, however, involves more than this primary reaction. In many situations, after all, an animal has to react appropriately to novelty or threat, but there can be a very rapid return to the initial baseline state as the threatening stimulus is withdrawn. To evoke the GAS the threat has to be maintained and the organism will eventually move to a secondary stage, to enable the production and utilization of energy. In the second stage the release of corticosteroids from the cortex of the adrenal gland is stimulated by the action of ACTH (adreno-cortico-trophic hormone) from the anterior part of the pituitary gland. There is increased production of red blood cells, which transport oxygen to the muscles, and there is secretion of stored sugar from the liver. In a sense this is the stage of resistance, a longer term attempt by the body mechanisms to deal with a continuing, threatening event.

So far, the reactions by the organism appear to be appropriate, useful reactions to a threat, helping the animal either to fight any threat with greater vigour, or to escape more effectively. Further reactions associated with the second stage are, however, likely to be damaging over time. The action of corticosteroids aggravates the natural inflammatory reaction, and there is a reduction of the immune reaction to infection or to physical damage. There is also an inhibition of the repair of cells which have a higher turnover. So, while the organism can, at least temporarily, react with vigour to the external threat, there is a longer term decline in the amount of resources which will be used. The body uses its resources faster than they are replaced, it is more reactive to damage and it can repair the damage less efficiently.

If the external stressor is withdrawn during this stage, then the organism seems naturally to be able to recover, and return to the baseline state existing prior to exposure. Should the stressor continue to exist, however, then the organism will eventually move into a third stage, of exhaustion, and in many cases, death.

There are a number of points to be drawn from such an analysis of the GAS in animal subjects, to help us to understand the nature of the stress reaction:

1. The stress reaction, at least in its early stages, is an <u>appropriate protective response</u> by an organism to threat.

2. The damage caused by the stress reaction will arise through long term, <u>chronic,</u> exposure to threat.

3. The GAS appears to be <u>stereotyped</u> in nature, that is, there is a

strong similarity in the responses made to a variety of different environmental stressors.

4. The identification of the GAS occurred largely through the use of animal subjects which were passively exposed to the stressors, that is, they were not provided with an opportunity to act upon the environment to change, in some way, what was happening to them.

SOCIAL INFLUENCES ON THE USE OF THE STRESS CONCEPT

At this point, we may take some time to point to the ways in which the concept of stress began to be used in medical and social research. The work on the evocation of the GAS in animals stimulated the view that such a chronic exposure to threat could be generalized to humans. The view was also expressed in many medical and social-scientific journals that chronic stress in humans, as experienced, for example, in time of war both for combat soldiers and for civilians, or in occupational settings could result in an eventual inability of sections of the community to cope with the events which impinged upon them.

In parallel with these beliefs, there were changes to the pattern of illness observed in the community. The development of medical treatment, especially the availability of early diagnostic techniques, the widespread availability of drugs, and, especially, much improved community standards for environmental hygiene, was associated with a change after the Second World War in the nature of the causes of death. Rather than infectious diseases being the main cause of death - diptheria, tuberculosis, whooping cough, for example - the new epidemics were of diseases which had no identifiable single cause, such as heart disease and cancer. Such diseases, however, could be viewed as general degenerative conditions of the body, with a number of internal changes contributing to the eventual fatal condition. It was possible to consider these conditions as psychosomatic (Christie, 1982), with the organism in a sense participating in the creation of its own pathology. The additional concept of stress could then be invoked. Exposure to environmental threat, from which an organism could not easily escape, could be conceived as leading to eventual pathological conditions, acting through particular organs of the body, so that stress could be a factor in the increased incidence of heart disease and cancer.

Such a generalization, from the studies of the GAS in passive animal subjects to the reactions of active humans exposed to everyday life, could not be substantiated by the available evidence, but the possibility of such a train of events was enough to encourage a wide range of research into a number of questions concerned with the concept of stress, especially in humans.

Specifically, the questions which had to be asked, in order for the stress concept to have value in explaining human illness, were these:

1. What may be some of the pathways from the physiological responses in stress to the pathological states observed? Is it possible to predict the nature of an illness that will follow from exposure to chronic stressors?

2. What are the environmental events which induce a stress reaction? Do certain stimuli evoke more reliably or with greater degree a form of the GAS? Are there dimensions across which it is possible to differentiate potential stressors?

3. Is there any influence of the organism upon the nature of the stress response? Can a reaction by the organism lead to a lessening of the stress reaction, instead of merely passively accepting it, or are there conditions in which reaction can exacerbate the response?

4. While an analysis of the stressors which elicit reactions in laboratory studies under controlled conditions may tell us something of value about the nature of stress, can anything be learned from a study of possible stressors in society at large? Is it possible to generalize to the nature of occupational and psycho-social events to understand what may result in stress?

5. As, by observation, there are clear differences between the reactions of people to environmental events and in the distribution of so-called psychosomatic illness, are there reliable measures of personal conditions which will predict people who will be resistent to stress, as against those who will be more susceptible? And connected with this, are there social and cultural differences which may contribute to such predictions?

6. If it is posible to show, by answering questions 3 and 5, that reactions modify the stress response and that people naturally vary in their reactions, then is it possible to help to provide people with beneficial reactions? Can people be trained to cope effectively with stressors and, therefore, experience less stress?

We shall attempt to give some answers to these questions with the aid of empirical studies. There are many more studies available to substantiate the point to be made, and indeed many which do not support some of the answers. The reader will be provided with some structure of the state of research into the nature of the stress reaction in humans, and will have some idea of the directions it is likely to take.

PHYSIOLOGICAL PATHWAYS TO DISEASE

The GAS identifies a set of responses which may create the conditions which will eventually lead to the development of irreversible pathology. If stress is to be considered one factor in the aetiology of disease, then we need to have some idea of what may be plausible routes from the initial physiological change to pathology. In considering such pathways, we may examine three.

The decreased immunological function with the secretion of corticosteroids may increase the susceptibility of the organism to any pathogen which is present in the environment: if any organism is stressed then it could be more susceptible to any prevalent infection (for example, Kasl, Evans and Niederman, 1979; Rogers, Dubey and Reich, 1979). A problem with testing any such view of the process of pathology is that, while it is a plausible one, it is virtually impossible to falsify the hypothesis. If a population is chronically exposed to a stressor, then all the members of that population should, theoretically, have an increased probability of falling ill. There is, however, no prediction about the specific illness. Any illness which afflicts a member of the population will support the hypothesis (Cassel, 1976). If someone contracts pneumonia, another the common cold, and yet another lung cancer, then these could be read as support for the illness-producing effects of stress. Until the reaction of the stressed organism to specific pathogens can be identified, the hypothesis remains just that, an hypothesis without adequate empirical support. There are some recent suggestions, however, that particular forms of illness may be predictable (cf. Bahnson, 1981; Fox, 1981).

Stress may be related to general somatic disorders, however, directly through the action of hormones, upon physiological activity. The action of the pituitary gland to increase the level of ACTH under stress acts through a variety of pathways to increase blood pressure. Sodium and water retention is increased and this increases both vasoconstriction (the constriction of blood vessels) and also the volume of the blood which is pumped through the vessels (Henry and Stephens, 1977; Sterling and Eyer, 1981). Vasoconstriction is also increased through the action of noradrenaline. While this latter action during a primary stage of the GAS can be beneficial for the organizer, with quicker blood flow and oxygen transport, chronic high blood pressure, or hypertension, is a risk factor for a number of ailments without the need for any further external agent to produce an effect. The increased blood flow can damage the linings of the arteries, which, it has been suggested, can help to increase the rate of deposition of atherosclerotic plaque (the material which leads to the blocking of arteries associated with coronary heart disease and stroke; Steinberg, 1979), and is also associated with impaired kidney function. So chronic levels of stress may lead to physical damage to the body.

Stressful events may also have direct influence upon the cardiovascular system, other than through the mediation of hormonal activity. While coronary artery disease is a major killer, with the blocking of arteries which lead into the heart acting to prevent the flow of oxygen to the heart muscle, sudden death from heart attacks in humans need not be associated with it alone (Friedman et al., 1973). Heart attacks and death have been associated with very rapid heart beat (tachycardia), which can lead to a loss of rhythm in the heart muscle (arrhythmia). The induction of tachycardia has been shown to be induced by exposure to stressful events, possibly through an enhancement of activity in the sympathetic nervous system and the withdrawal of the inhibitory influence of the parasympathetic nervous system (Lown, DeSilva and Renson, 1978; Natelson and Cagin, 1979). Repeated exposure to stress, even though it may only be at the primary stages of the reaction, could lead to ventricular damage and perhaps, eventually, death.

There are other routes whereby the very complex set of events in the central and peripheral nervous systems and in the hormonal systems which are evoked under stress may influence the ability of the body to maintain a stable state and resist pathogenic influences (Ader, 1981; Rogers, Dubey and Reich, 1979). That there are such theoretical pathways from stressor to illness seems clear. What needs to be considered is what are the kinds of things which elicit the broad range of reactions we term stress.

CHARACTERISTICS OF THE STRESSORS

Subjective reaction

The stereotyped nature of the GAS to any stimulus has been mentioned. Recent work has shown, however, that the reaction may vary in response to different stimuli (Frankenhaeuser, 1976; Mason, et al., 1976). Mason, for example, has shown that in humans, contrary to effects with animals, exposure to strong aversive stimulation, such as heat, noise and exertion, will elicit catecholamine production as part of the primary stage, but will fail to produce the corticosteroid, cortisol, a part of the secondary stage, provided that any subjective feelings of evaluation and competition are minimized. Given the crucial role that cortisol plays in the inhibition of the immunological response, the psychological factors involved in stressor presentation would seem to be highly important.

Of course, in human society, elements of the subjective experience of being evaluated, or of being in competition with some other person or group are likely to be prevalent. But exposure to a physically aversive stimulus alone need not lead to a stress response. There will be catecholamine activity, with increased respiration rate, heart rate, increase in blood pressure, etc., but not necessarily the development of inflammatory and immunological reactions.

Work on such topics with humans, as against animal subjects, alerts one to the need to take account of the subjective reaction of the organism. Essentially, stress can be viewed as a product of the 'cognitive appraisal' by the person (McGrath, 1979). The manner in which the stimulus is categorized appears to be a mediating factor relating exposure to reaction.

Predictability

Another feature, which seems in many cases to be crucial, is the predictability of a stimulus. Glass and Singer (1972) showed in several experiments with physical stressors that when the onset of the stimuli was unpredictable there were debilitating short and long-term effects. Even when the stimulus has been removed there were measurable deleterious effects upon behaviour and upon bodily function. Predictability will presumably help the appraisal of the stressor to be classified in a different way.

THE REACTIONS OF THE ORGANISM

In initial experiments, the animals were passive. Perhaps having no opportunity to react is itself stressful; after all, organisms exist in an environment which requires them to seek nutrition and avoid damage. Passivity may not be an ecologically valid test of the generality of the stress concept. Research on humans does show a physiologically differentiated response when the participant is able to respond actively to a stimulus threat and not merely passively. In the former condition, there is a greater secretion of the catecholamine noradrenaline, which other studies suggest is secreted in conditions which stimulate a fighting reaction by the organism. In the latter, passive, condition, on the other hand, there is a proportionately greater secretion of adrenaline, associated with a fleeing, flight reaction (Frankenhaeuser, 1976).

Control over presentation

Simply not being able to do something has an influence upon the nature of the stress response. To be able to control when a stressor will occur appears to have an effect, and, importantly, this seems to influence the nature of the secondary, resistance stage. Frankenhaeuser (1976), in her studies of the effect of stressors in occupational settings such as factories and continuous production plants, showed that the opportunity for control lowered cortisol secretion, compared with exposure to an uncontrollable stimulus. In view of the suppressive role of cortisol upon the immune response, this effect seems to be especially important.

It may not even be the case that the person has to exercise any control. Provided that a person believes that they can shut off the stimulus when they wish to, then they will endure exposure to a stressor, and will not show an enhanced physiological reaction (Miller, 1979). It has been postulated that such a beneficial result is due to a person's belief that their own response is a reliable one and that therefore they know they can do it if required.

Beliefs and control

The subjective beliefs about the amount of control that is available may also play a part in the influence upon the stress response. It has been demonstrated (for example, Seligman, 1975) that the expectations which exist concerning the relationship between an outcome and a reaction can play a large part in determining later behaviour. If an organism can be induced to expect that there is no correlation between what it does and what happens to it, then something akin to a state of 'learned helplessness' is induced, with an elevated stress reaction. Thus, if an organism learns that whatever response it makes it is just as likely to receive an aversive stimulus as not, then there is a failure by that organism to react appropriately when later allowed to do so. The organism learns to be helpless in response to the environment.

This can be taken a stage further. Rather than training an organism that there is no relationship between behaviour and outcome, it is possible to see to what extent people believe that they have control over what happens to them. Human beings do not simply react to events; they try to work out why particular things occurred (Nisbett and Ross, 1980). There is a proclivity to analyse the causal relationship between experience and outcome.

So, for example, if in an examination I do very badly, there is a likely causal analysis by me to account for the failure. I may not know all the factors that were at work on the particular day of the exam, but I try to make sense of the event. I can try to explain, or attribute, the failure to the fact that the examination was very difficult or the day was too hot. I may say to myself that I didn't try hard enough or, if I am very honest, that I wasn't clever enough to cope. But very basically I can attribute the cause of my poor performance, and its likely stressful effect, to either something which was external (the temperature or the difficulty) and outside my control, or internal (my motivation or effort), which may to some extent be under my control. The stress reaction may then vary with the nature of my attribution.

If it is believed that the failure, or the stress, occurred because of lack of control, then is there likely to be less stress than where it is believed that there was control? If, for example, chance or luck is believed to play a part in determining the outcome, then will the stress be less than if the outcome was thought to be the individual's fault?

One might think that, in a stressful situation such as recovering from an accident or in attempting to adjust to the loss of property or a spouse, a belief that chance played a part might reduce stress. However, rather the opposite seems to be the case. As was mentioned above, we seem to be less stressed if we believe we have control. We are also less stressed if we believe that we could have had control, but we didn't avail ourselves of it. So, for example, the victim of an accident which has resulted in grave damage will apparently come to show less stress and will make a better recovery if that person believes that the accident was their fault rather than due to someone or something else (for example, Wortman et al., 1980). A belief that one can cause things to occur seems to be an important mediator influencing the magnitude of a stress reaction.

It appears, therefore, that the degree of stress experienced by an individual will be strongly influenced by the perception by that individual of the circumstances around the stressor. Not only the magnitude of the stressor will have an effect; the expectations of predictability and control, even the sense that control is possible, can act to modify the amount of stress which results.

An analysis in terms of the subjective classification of stimuli and the importance of perceived control leads to a modified view of the stress reaction. Stress needs now to be defined, not in terms of a reaction to noxious stimuli, but rather as an attempt by the individual to adjust to some environmental demand. If that demand exceeds the capacity of the person to cope, or if there is a belief that matters are out of control, then there will be stress. The degree of 'fit' between the environmental demands and the capacities of the person will define the degree of stress (Caplan et al., 1975). Stressors will vary in the degree of stress they induce as a function of the resources that the person has to deal with them. On this view, therefore, stress is a function of an interaction between person and environment.

So far, we have been concerned with the stress reaction, saying little about the nature of the stressors. Physical stressors, stimuli such as excessive heat, noise, etc., have been the factors used to study the nature of the stress response. But in everyday life it seems likely that the majority of stress reactions will occur in connection with non-physical stimuli, with contact with the experiences of living in a social community.

PSYCHOSOCIAL SOURCES OF STRESS

Reference was made earlier to the finding by Mason et al. (1976) that physical stressors only appear to elicit a stress reaction, one that is likely to have long-term physiological effects, where there is a degree of social evaluation or competition associated with them; if, for example, endurance of heat or exercise is seen as a challenge. Indeed, failure at a task can be seen as a most stressful event, in the workplace as well as in the laboratory or examination room (Kasl and Cobb, 1970). We should note here that one person's failure may be another's success; we shall take up this point in the section on individual differences.

The concept that social events can precipitate a stress reaction, and perhaps lead to illness is a difficult one to test properly. What is required is a method to measure the degree to which people experience social relationships which are likely to require a response which entails a stress reaction. What can we consider as social events which act in this way?

We may conceive changes in personal circumstances as requiring an adjustment to those changes; there will be an alteration in the normal way of coping. If such a change is large, or if there are too many of these 'life events', then the individual's capacity may be exceeded and stress will ensue. Thus a new job, or the loss of a job, or divorce can be considered life events. Even minor events, if there are enough of them, may have an eventual effect (Dohrenwend and Dohrenwend, 1974).

The research has mainly required people to recall the number of such events experienced over a set period of time (for example, six months). The events can be subjectively weighted, by getting estimates from other people about the amount of adjustment required. In one of the scales most commonly used, the Social Readjustment Rating Scale (SRRS) (Holmes and Rahe, 1967), for example, the event of marriage is given an arbitrary value of 50 and the death of a spouse the maximum value of 100, with other events scaled around these scores. The total figure for an individual, which summarizes the amount of change experienced in the defined time period, can then be related to the number of illnesses experienced by that individual.

Note that this scale attempts to measure change, not whether the event is particularly pleasant or unpleasant. So marriage is rated at 50, loss of a job at 47. Given that pleasant and unpleasant stressors induce different reactions (for example, Patkai, 1971), it seems reasonable to consider that different measures may obtain different results. Some attempts have been made to examine such factors (Johnson and Sarason, 1978), with expected differences in the magnitude of the impact of differently rated events. Those measures of life events, however, which do scale the amount of change and the amount of distress (for example, Tennant and Andrews, 1976), do find strong correlations between the measures.

Studies using such scales have shown a relationship between events and a range of physical and mental illnesses (for example, Clarke and Innes, 1983; Holmes and Masuda, 1974). The problem with such studies, however, is that they require people to recall events, and there is good evidence to indicate a poor ability to do so (Jenkins, Hurst and Rose, 1979). Prospective studies, which measure events and then follow-up over time to examine the incidence of illnesses, do not show such strong relationships (Rahe, 1968).

There are a number of problems of a statistical nature associated with the scales (Hurst, Jenkins and Rose, 1978; Rabkin and Streuning, 1976). From the point of view of the study of stress, however, there is a larger problem. There is little known about the way in which the life events may produce stress. The study of a plethora of events in large populations does not enable us to pin-point what may be the mediating physiological and psychological changes. Perhaps more may be learned by the study of the impact of single major events, following such change over an extended period of time (Kasl, 1977).

A different approach to the study of social stress assumes that major life events may not be such a potent source of stress for most people. Much stress, or at least subjective feelings of tension, may stem from minor upsets or 'hassles'. Worries about leaking pipes, shopping, the kids' marks at school, may all act cumulatively to produce chronically high degrees of stress. Some studies using 'hassles' scales have suggested that minor upsets and worries may be better predictors of physical and psychological complaints than are major life events (Kanner et al., 1981).

It should be pointed out here that, while there does seem to be a good degree of consensus about the likely stress of particular problems, such as doing jobs around the house (Delongis et al., 1982), the nature of hassles that are identified as such will depend upon characteristics of the individual. The identification of a hassle as 'continual calls from colleagues', or 'interruptions by the telephone' may tell us a great deal about the strengths and weaknesses of the individual. Whatever may be the problems of measuring social stress, the range of studies which have demonstrated a relationship between social events and illness suggests that it is robust. We have had to mention the possibility of individual reactions, however, and the role of the characteristics of the person must be examined before we can properly begin to understand what may be the nature of stress.

Before looking at individual differences we should consider what is a major underlying approach to the study of stress. Specifically, there is an emphasis upon the experiences of the individual person. Such experiences will indeed be varied, around some general mean level. But such an emphasis can ignore the possibiity that the general mean value, the endemic level of stress experienced by a population, may alter over time or over place.

By this two things are meant. First, there is a tendency to ignore cultural differences. The categorization of events as stressful or not may well be different in different societies. In our consideration, the value of control as a stress-reducing factor has been noted. But such results have been obtained from a narrow range of social groups. In societies other than industrialized Westernized ones a general approach which views the events in life as controlled by others may be a more appropriate one to enable a person or a group to cope with stressful times and events.

The second consideration is that there are possible differences in a culture over time; the experiences of a generation or cohort may differ from another cohort in very substantial ways. While we have been concerned to date with the impact of such events as marital or financial crises upon the general well-being of individuals, the general background of expectations about the likelihood of such cases can vary. The way in which a financial crisis will be defined will be at least partially dependent upon the prevailing world view which accompanies a particular cohort of people.

Long-term studies (for example, Eyer and Sterling, 1977) have suggested that stress-related illness can be related to growth in economic factors, with more work leading to more hours on the job, overtime and poorer working conditions. If a person is born into a small cohort then the kind of stress that may be experienced with demand for labour and higher employment will differ from that experienced by a person born into a large cohort, where there may be surplus labour and the stress will come from unemployment and employer demands. Obviously, it is not only the size of a cohort that affects the level of work stress or unemployment stress, but the experiences and the nature of stress will be partly a function of such a social or demographic variable (Easterlin, Wachter and Watcher, 1978). Stress cannot be studied solely from a psychological perspective, focused upon the degree of control or freedom to choose that an individual believes himself or herself to have. The psychological study of stress may benefit greatly from a wider view of sociological methods that are relevant (for example, Elder, 1981).

Whatever may be the prevalence of stress-inducing factors in a society, it is clear that people will vary within a group in the degree to which they can cope. The ability to cope may be a function of social factors; economic resources or social status will buffer the impact of many social stressors (Elder and Liker, 1982). But psychological resources may enable a person better to resist stress or, on the other hand, the possession of some characteristics may make a person more susceptible to the effects of stress.

INDIVIDUAL DIFFERENCES IN REACTION

Psychologists have always been interested in the extent to which people react differentially to stress, with an emphasis usually on how people breakdown rather than on how they cope. Studies of how people respond to such events as natural disasters or accidents strongly suggest that the more poorly adjusted they are prior to the event, then the more poorly they recover from the trauma (Andreassen, Noyes and Hartford, 1972).

A characteristic manner of psychological investigation into susceptibility to stress has been to identify a particular psychological characteristic and examine the outcome when studied in interaction with an external stressful event. One such factor which has been repeatedly implicated in stress research is low self-esteem, that is, feelings of incompetence, depression and anxiety. Caplan et al. (1975), for example, found a strong relationship between illness and low esteem in a sample of men in several different occupations. Kasl and Cobb (1970) found a similarly poor adjustment in unemployed men with low self-esteem, with a greater incidence of subjective and physiological stress.

A factor which has been related to a stress-related physical illness is the Type A proneness to coronary-heart disease (CHD) behaviour pattern (for example, Innes, 1981). Early intuitions that a person who manifested heart disease showed a particular syndrome of behaviour were supported in a number of studies, best exemplified by the Western Collaborative Group Study (Rosenman et al., 1975). In this study, followed up over a period of 8.5 years, a group of men were interviewed to establish their characteristic behaviour pattern, and their health status was subsequently examined. Men showing the Type A pattern were twice as likely to die of myocardial infarction (death of portions of the heart muscle) and to report symptoms of angina (chest pain) than were men who did not show the pattern, even when other risk factors for heart disease were controlled for. It is well known that the accepted biological risk factors will only account for half of the variation in CHD. So it is certainly plausible that psycho-social factors play a part.

The Type A pattern has been characterized by the combination of a strong tendency to be competitive, with feelings of time urgency and a need to strive hard to achieve. The Type A person can be characterized as being self-stressed: people and events are seen as providing problems and impediments which must be overcome, quickly. A number of psychological studies (for example, Glass, 1977) have related the Type A pattern to an overly strong need to control stimulus events. As considered earlier, a feeling of control can help to alleviate stress. The Type A individual, however, appears to require a degree of control over almost everything and will work towards that end. Stress can thus be induced in at least two ways. First, the strong need to achieve control can lead to a persistence to gain control, when it is clear that such control cannot be achieved. Since people are often uncontrollable events with which we have to engage, it is not surprising that the Type A person does not like working with other people (Dembroski and MacDougall, 1978), and will attempt to do all jobs himself rather than waste time having other people do them.

There is an additional moderating factor here, introducing a social variable. People in organizational settings obviously cannot do all the jobs they are responsible for. But this is where the need for control experienced by the Type A person can enter. When a person has the power to control outcomes to another person, then there will be less stress than where one is under another person's control. So Type A individuals who are in positions of power in organizations may be expected to show less stress than those who are in positions where they are under control. Such an outcome has been shown to exist (Howard, Cunningham and Rechnitzer, 1977). There is a greater risk of experiencing a cardiovascular event if you are a Type A person in the middle levels of an organization than if you are at the top.

A second pathway to increased stress for the Type A individual is when the continual expression of a need for control is followed by clear evidence that control has been lost or cannot be achieved. The evidence that it is not possible to achieve what one wishes seems to induce extremely strong stress responses. Glass (1977) has shown, for example, that Type A sufferers from CHD are far more likely than other sufferers to have experienced some event which indicates that control has not been achieved.

There has been considerable debate regarding the primary factor which leads to increased risk for CHD. The early workers emphasized the totality of the syndrome (Jenkins, Zyzanski and Rosenman, 1978). More recent work, however, points to the centrality of the aggressiveness associated with competitiveness and achievement. Mere achievement motivation, or job involvement do not seem to be significant predictors of CHD (Dembroski et al., 1981). Aggression and hostility, however, have been shown to predict later illness and death, not only from heart disease but from a range of diseases (Shekelle et al., 1983; Williams et al., 1980). It is known that Type A individuals will show generalized aggression, not only to those who frustrated their attempts, but also to anyone who happens to be standing by (Carver and Glass, 1978). The extreme Type A person prefers to work alone and is apparently also difficult to get along with as a spouse (Burke, Weir and DuWars, 1979). Just whether aggression, with the associated arousal of the autonomic nervous system, or the need for control are the factors predictive of CHD remains to be seen. That some form of the Type A pattern is associated with CHD does, however, seem clear, suggesting that stress, self-created, may be related to later illness.

But susceptibility to stress is only one side of the picture. There are people who are more resistant to stress and possible subsequent illness. While clearly there are breakdowns in highly stressful conditions such as armed combat, there is also evidence of courage and ability to deal with severe problems (cf. Berkun et al., 1962; Rachman, 1978).

Resistance to illness may be related to the positive presence of characteristics rather than merely the absence of negative features. People who seek arousal, who are sensation-seekers (Zuckerman, 1979), appear to be less prone to illness than are those who are low on the dimension (Cooley, and Keesey, 1981), the reason being perhaps that continued experience of psychologically arousing situations will enable more moderate responses to be made to stress than is possible for those people who have not had the experience (cf. Berkun et al., 1962).

High self-esteem is also associated with stress resistance (Moos, 1974). A belief in the value of one's own work, that one's skills and values are important, has been shown to be a strong predictor of an absence of illness (Kobasa, Maddi and Puccetti, 1982).

It should be noted, however, that too great an adherence to such beliefs could lead to compulsive behaviours to cope, and such activities could be similar in effect to the Type A pattern. The manifest nature of some behaviours may not be the crucial factors to study in relation to stress and illness. What is central is the relationship between the person's aspirations or goals and achievements. If the aspirations are set too high and cannot be achieved, or if even the very achievements are used to define the goals, as may be the case with the Type A person, then the basis has been laid for stress reactions. If the person sets realistic goals and feels content that they have been achieved, or knows when they cannot be achieved and still does not feel a failure, then stress may not take its toll. Failure need not be a stressor, if that failure is set within the context of realistic aspirations and perception of achievements.

What clearly becomes important, in this view of stress, is to ask where and how the standards for judging behaviour and success/failure were established. Presumably this will be related to early socialization experiences. The study of stress may require us to look at early ways to resolving conflicts. In this sense also, the link between coping with stress and psychosomatic illness becomes clear; both are concerned with the analysis of early experience to later, adult, behaviour. An analysis of possible relationships between mechanisms of conflict resolution and later stress may enable the prediction of particular somatic illnesses to be made (Bahnson, 1981).

LEARNING TO COPE WITH STRESS

The last question is concerned with whether people who may be identified as susceptible to stress may learn to deal with stress by adopting some of the techniques or skills that are used by those more resistant.

A number of avenues can be suggested from our brief review. If stress is seen as a lack of fit between a person's circumstances and reaction, then training may enable the gap to be filled. At a physiological level, it may be possible to provide the body with higher degrees of activity so that the body tone is better and reacts with fewer peaks and troughs when stressed. Physical exercise may keep a body at a higher level of arousal, making adjustment to psychological stress less traumatic.

If we establish that a belief in control is beneficial, then it may be possible to help people to establish control over the events that affect them. While this is clearly impossible for many life events (one just does not have control over a natural disaster or over the death of a spouse), nevertheless, achieving what Averill (1973) identified as important, namely believing that there is some control and that one should not give up, may be sufficient to reduce stress.

At the other extreme of the dimension, where people attempt to achieve too much control, then it may be possible to give such individuals insight into the lack of fit between their aspirations and their behaviour, and thereby reduce the degree of striving which is self-stressing (Friedman et al., 1982).

The realization that training to cope actively with a stressor is not the only means of reducing stress is an important one. Avoidance of a problem, even denial, can be beneficial in some circumstances. There are two components in any attempt to deal with a problem, or stressful event. There may need to be an attempt at the problem itself; there is also dealing with the emotional response to the problem. Distraction, distancing oneself from the arousal, can help to reduce the arousal and hence alleviate the stress. Naturally it will not do always to deny a problem, but also it is not always beneficial to think about the emotional problem, to meet it head on (Lazarus and Launier, 1978).

SUBJECTIVE REACTIONS TO STRESS

A feature of a stress reaction which has not so far been treated explicitly in this chapter is the subjective, feeling response made by the person, although such a factor has been touched upon indirectly. Exposure to a stressor can bring with it a range of feelings. Associated with exposure to acute stress, where there is a loss of feeling of control, there may be experience of panic, with loss of cognitive or behavioural co-ordination. With more chronic stress, there may be feelings of anxiety or dread that 'something' is looming, about to occur. Such long-term anxiety can be debilitating, leading to a loss of cognitive capacity to deal with problems or events. Feelings of psychological distress associated with stress exposure can include depression, feelings of loneliness and anhedonia (lack of ability to feel happiness or joy) (Mechanic, 1979), and these feelings in turn have been related to poor coping styles (Coyne, Aldwin and Lazarus, 1981) and to poor physical health (for example, Stewart and Salt, 1981).

Measures designed to assess such a range of feelings of distress have been developed both for clinical populations (the Beck Depression Inventory, Beck et al., 1961), and also for non-clinical groups (the Psychiatric Epidemiology Research Inventory, Dohrenwend et al., 1980). Both of these measures provide a variety of feelings, although they do seem to have a similar structure comprising three basic factors.

The assessment of subjective distress is clearly an important factor in the understanding of stress reactions. We may primarily identify people under stress by assessment of their subjective state, and physiological identification may be a secondary feature. Whether the subjective feelings themselves are primary causes of the stress, however, is another matter. People may feel 'blue' because they are stressed, they may not be stressed because they feel low. Unravelling the causal relationships between stimulus conditions, physiological, behavioural, cognitive and affective reactions is a fundamental problem for stress research, just as it is for psychological research in general. Indeed, the primacy of affective reactions to an event as against the cognitive appraisal of the same event is re-emerging as a central problem in psychology (Lazarus, 1984; Zajonc, 1984) and research into stress reactions is relevant to such issues.

The differentiation of subjective feelings from the stress reaction can have other implications, especially for attempts to reduce such stress responses. Some people seem to react to stressors more cognitively than others, showing reactions of worry and anxiety. Others may react more somatically, that is with bodily, physical reactions. The nature of the intervention that is required to reduce 'cognitive' anxiety seems to be of a different kind from those required to reduce 'somatic' anxiety (Davidson, 1978). So the stress reaction has several components and an understanding of this is necessary for the development of any treatment.

CONCLUSION

The study of stress, and the investigation of the means characteristically used to deal with stress, raises classic problems in psychological research. Stress can be regarded as the interaction between a stimulus event and the person experiencing the event, and the skills, resources and deficiencies of that person, to produce a reaction within the person and also acting upon the external world. Understanding of stress can come only from a realization that different disciplines, from physiology to sociology, can contribute to the psychologist's armamentarium of method and theory and that consideration of almost the entire range of psychology is needed. This chapter has suggested some ways in which social and personality psychology can contribute; other avenues are equally valid.

REFERENCES

ADER, R. (1981) **Psychoneuroimmunology.** New York: Academic Press

ANDREASSEN, N.J., NOYES R. and HARTFORD, C.E. (1972) Factors influencing adjustment of burn patients during hospitalization. **Psychosomatic Medicine, 34,** 517-523

AVERILL, J.R. (1973) Personal control over aversive stimuli and its relationship to stress. **Psychological Bulletin, 80,** 286-303

BAHNSON, C.B. (1981) Stress and cancer: the state of the art. Part 2. **Psychosomatics, 22,** 207-220

BECK, A.T., WARD, C.H., MENDELSON, M., MOCK, M. and ERBAUGH, J. (1961) An inventory for measuring depression. **Archives of General Psychiatry, 4,** 561-571

BERKUN, M.M., BIALEK, N.M., KERN, R.P. and YAGI, K. (1962) Experimental studies of psychological stress in man. **Psychological Monographs, 76,** (Whole No 534)

BURKE, R.J. WEIR T. and DUWARS, R.E. (1974) Type A behaviour of administrators and wives' report of marital satisfaction and well-being. **Journal of Applied Psychology, 65,** 57-65

CAPLAN, R.D., COBB, S., FRENCH, J.R.P., VAN HARRISON, R. and PINNEAU, S.R. (1975) **Job Demands and Worker Health.** Washington DC: U.S. Department of Health, Education and Welfare

CARVER, C.S. and GLASS, D.C. (1978) Coronary-prone behaviour pattern and interpersonal aggression. **Journal of Personality and Social Psychology, 38,** 361-366

CASSEL, J. (1976) The contribution of the social environment to host resistance. **American Journal of Epidemiology, 104,** 107-123

CHRISTIE, M. (1982) Psychosomatics, an historical perspective. In: J. Nicholson and B. Foss (eds) **Psychology Survey No. 4** Leicester: The British Psychological Society

CLARKE, A. and Innes, J.M. (1983) Sensation-seeking motivation as a moderator of the life stress/illness relationship. **Personality and Individual Differences, 4,** 547-550

COOLEY, E.J. and KEESEY, J.C. (1981) Moderator variables in life stressand illness relationship. **Journal of Human Stress, 7(3),** 35-40

COYNE, J.C. and LAZARUS, R.S. (1981) Depression and coping in stressful episodes. **Journal of Abnormal Psychology, 90,** 439-447

DAVIDSON, R.J. (1978) Specificity and patterning in biobehavioural systems: Implications for behaviour change. **American Psychologist, 33,** 430-436

DELONGIS, A., COYNE, J.C., DAKOF, G., FOLKMAN, S. and LAZARUS, R.S. (1982) Relationships of daily hassles, uplifts and major life events to health status. **Health Psychology, 1,** 119-136

DEMBROSKI, T.M. and MACDOUGALL, J.M. (1978) Stress effects on affiliation preferences among subjects possessing the Type A coronary-prone behaviour pattern. **Journal of Personality and Social Psychology, 36,** 23-33

DEMBROSKI, T.M., MACDOUGALL, J.M., BUELL, J.C. and ELIOT, R.S. (1981) Type A, stress and autonomic reactivity. In: J. Siegrist and M.J. Halhuber (eds) **Myocardial Infarction and Psychosocial Risks.** New York: Springer-Verlag

DOHRENWEND, R.S. and DOHRENWEND, S.P. (1974) **Stressful Life Events.** New York: Wiley

DOHRENWEND, B.P., SHROUT, P.E., EGRI, G. and MENDELSOHN, R.S. (1980) Nonspecific psychological distress and other dimensions of psychopathology. **Archives of General Psychiatry, 37,** 1229-1236

EASTERLIN, R.A., WACHTER, M.L. and WACHTER, S.M. (1978) Demographic influences on economic stability: The United States experience. **Population Development Review, 4** 1-22

ELDER, G. (1981) History and the life course. In: D Bertaux (ed) **Biography and Society: the Life History Approach in the Social Sciences.** London: Sage

ELDER, G.H. and LIKER, J.K. (1982) Hard times in women's lives: historical influences across forty years. **American Journal of Sociology, 88,** 241-269

EYER, J. and STERLING, P. (1977) Stress-related mortality and social organization. **Review of Radical Political Economics, 9,** 1-44

FOX, B.H. (1981) Psychosocial factors and the immune system in human cancer. In: R. Ader (ed.) **Psychoneuroimmunology.** New York: Academic Press.

FRANKENHAEUSER, M. (1976) The role of peripheral catecholamines in adaptation to under-stimulation and over-stimulation. In: G. Serban (ed.) **Psychopathology of Human Adaptation.** New York: Plenum

FRIEDMAN, M., THORESSEN, C.E., GILL, J.J., ULNER, D., THOMPSON, L., POWELL, L., PRICE, V., ELCK, S.R., RABIN, D.D., BEALL, W.S., PIAGET, G., DIXON, T., BOURG, E., LEVY, R.A., and TASTO, D.L. (1982) Feasibility of altering Type A behavior pattern in post myocardial infarction patients. **Circulation, 66,** 83-92

FRIEDMAN, M., MANWARING, J.H., ROSENMAN, R.H. DONLON, G., ORTEGA, P. and GRUBE, S.M. (1973) Instantaneous and sudden deaths: clinical and pathlogical differentiation in coronary artery disease. **Journal of American Medical Association, 225,** 1319-1328

GLASS, D.C. (1977) **Behavior Patterns, Stress and Coronary Disease.** Hillsdale, N.J.: Erlbaum

GLASS, D.C., and SINGER, J.E. (1972) **Urban Stress.** New York: Academic Press

HENRY, J.P., and STEPHENS, P.M. (1977) **Stress, Health and the Social Environment.** New York: Springer-Verlag

HINKLE, L.E. (1973) The concept of 'stress' in the biological and social sciences. **Science, Medicine and Man, 1,** 31-48

HOLMES, T.H. and MASUDA, M. (1974) Life change and illness susceptibility. In: B.S. Dohrenwend and B.P. Dohrenwend (eds) **Stressful Life Events.** New York: Wiley

HOLMES, T.H., and RAHE, R.H. (1967) The Social Readjustment Rating Scale. **Journal of Psychosomatic Research, 11,** 213-218

HOWARD, J.H., CUNNINGHAM, D.A. and RECHNITZER, P.A. (1977) Work patterns associated with Type A behavior: a managerial population. **Human Relations, 30,** 825-836

HURST, M.W., JENKINS, D. and ROSE, R.M. (1978) The assessment of life change stress: a comparative and methodological inquiry. **Psychosomatic Medicine, 40,** 126-141

INNES, J.M. (1981) Social psychological approaches to the study of the induction and alleviation of stress. In: G.M. Stephenson and J.H. Davis (eds) **Progress in Applied Social Psychology, Volume 1.** London: Wiley

JENKINS, C.D., HURST, M.W., and ROSE, R.M. (1979) Life changes: do people really remember? **Archives of General Psychiatry, 36,** 379-384

JENKINS, C., ZYZANSKI, S.J., and ROSEMAN, R.H. (1978) Coronary-prone behavour: one pattern or several? **Psychosomatic Medicine, 40,** 25-43

JOHNSON, J.H., and SARASON, I.G. (1978) Life stress, depression and anxiety: internal-external control as a moderator variable. **Journal of Psychosomatic Research, 22,** 205-208

KANNER, A.D., COYNE, J.C., SCHAEFER, C. and LAZARUS, R.S. (1981) Comparison of two modes of stress measurement: daily hassles and uplifts versus major life events. **Journal of Behavioral Medicine, 4,** 1-39

KASL, S.V. (1977) Contributions of social epidemiology to studies in psychosomatic medicine. **Advances in Psychosomatic Medicine, 9,** 160-223

KASL, S.V. and COBB, S. (1970) Blood pressure change in men undergoing job loss: a preliminary report. **Psychosomatic Medicine, 32,** 19-38

KASL, S.V., EVANS, A.S., and NIEDERMAN, J.C. (1979) Psychosocial risk factors in the development of infectious mononucleosis. **Psychosomatic Medicine, 41,** 445-466

KOBASA, S.C., MADDI, S. and PUCCETTI, M.C. (1982) Personality and exercise as buffers in the stress-illness relationship. **Journal of Behavioral Medicine, 5,** 391-404

LAZARUS, R.S. (1984) On the primacy of cognition. **American Psychologist, 39,** 124-129

LAZARUS, R.S. and LAUNIER, R. (1978) Stress-related transactions between person and environment. In: G.A. Pervin and M. Lewis (eds) **Perspectives in Interactional Psychology.** New York: Plenum

LOWN, B., DeSILVA, R.A. and RENSON, R. (1978) Roles of psychological stress and autonomic system changes in provocation of ventricular premature complexes. **American Journal of Cardiology, 41,** 979-985

McGRATH, J.E. (1970) **Social and Psychological Factors in Stress.** New York: Holt, Rinehart and Winston

MASON, J.W., MAHER, J.J., HARTLEY, L.H., MOUGEY, G.H., PERLOW, H.J., and JONES, L.G. (1976) Selectivity of corticosteroid and catecholamine responses to various natural stimuli. In: G. Serban (ed.) **Psychopathology of Human Adaptation.** New York: Plenum Press

MECHANIC, D. (1979) Development of psychological distress in young adults. **Archives of General Psychiatry, 36,** 1233-1239

MILLER, S.M. (1979) Controllability and human stress. **Behavior Research and Therapy, 17,** 287-304

MOOS, R.H. (1974) Psychological techniques in the assessment of adaptive behavior. In: G.C. Coelho, D.A. Hamburg and J.E. Adams (eds) **Coping and Adaptation.** New York: Basic Books

NATELSON, B.H., and CAGIN, N.A. (1979) Stress-induced ventricular arrhythmias. **Psychosomatic Medicine, 41,** 259-262

NISBETT, R. and ROSS, L. (1980) **Human Inference.** Englewood Cliffs, N.J.: Prentice-Hall

PATKAI, P. (1971) Catecholamine secretion in pleasant and unpleasant situations. **Acta Psychologica, 35,** 352-363

RABKIN, J.G. and STREUNING, E.L. (1976) Life events, stress and illness. **Science, 194,** 1013-1020

RACHMAN, S. (1978) **Fear and Courage.** San Francisco: Freeman

RAHE, R.H. (1968) Life change measurement as a predictor of illness. **Proceedings of the Royal Society of Medicine, 61,** 1124-1126

ROGERS, M.P., DUBEY, D., and REICH, P. (1979) The influence of the psyche and the brain on immunity and disease susceptibility: a critical review. **Psychosomatic Medicine, 41,** 147-164

ROSENMAN, R.H., BRAND, R.J., JENKINS, C.D., FRIEDMAN, M., STRAUSS, R., and WURM, M. (1975) Coronary heart disease in the Western Collaborative Group Study. **Journal of the American Medical Association, 233,** 872-877

SELIGMAN, M.E.P. (1975) **Helplessness.** San Francisco: Freeman

SHEKELLE, R.B., GALE, M., OSTFELD, A.M., and PAUL, O. (1983) Hostility, risk of coronary heart disease and mortality. **Psychosomatic Medicine, 45,** 109-114

STEINBERG, D. (1979) Research related to underlying mechanisms in atherosclerosis. **Circulation, 60,** 1559-1565

STERLING, P., and EYER, J. (1981) Biological basis of stress-related mortality. **Social Science and Medicine, 15E,** 3-42

STEWART, A.J. and SALT, P. (1981) Life stress, life-styles, depression and illness in adult women. **Journal of Personality and Social Psychology, 40,** 1063-1069

TENNANT, C. and ANDREWS, G. (1976) A scale to measure the stress of life events. **Australian and New Zealand Journal of Psychiatry, 10,** 27-32

WILLIAMS, R.B., HANEY, T.L., LEE, K.L., KONG, Y., BLUMENTHAL, J.A., and WHALEN, R.E. (1980) Type A behavior, hostility and coronary atherosclerosis. **Psychosomatic Medicine, 42,** 539-549

WORTMAN, C.B., ABBEY, A., HOLLAND, A.E., SILVER, R.L., and JANOFF-BULMAN, R. (1980) Transitions from the laboratory to the field. In: L. Bickman (ed.) **Applied Social Psychology Annual, Volume 1.** London: Sage

ZAJONC, R.B. (1984) On the primacy of affect. **American Psychologist, 39,** 117-123

ZUCKERMAN, M. (1979) **Sensation Seeking.** Hillsdale, N.J.: Erlbaum

COGNITIVE APPROACHES TO CLINICAL PSYCHOLOGY

I.M. Blackburn

The emergence of interest in mediational or cognitive factors in clinical psychological theory and practice over the last 20 years, after a period of strictly behavioural paradigms, has been called the cognitive revolution. As with all revolutions, this one has been welcomed by many and reviled by others. Though only the future can reveal the full benefits to clinical psychology of this new stream of interest, it cannot but be recognized that the current level of enthusiasm, as reflected by journal articles, text-books and clinical practice, does suggest a dissatisfaction with purely behavioural models for the understanding and treatment of the emotional and behavioural disorders.

The first section of this chapter will trace briefly the development of the cognitive approaches and delineate the general assumptions made by practitioners of cognitive therapy. The second part will describe clinical applications, while the final section will describe some of the empirical evidence from experimental, correlative and treatment outcome studies. The main emphasis will be on depressive illness as an example of the application of cognitive approaches to a clinical problem, partly because of the author's personal interest and partly because the theoretical aspect has been more clearly articulated and better controlled treatment studies have been carried out in this area. However, as reviewed by Mahoney and Arnkoff (1978), cognitive approaches were first applied to clinical problems in areas of behavioural excess, for example, smoking and obesity, and of anxiety and phobic problems.

DEVELOPMENT OF COGNITIVE APPROACHES AND GENERAL ASSUMPTIONS

Cognitive approaches to treatment are probably more accurately described as cognitive-behavioural in that they attempt a synthesis of two traditionally opposed paradigms. This combined approach involves a recognition of the importance of mediational factors, while adhering to methodological behaviourism. Methodological behaviourism was first contrasted with metaphysical behaviourism by

Watson (1913). The central features of metaphysical or radical behaviourism were the denial of the existence of mind and the assertion that conscious or mental processes are beyond the realm of scientific enquiry, while methodological behaviourism is concerned mainly with scientific method. It emphasizes observability, operationalism, falsifiability or testability, experimentation, and replication. Cognitive-behavioural therapists and researchers can and do accept methodological behaviourism, as they assume that thoughts are observable at least by an n of 1. Thus, they reject the stimulus-response (S-R) theory of human behaviour as propounded by Skinner (1945) and adopt the mediational learning model of such early learning theorists as Tolman (1932). However, Skinner's metaphysical behaviourism is often exaggerated by his followers. It is interesting to note that he makes several references to the essential study of thoughts in the science of psychology:

> Some of the objects of introspection are private (covert) responses ... The stimuli they generate are weak but nevertheless of the same kind as those generated by overt response. It would be a mistake to refuse to consider them as data just because a second observer cannot feel or see them, at least without the help of instruments. (Skinner, 1969, p.242)

The main premise of mediational approaches is that the processes and principles which are applicable to overt behaviours are also applicable to covert phenomena. Mahoney (1974, p.51) lists important differences between the covert phenomena invoked by cognitive-behavioural psychology and those invoked by traditional psychodynamic theory:

1. Covert mediators are often assigned an implicit 'response' status which emphasizes their specific function in a particular relationship and facilitates their empirical evaluation.

2. In contrast to the extensive inferences made in psychodynamic theory, the inferences in cognitive-behavioural psychology are more direct and proximal, often involving only one step; for example, from verbal report to covert response.

3. The individual is often unaware of the mediating variables proposed by psychodynamic theory, for example, libidinal cathexes or repressed impulses, whereas in cognitive-behavioural approaches, inferred mediators are observable by a public of one, that is, the person who is experiencing them, and thus need not be inferred by their owner.

All cognitive-behavioural therapies assume a cognitive learning model, some more explicitly than others, which is derived from the systematic theories of, among others, Bandura (1971) and Bem (1972), where man is seen as an active agent who controls and is controlled by his environment. He selectively filters environmental stimuli, interprets them, categorizes them and stores them. The mediating processes, which can be both adaptive and maladaptive, involve different factors, which have been summarized by Mahoney (1974). These are listed in Table 1.

Table 1. Maladaptive processes from the cognitive-learning model of psychological disorders

FACTORS	PROCESSES
Attentional	Selective inattention, misperception, maladaptive focusing
Relational	Mis-classification, evaluative errors, retentional deficiencies, inferential errors
Response/Repertoire	Lack of problem-solving skills, lack of coping skills
Feed-back	Lack of positive self-evaluative feed-back

The maladaptive processes from the cognitive-learning model are:

Attentional factors. Maladaptive processes in attention for example, would include selective inattention (ignoring salient aspects of a situation); mis-perception or mis-labelling stimuli (as do anorexics who perceive themselves as obese or the depressed person who perceives disapproval in a passer-by's frown); and maladaptive focusing (attention to distracting stimuli in hyperactive children or focusing on a negative detail in a situation irrespective of other more positive aspects in a depressed individual).

Relational factors. After stimuli have been encoded and attended to, they can be subjected to several transformational errors, for example:

classification errors (classifying a stimulus as dangerous or bad when it is not, or dichotomous thinking in terms of good-bad, success-failure, etc.);

evaluative errors (setting excessively high performance standards in the perfectionist individual or fear of evaluation in the anxious individual);

retentional deficiencies (lack of rehearsing skills or the preponderance of negative over positive memories in the depressed);

inferential errors (inferring conclusions wrongly supported by data, distorted anticipation of consequences and inaccurate cognitive contingencies, which are the individual's rules or plans).

Response repertoire features. In addition to attentional and relational processes, the individual needs appropriate response repertoires to ensure adaptive performance. Lack of problem-solving skills or of coping skills will impede performance and many cognitive-behavioural therapies address this problem.

Feed-back. Finally, feed-back, whether in the form of external incentives or at the experiential level, has been stressed in learning theories. Self-evaluative feed-back is stressed in cognitive-behaviour therapy for modulating adaptive behaviour and mood.

To conclude this section about influences and assumptions in cognitive approaches to clinical psychology, several factors from basic and clinical psychology were identified:

1. Dissatisfaction with the S-R model in accounting for complex human behaviour and in particular for psychopathology.

2. The adoption of mediational learning models and in particular, the cognitive learning model.

3. The adherence to methodological behaviourism.

4. The proposition that thoughts are subject to the same laws of learning as are overt behaviours.

5. The assertion that attitudes, beliefs, expectancies and other cognitive activities are central to producing, predicting and understanding adaptive and maladaptive behaviour.

Table 2. Cognitive-behavioural theories of depression

APPROACH	THEORY	PROCESS OF CHANGE IN THERAPY	THERAPY TECHNIQUES
Cognitive (Beck)	Dysfunctional schemata → distorted information processing →negative thinking →depression	Alter information processing distortions and modify schemata	Training in thoughts monitoring; behavioural and cognitive tasks to test hypotheses inductive reasoning cognitive restructuring
Rational-emotive (Ellis)	Maladaptive beliefs →depression	Change beliefs	Deductive reasoning and persuasion
Self-control (Rehm)	Deficits in self-monitoring, self-evaluation & self-reinforcement →depression	Increase self-reinforcement & decrease self-punishment	Training in self-monitoring self-evaluation & self-reinforcement
Learned helplessness (Seligman)	Expected aversiveness expected uncontroll-ability, attributional style →depression	Increase expectation of positive outcomes and sense of control, alter attributional style	Environmental enrichment, personal control training, resignation training, attribution retraining

CLINICAL APPLICATIONS

Depressive illness

As pointed out in the introduction, though cognitive approaches have been applied to several other areas of psychopathology, in particular phobic disorders and behavioural excesses such as addictions, this chapter will concentrate on depressive illness to illustrate the principles involved. Cognitive theory and cognitive therapy (Beck, 1976), rational-emotive-therapy (Ellis, 1962), self-control (Rehm, 1977), learned helplessness (Seligman, 1975) and the reformulated learned helplessness theory (Abramson, Seligman and Teasdale, 1978) have been the main approaches which have inspired a whole generation of clinicians. Table 2 summarizes the main aspects of these approaches to depression and of the therapeutic techniques derived from them.

Traditionally, the emphasis has been put on the mood disorder in depression, hence the term affective disorder, though several other functions, cognitive, motivational, behavioural, and biochemical, are also affected. According to Beck (1976) the most salient psychological symptom in clinical observation is the profoundly altered thinking. Kovacs and Beck (1978) identify cognitive dysfunctions at three different levels: in the content of thought; in the processing of thought (that is, appraisal, attention, retention, abstraction and encoding of information); and finally in superordinate cognitive structures, that is, in beliefs and attitudes.

1. Cognitive content

The thought content of depressed individuals is predominantly negative and relates to themes of loss or perceived subtractions from what Beck called the 'personal domain'. The personal domain includes the individual, significant others, valued objects, attributes and ideas, principles, and goals held to be important. Thus, the negative thematic content is related to the self, the world and the future. Beck has called this negative content of thought 'the negative cognitive triad'.

Typically, the depressed person sees himself as inadequate or unworthy and he tends to attribute his unpleasant experiences to a physical, mental or moral defect in himself. He believes that he is undesirable because of these presumed defects and, therefore, he tends to underestimate or criticize himself. Finally, he believes that he lacks the attributes which are essential to happiness and contentment, that is, he sees himself as helpless.

He sees the world as making exorbitant demands upon him or as putting obstacles in his way, so that he interprets his on-going experiences in a negative way. He misinterprets his interactions with the world as representing defeat and deprivation.

As he looks into his future he anticipates that his current difficulties or suffering will continue indefinitely, so that the expectation of failing interferes with his motivation to try.

According to cognitive theory, these pervasive negative cognitions inevitably lead to dysphoria, to reduced desire to provide for one's welfare, to passivity and ultimately to giving up.

2. Cognitive processing

A number of systematic errors can be seen in the thinking style of the depressed individual which seem to maintain his invariant, stereotypic negative conclusions. These have been catalogued as: arbitrary inferences, over-generalization, selective abstraction, magnification and minimization, personalization, and dichotomous thinking. These logical errors are not mutually exclusive and several examples can be seen in one negative thought. For example, a depressed housewife and mother thinks 'I am a complete failure' after her son fails a class examination. She thus magnifies the importance of an admittedly undesirable event; she overgeneralizes from one event to all aspects of her life; she selectively abstracts one aspect of a complex situation and interprets a whole experience on the basis of this one aspect; she is probably making an arbitrary inference in that her conclusion that her son failed because of her is not likely to be supported by the evidence; she is personalizing in that she attributes to herself the cause of an external negative event, and she is thinking in black and white terms, or showing dichotomous thinking.

These cognitive distortions are most apparent in what is called 'automatic thoughts' in cognitive theory, that is in the 'self-talk' or the rapid, habitual cognitive reaction that each individual has. These thoughts are autonomous, plausible, repetitive and idiosyncratic.

3. Cognitive structures or schemata

These refer to basic beliefs, attitudes or premises, and are a major component of the cognitive model in that they allow for an integration of the thematic content of depressive cognitions and the particular transformation that stimuli are subjected to. Schemata have been defined (for example, Neisser, 1967) as non-specific but organized representations of prior experience which facilitate recall as well as systematically distort new constructions. In Piagetian terms, a schema refers to a basic structure or process which underlies sensorimotor behaviour or complex mental activity and explains the organization and regularity of acts. Problem-solving and reasoning experiments essentially address some aspect of the selective use of prior experience and of premises in complex activity. Thus, in both everyday and pathological reasoning, the nature of the premise taken is of particular importance. An individual selectively attends to specific stimuli, combines them in a pattern and thus conceptualizes a situation. Although different people may conceptualize the same situation in different ways, a particular person tends to be consistent in his response to similar types of events. These relatively stable cognitive patterns form the basis for the regularity of interpretations of a particular type of situation. The schema designates these stable cognitive patterns and is thus the basis for screening out, differentiating and coding the stimuli which confront an individual.

According to Beck, a schema can be inactive for long periods of time, but can be elicited by specific environmental stimuli. The types of schemata elicited in depressed patients are of the type:

> 'In order to be happy I have to be successful in whatever I undertake.'
>
> 'To be happy I must be accepted by everybody at all times.'
>
> 'My value as a person depends on what others think of me.'

It is proposed that as depression progresses, the patient's conceptualization of specific situations becomes distorted to fit these types of prepotent dysfunctional schemata, so that the orderly matching of appropriate schemata with particular stimuli becomes disrupted. The formal characteristics of these dysfunctional schemata are their excessive use of the directive 'should' or 'must', the use of quantifiers such as 'all', 'none', 'always', the use of pre-emptive class assignments, for example 'nothing-but', 'either-or', and the fact that they relate to the self. It is hypothesized that they are learnt in early childhood and that predisposing factors may be the early loss of a parent, a depressed parent who plays the role of a model or, an over-strict parent who selectively attends to the child's deficiencies and does not reward good behaviour.

It can be seen that these explanatory concepts, as evoked by Beck, fit quite neatly into the various processes of the cognitive learning model described in the first section. As applied to depression, there would be dysfunctions at every level:

1. Attentional factors - selective abstraction; inattention to positive elements in a situation.

2. Relational processes - negative evaluation; errors of inference in the form of arbitrary inferences; classificatory errors as evidenced by personalization and negative view of the world; retentional deficiencies in that past negative experiences are more easily remembered.

3. Response repertoire deficiencies - lack of alternative behaviours.

4. Experiential feed-back - underestimation of performance and therefore lack of self reinforcement.

More recently (Beck, Epstein and Harrison, 1983), Beck has hypothesized that in addition to automatic thoughts and schemata, there is a third, more stable level in personality structure, which may predispose an individual to depression in response to particular types of environmental stresses, determine the pattern of symptoms and even influence response to particular forms of treatment. He has identified two such personality characteristics as autonomy and social dependence:

> Autonomy involves an investment in independent functioning, mobility, choice, achievement and integrity of one's domain. Blocking of these valued conditions is perceived as a major loss by the autonomous individual. The socially dependent person is invested in positive interchange with others, focusing on acceptance, intimacy, support and guidance. Interruption of these interpersonal 'resources' is perceived as a major loss by such an individual. (Beck, Epstein and Harrison, 1983)

Beck's theoretical approach has led to a specific type of therapy, cognitive therapy, which has been clearly operationalized in a manual (Beck et al., 1979). It is a short-term psychotherapy (lasting approximately 12 to 15 weeks) which aims to relieve depressed affect and behaviour through the application of cognitive and behavioural techniques. Behavioural techniques are used not only to change behaviour (for example, teaching of coping skills, such as relaxation or assertion), but also to change cognition through behavioural change. Though this process is presumably taken for granted in behaviour therapy and remains implicit, in cognitive therapy it is stressed explicitly as a test of cognitive hypotheses. The main steps of therapy are described in Table 3.

Table 3. Summary of cognitive therapy (duration approximately 12 weeks)

PROCEDURES

1. Explain rationale of therapy and epistemological difference between thoughts and reality.
2. Train to monitor automatic thoughts.
3. Graded tasks or assigned tasks to increase activity, pleasure and mastery experiences.
4. Modify automatic thoughts through inductive reasoning and empirical verification.
5. Elicit basic attitudes or schemata.
6. Modify basic attitudes through inductive reasoning and empirical tests.

All the steps of therapy are accompanied by specific tasks to help the patient gather information, test out an unrealistic expectation or engage in alternative behaviours. Cognitive therapy of depression has now been tested, with encouraging results in several outcome studies which will be described in the next section. It is a complicated package which requires intense training. The process of change has not been sufficiently tested yet, so that it is possible, as suggested by Bandura (1977a), that though the processes of change may be cognitive, as proposed by the theory, the procedures which are most effective in changing these processes may be behavioural. The latest development in Beck's theoretical approach with regard to personality characteristics has not been tested yet for its heuristic or theoretical value and will therefore not be considered further, whereas evidence for the other aspects of his theory will be considered in the next section.

Ellis's (1962, 1970) rational emotive therapy (RET) approach is similar to Beck's in its view of maladaptive thoughts as mediators of maladaptive feelings and behaviours, but the emphasis is on basic assumptions or beliefs, ignoring much of the subordinate levels of thinking, such as automatic thoughts. An implicit premise in Ellis's view of man is the role of logic in thought-patterns. He appears to assume that the discovery of irrationality in one's beliefs will automatically lead to change, whereas the social psychology of cognitive consistency and belief systems casts serious doubts on whether we are inherently logical organisms (McGuire, 1968). In his 1970 summary, he states:

> The rational-emotive therapist - often within the first session or two of seeing a client - can almost always put his finger on a few central irrational philosophies of life which this client is vehemently propounding to himself. He can show the client how these ideas inevitably lead to his emotional problems and hence to his presenting clinical symptoms, can demonstrate exactly how the client can forthrightly question and challenge these ideas, and can often induce him to work to uproot them and to replace them with scientifically testable hypotheses about himself and the world which are not likely to get him into future emotional difficulties.

He lists twelve irrational beliefs which he believes to be at the root of most emotional disturbances:

1. The idea that it is a dire necessity for an adult to be loved by everyone for everything he does.

2. The idea that certain acts are awful or wicked, and that people who perform such acts should be severely punished.

3. The idea that it is horrible when things are not the way one should like them.

4. The idea that human misery is externally caused and is forced on one by outside people and events.

5. The idea that if something is or may be dangerous, one should be terribly upset about it.

6. The idea that it is easier to avoid than to face life-difficulties and self-responsibilities.

7. The idea that one needs something other or stronger or greater than oneself on which to rely.

8. The idea that one should be thoroughly competent, intelligent and achieving in all possible respects.

9. The idea that because something once strongly affected one's life, it should indefinitely affect it.

10. The idea that one must have certain and perfect control over things.

11. The idea that human happiness can be achieved by inertia and inaction.

12. The idea that one has virtually no control over one's emotions and that one cannot help feeling certain things.

RET techniques differ considerably from those of cognitive therapy. Greater reliance is put on semantic and persuasive techniques and as described by Hollon and Beck (1979):

> The specific approach has been traditionally structured as a deductive debate; the therapist knows in advance what types of irrational beliefs the client holds and frequently relies on verbal persuasion to produce changes in beliefs.

The effectiveness of RET has unfortunately tended to rely more on uncontrolled case studies than on more rigorous controlled trials.

Rehm (1977) has put forward a self-control model of depression derived from Kanfer's (1970) self-regulation model. Self-control refers to those processes by which an individual alters the probability of a response in the relative absence of immediate external supports. Three processes are postulated in a feed-back loop model: self-monitoring, self-evaluation and self-reinforcement. There may be defects in any one or all of these processes in depression.

1. **Self-monitoring:** Depressed patients tend to attend selectively to immediate versus delayed outcomes of their behaviour.

2. **Self-evaluation:** (a) depressed patients fail to make accurate internal attributions of causality; (b) they set over-stringent criteria for self-evaluation; (c) they perceive themselves as lacking in ability to obtain positive consequences.

3. **Self-reinforcement:** Depressed patients have low rates of self-reward and high rates of self-punishment.

It can be seen that these concepts can be easily incorporated within Beck's cognitive theory (though they are couched in more behavioural, operational terms) and within the cognitive-learning model described in the first section. For example, self-monitoring deficits are presumably due to systematic logical errors like selective abstraction; that is, to attentional deficits. Self-evaluation errors would be due to relational processes like arbitrary references and classification errors. Self-reinforcement deficits relate to experiential feed-back, which reflects underestimation of performance and attributional style.

Therapy involves training in these three processes, which are deemed to be deficient, and involves a combination of behavioural and cognitive techniques, not dissimilar to Beck's cognitive therapy, though basic operational differences do exist. No study has compared the relative efficacy of self-control therapy and cognitive therapy, but Fuchs and Rehm (1977) compared self-control therapy with waiting-list controls and non-specific treatment controls. They found self-control therapy superior on several dependent measures at termination of therapy and at one month follow-up.

Seligman's (1975) 'learned helplessness' model was derived from animal experiments where inescapable noxious stimuli were administered. In a reformulation of the theory by Abramson, Seligman and Teasdale (1978), the old learned helplessness hypothesis was criticized, in that when applied to humans:

1. It does not distinguish between cases in which outcomes are uncontrollable for all people and cases in which they are uncontrollable for some people (universal versus personal helplessness).

2. It does not explain when helplessness is general and when specific, or when chronic and when acute.

A reformulation based on a revision of attribution theory was proposed to resolve these inadequacies. Seligman (1981) summarizes the reformulated helplessness model in four premises:

PREMISE 1 (expected aversiveness). The individual expects that highly aversive outcomes are probable or that highly desired outcomes are improbable.

PREMISE 2 (expected uncontrollability). The individual expects that no response in his or her repertoire will change the likelihood of these events.

PREMISE 3 (attributional style). The individual possesses an insidious attributional style that governs the duration and breadth of depression deficits and whether self-esteem is lowered. The depressive attributional style consists of a tendency to make internal attribution for failure, but external attributions for success; stable attributions for failure, but unstable attributions for success; and global attributions for failure, but specific attributions for success. Internal attributions for failure (and external ones for succcess) produce long-lasting depressive deficits, and global attributions for failure (and specific ones for success) produce depressive deficits over a variety of situations.

PREMISE 4 (severity). The strength of the motivational and cognitive deficits of depression depends jointly on the strength (that is, the certainty) of the expectation of the aversive outcome (premise 1) and the strength of the uncontrollability expectancy (premise 2). The severity of the affective and self-esteem deficits is governed by the importance of the uncontrollable outcome.

According to Seligman (1981) these few premises and their co-occurrence are deemed sufficient but not necessary to account for the four sets of deficits seen in depression; that is, motivational, cognitive, affective-somatic, and self-esteem. Following from these premises, four sets of strategies are proposed for treatment:

1. Environmental enrichment by environmental manipulation and/or provision of better medical care.

2. Personal control training by training in coping skills and modifying expectation of failure.

3. Resignation training by providing more realistic goals, challenging basic assumptions, reducing desirability of highly valued, but unrealistic goals.

4. Attribution retraining by changing unrealistic attributions for failure and success.

This approach to therapy has yet to be tested with clinical groups, though the theoretical approach has been extensively researched. Some of this empirical work will be reviewed in the next section. Selgiman (1981) makes the provocative assertion that cognitive theory and therapy are diffuse and unsystematic and can be subsumed by the reformulated learned helplessness model, which is more systematic and parsimonious. It is, however, apposite to note that the experimental evidence that is purported to underpin his theory does not always support the theory.

Other psychological disorders

The emergence of interest in the concept of self-control in the early 60s, emphasizing the causal interaction between the organism and the environment, underlined the role of cognitive factors in self-regulatory processes. R. Lazarus (1966), A. Lazarus (1971), Bandura (1971) and Thoresen and Mahoney (1974) have described the new philosophical approach of reciprocal determinism where the person is no longer seen as a passive product of his environment, but as an active participant in his development. Several studies were published in the 60s describing various cognitive-behavioural approaches to behavioural problems; for example, coverant control (Homme, 1965) and covert conditioning (Cautela, 1966), where thoughts, imagery and feeling are used as targets of therapy and as cues to induce behaviour change. More recently, there has been a burgeoning cognitive literature in various areas of psychopathology. This treats, among others, the treatment of impulsive and hyperactive children (Miechenhaum and Goodman, 1971), of anxiety (Meichenbaum, 1977; Goldfried, 1979), of anger (Novaco, 1976), of pain patients (Turk, 1978) and of eating disorders (Garner and Bemis, 1982). Since it is not within the scope of this chapter to review these different areas in detail, interested readers are referred to excellent reviews by experts in their field in Kendell and Hollon (1979).

Some of the impressive work with impulsive children, using self-instruction or self-control strategies, will be described because it deals with a different population, children instead of adults, and uses somewhat different therapeutic methods from those described in the depression section. Impulsivity has been conceptualized as a cognitive style or an approach to problem-solving tasks, with cognitive and behavioural components.

Studies comparing impulsive with reflective children have indicated that impulsive children spend less time in search-and-scan behaviour, make more errors and employ less mature information-seeking skills, and show more generally impulsive behaviour in that they are more likely to blame others unfairly, to be aggressive and to threaten to injure themselves (Kendall and Finch, 1979). Various behavioural techniques, for example, imposed delay, modelling and reward contingencies, have been used to modify impulsivity in children. More recently, a cognitive-behavioural approach, self-instructional training (Meichenbaum, 1977), has been used with promising results. Self-instructional procedures involve a sequence which parallels the developmental progression of the normal child's internalization of speech and control of behaviour, as described by Luria (1963). These procedures are described in Table 4.

In his thinking out loud, the model displays several performance-relevant skills: problem definition, focused attention, self-reinforcement, self-evaluation and error-correcting options. Meichenbaum and Goodman (1971) in two studies with young impulsive children, found that modelling plus self-instructional training were superior to modelling alone in increasing response latencies and decreasing errors. Douglas et al. (1976) demonstrated the effectiveness of cognitive training procedures in hyperactive children by using the techniques described above to induce a less impulsive approach to cognitive tasks, academic problems and social situations. Though some measures did not show the desired changes, they obtained increased latency and fewer errors in the matching of figures, improvements on measures of reading ability and improved performance on the Porteus mazes test.

Self-instructional procedures have likewise been applied to test and speech anxiety subjects, to phobic patients and to institutionalized schizophrenics (Meichenbaum, 1977). These studies have usually compared self-instruction with desensitization or no treatment controls and found self-instructional methods in addition to modelling superior.

Table 4. Self-instructional treatment techniques with hyper-active children

PROCEDURES	TECHNIQUES
1. Cognitive modelling	Therapist models task performance while talking out loud to himself
2. Overt external guidance	Child performs task with therapist's instruction
3. Overt self-guidance	Child performs task while instructing himself out loud
4. Faded overt self-guidance	Child performs task while whispering the instruction to himself
5. Overt self-instruction	Child performs task while guiding his peformance by private speech

Cognitive-behavioural approaches to training in self-control appear promising and will, it is to be hoped, generate more research to test the range of applicability, generalization and relative relevance of different tasks.

EMPIRICAL EVIDENCE FOR COGNITIVE APPROACHES

As the emphasis in this chapter has been on depressive illness, empirical evidence for the cognitive model will rely solely on research in this field of psychopathology as an illustration of clinical and experimental studies in this area. A selection of studies are described below as correlative, experimental or treatment related.

Correlative studies

1. Cognitive distortion. A vast number of studies have shown that depressed patients differ from control groups in their thought content and in their thought processing. Some early studies (for example, Beck and Ward, 1961) indicated differences between depressed and non-depressed individuals in terms of manifest dream contents, with the depressed reporting themes of personal loss and failure. Weintraub, Segal and Beck (1974), using a multiple choice measure of expectancy, found that the tendency to endorse negatively distorted outcome correlated significantly with ratings of depressed affect. Nelson (1977) found significant correlation between a self-rating scale of depression, the Beck Depression Inventory (BDI) (Beck, Ward, Mendelson, Mock and Erbaugh, 1961) and various depressogenic attitudes. Blackburn and Bishop (1983), in their treatment outcome study, found highly significant correlations ($p < .001$) between the BDI and the negative view of self, the world and the future as measured by semantic differential techniques. An observer rating scale, the Hamilton Rating Scale for Depression (HRS-D) (Hamilton, 1960) correlated at the .05 level with the negative view of self, the correlations with view of the world and view of the environment being non-significant. Though the BDI and the HRS-D were correlated at the .001 level ($r = .51$, $df = 62$), the cognitive bias of the BDI items relative to the HRS-D was evident. Thus, the correlations of the BDI with other putative depressive cognitive variables may be less meaningful than is sometimes assumed.

No study, to the author's knowledge, has addressed the question of how necessary or sufficient are the elements of the cognitive triad to depression. Nekanda-Trepka, Bishop and Blackburn (1983), in a study of hopelessness in patients diagnosed as primary major depressives according to research diagnostic criteria, reported that on the Hopelessness Scale (Beck et al., 1974), 13 per cent of patients scored within normal limits and thus did not show a negative view of the future. They also found a significant correlation with self-rated depression on the BDI ($r = .47$, $P < .001$), but not with the HRS-D ($r = .12$).

Several questionnaires have been developed recently to measure some of the factors described by Beck as important in the causation and maintenance of depression. The Automatic Thought Questionnaire (ATQ) (Hollon and Kendall, 1980) attempts to measure the frequency of negative thoughts, the Dysfunctional Attitude Scale (DAS) (Weissman and Beck, 1978) aims to tap the degree of belief in the basic attitudes which have been described as depressogenic schemata and the Cognitive Style Test (CST) (Wilkinson and Blackburn, 1981) attempts to measure negative bias in views of self, the world and the future relating to pleasant and unpleasant situations. All these scales have been shown to discriminate between depressed and non-depressed populations and to correlate significantly with the BDI. A general weakness of these studies is that they often do not attempt to demonstrate the specificity of the dysfunctional thinking to depressive illness, as comparisons are not generally made with other pathological groups.

The cognitive theory of depression has been criticized for interpreting in a causative role what others have considered to be effects of depression. The question of whether distorted cognitive style is a symptom or a trait has been addressed by several authors recently. Wilkinson and Blackburn (1981) failed to differentiate recovered depressed patients, patients recovered from other psychiatric disorders and normals on several cognitive measures. More recently, Hamilton and Abramson (1983) showed a dramatic change on several measures in depressed patients when tested at admission to hospital and just before discharge. In addition, they showed that the recovered depressed did not differ from recovered psychiatric controls and normal controls on any of the dependent measures. They concluded, as have other researchers, that 'the cognitive style exhibited by clinically depressed individuals appeared to be more a feature of the depressive episode itself than an enduring cognitive characteristic of the depressed individual'.

Blackburn and Bishop (1983) and Simons, Garfield and Murphy (1984) reported similar results in two outcome studies comparing the efficacy of cognitive therapy and pharmacotherapy. At the end of treatment, there were significant changes on all dependent cognitive measures whether the patients had received cognitive therapy or pharmacotherapy, and changes in cognitive measures paralleled changes in measures of mood and severity level. Simons et al. concluded that 'the cognitive distortions that are the focus of cognitive therapy appear to behave more as symptoms of depression than as causes'. It is possible, however, that both pharmacotherapy and cognitive therapy work through facilitating cognitive changes, so that the processes of change would be cognitive, though different procedures would be altering these processes (Bandura, 1977a). It must therefore be concluded, at this point, that though cognitive distortions in depression have been satisfactorily demonstrated, their exact role in the development of a depressive episode has not yet been established.

2. Attributional style. A large number of studies have investigated the attributional processes postulated by the reformulated learned helplessness model, with inconsistent results. Most studies have shown that depressed subjects (university students) made more internal attributions for failure than do non-depressed subjects (for example, Klein, Fencil-Morse and Seligman, 1976). Abramson, Garber et al. (1978) could not replicate these results in patient groups. Similarly, differences in attributions to stability have not been supported (Kuiper, 1978), nor have attributions to effort, luck and task difficulty and perceived control (Garber and Hollon, 1980). Using the Attributional Style Questionnaire (ASQ), Seligman et al. (1979) reported that depressed students made more internal stable and global attributions for bad outcomes than did non-depressed students. Several other studies, however, have reported weak correlations or negative results (Manly et al., 1982).

Experimental studies

Demonstrating the existence of differences in cognitive content and processes between depressed and non-depressed subjects establishes co-variation, without establishing that these differences are causal in depression. Experiments linking shifts in cognitive content and processes with subsequent changes in affective, behavioural and motivational components of the depressive syndrome are stronger tests of the theory.

1. Cognition and changes in mood. The most common method has been the use of cognitive induction procedures to induce a happy or depressed mood. Velten (1968) had subjects read depressing, elating or neutral statements and measured subsequent mood. Subjects reading the negative statements reported increase in dysphoric affect. Similar results have been reported by several other studies. Teasdale and Bancroft (1977), in five single-case experiments, found that mood was significantly more depressed after unhappy thoughts than after happy thoughts and corrugator EMG was higher in the unhappy than in the happy condition. Blackburn and Bonham (1980) partially replicated these results and also demonstrated that using a cognitive therapy technique, 'distancing', reversed that effect. Blackburn, Lyketsos and Tsiantis (1979), using cross-lagged correlations, demonstrated that in depressed in-patients treated by physical methods of treatment, changes in negative attitudes preceded changes in mood. Teasdale and Fennell (1982) have demonstrated the superior effects on clinical depression of brief interventions designed to modify depressive thinking and of distractions techniques, relative to control conditions. These experiments appear to indicate that specific thoughts induce affective and physiological states and that thought change techniques have a direct effect on mood.

2. Memory and recall of feed-back. Several studies have indicated that memory functions differ between depressives and non-depressives. For example, Lloyd and Lishman (1975) found that depressed subjects were more likely to recall negative events than were non-depressed controls. Isen et al. (1978) found that induced depressed mood led to increases in recall of negatively toned materials, while Teasdale and Fogarty (1979) found that induced depressed mood lengthened retrieval time for pleasant memories. They postulated a feed-back mechanism between depressed thought, depressed mood and depressed memories. In a later study (Teasdale and Taylor, 1981), accessibility to pleasant or unpleasant experiences was found to co-vary with induced happy or depressed mood. Derry and Kuiper (1981) predicted that depressed individuals should demonstrate superior recall for depressive adjectives, whereas non-depressed controls should show superior recall for non-depressed adjectives. Consistent with their prediction, they found that depressed subjects showed superior recall for self-referrent depressed adjectives, whereas two non-depressed groups showed superior recall for selfreferrent non-depressive adjectives.

Several studies have investigated the recall of positive feed-back and negative feed-back in laboratory tasks with predetermined feed-back levels. Wener and Rehm (1975) and Kuiper (1978) reported differences between depressed and non-depressed groups, with the depressed estimating less positive feed-back. Nelson and Craighead (1977), Demonbreun and Craighead (1977) and Alloy and Abramson (1979) have investigated recall of feed-back in relation to the actual amount of feed-back given. In general, the findings indicated that depressed patients underestimate reward in high percentage reward conditions relative to non-depressed, and non-depressed underestimate punishment in low level punishment conditions, the depressed group being more accurate. All subjects tend to overestimate low rate of positive feed-back and often no signficant differences are obtained between depressed and non-depressed. Coyne and Gotlib (1983) concluded that the recall of information experiments provided equivocal evidence for predictions from the cognitive model.

3. Cognition and behaviour. Other experiments have attempted to show that cognitive factors influence behavioural performance and motivational factors. Seligman and his colleagues (for example, Klein and Seligman, 1976) have demonstrated that the experience of non-contingent failure, that is, lack of control, appears to produce subsequent deficits on performance measures (speed and anagram-solving). On the other hand, increases in expectation following successful task performance were associated with subsequent increases in performance levels. Friedman (1964) had argued earlier that psychomotor retardation in depression was largely explained by cognitive variables such as indecision and negative expectations, as depressives did not differ from non-depressives on a battery of performance tasks, once they were encouraged to begin and continue working.

Treatment studies

Though the effectiveness of a therapy cannot fully validate the theory from which it is derived in that the techniques and processes of change may be different, as argued earlier, it nevertheless stands to reason, as pointed out by Seligman (1981) 'that one criterion of adequacy of a more complete theory of a disorder is that it deduces the effective therapeutic procedures from its etiological considerations'.

Several methodologically adequate outcome studies of cognitive therapy of depression, with consistently promising results, have appeared in the literature over recent years. These have already been reviewed by several authors, for example, Rush and Giles (1982). These studies will, therefore, not be examined in detail here and are summarized in Table 5.

The studies in Table 5 are the main clinical trials published to date. Other treatment studies have been conducted on student or community volunteers and are not included here. As can

Table 5. Outcome studies of cognitive therapy in depression

STUDY	MEASURES	TREATMENT	RESULTS
Rush, Beck, Kovacs and Hollon (1977) (N = 41)	BDI, HRSD	CT; Imipramine	CT > Imipramine
Beck, Rush, Shaw and Emery (1979) (N = 26)	BDI, HRSD	CT; CT + Amitriptyline	CT = CT + Amitriptyline
McLean and Hakstian (1979) (N = 154)	BDI, DACL	CBT; relaxation training; insight therapy; Amitriptyline	CBT > Amitriptyline = relaxation > insight therapy
Blackburn, Bishop Glen, Whalley and Christie (1981) (N = 64)	BDI, HRSD	CT; Anti-depressant medications, combination	Hospital clinic: combination CT = anti-depressant; General practice CT = combination anti-depressant
Murphy, Simons, Wetzel and Lustman (1984) (N = 70)	BDI, HRSD	CT; pharmacotherapy; CT + pharmacotherapy, CT + placebo	CT = pharmacotherapy = CT + pharmacotherapy = CT + placebo
Rush and Watkins (1981) (N = 38)	BDI, HRSD	Group CT; individual CT; individual CT + anti-depressants	Individual CT = individual CT + anti-depressants >group CT
Shaw (1977) (N = 32)	BDI, HRSD	Group CT; BT; non-directive therapy; waiting list.	CT > BT; CT >non-directive therapy; BT = non-directive therapy. > Each waiting list

Note:
> denotes more effective than; = denotes equivalent efficacy; CT = Cognitive therapy; BT = Behaviour therapy; CBT = Cognitive-behavioural therapy; BDI = Beck depression inventory; HRSD = Hamilton rating scale for depression; DACL = Depression adjective check list

be seen, the general finding is that cognitive therapy is effective in depressed patients. It is, however, important to note that cognitive therapy has, so far, been shown to be effective on a sub-group of depressed patient, that is, unipolar, non-psychotic depressed out-patients, satisfying research diagnostic criteria for major or minor depressive illness. Blackburn et al. (1981) reported that the presence of an endogenous pattern of symptoms did not prove to be a negative predictor of response.

CONCLUSION

This chapter has attempted to show the influences from general psychology and from applied clinical psychology which have led to the current high level of interest in the cognitive approaches to psychopathology. Various theoretical approaches have been described and some pertinent research evidence has been reviewed. The main criticisms which should qualify the research findings are, firstly, that many studies have used 'depressed' college students instead of clinical populations. It is doubtful that mildly depressed students or experimentally-induced depressions have much in common with clinical depression. These subjects are often not diagnosed according to recognized criteria, but labelled as depressed according to an arbitrary score on a severity scale. Secondly, many studies have not used psychiatric control groups, so that serious doubts must be raised as to the specificity of cognitive distortions to the illness group being investigated. However, there is no doubt that much ground has already been covered and that cognitive approaches to the understanding, explanation and treatment of psychological disorders offer an exciting and fruitful avenue to more and better research.

REFERENCES

ABRAMSON, L.Y., SELIGMAN, M.E.P. and TEASDALE, J.D. (1978) Learned helplessness in humans: critique and reformulation. **Journal of Abnormal Psychology, 87,** 49-74

ABRAMSON, L.Y., GARBER, J., EDWARDS, N.B. and SELIGMAN, M.E.P. (1978) Expectancy changes in depression and schizophrenia. **Journal of Abnormal Psychology, 87,** 102-109

ALLOY, L.B. and ABRAMSON, L.Y. (1979) Judgment of contingency in depressed and non-depressed students: sadder but wiser? **Journal of Experimental Psychology: General, 108,** 441-485

BANDURA, A. (1971) **Social Learning Theory.** New Jersey: General Learning Press

BANDURA, A. (1977) **Social Learning Theory.** Englewood Cliffs,NJ: Prentice Hall

BANDURA, A. (1977a) Self-efficacy: toward a unifying theory of behavioural change. **Psychological Review, 84,** 191-215

BECK, A.T. (1976) **Cognitive Theory and the Emotional Disorders.** New York: International Universities Press

BECK, A.T. and WARD, C.H. (1961) Dreams of depressed patients: characteristic themes in manifest content. **Archives of General Psychiatry, 5,** 462-467

BECK, A.T., WARD, C.H., MENDELSON, M., MOCK, J.E. and ERBAUGH, J.K. (1961) An inventory for measuring depression. **Archives of General Psychiatry, 4,** 561-571

BECK, A.T., WEISSMAN, A., LESTER, D. and TREXLER, L. (1974) The measurement of pessimism: the hopelessness scale. **Journal of Consulting and Clinical Psychology, 42,** 861-865

BECK, A.T., RUSH, A.J., SHAW, B.F. and EMERGY, G. (1979) **Cognitive Therapy of Depression: A Treatment Manual.** New York: Guilford Press

BECK, A.T., EPSTEIN, N. and HARRISON, R. (1983) Cognitions, attitudes and personality dimensions in depression. **British Journal of Cognitive Psychotherapy, 1,** 1-16

BEM, D.J. (1972) Self-perception theory. In: L. Berkowitz (ed.) **Advances in Experimental Social Psychology, Volume 6.** New York: Academic Press

BLACKBURN, I.M., LYKETSOS, G. and TSIANTIA, J. (1979) The temporal relationship between hostility and depressed mood. **British Journal of Social and Clinical Psychology, 18,** 227-235

BLACKBURN, I.M. and BONHAM, K.G. (1980) Experimental effects of a cognitive therapy technique in depressed patients. **British Journal of Social and Clinical Psychology, 19,** 353-363

BLACKBURN, I.M., BISHOP, S., GLEN, A.I.M., WHALLEY, L.J. and CHRISTIE, J.E. (1981) The efficacy of cognitive therapy in depression: a treatment trial using cognitive therapy and pharmacotherapy, each alone and in combination. **British Journal of Psychiatry, 139,** 181-189

BLACKBURN, I.M. and BISHOP, S. (1983) Changes in cognition with pharmacotherapy and cognitive therapy. **British Journal of Psychiatry, 143,** 609-617

CAUTELA, J.R. (1966) Treatment of compulsive behavior by covert sensitization. **Psychological Record, 16,** 33-41

COYNE, J.C. and GOTLIB, I.H. (1983) The role of cognition in depression. A critical appraisal. **Psychological Bulletin, 94,** 472-505

DEMONBREUN, B.G. and CRAIGHEAD, W.E. (1977) Distortion of perception and recall of positive and neutral feedback in depression. **Cognitive Therapy and Research, 1,** 311-329

DERRY, P.A. and KUIPER, K.A. (1981) Schematic processing and self-reference in clinical depression. **Journal of Abnormal Psychology, 90,** 286-297

DOUGLAS, V.I., PARRY, P., MARTON, P. and GARSON, C. (1976) Assessment of a cognitive training programme for hyperactive children. **Journal of Abnormal Child Psychology, 4,** 389-410

ELLIS, A. (1962) **Reason and Emotion in Psychotherapy.** New York: Lyle Stuart Inc

ELLIS, A. (1970) **The Essence of Rational Psychotherapy. A Comprehensive Approach to Treatment.** New York: Institute of Rational Living

FRIEDMAN, A.S. (1964) Minimal effect of severe depression on cognitive functioning. **Journal of Abnormal and Social Psychology, 69,** 237-243

FUCHS, C.Z. and REHM, L.P. (1977) A self-control behaviour therapy program for depression. **Journal of Consulting and Clinical Psychology, 45,** 206-215

GARBER, J. and HOLLON, S.D. (1980) Universal versus personal helplessness. Belief in uncontrollability or incompetence? **Journal of Abnormal Psychology, 89,** 56-66

GARNER, D.M. and BEMIS, K.M. (1982) A cognitive-behavioural approach to anorexia nervosa. **Cognitive Therapy and Research, 6,** 123-150

GOLDFRIED, M.R. (1979) Anxiety reduction through cognitive-behavioural intervention. In: P.C. Kendall and S.D. Hollon (eds) **Cognitive-Behavioural Intervention. Theory, Research and Procedures.** 117-152. New York: Academic Press

HAMILTON, M. (1960) A rating scale for depression. **Journal of Neurology, Neurosurgery and Psychiatry, 23,** 56-62

HAMILTON, E.W. and ABRAMSON, L.Y. (1983) Cognitive patterns and major depressive disorder. A longitudinal study in a hospital setting. **Journal of Abnormal Psychology, 92,** 173-194

HOLLON, S.D. and BECK, A.T. (1979) Cognitive therapy of depression. In: P.C. Kendall and S.D. Hollon (eds) **Cognitive-Behavioural Interventions, Theory, Research and Procedures.** 153-203. New York: Academic Press

HOLLON, S.D. and KENDALL, P.C. (1980) Cognitive self-statements in depression: development of an Automatic Thoughts Questionnaire. **Cognitive Therapy and Research, 4,** 383-395

HOMME, L.E. (1965) Perspectives in mythology XXIV. Control of coverants, the operants of the mind. **Psychological Record, 15,** 501-511

ISEN, A.M. Shalker, T.E., CLARK, M. and KARP, L. (1978) Affect, accessibility of material in memory, and behaviour. A cognitive loop? **Journal of Personality and Social Psychology, 36,** 1-12

KANFER, F.H. (1970) Self-regulation. Research issues and speculations. In: C. Neuringer and J.L. Michael (eds) **Behaviour Modification in Clinical Psychology.** New York: Appleton-Century-Crofts

KENDALL, P.C. and FINCH, A.J. (1979) Developing non-impulsive behaviour in children. In: P.C. Kendall and S.D. Hollon (eds) **Cognitive-Behavioural Interventions. Theory, Research and Procedures.** 37-79. New York: Academic Press

KENDALL, P.C. and HOLLON, S.D. (1979) **Cognitive Behavioural Interventions. Theory, Research and Procedures.** New York: Academic Press

KLEIN, D.C., FENCIL-MORSE, E. and SELIGMAN, M.E.P. (1976) Learned helplessness, depression and the attribution of failure. **Journal of Personality and Social Psychology, 33,** 508-516

KLEIN, D.C. and SELIGMAN, M.E.P. (1976) Reversal of performance deficits and perceptual deficits in learned helplessness and depression. **Journal of Abnormal Psychology, 85,** 11-26

KUIPER, N.A. (1978) Depression and causal attribution for success and failure. **Journal of Personality and Social Psychology, 36,** 236-246

KOVACS, M. and BECK, A.T. (1978) Maladaptive cognitive structure in depression. **American Journal of Psychiatry, 135,** 525-535

LAZARUS, A.A. (1971) **Behavior Therapy and Beyond.** New York: McGraw-Hill

LAZARUS, R.S. (1966) **Psychological Stress and the Coping Processes.** New York: McGraw-Hill

LLOYD, G.G. and LISHMAN, A.A. (1975) Effect of depression on the speed of recall of pleasant and unpleasant experiences. **Psychological Medicine, 5,** 173-180

LURIA, A. (1963) Psychological studies of mental deficiency in the Soviet Union. In: N.R. Ellis (ed.) **Handbook of Mental Deficiency.** New York: McGraw-Hill

McGUIRE, W.J. (1968) Theory of the structure of human thought. In: R.P. Abelson, E. Aronson, W.J. McGuire, T.M. Newcomb, M.J. Rosenberg and P.H. Tannenbaum (eds) **Theories of Cognitive Consistency. A Source Book.** 140-162. Chicago: Rand McNally

McLEAN, P.D. and HAKATIAN, A.R. (1979) Clinical depression. Comparative efficacy of outpatient treatments. **Journal of Consulting and Clinical Psychology, 47,** 818-836

MAHONEY, M.J. (1974) **Cognition and Behaviour Modification.** Cambridge Mass: Ballinger Publishing Co

MAHONEY, M.J. and ARNKOFF, D.B. (1978) Cognitive and self control therapies. In: S.L. Garfield and A.E. Bergin (eds) **Handbook of Psychotherapy and Behavior Change.** 689-722. Chichester: Wiley

MANLY, P.C., McMAHON, R.J., BRADLEY, C.F. and DAVIDSON, P.O. (1982) Depressive attributional style and depression following childbirth. **Journal of Abnormal Psychology, 91,** 245-254

MEICHENBAUM, D.H. (1977) **Cognitive Behaviour Modification. An Integrative Approach.** New York: Plenum Press

MEICHENBAUM, D.H. and GOODMAN, J. (1971) Training impulsive children to talk to themselves. A means of developing self-control. **Journal of Abnormal Psychology, 77,** 115-126

MURPHY, G.E., SIMONS, A.D., WETZEL, R.D. and LUSTMAN, P.J. (1984) Cognitive therapy and phamacotherapy. **Archives of General Psychiatry, 41,** 33-41

NEISSER, U. (1967) **Cognitive Psychology.** New York: Appleton-Century-Crofts

NEKANDA-TREPKA, C.J.S., BISHOP, S. and BLACKBURN, I.M. (1983) Hopelessness and depression. **British Journal of Clinical Psychology, 22,** 49-60

NELSON, R.E. (1977) Irrational beliefs in depression. **Journal of Consulting and Clinical Psychology, 45,** 1190-1191

NELSON, R.E. and CRAIGHEAD, W.E. (1977) Selective recall of positive and negative feedback, self-control behaviours and depression. **Journal of Abnormal Psychology, 86,** 379-388

NOVACO, R.W. (1976) The function and regulation of the arousal of anger. **American Journal of Psychiatry, 133,** 1124-1128

REHM, L.P. (1977) A self-control model of depression. **Behavior Therapy, 8,** 787-804

RUSH, A.J., BECK, A.T., KOVACA, M. and HOLLON, S.D. (1977) Comparative efficacy of cognitive therapy and pharmacotherapy in the treatment of depressed out-patients. **Cognitive Therapy and Research, 1,** 17-37

RUSH, A.J. and WATKINS, J.T. (1981) Group versus individual cognitive therapy. A pilot study. **Cognitive Therapy and Research, 5,** 95-103

RUSH, A.J. and GILES, D.E. (1982) Cognitive therapy. Theory and research. In: A.J. Rush (ed.) **Short-Term Psychotherapies for Depression.** Chichester: Wiley

SELIGMAN, M.E.P. (1975) **Helplessness.** San Francisco: Freeman

SELIGMAN, M.E.P. (1981) A learned helplessness point of view. In: L.P. Rehm (ed.) **Behaviour Therapy of Depression.** 123-141. New York: Academic Press

SELIGMAN, M.E.P., ABRAMSON, L.Y., SEMMEL, A. and VON BAEYER, C. (1979) Depressive attributional style. **Journal of Abnormal Psychology, 88,** 242-247

SHAW, B.F. (1977) Comparison of cognitive therapy and behaviour therapy in the treatment of depression. **Journal of Consulting and Clinical Psychology, 45,** 543-551

SIMONS, A.D., GARFIELD, S.L. and MURPHY, G.E. (1984) The process of change in cognitive therapy and pharmacotherapy for depression. **Archives of General Psychiatry, 41,** 45-51

SKINNER, B.F. (1945) The operational analysis of psychological terms. **Psychological Review, 52,** 270-277

SKINNER, B.F. (1969) **Contingencies of Reinforcement: A Theoretical Analysis.** New York: Appleton-Century-Crofts

TEASDALE, J.D. and BANCROFT, J. (1977) Manipulation of thought content as a determinant of mood and corrugator electromyographic activity in depressed patients. **Journal of Abnormal Psychology, 86,** 235-241

TEASDALE, J.D. and FOGARTY, S.J. (1979) Differential effects of induced mood on retrieval of pleasant and unpleasant events from episodic memory. **Journal of Abnormal Psychology, 88,** 248-257

TEASDALE, J.D. and TAYLOR, R. (1981) Induced mood and accessibility of memories: an effect of mood state or of mood induction procedure? **British Journal of Clinical Psychology, 20,** 39-48

TEASDALE, J.D. and FENNELL, M.J.V. (1982) Immediate effects on depression of cognitive therapy interventions. **Cognitive Therapy and Research, 6,** 343-351

THORESEN, L.E. and MAHONEY, M.J. (1974) **Behavioral Self-Control.** New York: Holt, Rinehart and Winston

TOLMAN, E.C. (1932) **Purposive Behavior in Animals and Men.** New York: Appleton-Century-Crofts

TURK, D.C. (1978) Cognitive-behavioral techniques in the management of pain. In: J.P. Forsyt and D.J. Rathjen (eds) **Cognitive Behavior Therapy: Research and Application.** New York: Plenum Press

VELTEN, E. (1968) A laboratory task for the induction of mood states. **Behaviour Research and Therapy, 6,** 473-482

WATSON, J.B. (1913) Psychology as the behaviorist views it. **Psycholoical Review, 20,** 158-177

WEINTRAUB, M., SEGAL, R.M. and BECK, A.T. (1974) An investigation of cognition and affect in the depressive experience of normal men. **Journal of Consulting and Clinical Psychology, 42,** 911

WEISSMAN, A. and BECK, A.T. (1978) Development and validation of the Dysfunctional Attitude Scale: a preliminary investigation. Paper presented at the Annual Meeting of the American Eductional Research Association, Toronto.

WENER, A.E. and REHM, L.P. (1975) Depressive Affect: a test of behavioral hypotheses. **Journal of Abnormal Psychology, 84,** 221-227

WILKINSON, I.M. and BLACKBURN, I.M. (1981) Cognitive style in depressed and recovered depressed patients. **British Journal of Clinical Psychology, 20,** 283-292

WOMEN AND MENTAL ILLNESS

Jennifer A. Williams

Mental illness in women has been studied with considerable enthusiasm over the last decade, and the intention here is to identify some of the key issues and debates which are energizing this inquiry. It will not be feasible to give due consideration to the ways in which this work is being translated into clinical practice (for example, Brodsky and Hare-Mustin, 1980), though clearly this a matter of considerable significance.

RATES OF MENTAL ILLNESS

This literature, which has flourished under the pervasive influence of feminism, is rooted in the observed over-representation of women in mental illness statistics. However, this phenomemon is neither as clear cut as it appears, nor is its interpretation as simple as some people are inclined to believe. The data which are the least contentious are those based on treatment rates. There is little doubt that women are more likely to receive in-patient mental hospital treatment than men, both in Britain (DHSS, 1980), and the United States (Gove, 1980). Furthermore, this excess of women seems to occur largely because they are more likely to be admitted for disorders with a neurotic or depressive component. Men, in turn, are more likely to be admitted for problems relating to drug and alcohol use, though not in sufficient numbers for this to result in a balanced equation. So, do these figures reflect a sex difference in mental health or a sex difference in the chance that people will be admitted to mental hospital?

To try to gauge the meaning of the sex differential in treatment statistics theorists have turned to community surveys of mental illness. Those who have collated the available findings agree that women report more symptoms than men, but don't agree on how this should be interpreted. Gove and Tudor (1973), for example, argue that as these findings corroborate treatment statistics, it is reasonable to assume that women are more vulnerable to mental illness than men. Other writers have countered this position by drawing attention to the fact that what is called mental illness in community surveys bears very little resemblance to the psychiatrically defined disorders which provide the structure for treatment statistics. This criticism is well grounded. Community studies rarely investigate the prevalence of psychosis and personality disorders, and often detect and quantify other symptoms which have a tenuous relationship with formal definitions of mental illness. This discrepancy seems to have arisen, as the Dohrenwends pointed out some time ago (1969), because of the methodology now being used in community studies. Data are typically self-reported and collected by questionnaire and this has placed limits on the symptoms and disorders receiving consideration. As a result, it is not possible to talk with any confidence about sex differences in the 'true' prevalence of mental illnesss. A more acceptable interpretation of these findings is that more women than men report the symptoms on which these studies concentrate.

On closer examination, therefore, there is more than one basic problem to be explained. Women's over-representation in treatment rates and in 'true' prevalence rates deserve to be regarded as separate issues. Data from both sources also permit a further phenomemon to be identified, which is that certain disorders and symptoms appear to be sex-typed. Now while some writers (for example, Dohrenwend and Dohrenwend, 1975) have argued that the origins of this sex-typed pattern is the only issue worth pursuing, there is little evidence that this advice has been taken seriously. First, the contemporary literature on women's specific vulnerability to depression is not juxtaposed by a similar consideration of men's specific vulnerability to disorders. Second, the broader issues of women's over-representation in both treatment rates and 'true' prevalence rates have commanded a good deal of attention.

APPROACHES

Workers in this field tend either to interpret women's over-representation in these figures as an artefact or as a real indication of the psychological vulnerability of women. Both perspectives have stimulated theory and research which have, not infrequently, acquired their own impetus and rationale. It is, therefore, not simply a matter of which approach is right, but what both can tell us. As the work to be discussed indicates, both may be needed to explain women's over-representation in these statistics, and also to unravel the more subtle connections between gender and mental illness. First to be examined will be the literature generated by the view that, contrary to the apparent findings, women are not more psychologically vulnerable than men.

THE EXCESS OF WOMEN IS AN ARTEFACT

1. The definition of mental illness

Writers who invoke this type of explanation draw our attention to the fact that definitions of mental illness are socially constructed. They then argue that how they are constructed is responsible for the observed preponderance of women in mental illness statistics. However, they arrive at this conclusion by different routes.

First, following the Dohrenwends (1969) it has been argued that the way in which mental illness is defined in community surveys favours the detection of symptoms of distress more common amongst women. It is noted that the sex-typing of symptoms and disorders has an important characteristic. Busfield (1982) summarizes this point, which has been made elsewhere (for example, Goldman and Ravid, 1980):

> The 'female' disorders are structured in relation to states that are essentially disturbing to the woman herself, whereas the 'male' disorders relate to what tends to be more disturbing to others than to the man himself. (p.118)

Hence, is argued, women predominate in community surveys because the methods invariably require that symptoms are self-defined and self-reported. Insofar as this analysis is correct, and it does have considerable substance, it suggests that theorists and researchers may be puzzling over only half a problem. If comparable data had been available on 'male' disorders and symptoms, they might now be trying to figure out why men appear especially vulnerable in this respect.

The second line of argument is more radical and has only been proposed in detail by a few writers (Busfield, 1982; Kaplan, 1983). The basic contention is that diagnostic categories have largely been constructed by men, who are more inclined to construe the ways that women respond to life's pressures as pathological. It is not suggested that this has affected the identification and conceptualization of all disorders, but that it has happened to a sufficient extent to explain a substantial proportion of the sex differential in mental health statistics. This thesis is therefore of relevance to the interpretation of both survey data and treatment statistics. But how is it to be supported? The typical strategy has been to draw attention to the fact that the criteria used to define certain diagnostic categories are weighted in favour of labelling women as psychiatrically disturbed or distressed.

Depression, hysteria, and certain personality disorders and sexual difficulties have been selected by these authors (Busfield, 1982; Kaplan, 1983), to make this point. Such analyses do not find ready acceptance in psychiatric circles, largely because of the disinclination to accept the basic assumption that diagnostic categories are socially constructed. The traditional view is that certain types of disorders exist, so if women report them more frequently that says something about women. The diagnostic system itself is beyond criticism. The predominance of men in several diagnostic categories is also used to directly oppose the suggestion that the system of classification is sex-biased (for example, Williams and Spitzer, 1983).

There is an apparent impasse: the data are equally amenable to interpretations from either of the positions outlined here. Furthermore, no attempts have as yet been made to resolve these matters by deriving testable hypotheses. However, there are several reasons for suspecting that the arguments proposed by Busfield (1982) and Kaplan (1983) are not fallacious. For example, the writings of historians in this field indicate that the psychiatric profession's involvement with women has often been excessive (for example, Ehrenreich and English, 1973; Lenanne and Lenanne, 1973). There has been a long-standing enthusiasm for identifying psychopathology in women, and this has been expressed in fanciful theories and dubious, if not pernicious, therapies. That this, as a number of writers have argued (Chesler, 1972; Bart and Scully, 1979), has been one of the institutionalized ways in which women have been kept in their place, does not seem implausible. This suggests an additional element which may be added to the argument that definitions of mental illness are sex-biased. More specifically, they may be biased in a way which supports rather than undermines the power differential between the sexes. If this is so, we might expect a reticence to label as pathological extreme forms of those specific behaviours which help preserve the dominance of men. There is some evidence which supports this notion. For example, both an excessive preoccupation with personal achievement (Unger, 1979), and emotional inexpressiveness (for example, Sattel, 1975), have been recognized as functional for preserving male power, but concomitantly dysfunctional for individuals and their relationships with others (Feldman, 1982). Nonetheless, these have not surfaced as clearly defined diagnostic categories in the psychiatric classification system. Rather, it is the behaviours associated with the ways that men fail to cope with the demands of their roles which are synthesized in psychiatric definitions of mental illness, such as alcohol and drug abuse, and personality disorders. Those that relate to an over-zealous search for dominance appear to be under-represented.

Attention is drawn to this specific debate, not because it is well established but because perhaps it should be. It is not necessary to assume that diagnostic categories are simply fabrications but that social processes can exert an influence on their construction. That these processes include those which maintain inequality between the sexes is a possibility worthy of consideration. Discussions which centre on definitons of mental illness are notoriously difficult and this may well be one of the reasons why they have largely been side-stepped in this literature.

In summary, the work considered here has identified two ways in which gender bias may have affected the definitions of mental illness and hence introduced a distortion into the statistics. First, it has been argued that the methods used in community studies have selectively drawn attention to psychological disorders and symptoms more common amongst women. This case appears to be well founded. Second, it has been argued that gender bias exists at a more fundamental level, and is built into the psychiatric classification system. This case, is less well developed and more difficult to test. However, the issue is central and the analyses sufficiently convincing to suggest that it should not be dismissed lightly. A further point to be drawn from both lines of argument is that because of the ways that gender bias is expressed in mental illness statistics, mental illness in men is currently being under-investigated. However, there are no grounds for assuming that in the absence of these possible artefacts the sexes would then be equally vulnerable to mental illness per se. While some writers believe this to be the case, this remains to be seen.

2. Diagnosis of mental illness

In contrast to the arguments outlined above, those considered here focus on the ways that definitions of mental illness are used rather than constructed.

The basic contention is that clinical judgements of mental health are affected by gender stereotypes in which beliefs about women's inferiority are embedded and that, as a result, women are more likely to be diagnosed as mentally ill (for example, Morgan, 1980). It is assumed, therefore, that clinicians unwittingly perpetuate the sexual status quo, though not all theorists who share this assumption believe it has the same clinical consequences. A counter thesis proposed by Tudor et al. (1977) and Rushing (1979) is that because men are accorded more status and power than women, any deviancy on their part is taken more seriously and judged more stringently. So, are clinicians more predisposed to diagnose women or to diagnose men as mentally ill? There is now a large body of research exploring a number of facets of clinical gender bias and, in principle, this should help resolve this debate.

The seminal study in this area is that carried out by Broverman et al. (1970). A sample of mental health professionals were asked to complete a bipolar adjective checklist which contained a number of items known to be stereotyped as masculine or feminine. They were then instructed to describe, using this checklist, one of the following: a mature, healthy, socially competent adult; a mature, healthy, socially competent woman; or a mature, healthy, socially competent man. Analysis of the data confirmed the expectation that clinical judgements would paralled sex-role stereotypes. Furthermore, while the concepts of a psychologically healthy man and a psychologically healthy adult were found to be similar, a psychologically healthy woman was perceived as significantly different from both these concepts. Although these findings have now been replicated, Whitley's (1979) careful examination of this series of studies suggests that until a number of methodological and interpretive points are adequatly dealt with, the findings of this research should be regarded as tentative.

Perhaps rather more important than whether clinicians have double standards of mental health for the sexes, is whether they actually use them. The studies exploring this possibility are legion, and reviewers of this work (for example, Davidson and Abramowitz, 1980; Whitley, 1979; Zeldow, 1978) concur that there is little to suggest the operation of sex bias of this or indeed any other sort. However, the status of these studies is questionable as they invariably use paper and pencil ratings derived from experimental studies that are far removed from the real business of clinical work. This criticism cannot be levelled at the small number of naturalistic studies which have used patients' records as their database. It is therefore of note that often these studies do report sex-effect, though not consistently nor in a way which is readily interpretable in terms of either argument under consideration here. Although some workers are doggedly refining their methods to sort out this confusion (for example, Abramowitz and Herrera, 1981) the currently available data are not good enough to sustain any pronouncement about the influence of clients' sex on clinical decision making. Nonetheless, those who theorize about this relationship are often inclined to take liberties with these research findings. For example, studies which suggest that clinicians might hold double standards are used both as support for the argument that clinical bias leads to an over-inclusion of women in treatment statistics (for example, Morgan, 1980) and as support for the argument that it leads to an over-inclusion of men (Tudor et al., 1977). In such instances, writers tend not to draw attention to the fact that available evidence does not, as yet, indicate that this attitudinal bias has any predictable effect on behaviour.

So, depending on the theoretical perspective adopted, women's lack of social status and resources can be argued to increase or decrease the likelihood they will be labelled as mentally ill. When the cumulative evidence is examined, there is little to support either of these two popular arguments, though it has been noted that there is a tendency for theorists to believe that this is the case. The debate is not closed and its resolution is likely, as Davidson and Abramowitz (1980) argue, to be contingent on much-needed innovation in the traditional research paradigms which have been used.

3. Sex differences in response to mental illness

There are now well documented differences between the sexes in psychological functioning and this has led to wide speculation that this might result in women appearing to be more vulnerable than men.

First, it has been argued that help-seeking comes more easily to women than to men. This has been derived on various grounds. For example, it is noted that women are taught to think of themselves as helpless (Chesler, 1972), and that whereas help-seeking is compatible with femininity, stoicism tends to be more compatible with masculinity (Phillips and Segal, 1969). However, while there is some evidence that the pathways to treatment are different for men and women (Horwitz, 1977; Tudor et al., 1977), this has not convincingly been shown to affect the actual likelihood of receiving treatment. The only study (Kessler et al., 1979) which has detected such an effect is limited in generalizability because of the population studied. Large scale surveys (Gove, 1978; Kessler et al., 1981) fail, when other variables are controlled, to find a sex difference in willingness to seek help. While these surveys have inevitable weaknesses, some of which are detailed by Kessler et al. (1981), it seems unlikely that this particular bias will emerge as a powerful explanation for the observed sex differential in treatment statistics.

A second explanation, which may need to be taken more seriously, argues that one of the reasons for women's over-representation in treatment statistics is that they are better able than men to recognize that they have a psychological problem. This is rooted in observation and research which suggest that women are more generally sensitive to emotional states of self and others. Now while this proposition has some face validity, it is not easy to test. Often there are no external criteria against which to judge the accuracy of a person's insight into their psychological state. Still, some headway has been made by researchers looking for patterns between different types of self-reported data. For example, Phillips and Segal (1969) inferred from their data that women had a greater readiness to detect signs of emotional distress, and Kessler et al. (1981) reached similar conclusions from the careful analysis of data from several large surveys. In the latter instance, the authors tentatively suggested that this might account for between 10 per cent and 28 per cent of the excess of women in treatment statistics. There is some indication, therefore, that this is a factor which needs to be taken seriously, and the findings of a small British study (Briscoe, 1982) add weight to this view. A further point needs to be made explicit. These studies only suggest that women may be more prepared to recognize diffuse feeling of distress; neither the arguments nor the findings pertain to any other psychological symptoms or syndromes. Women, it appears, may be more finely tuned to the symptoms and distress more common in their sex, in which case it is interesting to contemplate whether men show a comparable sensitivity to the symptoms and disorders more common in their sex.

There has been a long-standing speculation that psychological sex differences might explain the excess of women receiving clinical treatment and two popular explanations have been considered here. While current evidence does not rule out the possibility that there are sex differences in willingness to seek help, it seems unlikely that this will account for much of the variance in treatment rates. More convincing is the argument that women are better able, or more prepared, to define experienced distress as a psychological problem. Evidence suggests that this may be one of the reasons for their over-representation in the rates of 'female' disorders such as depression and anxiety. Such findings are provocative, though they should not be interpreted as an indication that women are more inclined to use all psychiatric constructs to give meaning to their behaviour and feelings.

4. Sex role effects on response to mental illness

A related form of analysis employs role concepts rather than psychological sex differences. It is proposed that certain characteristics of the female role make it easier for women to take advantage of clinical services. It has been suggested, for example, that women have time (or more flexible time) to engage in such activities, and that loss of household income is less likely to be a deterrent in their case (Nathanson, 1975). To date, the influence of these factors on seeking clinical help does not appear to have been systematically examined. However, as this type of analysis has also been invoked to explain women's greater use of the health services per se (Waldron, 1983), future development may well take place in this literature.

5. Summary

The findings from this literature are perhaps less conclusive than it is ofter assumed. However, there are interesting patterns which are amenable to tentative interpretation. It seems that, while sex may predict how people get to treatment and perhaps what happens when they get there, these factors do not produce strong artefacts in treatment rates, though quite clearly these issues deserve consideration in their own right. Less easy to rule out is the possibility of gender bias at a more fundamental level. The association between women and mental illness appears, in several ways, to be contrived. There is some indication that the psychiatric profession is more inclined to attribute pathology to the experiences and behaviour of women. This association is then amplified by community surveys which tend to focus on the prevalence of symptoms and disorders which are common among women. Finally, by their greater readiness to identify these symptoms, women make their own contribution to establishing this relationship. If this interpretation is valid, it suggests that the important question may not be whether women's over-representation in mental illness statistics is an artefact, but why mental illness in women has been singled out for such attention. It may well be fruitful, as some of the work discussed here indicates, to look for answers to this question in the dynamics of the relationship between the sexes. Currently, the majority of people working in this field do not appear inclined to ponder such issues. They have the bit firmly betwen their teeth: why, they ask, are women more vulnerable to mental disorders?

THE EXCESS OF WOMEN IS REAL

While it has been suggested that women's structural position in society may be one of the reasons why they continue to be bonded to the category of mental illness, this position may in itself take a toll on their mental health. If this is the case, it should be evident in the flurry of research into the origins of women's psychological well-being. This literature, to which Al-Issa's (1980) book provides a useful introduction, is too extensive to be dealt with here in any depth. However, it is possible to identify a number of themes and engage in some reflection on the findings that have emerged. Two major quests have dominated this literature. One has been directed to identifying which aspects of women's lives affect their mental health, and the other to finding out what it is about being a woman that might predispose them to mental illness. Though these inquiries are sometimes pursued in tandem (for example, Radloff and Rae, 1979), they are sufficiently distinct to be discussed separately.

1. Women's home roles

Gove (1972) was one of the first people to identify women's home roles as an important area for study and continues to be the main protagonist in this field. Before considering his work, it is necessary to note that this author conceptualizes mental illness in a particular way. In the original (Gove, 1972a) and subsequent papers (for example, Gove, 1979a, 1980) a precise definition of mental illness has consistently been advocated on the grounds that not all people who receive psychiatric treatment are mentally ill. Gove favours the following definition of mental illness:

> A disorder that involves personal discomfort (as indicated by distress, anxiety, depression, etc...) and/or mental disorganization (as indicated by confusion, thought blockage, motor retardation, and in the most extreme cases by hallucinations or delusions) that is not caused by organic or toxic conditions. (Gove, 1979a, p.24)

Excluded from consideration are disorders such as acute and chronic brain disorders, personality disorder, and problems relating to alcohol and drug abuse. These, Gove argues, have become labelled as mental illness as a result of an 'historical accident and the successful entrepreneurship of the psychiatric profession' (Gove, 1980, p.347). On the basis of the earlier discussion, it should be evident that this definition is female-orientated. A point which has now been made by a number of writers (for example, Dohrenwend and Dohrenwend, 1975, 1977; Johnson, 1980). It needs to be borne in mind, therefore, that research employing this definition may underestimate the detrimental effects that men's lives have on their mental health. That said, how has Gove's exploration into the relationship between women's home roles and this specific range of psychological disorders been conducted, and what can we gather from it?

In the article published in 1972, Gove speculated that the apparently higher treated and untreated rates of mental illness in women might be causally related to psychogenic aspects of women's marital roles in modern industrial society. Several reasons were offered for advancing this proposition. First, it was noted that women are typically restricted to one major societal role, that of housewife, whereas men usually have both a home and a work role. It was argued that this might make it more difficult for women to attain a satisfactory identity and self esteem. Attention was then directed to what was perceived as the common denominator in women's marital roles - the role of housewife. It was suggested that because this role has a low ascribed status and does not fully utilize the competencies of modern women, that is has potential to generate frustration. The lack of formal structure and the invisibility of this role were also argued to create a 'breeding ground' for psychological difficulties. While it was recognized by Gove that many women supplement this role with paid work outside the home, it was argued that the potential psychological advantages accrued were offset by the fact that women's work roles were often of low status and in conflict with their home roles. Gove's specific gender-role theory contains a wealth of ideas about causal processes. While none are specified with sufficient clarity to be amenable to direct testing, this author has made several attempts to test predictions about their cumulative effects on women's mental health.

Initially, Gove supported his thesis by drawing attention to the historical patterning of mental illness in the sexes (Gove and Tudor, 1973). The comparative higher rate of mental illness in women after 1950 was argued to coincide with the time when the role of housewife changed and became less meaningful, less socially valued, and more stressful. However, interpreting historical data is a highly contentious business, and in this instance a lively debate ensued between these authors and the Dohrenwends (1975, 1977). Probably the most important criticism raised was that the observed increase in women's susceptibility to mental illness in the post-war period may well be a function of change in the method used to collect these data. It was at this time that self-report questionnaires became a popular means for estimating the 'true' prevalence of mental illness, a method which has been noted earlier to favour the inclusion of women in statistics. Historical trends in community survey data, therefore, do not provide unequivocal support for Gove and Tudor's (1973) case.

Taking a different tack, Gove (1972) derived and tested predictions about sex and marital status effect on the incidence of mental illness. Although previous research had invariably found that married people had fewer psychological difficulties that the unmarried, it was proposed that this difference would be less discernible in women than men. Gove (1972) predicted that rates of mental illness in unmarried men and women would be the same, reflecting as assumed similarity in their social roles, and that the rates of mental illness in married women would be higher than those found in married men, reflecting the processes identified in his specific gender role-theory. Data were collated from published studies and the expected patterning was detected, with the exception that unmarried men tended to be more at risk than unmarried women. The author then concluded: 'it is the relatively high rates of mental illness in married women that account for the higher rates of mental illness among women' (Gove, 1972, p.34).

While this study has been well received and widely cited, there are grounds for suspecting that the findings may not have been appropriately interpreted. Fox's (1980) comments are particularly pertinent in this respect. He noted that the database for this study consisted primarily of treatment rates. This is important; it is widely recognized that treatment rates are multiply determined and are not the best means for testing aetiological theories of mental illness. Fox (1980) also drew attention to the fact that Gove's analyses lacked internal validity because he was unable to use the definition of mental illness which is specified in the theory. The same criticisms can also be made of a later study by Gove (1979b) which replicated the previously-found relationship between sex, marital status and mental illnes. It cannot be said that Gove has tested the specific gender-role theory in an entirely satisfactory manner. However, several community studies have now been carried out which permit these ideas to be examined more directly. Data from this source are better suited to examing aetiological theories than treatment rates, and also provide a closer approximation to Gove's conceptualization of mental illness. Three such surveys are examined by Fox (1980), and to these can be added several further studies (Bebbington et al., 1981; Cochrane and Stopes-Roe 1981; Warheit et al., 1976). With the exception of Bebbington et al. (1981), the findings do not support Gove's theory. Women are found to have higher rates of symptoms than men in all marital status categories.

A number of tentative conclusions can be drawn from this examination of the merits of Gove's specific gender-role theory. First, it has received little support from the analysis of 'true' prevalence data. This suggests that women's susceptibility to these particular symptoms is not located precisely in the psychogenic aspects of their marital role. Second, while the predicted effects have been detected in the patterning of treatment rates, the lack of concordance between these findings and those reported in community surveys suggests that they are not explicable in terms of the specific gender-role theory. Indeed given the discrepancy between Gove's exclusive definition of mental illness and the inclusive psychiatric definiton on which these treatment statistics were based, it would have been less surprising if the predicted pattern had not been found in treatment rates. Third, while Gove's theory may not have been supported, it appears to have identified an interesting phenomenon: being married seems to increase the chance that women will receive treatment for mental illness. Cochrane and Stopes-Roe (1981) observing a similar pattern in the data from their study, consider that this might reflect the fact that wives are more able to look after psychologically distressed husbands than vice versa. However, neither this nor any other intepretation appears to have been directly examined. Finally, the overall conclusion to be reached is that despite the plausibility of the specific gender-role theory, by itself it is not sufficient to explain women's preponderance in mental illness statistics.

2. Other aspects of women's lives

Marital status has continued to be included in the search for the parameters of women's mental health, though changes are taking place in how researchers are exploring its effects. It has become less common for this single variable to be the focus of inquiry, and it is now included in analyses with a variety of other possible predictors. The net has been cast wide in the search to identify further factors. In contradistinction to this particular growth industry, mental illness itself has received less attention. Typically, operational definitions of mental illness have continued to be employed in studies, and researchers often freely admit that the relationship betwen their measures and psychiatrically defined disorders is an unknown quantity. So while many studies now report significant connections between characteristics of women's lives and depressive symptoms, it is often difficult to know what these mean. Such symptoms are not only quite mundane but are also common to many different types of psychological disorders. Bearing in mind this interpretive problem, some brief comments on recent developments in this field will now be made.

Amongst the variables currently under investigation, those that have received the most attention include: employment status (for example, Krause, 1984); social class (for example, Brown and Harris, 1978); marital status (for example, Bebbington et al., 1981); and the number and ages of children at home (for example, Gove and Geerken, 1977). There are also signs of an emerging interest in social support (for example, Roberts et al., 1982) and life stress (for example, Stewart and Salt, 1981). In the main, studies which have examined these variables singly tend to report contrary findings. It is, for example, hard to decide on balance whether women who are not in paid employment are more psychologically vulnerable than those who are (Roberts et al., 1982). Studies which take a multivariate approach tend to yield more interesting and persuasive results. The work described below serves to illustrate this point.

Warr and Parry (1982a) have reviewed, from a fairly critical position, the research on women's employment status and mental health. They argue that future analyses need to take account of both the quality of women's employment relationship and the quality of their non-occupational environment. The support they offer for the latter point is particularly interesting. Their secondary analysis of data from other sources (Brown and Harris, 1978; Bebbington et al., 1981) indicates that employment is a stronger predictor of psychological well-being in working class compared to middle class women. These findings also support their more specific proposition that employment is more likely to be psychologically beneficial for women whose non-occupational environment is adverse. This and a further study (Warr and Parry, 1982b) indicate that their perspective may have a useful contribution to make to this particular inquiry.

A number of studies have also identified women who have young children at home as a high risk group (for example, Ensel, 1982; Radloff, 1975), and that this risk may be amplified by low socio-economic status (Brown and Harris, 1978; Cleary and Mechanic, 1983). Now while this is often taken as a salutary reminder of the difficulties of child-rearing in modern society, the authors of one study reach a different conclusion. The statistical model Bebbington et al. (1981) applied to their data led them to conjecture that having children living at home may not directly affect women's mental health, but that children make it more difficult for women to gain psychological benefits from going out to work. A more recent study (Krause, 1984) also did not find that young children at home directly affected women's mental health, but did find that dissatisfaction with child care was a predictor of depression. This author (Krause, 1984) argues that future research needs to give precedence to women's attitudes towards their children. These different findings, interpretations, and analyses convey the complexity of the causal processes awaiting investigation. Certainly, on the basis of clinical observation (for example, Maracek and Ballou, 1981), it would seem ill-advised to treat lightly the difficulties entailed in bearing and rearing children.

It is not easy to piece together a coherent picture from this now extensive literature exploring the relationship between women's lives and their mental health. This may be explicable in terms of the developmental stage of this work. It is, for example, at the difficult point of shifting from the use of single to multiple variables and, as yet, no agreement has emerged about which variables should be investigated and in what way. This appparent confusion may also be a function of the way in which this enterprise is being conducted. It was noted earlier that in these studies mental illness is often estimated in a cursory fashion, and implicit in this is a disinterest in the aetiology of psychological symptoms and disorders. With few exceptions (Brown and Harris, 1978; Radloff and Rae, 1981), researchers in this area have not drawn on what is known about the origins of psychological disorders to help them identify potentially psychogenic characteristics of women's lives. The preference has been for empiricism. As a result, a large body of findings has been generated, which lacks internal consistency and offers few insights into the nature and direction of causal processes.

Although the research on women and mental illness is dominated by a concern to identify the aetiological factors that are embedded in women's lives and roles, this does not constitute the only perspective. There has been a concomitant interest in what it is about being female that might increase women's vulnerability to mental illness. Important strands of this particular inquiry will now be identified.

3. Femininity

The feminist movement has injected new life into the study of psychological differences between the sexes, and theorists and researchers concerned about the mental health of women have both drawn from this literature and contributed to its development.

One way in which both lay people and psychologists differentiate between the sexes is in terms of the personality traits of masculinity and feminity. This is only an approximation to reality, and there is now ample evidence (Bem, 1981; Spence and Helmreich, 1978) that members of both sexes can be feminine, or masculine, or various admixtures of both. This realization has prompted researchers to re-examine previously-assumed relationsips between biological sex, sex-typed traits, and mental health. Their work may therefore help to clarify the relationship between femininity and mental health. For example, does the cluster of characteristics which are normative for women lie at the root of their psychological vulnerability?

From major reviews of this literature (Whitley, 1983; Worrell, 1978) it does not appear that feminine traits are an important determinant of the mental health of either women or men. In contrast, for both sexes, masculine traits appear to have a strong positive association with mental health. On face value, women seem relatively disadvantaged by the characteristics considered to be normal in their sex. However, the authors of these reviews, quite reasonably, urge us not to jump to such conclusions. They draw attention to fairly serious methodological problems in this field, including the lack of independence in the measures, and the use of self-reports. It seems appropriate, therefore, to await further developments in this field. This particular inquiry also needs to be supplemented by other considerations.

Following Bakan (1966) it is now recognized that the identities of the sexes not only differ in content but have different sources. Whereas identity for women is primarily derived communally, that is in relationship with others, for men it is primarily derived agentically, that is by differentiating the self from others. This implies that identities structured in these ways are likely to come under threat for different reasons and that the coping strategies used may also be different. This type of analysis may well prove central to understanding the much neglected issue of the sex-typing of specific symptoms and disorders in both women and men. As yet, it is not well established in this field and has primarily been limited to exploring women's particular vulnerability to depressive symptoms. For example, depression in women has been linked to problems in sustaining an other-oriented identity at different stages of life (Bart, 1971), and in different historical periods (Bernard, 1976).

4. Power and status

Most of the literature discussed so far has been concerned with the ways that the sexes are differentiated socially and psychologically and how this might explain women's apparent vulnerability to mental illness. The mental health implications of the stratification of the sexes in society have received little direct attention. Exceptions to this will now be examined.

Interestingly, it is clinical writers who have directed attention most forcefully to the mental health implications of sexual inequality. As these writers probably have the best empirical data at hand, it can be considered unfortunate that their theorizing has exerted little influence on the research literature. Those working from a psychodynamic perspective have been especially concerned to delineate problems arising from inequality between the sexes. Analyses have now been derived from a number of different models of the ways that intrapsychic processes reproduce and are shaped by male dominance (for example, Chodorow, 1978; Dinnerstein, 1978; Eichenbaum and Orbach, 1982). Related, but less well developed analyses have also been offered by theorists working from intergroup (for example, Miller, 1971) and family (for example, Lerner, 1983) perspectives. The work generated by these different levels of theorizing is exerting considerable influence on clinical practice (Llewelyn and Osborn, 1983) but has yet to make its mark on the research literature. This may partly reflect difficulties in adequately testing many of these formulations within conventional research paradigms. Certainly, the only clinically inspired theorizing on the mental health implications of sexual inequality to receive empirical examination is that which is particularly amenable to investigation using the classical experimental method. This work accords importance to cognitive processes and it is its potential to explain women's vulnerability to depression that is receiving most attention. This approach and its development will now be broadly described.

Reviewing the research on the causes of depression, Weissman and Klerman (1977) suggested that sexual inequality might be one of the factors contributing to women's vulnerability to this disorder. They argued that women's position in society has the potential to engender feelings of helplessness and hopelessness, which are the precursors of depression. This analysis has now been adopted and elaborated by Radloff and her colleagues (for example, Radloff and Rae, 1981; Radloff and Monroe, 1978) who have used the sex role literature to identify a number of ways in which women learn to be helpless. They also draw attention to the various links that are now being made betwen helplessness, perceived lack of power, and depression. These links, in which attributions and beliefs play a central role, have achieved some respectability in experimental studies (for example Abramson et al., 1978). The potential of this analysis to explain women's vulnerability to negative affective states, and depression specifically, has also received some empirical support (for example, Baucom, 1983; Horowitz, 1982; Warren and McEachren, 1983). While this enquiry is still in its youth, it does illustrate two important points. First, that it is both appropriate and necessary to consider the relationship between sexual inequality and women's mental health. Typically, this has been disregarded in theory and research which taken women's roles and traits as units of analyses. Second, that there are theories that can help advance this field, and that it is by default that empiricism has been favoured. In the work described above, for example, theories of depression and women's psychological development have been integrated to prescribe the issues that require empirical investigation.

Whilst there are no definitive answers to what it is about being a women that increases vulnerability to mental illness, there are some clues. It has yet to be proven to satisfaction that feminine traits are intrinsically problematic for women, and perhaps the question that needs to be asked is under what circumstances do these, or indeed any other combination of sex-typed traits, militate against psychological health. The trait approach may provide some insights but it leaves untouched the dynamics of women's self-definition in society and the difficulties this entails. This is familiar ground for identity theorists, and there are indications that their work on the structure and source of identity provides a stronger platform for exploring the social origins of women's mental health. Finally, there is a growing interest in relating psychological distress in women to sexual inequality. That women's structural position in society is causally related to their vulnerablity to depression has been well argued, and receives some empirical support. In view of this it may well be time to broaden the focus and systematically examine whether this type of analysis can help explain the sex-typing of other disorders and symptoms.

5. Summary

The literature considered here amply illustrates the complexity of the issues under consideration. The aetiological role of gender in the development and manifestation of psychological distress in women is not going to be pinned down easily. Although gereralizations are often well received, on closer examination they invariably need qualification, or are not substantiated. It has also been noted throughout this discussion that the difficulties of the subject matter are often compounded by the way investigations are conducted. Conceptual and methodological problems remain unresolved, and the elected a-theoretical stance of many researchers has done little to advance this field.

CONCLUSION

Within its own frame of reference the study of women and mental illness appears legitimate. Nonetheless, there is reason for disquiet. From this examination of the literature, it is evident that at all decision points attention has not been given to issues concerning men's mental health. Now, at this juncture, a plea could be made for an equivalent exploration of the psychological problems of men; that is not my intention. Rather, I consider it more important to reflect upon why women have become the 'identified patient' in the social system. I suggest that when 'women have problems', the problems in the social system itself are not singled out for attention. In short, it is functional for the sexual status quo. Furthermore, I would argue that the fundamental problem of this system that needs to be acknowledged in this field is its inequality. To date, theorists and researchers have been reluctant to examine directly how inequality affects women's mental health. While this constitutes one area for future development, a different type of inquiry can be advocated on the basis of the analysis offered here. I would argue that attention needs to be given to the processes which operate to maintain and change the essentially irrational system of sexual inequality, and the ways in which they affect the mental health of both women and men. This would require a shift of focus from women to the relationships between women and men, and from conceptualizing power and status as static variables to conceptualizing them as dynamic processes central to these relationships. In this event, there are literatures which are pertinent to this inquiry. Family process and system theorists, though they have demonstrated little interest in sex and gender, have concepts and methods for exploring the psychogenic properties of micro-systems (for example, Gurman and Kniskern, 1981). Theorists concerned with the dynamics of the social arrangement between the sexes (for example, Williams and Giles, 1978; Williams, 1984) also offer a level of analysis which is vital to this enterprise. Their work can help us to understand the processes which have sustained, and no doubt will continue to sustain, the strong association between women and mental illness.

REFERENCES

ABRAMOWITZ, W.I. and HERRERA, H.R. (1981) On controlling for patient psychopathology in naturalistic studies of sex bias: a methodological demonstration. **Journal of Consulting and Clinical Psychology, 49,** 597-603

ABRAMSON, L.Y., SELIGMAN, M.E.P. and TEASDALE, J.D. (1978) Learned helplessness in humans: Critique and reformulation. **Journal of Abnormal Psychology, 87,** 49-74

AL-LSSA, I. (1980) **The Psychopathology of Women.** Englewood Cliffs, New Jersey: Prentice-Hall

BAKEN, D. (1966) **The Duality of Human Existence.** Chicago: Rand McNally

BART, P.B. (1971) Depression in middle-aged women. In: V. Gornick and B.K. Moran (eds) **Woman in Sexist Society.** New York: Basic Books

BART, P.B. and SCULLY, D.H. (1979) The politics of hysteria: a case of the wandering womb. In: E.S. Gomberg and V. Franks (eds) **Gender and Disordered Behaviour: Sex Differences in Psychopathology.** New York: Brunner/Mazel

BAUCOM, D.H. (1983) Sex role identity and the decision to regain control among women: a learned helplessness investigation. **Journal of Personality and Social Psychology, 44,** 334-353

BEBBINGTON, P., HURRY, J., TENNANT, C., STURT, E. and WING, J.K. (1981) Epidemiology of mental disorders in Camberwell. **Pschological Medicine, 11,** 561-579

BECK, A.T. and GREENBERG, R.L. (1974) Cognitive therapy with depressed women. In: V. Franks and V. Burtle (eds) **Women in Therapy: Psychotherapies for a Changing Society.** New York: Brunner/Mazel

BEM, S.L. (1981) **Bem Sex-Role Inventory.** Palo Alto, Cal.: Consulting Psychologists Press

BERNARD, J. (1976) Homosociality and female depression. **Journal of Social Issues, 32,** 213-238

BRISCOE, M. (1982) Sex difference in psychological well-being. **Psychological Medicine. Monograph Supplement 1**

BRODSKY, A.M. and HARE-MUSTIN, R.T. (1980) **Women and Psychotherapy: An Assessment of Research and Practice.** New York: Guildford Press

BROVERMAN, I., BROVERMAN, D.M., CLARKSON, I.E., ROSENKRANTZ, P.S. and VOGEL S.R. (1970) Sex role stereotypes and clinical judgements of mental health. **Journal of Consulting and Clinical Psychology, 34,** 1-7

BROWN, G.W. and HARRIS, T. (1978) **Social Origins of Depression: A Study of Psychiatric Disorder in Women.** London: Tavistock

BUSFIELD, J. (1982) Gender and mental illness. **International Journal of Mental Health, 11,** 46-66

CHESLER, P. (1972) **Women and Madness.** New York: Doubleday

CHODOROW, N. (1978) **The Reproduction of Mothering.** London: University of California Press

CLEARY, P.D. and MECHANIC, D. (1983) Sex differences in psychological distress among married people. **Journal of Health and Social Behaviour, 24,** 111-121

COCHRANE, R. and STOPES-ROE, M. (1981) Women, Marriage, employment, and mental health. **British Journal of Psychiatry, 139,** 373-381

DAVIDSON, C.V. and ABRAMOWITZ, S.I. (1980) Sex bias in clinical judgement: later empirical returns. **Psychology of Women Quarterly, 4,** 377-395

DHSS (1980) **Statistical and Research Report Series No. 23. In-patient Statistics from the Mental Health Enquiry for England** 1977. London: HMSO

DINNERSTEIN, D. (1978) **The Rocking of the Cradle.** London: Souvenir Press

DOHRENWEND, B.P. and DOHRENWEND, B.S. (1969) **Social Status and Psychological Disorder.** New York: Wiley

DOHRENWEND, B.P. and DOHRENWEND, B.S. (1975) Sex differences and psychiatric disorder. **American Journal of Sociology, 80,** 1447-1454

DOHRENWEND, B.P. and DOHRENWEND, B.S. (1977) Reply to Gove and Tudor's comment on 'sex differences and psychiatric disorders'. **American Journal of Sociology, 82,** 1336-1345

EHRENREICH, B. and ENGLISH, D. (1973) **Complaints and Disorders.** New York: Feminist Press

EICHENBAUM, L. and ORBACH, S. (1982) **Outside In Inside Out. Women's Psychology: A Feminist Psychoanalytic Approach.** Harmondsworth: Penguin

ENSEL, W.M. (1982) The role of age in the relationship of gender and marital status to depression. **Journal of Nervous and Mental Disease, 170,** 536-543

FELDMAN, L.B. (1982) Sex roles and family dynamics. In: F. Walsh (ed.) **Normal Family Processes.** London: Guilford Press

FOX, J.W. (1980) Gove's specific sex-role theory of mental illness: a research note. **Journal of Health and Social Behaviour, 21,** 260-267

GOLDMAN, N. and RAVID, R. (1980) Community surveys: sex differences in mental illness. In: M. Guttentag, S. Salasin, D. Belle (eds) **The Mental Health of Women.** London: Academic Press

GOVE, W.R. (1972) Sex roles, marital roles and mental illness. **Social Forces, 51,** 34-44

GOVE, W.R. (1978) Sex differences in mental illness among adult men and women: an evaluation of four questions raised regarding the evidence on the higher rates of women. **Social Science and Medicine, 12B,** 187-198

GOVE, W.R. (1979a) Sex differences in the epidemiology of mental disorders: evidence and explanations. In: E.S. Gomberg and V. Franks (eds) **Gender and Disordered Behaviour: Sex Differences in Psychopathology** New York: Brunner/Mazel.

GOVE, W.R. (1979b) Sex, marital status, and psychiatric treatment: a research note. **Social Forces, 58,** 89-93

GOVE, W.R. (1980) Mental illness and psychiatric treatment among women. **Psychology of Women Quarterly, 4,** 345-362

GOVE, W.R. and GEERKEN, M.R. (1977) The effects of children and employment on the mental health of married men and women. **Social Forces, 56,** 66-76

GOVE, W.R. and TUDOR, J.F. (1973) Adult sex roles and mental illness. **American Journal of Sociology, 78,** 812-835

GURMAN, A.S. and KNISKERN, D.P. (1981) **Handbook of Family Therapy.** New York: Brunner/Mazel

HORWITZ, A.V. (1977) The pathways into psychiatric treatment: some differences between men and women. **Journal of Health and Social Behaviour, 18,** 169-178

HORWITZ, A.V. (1982) Sex-role expectations, power and psychological distress **Sex Roles, 8,** 607-623

JOHNSON, M. (1980) Mental illness and psychiatric treatment among women: a response. **Psychology of Women Quarterly, 4,** 363-371

KAPLAN, M. (1983) A woman's view of DSM-111. **American Psychologist, 38,** 786-792

KESSLER, R.C., BROWN, R.L. and BROMAN, C.L. (1981) Sex differences in psychiatric help-seeking: Evidence from four large-scale surveys. **Journal of Health and Social Behaviour, 22,** 49-64

KESSLER, R.C., REUTER, J.A. and GREENLEY, J.R. (1979) Sex differences in the use of psychiatric outpatients facilities. **Social Forces, 58,** 557-571

KRAUSE, N. (1984) Employment outside the home and the women's psychological well-being. **Social Psychiatry, 19,** 41-48

LENNANE, M.B. and R.J. LENNANE (1973) Alleged psychogenic disorders in women - a possible manifestation of sexual prejudice. **New England Journal of Medicine, 288,** 1-13

LERNER, H.E. (1983) Female dependency in context: some theoretical and technical considerations. **American Journal of Orthopsychiatry, 53,** 697-705

LLEWELYN, S. and OSBORN, K. (1983) Women as clients and therapists. In: D. Pilgrim (ed.) **Psychology and Psychotherapy: Current Trends and Issues.** London: Routledge and Kegan Paul

MARACEK, J. and BALLOU, D.J. (1981) Family roles and women's mental health. **Professional Psychology, 12,** 39-46

MILLER, J.B. (1971) Psychological consequences of sexual inequality. **American Journal of Orthopsychiatry, 41,** 767-775

MORGAN, C.S. (1980) Female and male attitudes towards life: implications for theories of mental health. **Sex Roles, 6,** 367-380

NATHANSON, C.A. (1975) Illness and the feminine role: a theoretical review. **Social Science and Medicine, 9,** 57-62

PHILLIPS, D. and SEGAL, B. (1969) Sexual status and psychiatric symptoms. **American Sociological Review, 34,** 58-72

RADLOFF, L.S. (1975) Sex differences in depression: the effects of occupation and marital status. **Sex Roles, 1,** 249-266

RADLOFF, L.S. and MONROE, M.M. (1978) Sex differences in helplessness: With implications for depression. In: L.S. Hanson and R.S. Rapoza (eds) **Career Development and Counselling of Women.** Springfield, Illinois: Charles Thomas

RADLOFF, L.S. and D.S. RAE (1979) Susceptibility and precipitating factors in depression: sex differences and similarities. **Journal of Abnormal Psychology, 82,** 174-181

RADLOFF, L.S. and RAE, D.S. (1981) Components of sex differences in depression. **Research in Community & Mental Health, 2,** 111-137

ROBERTS, C.R., ROBERTS, R.E., and STEVENSON, J.M. (1982) Women, work, social support and psychiatric morbidity. **Social Psychiatry, 17,** 167-173

RUSHING, W.A. (1979) The functional importance of sex roles and sex-related behaviour in societal reactions to residual devaints. **Journal of Health and Social Behaviour, 20,** 208-217

SATTEL, J.W. (1975) The inexpressive male: tragedy or sexual politics? **Social Problems, 23,** 469-477

SPENCE, J.T. and HELMREICH, R. (1978) **The Psychological Dimensions of Masculinity and Femininity: Their Correlates and Antecedents.** Austin: University of Texas Press

STEWART, A.J. and SALT, P. (1981) Life stress, life styles, depression, and illness in adult women. **Journal of Personality and Social Psychology, 40,** 1063-1069

TUDOR, W., GOVE, W.R. and TUDOR, J. (1977) The effect of sex role differences on the social control of mental illness. **Journal of Health and Social Behaviour, 18,** 98-112

UNGER, R. (1979) The politics of gender. In: **Female and Male: Psychological Perspectives.** London: Harper Row

WALDRON, I. (1983) Sex differences in illness incidence, prognosis and mortality: issues and evidence. **Social Science and Medicine, 17,** 1107-1123

WARHEIT, G.J., HOLZER, C.E., BELL, R.A. and AREY, S.A. (1976) Sex, marital status, and mental health: a reappraisal. **Social Forces 55,** 459-470

WARR, P. and PARRY, G. (1982a) Paid employment and women's psychological well-being. **Psychological Bulletin, 91,** 498-516

WARR, P. and PARRY, G. (1982b) Depressed mood in working-class mothers with and without paid work. **Social Psychiatry, 17,** 161-165

WARREN, L.W. and McEACHREN, L. (1983) Psychosocial correlates of depressive symptomatology in women. **Journal of Abnormal Psychology, 92,** 151-160

WEISSMAN, M.M. and KLERMAN, G.L. (1977) Sex differences and the epidemiology of depression. **Archives of General Psychiatry, 134,** 98-111

WHITLEY, B.E. Jr (1979) Sex roles and psychotherapy: a current appraisal. **Psychological Bulletin, 86,** 1309-1321

WHITLEY, B.E. Jr (1983) Sex role orientation and self-esteem: a critical meta-analytic review. **Journal of Personality and Social Psychology, 44,** 765-778

WILLIAMS, J.A. (1984) Gender and intergroup behaviour: towards an integration. **British Journal of Social Psychology**

WILLIAMS, J.A. and GILES, H. (1978) The changing status of women in society. In: H. Tajfel (ed.) **Differentiation Between Social Groups: Studies in the Social Psychology of Intergroup Behaviour.** London: Academic Press

WILLIAMS, J.B.W. and SPITZER, R.L. (1983) The issue of sex bias in DSM-111. **American Psychological, 38,** 793-798

WORRELL, J. (1978) Sex roles and psychological well-being: perspectives on methodology. **Journal of Consulting and Clinical Psychology, 44,** 777-791

ZELDOW, R. (1978) Sex differences in psychiatric education and treatment. **Archives of General Psychiatry, 35,** 89-93

COUNSELLING PSYCHOLOGY

Stephen Murgatroyd

Counselling is defined variously in the psychological literature. Most definitions give emphasis to the attainment of personal growth objectives within the framework of the theory of self-actualization developed both by Maslow (1971) and Rogers (1957a). As an example, Arbuckle (1967) suggests that counselling is the process of 'assisting individuals towards responsible independence, development of maximum potentials, or self-actualization'. In addition, most definitions give emphasis to the importance of counselling as a process intended to enable change or development. Carl Rogers (1952) writes of counselling as 'the process by which the structure of the self is relaxed in the safety of the relationship with the counsellor, and previously denied experiences are perceived then integrated into an altered self'. Whilst some definitions give emphasis to the behavioural component of change and others place the emphasis upon the affective and cognitive components, these two features of counselling, personal growth and self-change, are common to almost all definitions.

In this chapter, as elsewhere (Murgatroyd, 1980a, 1983a), counselling is defined as those processes intended to 'enable an individual to make his/her own choices and live his/her own life without being more dependent than he/she wants to be upon the decisions of others'. It will be noted that this definition does not confine counselling to a one:one relationship between a counsellor and a client; nor does it imply that counselling is a soley psychological process. This definition enables counselling to be regarded as a term embracing the creation of social support networks, political actions intended to reduce dependence, or, self help activities conducted by a person seeking to become more independent of others or more like the self they wish to become. Whilst this concept of counselling is wider than many found in currently available standard texts, it does accurately reflect both general practice and the experience of counselling within organizations.

This definition of counselling suggests that a psychology of counselling will need to embrace the study of:

(a) the process of change in the person;
(b) the process of change in organizations;
(c) the necessary conditions for change and development;
(d) the processes by which personal and organizational change can be facilitated;
(e) the differences between individual and group-based counselling activity; and
(f) the extent to which counselling interventions can be effective under different conditions.

This emerging territory for psychological inquiry in Britain involves the psychologist in developing an understanding of personality theory, theories of interpersonal exchange, social psychology, organizational change and development and clinical psychology. Increasingly too, there is an interest in family therapy as a basis for counselling, especially in groups and in organizations.

These last remarks suggest another issue that needs to be addressed early in this chapter: what is the difference between counselling psychology and clinical psychology? Nelson-Jones (1982) observes that counselling takes place largely in non-medical settings with persons who are not severely disturbed. In contrast, a great deal of clinical psychology takes place in medical settings with a range of clients, some of whom are severely disturbed. In addition, counselling can be distinguished from clinical practice by its emphasis on well-being and personal development rather than on sickness or maladjustment. Finally, counselling is practised in a greater variety of settings - schools, industry, social organizations, community groups and organizations - and tends to be concerned with the whole person rather than specific aspects of that person's actions or behaviour. Whilst these differences do exist, in many cases they may be regarded as differences of degree or emphasis. In fact, there is a close relationship between clinical and counselling psychology. Perhaps the most significant difference concerns the professional recognition of clinical psychologists versus that of counselling psychologists: despite some recent attempts to change the situation, counselling psychology remains a sub-professional or para-professional activity.

Counselling psychology has a long history in America, Canada and Australia but is a relative newcomer to the psychological market-place in Britain. In part this is because the training of counsellors in Britain has taken place largely within departments of education in universities, polytechnics and colleges and in part because there is no single, structured career pattern for counselling psychologists in Britain. Counsellor education developed in the 1960s in Britain largely in response to the comprehensivization of schools. At this same time, social work education and the education of the clergy were also reviewed and counselling components began to appear. More recently, counselling skills have become a part of the initial training of general practitioners and nurses and there has been a significant growth in counselling training within the framework of in-service programmes for personnel managers in industry and in the provision of counselling services for participants of Manpower Services Commission schemes (especially the Youth Training Scheme). Most counselling skills training is, however, an adjunct or optional part of a training programme for some professional or para-professional activity.

Another reason for the late adoption of counselling psychology in Britain has been the absence of recognized professional bodies for counsellors. There are now several large counselling organizations, including the British Association for Counselling (BAC), the National Association of Counsellors in Education (NACE) and the British Psychological Society's Section of Counselling Psycholgy. None of these organizations has been able to impose training criteria for accreditation (though BAC is now seeking to do so), nor have they been able to establish and impose a code of conduct for counselling practice, though members of The British Psychological Society are bound by a code of conduct agreed by the Society. Indeed, unlike the situation in a great many other countries, the term 'counsellor' is not protected in law: anyone may establish themselves as a counsellor and advertise their services to the public. Whether or not this is a satisfactory state of affairs is an interesting question (Murgatroyd, 1983b); these circumstances do, however, help to explain the slow rate growth of counselling psychology in Britain.

KEY PSYCHOLOGICAL ISSUES

In a chapter of this kind it is not possible to review all of the features of counselling psychology which students are asked to consider in an optional programme of study. Some selection of issues is necessary. Here five topics are chosen since; (a) these represent the core psychological areas of concern to counselling psychology; and (b) an understanding of these areas is of importance to other issues in the field of counselling psychology. These five topics are:

1. What models of counselling intervention are available to

counselling psychologists to guide their thinking about the nature of intervention?

2. What are the necesary conditions for counselling?

3. What are the cognitive and social components of the counselling process?

4. How do different forms of counselling view the person?

5. What could studies of counsellor effectiveness tell us about counselling?

In a short chapter even these selected topics can only be briefly examined. More detailed consideration of these issues will be found in the books and papers referenced under each topic heading below.

MODELS OF INTERVENTION

As with psychotherapy and clinical psychology, counselling psychology takes a great many forms. Herink's (1980) 'Psychotherapy Handbook' briefly describes over 250 forms of therapy which could be regarded as descriptions of the variety of counselling interventions available. Since a great many counsellors describe themselves as eclectic (Garfield and Kurtz, 1974) the variety of forms of counselling practice is therefore considerable. The counselling psychologist needs to have some schema by which interventions can be classified.

One schema focuses upon the feature of the person to which the intervention is primarily addressed. For example, if the intervention is primarily concerned with the modification of behaviour then this is described as a behavioural intervention; in contrast, an intervention which seeks to unblock some emotional content is referred to as a cathartic intervention. Such models of intervention, advanced by Stewart (1983) amongst others, are weak in the sense that they tell us little about the style of the intervention since they concentrate upon the focus (behaviour, affect or cognition) for the intervention.

Heron (1976) suggests a six-fold classification of counsellor intervention which concentrates upon both the style and intention of the counsellor. These six categories are:

1. **Prescriptive:** giving advice, being judgemental. The counsellor seeks to direct the behaviour of the client, most especially that which occurs outside their own interaction.

2. **Informative:** being didactic, interpreting or giving instruction. The counsellor seeks to impart new information to clients which is intended to shape their subsequent behaviour, thoughts or feelings.

3. **Confronting:** giving direct feedback, challenging. The counsellor uses a variety of techniques to challenge the restrictive attitudes, values, behaviours, thoughts and/or feelings of the client so as to change these features of the person.

4. **Cathartic:** encouraging emotional discharge. The counsellor uses facilitative techniques to enable the client to release and directly experience emotion (sadness, joy, sorrow, etc.) hitherto kept 'locked' within them so that they may use this experience as a basis for personal growth and development.

5. **Catalytic:** being reflective, enabling self-direction. The counsellor encourages clients to take control of their own counselling programme by directing the attention of the counsellor to their needs and by negotiating a therapeutic contract in which rights and duties are clearly defined so that they may transfer these skills to other areas of their life.

6. **Supportive:** being approving, consolidating, suggesting organizational structures. The counsellor seeks to help the client accept their own development and create mutual support structures which are helpful to them so as to provide the basis for sustained growth and development.

These six categories of intervention are not a 'trait-like' classification of counselling as a process. They may be used to describe different phases of a counselling intervention. They may also be used to classify interventions which take place during a single session or across a fixed number of sessions. All are descriptions of counselling in action.

There are two groupings within these six categories. The first grouping (categories 1 to 3) can be described as **directive:** these interventions place the emphasis upon the counsellor's intervention and give the counsellor a significant role in determining both <u>what</u> happens and <u>how</u> it happens during counselling. The second grouping (categories 4 to 6) is more **facilitative:** there is a developing equality between the counsellor and the client and the concern is to encourage and enable clients to take control of their therapy as a basis for them taking control over their personal development outside therapy.

Whilst these categories have been available to counselling psychologists for some time, they are rarely used in studies of counselling orientation or process. More common are ad hoc classification systems. For example, Pallone and Di Bennardo (1967) classify careers counselling processes into one of four modes: (a) **interpretive;** (b) **interrogative;** (c) **reflective** and (d) **confrontative** during a series of five interviews with clients and showed that, overall, there was no change in counsellor intervention pattern across the five interviews. There is a considerable need for a classification system to be used systematically across a variety of counselling settings. That offered by Heron (1976) is a useful starting point.

Another starting point for the study of counselling orientation is the process rating scale offered by Hill (1978), similar in many ways to the classroom interaction scales of Flanders (1960) and Bales (1950). The Hill process orientation scale requires each statement made during a counselling session to be classified as belonging to one of 14 categories. These categories include **minimal encouragement, self-disclosure** and **reflection** . Research so far conducted with this process orientation schema shows its utility in both comparative studies (Hill, Thomas and Rardin, 1978) and in single case studies (Hill, Carter and O'Farrell, 1983). Its more widespread use in encoding the counselling process would be welcomed.

A final approach to the classification and study of counselling interventions is that offered by the psychotherapy orientation studies. Rating scales appropriate to clinical and counselling psychology and psychotherapy have been developed by Fey (1958), Rice et al. (1972), Sundland and Barker (1962), Wallach and Strupp (1964), Weissman, Goldschmid and Stein (1971) and Wile et al. (1970). Using rated attitude statements which are subsequently factor analysed, these scales seek to classify counsellors and therapists into categories based on their orientation towards key features of therapeutic practice. For example, Weissman, Goldschmid and Stein (1971) seek to classify counsellors into one of five categories (authoritarian, egalitarian, normalist, dogmatist or pragmatist) according to how they respond to such statements as: 'I use relaxation techniques', or: 'I plan activities for the patient'. These have been used extensively in studies of therapist orientation in America and Canada (see review by Sundland, 1977) but have yet to be used in Britain.

That the study of intervention processes is relevant to the psychology of counselling is clear from a number of studies of therapeutic outcome. Studies by Ashby et al. (1957) and by Friedman and Dies (1974) show that different styles of counselling (directive versus nondirective) affected different types of clients in different ways. Ashby and colleagues show that defensive clients increase their defensiveness when faced with a directive counsellor whilst clients matched for age, sex and degree of defensiveness were more self-disclosing and less defensive with a nondirective counsellor. Friedman and Dies show that clients with a high internal locus of control preferred and made progress in non-directive counselling whilst those who scored high on external control preferred and made more progress with directive counsellors. The orientation of the counsellor can thus be seen to be a contributory factor to the outcome of counselling (see also Heller, Myers and Kline, 1963; Parker, 1967).

NECESSARY CONDITIONS

Carl Rogers (1957b) a leading existential humanistic psychotherapist and counsellor, proposed that there were three necessary and sufficient conditions for effective counselling. These are:

Empathy. The ability to experience the phenomenological world of another person as if it were the counsellor's own world without losing the 'as if' quality.

Warmth. The ability to accept a person in need as a person in their own right without making this acceptance conditional upon some behavioural or attitudinal change.

Genuineness. The use of the counsellor's actual thoughts and feelings about the person in need as a basis for the counselling transaction rather than a set of skills or techniques simply acquired and 'turned on' for counselling purposes.

Fuller explanations of these conditions are given in Nelson-Jones (1982, pp.208ff). These three conditions are generally accepted as statements of some of the necessary conditions for effective counselling and therapy. They are similar in many respects to those proposed by Truax and Carkhuff (1967) and Leon Tyler (1969), though Carkhuff (1969) had suggested that there are three equally important conditions: **Concreteness** - working at the level of the client beginning with the client's presenting problem. **Immediacy** - focusing upon the 'here and now' rather than only on the past and the future. **Confrontation** - from the basis of warmth and genuineness, the counsellor is able to confront the client's defences, mismatches between talk and behaviour, or challenge irrational beliefs.

The addition of these three conditions by Carkhuff implies that Rogers' claim (based upon substantial empirical and phenomenological research) that empathy, warmth and genuineness are sufficient, is not widely accepted.

Despite the fact that these three core conditions (as empathy, warmth and genuineness are now regarded) are not thought to be sufficient statements of the nature of counselling interactions, these core conditions have been extensively studied in terms of the relationship between their presence in counselling and the outcome of counselling. Truax and Mitchell (1971), reviewing the studies completed before November 1970, suggest that 'therapists or counselors who are accurately empathic, non-possessively warm in attitude and genuine are indeed effective' and that this statement holds across a wide variety of client groups in a wide variety of counselling settings.

Mitchell et al. (1977), however, provide a very different picture of the outcome studies completed up until the end of 1975 (including all those completed prior to this date). Some studies continue to show that presence and effective communication of these core conditions are directly associated with positive outcome (for example, Cairns, 1972); other studies suggest that there is some limited support for this relationship (for example, Altmann, 1973); but there is a growing body of research that suggests that there is no relationship between these interpersonal skills and the outcome of counselling (see especially Garfield and Bergin, 1971). Summarizing the apparent conflict between these three sets of findings, Bergin and Suinn (1975) suggest strongly that these conditions are related to outcome only when the counsellor is client-centred or Rogerian. Mitchell et al. (1977), however, reach a different conclusion. Their review suggests that: (a) the relationship between these conditions and outcome is far more complex than had hitherto been understood; and (b) such interpersonal skills as represented by these conditions are related differently to client outcome as a function of the different stages of counselling, the nature of the client's presenting problem and the degree of integration of these conditions with the counsellor's other (perhaps more technical) skills.

A special topic within the study of the relationship between these core conditions and the outcome of counselling has been the part such conditions have in behavioural counselling. There are only three major studies of the relationship between the core conditions and outcome in behaviourally-oriented counselling. Of these, that by Cairns (1972) is the most direct study and the least technically flawed. Cairns found no significant difference in the behavioural outcomes for a group who experienced high levels of the core conditions versus a group with low levels in a systematic desensitization study of counselling. She did find, however, significant differences between these groups on measures of subjective (or emotional) change. Also, the group with a high level of the core conditions completed the systematic desensitization task significantly quicker that the comparison group. This study gives some support to the view that the core conditions, when displayed, have a place in affecting the outcome of a behavioural intervention.

A final point here. The communication of the core conditions is seen to be important by clients when rating their immediate reactions to counselling (Mitchell, 1971), irrespective of the longer-term outcomes of the counselling process. In other words, these conditions help the client decide on the level of involvement and immediacy of the relationship he or she will have with their counsellor.

COGNITIVE AND SOCIAL COMPONENTS

One way of viewing the core conditions briefly examined above is to regard them as the affective components of the counselling relationship: they are concerned with the interpersonal and affective tone of a relationship. Given that such relationships also have cognitive and social components, it is important to examine and review these with similar vigour.

The work of Irving Janis and his co-workers at Yale (Janis, 1982) in developing a decision-theory model of counselling is of particular significance in the study of the social psychological and cognitive features of the counselling process. Janis suggests that helping relationships, such as counselling, can best be understood in terms of a theory of social influence based upon the construct of the significant other who uses referent power. Put simply, counsellors seek to promote a high degree of cohesiveness between themselves and their clients by means of empathy, warmth, and genuineness, and the constant reference to the potential personal, social and emotional gains to be achieved from a given change. Furthermore, the counsellor operates by exposing the client to norm-setting communications or behaviours which indicate clearly the behavioural and emotional standards a person in counselling is expected to live up to. Thus a client seeking to curb her smoking behaviour is encouraged to view the consequences of not smoking (that is, saving up to £700 a year by giving up smoking 40 cigarettes a day). The counsellor exercises his/her power to influence the client through social influences within the counselling relationship and through social reinforcement.

Seeing counselling as essentially about the exercise of social influences involves a recognition that going to a counsellor is a significant social step. It also involves a recognition that social influence takes time to affect the social behaviour of a person. This is why Janis (1982) suggests that counselling typically proceeds through three stages.

1. **The counsellor builds up his/her referent power.** This is achieved by the encouragement of self-disclosure, the giving of positive feedback and the counsellor's use of self- disclosure to offer cognitive reappraisal of the client's social world.

2. **The use of referent power by the counsellor.** This is achieved by the counsellor making directive statements or endorsing specific actions which the client intends to take, attributing norms implicit in the client's intended actions to a respected secondary group, giving selective positive feedback and giving the client specific training in decision making and coping skills.

3. **Promoting internalisation whilst retaining referent power after the contact ends.** This is achieved by the counsellor offering reassurance of his/her continued interest in the client, making specific arrangements for contact in the event of need, and building up in a systematic way the client's belief in their own ability to succeed in the absence of a regular counselling appointment.

This model, summarized briefly here but described more fully in Janis (1982) provides a valuable operational analysis of counselling which is amenable to systematic scrutiny.

Indeed, Janis reports on 23 'field experiments' of short-term counselling which utilize this model. He shows:

(a) that short-term counselling (between 3 and 12 sessions) is effective in reducing the incidence of certain behaviours such as smoking and inappropriate eating;
(b) that short-term contracts for counselling are, in specific circumstances, more effective than longer-term contracts or contracts involving frequent appointments;
(c) that all forms of counselling have problems in sustaining some desired change over the long term, but that short-term counselling using the model outlined here is showing some early signs of success when used with specific clients under specific conditions to deal with a specific problem;
(d) positive feedback to clients is a crucial variable in

determining the outcome of counselling, indicating the strength of the social reinforcement role of the counsellor;

(e) positive feedback to the client increases both the rate and intensity of self-disclosure, thereby facilitating the shorter-term contract for counselling; and

(f) that these results offer some tentative support to the social learning hypotheses implicit in the model of counselling outlined here.

The work of Janis and his co-workers at Yale marks an important development in the scientific study of counselling as a practice. For these workers begin with a clear theory of the nature of counselling as a social process and examine the practice of counselling in terms of counsellor and client inputs to the counselling situation, the process which takes place and the outcomes of their interactions. Furthermore, their fieldwork methods for evaluating counselling represent a significant step forward from the laboratory experiments with students acting as both counsellors and clients. Though progress in the scientific study of counselling is snail-like, it is better to operate with care than to run like a hare and get nowhere.

Whilst Janis and his workers have been concerned with the social influence of the counsellor and the related cognitive components of this influence, others have been concerned with the role of cognition in the development of the client's 'problem' and the potential of cognitive interventions in affecting the client's presenting state. Indeed, there is now a British journal devoted to this and related topics, the 'British Journal of Cognitive Psychotherapy'.

The cognitive-behaviour modification workers and rational-emotive therapists take the view that much of the distress a person experiences arises from the beliefs that they hold or from the way in which they offer inappropriate cognitive interpretations of their experiences. For example, Albert Ellis (1962) suggests that there are a number of irrational beliefs which, if held and pursued actively will create distress. These include the belief that a person, to be liked by others, needs to be thoroughly competent, adequate and achieving in all things at all times, and that a failure or a mistake will produce dreadful practical and social consequences. A related belief is that one's past history is an all important determiner of one's present behaviour - past history invariably determines current performance. Both of these beliefs can operate at the same time - as students about to sit examinations will testify. When actively pursued as beliefs which shape behaviour they can and do lead to distress. Donald

Meichenbaum (1977) has gone further in suggesting that these beliefs give rise to interior monologues which shape and direct all actions which are associated with some particular activating event which is distressing the person. Because of the existence of the cognitive set associated with the beliefs outlined here, these monologues are repeated interminably and give rise to further distress. Not only is the person woried about, say, an examination but they are also worried about worrying about the examination.

Windy Dryden (1984) outlines a number of interventions thought to be appropriate in affecting the client's cognitive set and monologue. These include:

(a) disputation and Socratic argument about the value of the beliefs held;
(b) rational-emotive imagery in which the person fantasizes about the emotional impact of holding alternative beliefs about their situation;
(c) shame-attacking exercises in which some practical task is set which will involve the person experienceing discomfort and shame but which are not harmful to themselves and others; and
(d) skill training, especially in social skills and assertiveness.

These techniques are in the 'classic' traditions of rational-emotive therapy (RET) and rely heavily upon the technical skill and competence of the therapist. Alternative forms of cognitive intervention have been suggested and operated by Meichenbaum (1977) and refined by Meichenbaum and Jaremko (1982). These latter procedures rely heavily upon training the client in the use of alternative monologues coupled with desensitization. This territory of intervention techniques is growing and has attracted a great deal of interest and support (Rachman and Wilson, 1980).

What is interesting about both these sets of cognitive concerns with counselling - those of Janis and his co-workers on the one hand and the RET/cognitive-behavioural workers on the other - is that both are based upon little empirical evidence of efficacy. Rachman and Wilson (1980) observe: (a) that there is little evidence linking RET to established theories of social and personal development; (b) some of the claims of RET cannot be sustained empirically, that is, that there are 12 irrational beliefs commonly observed in clinical practice; (c) the value of shame-attacking exercises is untested; and (d) the outcome studies so far conducted are with specific populations (mainly public speaking anxiety, stuttering, and mild phobia) and the appropriateness of RET to other neurotic groups of clients is not empirically established. Whilst it is possible to criticize the value of these outcome studies as studies (for example, Wessler, 1983), the fact remains that much of what takes place in the name of cognivive-behavioural intervention is untested.

The problem of the relationship between claims about therapeutic value of some intervention procedure and empirical studies of outcome is not unique to RET and cognitive-behavioural change strategies. For example, there is little research on the efficacy of counselling the bereaved person or of the theoretical constructs on which such counselling is based (but see Raphael, 1977). Virtually all stress-reduction workers will utilize a variant of progressive or systematic relaxation techniques, despite research showing clearly that for some subjects such techniques <u>increase</u> the level of anxiety and stress experienced (Heide and Borkovec, 1983). Very few of the prodedures outlined in smoking reduction counselling have been shown to be effective over time (Hunt and Bespalec, 1974). A claim made by the American Psychological Association that brief counselling (2-6 sessions) was less effective than longer-term counselling in promoting behavioural change was based upon a single study on counselling young children in the skills of toothbrushing ('American Psychologist', 1976). And so the catalogue could continue. The point to note is that counselling is a complex enterprise in which outcomes are many and varied and change over time. Counselling and therapy are explicitly not tied to working on the basis of current outcome studies; there are few. Rarely are they technically competent, and only occasionally do they mirror the experience of counsellors and therapists working in Britain. Counselling is not anti-scientific - outcome studies are reviewed so that counsellors may learn from them - and it is not wholly mechanical. But there is a marked separation between those who undertake the task of counselling and those who undertake the task of research. This unfortunate separation needs to be healed.

These comments about the relationship between the practice of counselling and the findings of outcome research should not belittle the finding of the major review by Rachman and Wilson (1980) that, of all the psychological therapies they reviewed (and there were many), cognitive-behavioural interventions are producing some of the most striking effects at this time. In particular, the procedures outlined in Meichenbaum and Jaremko (1982) are thought to hold promise and are currently subject to a great deal of critical and experimental scrutiny.

THINKING, FEELING AND ACTION

The previous section suggested that an important issue for the development of counselling psychology was the relationship between practice and research - a point that we shall return to below. Also implicit in the last three sections is the suggestion that counselling psychologists need to have a theory about how their interactions with clients are shaped by both interpersonal imperatives and social assumptions. This is why several strands of contemporary research in counselling psychology are concerned with the matching of counsellor and client variables (for example, outcome differences for different sex pairings and race pairings of counsellor and client: see Bernstein and Figioli, 1983); with the effects of cotherapy versus single counsellor intervention (Mehlman et al., 1983); and with the impact of specific client presenting problems upon the counselling process (for example, the differences between clients in crisis and clients presenting with existential or developmental concerns).

This section examines a further imperative for counselling psychologists. It is that they need to develop and refine a theory of the person so that this too can be examined both in the context of the counselling process and in terms of the utility of such theories about the person per se. Counselling psychologists interact with clients on the basis of their models of personal growth, personal development, change, interpersonal effectiveness, family life and the behaviour of a person in an organizational climate. These theories, so important in shaping the actions of the counsellor, need to become explicit if counselling psychology is to interact with other areas of psychological concern. For what the counselling psychologist seeks to do is to encourage the client to implement a model of the person in a social environment - hence the definition at the beginning of this paper. Making explicit these assumptions is likely to be the major contribution counselling psychologists can make to the development of psychology as the 'science of the person' interacting in their own environment.

Fortunately, this has been the particular concern of a number of British counsellors and counselling psychologists. Brigid Proctor's edited collection of theoretical and practical explorations by ten of Britain's leading counsellors (Proctor, 1978) is a valuable starting point for the study of the relationship between cognition, affect and action (see especially pp.256-265) as seen by counsellors working in traditions as varied as Gestalt, transactional analysis and object-relations.

More recently, Windy Dryden has edited a collection of papers in which a variety of counselling psychologists systematically describe their work in terms of their image of the person, the conceptions they have of psychological health and disturbance and their understanding of the change process which a person is enabled to use through counselling (Dryden, 1984). This collection includes contributions from counsellors and therapists describing Freudian and Kleinian psychodynamic approaches, Jungian, existential and personal construct psychotherapy and an eclectic approach from a reversal theory perspective, amongst others. The importance of this collection is that these contributors make explicit vital assumptions often neglected in studies of counselling processes and outcome. It moves the emphasis from questions about techniques of intervention (is a shame-attacking exercise likely to be more effective than a family sculpting exercise for a particular presenting problem?) to questions about the nature of a counselling strategy as it derives from a comprehensive theory about people and their ability to change.

A critical difference between the various approaches to the understanding of the person offered by the different schools of counselling theory is the way thinking, feeling and action are seen to be related. Some counselling theory places behaviour in the foreground and regards cognition and affect as consequential upon behavioural reinforcement (behavioural counselling). Other counselling theories place cognition in the foreground and regard behaviour and affect to be contingent upon beliefs, values and thought (RET/cognitive therapy). Yet others place affect in the foreground and see thinking and action to be contingent upon the emotional state of the person (Gestalt and some humanistic counselling). Whilst some have attempted integration of these competing and contrasting views of the person (Sheehy, 1981; Golan, 1981), counselling psychology needs now to show greater interest in and a development of theories of human action, especially in respect of the potential of the person for change. Whilst this process is difficult, it is starting to emerge as a feature of counselling psychology in Britain (Murgatroyd and Apter, 1984).

A final point here. Few major theoretical insights into the nature of the person originate in the laboratory (Bruner, 1983). Counselling psychologists are especially well placed to make contributions to the psychological understanding of the person in distress and the person able or unable to change. This is both a pragmatic task and a theoretical one. It may be argued that the ability of counselling psychologists to contribute to this important territory is unduly constrained by the over-experimentalism of a great many of the British psychological journals. Fortunately, counselling psychologists in Britain have access to the 'British Journal of Guidance and Counselling', the 'British Journal of Cognitive Psychotherapy', the 'European Journal of Humanistic Psychology', 'Self and Society' and 'Changes' as vehicles for the development of phenomenological and theoretical concerns (see note 1). The 'third-force' of psychology - the humanistic force - is growing through such publications.

OUTCOME STUDIES AND COUNSELLING

The question which this section is addressing is: What could studies of counsellor effectiveness tell us about counselling? This is a very different question from: What do such studies tell us about counselling?

This latter question has been examined briefly in the previous sections and can be explored more fully by studying Rachman and Wilson (1980) and Gurman and Razin (1977). It is not addressed directly here for two reasons. First, a great many outcome studies are, quite simply, badly designed and executed. Almost all reviews of such studies suggest that the methodological weaknesses are such that the degree of outcome variance that can be 'explained' by a predictor variable (for example, the therapist's skill) may just as well be due to errors in the statistical assumptions made. For example, Wells et al. (1972) comprehensively reviewed all the available outcome studies of family therapy between 1950 and 1970. Of the 18 studies available, only two were deemed by appropriate criteria to be satisfactory as research designs. These two studies were in fact different reports of the same project at different stages in the development of that project. The study shows that 69 per cent of those who engaged in family therapy as adult clients and 79 per cent of child and adolescent clients showed some improvement in symptoms at completion (Langsley et al., 1969) - a rate similar to that reported by Eysenck in his review of individual therapeutic effectiveness (Eysenck, 1952). The more recent review by DeWitt (1978) of this same field - a commendable piece of work in itself - also complains of the poor quality of outcome studies, of the failure to use randomized control trials or (in some cases) control groups, of the lack of specificity of outcome-anticipation by counsellors, and of the poor quality of process specification and description.

A more substantive reason for not reviewing the outcome studies here (except indirectly) is that so few reflect the practice of counselling in Britain. Whilst some attention has been given to the outcome of crisis intervention through the Samaritans (see Aurebach and Killman, 1977), and others have looked at the outcome of counsellor education programmes (Law, 1978; Murgatroyd, 1983c), British outcome studied have not really begun to be offered for critical scrutiny. This becomes especially clear in reading Rachman and Wilson (1980), who are not able to review many British studies of key therapeutic practices. That there are critical cultural differences is self-evident. For example, no major British studies have been able to replicate the frequently-found correlation beteen the incidence of ischaemic heart disease and coronary-prone (Type A) behaviour, yet such correlations are regularly found in the American studies of Type A behaviour (see Price, 1982). Since Type A behaviour is clearly a cognitive-social stress indicator, such differences between cultures are not without significance. Recent attempts to replicate studies of the coping behaviour of students faced with final-year examinations show that the psychometric instruments used in American studies factor differently when used in Britain (note 2). The nature of professional training for counselling and the level of ongoing supervision differs dramatically between Britain and the United States. For these and many other reasons, care should be taken in translating studies from one culture to another. For this reason too, there is a need for British outcome studies that examine counselling processes and efficacy.

Given that there is a need for British outcome studies, what questions might they now most usefully address? There are three. The first concerns methodology, the second the outcome of complex processes and the third concerns the insights that counselling provides into the nature of personal growth and development through change.

The methodological concern relates to the design of outcome and process studies in counselling. Rachman and Wilson (1980) comment on the quality of these designs to date and suggest some alternative paradigms for studying counselling as a process. A special edition of the 'Journal of Consulting and Clinical Psychology' (February, 1983) contains a description of meta-analysis - a valuable tool in the armoury of evaluators seeking to examine counselling processes and outcomes (see especially Rosenthal, 1983). Eysenck and his collaborators (Eysenck, 1976) have shown the potential of case studies in the study of clinical and counselling psychology, as did Murgatroyd (1980b). What is needed is a rigorous, eclectic, structural-phenomenological (Apter, 1981) approach to the study of counselling processes and outcome.

The methodological issues do need scrutiny and development. They also need to be focused upon the complexity of the outcomes that result from a complex human interaction. Far too many outcome studies focus upon a single outcome variable (for example, scores on a rating scale for social adjustment) when the intended outcome by both client and counsellor is far more complex and relates to a variety of emotions, thoughts and actions which will be brought to bear upon social and personal situations in different ways over a long time-span. The work of Janis and his co-workers (Janis, 1982) already cited, shows promise as a way of evaluating both the process and outcome of deliberate counselling intervention over time. In studying outcome, we need also to have a much better description of the processes which have been utilized in the course of counselling. Simply describing the counsellor's work as 'cognitive-behavioural' tells us little about what actually transpired. There is a need for interaction studies similar to those which have taken place in school classrooms (Amidon and Hough, 1967).

The purpose of undertaking such studies is in part to illuminate counselling processes and outcomes and to provide a scientific basis for counselling contracts. But this is only a part of the purpose of such research. The other purpose is to illuminate the nature of change processes which individuals and groups use when faced with challenge or distress. It is this that ties counselling psychology so closely to the mainstream of psychological concerns, as a reading of Kanfer and Goldstein (1980) will testify. Just as a stream of social psychology is concerned with the nature of coping processes, so counselling psychology is primarily concerned with the capacity individuals have to cope and change. The early work of Carl Rogers (Rogers, 1955) illuminates the powerful way in which counselling as a process provides insights into personality structure and the capacity for change. More work directed at this issue is needed to provide a comprehensive theoretical insight into the nature of counselling.

CONCLUSION

This chapter has reviewed a number of areas of current interest in the field of counselling psychology and has speculated on the areas of this growing field now in need of development. From the number of references cited and their time-span, it is clear that counselling psychology has a history and a future. The question that now needs to be asked by those with an interest in this field is how can the scientific study of counselling best proceed in a way that is benefical to psychology as a discipline and counselling psychologists in particular.

REFERENCES

ALTMANN, H.A. (1973) Effects of empathy, warmth and genuineness in the initial counseling interview. **Counselor Education and Supervision, 12,** 225-228

AMERICAN PSYCHOLOGIST (1976) The contributions of psychology to health research (feature). **American Psychologist, 31,** 263-274

AMIDON, E. and HOUGH, J.B. (eds) (1967) **Interaction Analysis - Theory, Practice and Application.** Reading, Mass: Addison-Wesley

APTER, M.J. (1981) The possibility of a structural phenomenology **Journal of Phenomenological Psychology, 12,** 173-187

ARBUCKLE, D. (1967) **Counseling and Psychotherapy.** New York: McGraw Hill

ASHBY, J.D., FORD, D.H., GUERNEY, B.G. and GUERNEY, L.F. (1957) Effects on clients of a reflective and a leading type of psychotherapy. **Psychological Monographs, 71,** (whole no 453)

AUREBACH, S.M. and KILLMAN, P.R. (1977) Crisis intervention - a review of outcome research. **Psychological Bulletin, 84,** 1189-1217

BALES, R.F. (1950) **Interaction Process Analysis.** Reading, Mass:Addison Wesley

BERGIN, A.E. and SUINN, R.M. (1975) Individual psychotherapy and behaviour therapy. **Annual Review of Psychology, 26,** 509-556

BERNSTEIN, B.L. and FIGIOLI, S.W. (1983) Gender and credibility introduction effects on perceived counselor characteistics. **Journal of Consulting Psychology, 30,** 506-513

BRUNER, J. (1983) **In Search of Mind - Essays in Autobiography.** New York: Harper and Row

CAIRNS, K.V. (1972) **Desensitisation and relationship quality.** Calgary, Canada: Unpublished Master's Thesis, University of Calagary, Canada

CARKHUFF, R.R. (1969) **Helping and Human Relations: A Primer for Professional and Lay Helpers.** New York: Holt, Rinehart and Winston

DEWITT, K.N. (1978) The effectiveness of family therapy - a review of outcome research. **Archives of General Psychiatry, 35,** 549-561

DRYDEN, W. (ed.) (1984) **Individual Psychotherapy.** London: Harper and Row

ELLIS, A. (1962) **Reason and Emotion in Psychotherapy.** New York: Citadel Press

EYSENCK, H.J. (1952) The effects of psychotherapy - an evaluation. **Journal of Consulting Psychology, 16,** 319-324

EYSENCK, H.J. (ed.) (1976) **Case Studies in Behaviour Therapy.** London: Routledge and Kegan Paul

FEY, W.F. (1958) Doctrine and experience - their influence upon the psychotherapist. **Journal of Consulting Psychology, 22,** 403-409

FLANDERS, N.A. (1960) **Interaction Analysis in the Classroom: A Manual for Observers.** Michigan: University of Michigan Press

FRIEDMAN, M.L. and DIES, F.R. (1974) Relationship of internal and external test anxious students to counseling and behaviour therapies. **Journal of Consulting and Clinical Psychology, 42,** 921

GARFIELD, S.L. and BERGIN, A.E. (1971) Therapeutic conditions and outcome. **Journal of Abnormal Psychology, 77,** 108-114

GARFIELD, S.L. and KURTZ, R. (1974) A survey of clinical psychologists: characteristics, activities and orientations. **Clinical Psyschologist, 28,** 7-10

GOLAN, N. (1981) **Passing Through Transitions - A Guide for Practicioners.** New York: Free Press

GURMAN, A.S. and RAZIN, A.M. (eds) (1977) **Effective Psychotherapy - A Handbook of Research.** Oxford: Pergamon

HEIDE, F.J. and BORKOVEC, T.D. (1983) Relaxation induced anxiety - paradoxical anxiety enhancement due to relaxation training. **Journal of Consulting and Clinical Psychology, 51,** 171-182

HELLER, K., MYERS, R.A. and KLINE, L.V. (1963) Interview behaviour as a function of standardized client roles. **Journal of Consulting Psychology, 27,** 117-122

HERINK, R. (ed.) (1980) **Psychotherapy Handbook - the A-Z Guide to More than 250 Therapies in Use Today.** New York: Meridian Books

HERON, J. (1976) A six category intervention analysis. **British Journal of Guidance and Counselling, 4,** 143-155

HILL, C.E. (1978) Development of a counselor verbal response category. **Journal of Counseling Psychology, 25,** 106-117

HILL, C.E., CARTER, J.A. and O'FARRELL, M.K. (1983) A case study of the process and outcome of time limited counseling. **Journal of Counseling Psychology, 30,** 3-18

HILL, C.E., THOMAS, T.B. and RARDIN, D.K. (1978) Comparison of Rogers, Perls and Ellis on the Hill Verbal Response Category System. **Journal of Counseling Psychology, 26,** 198-203

HUNT, W.A. and BESPALEC, D.A. (1974) An evaluation of current methods of modifying smoking behaviour. **Journal of Clinical Psychology, 30,** 431-438

JANIS, I. (ed.) (1982) **Counseling and Personal Decisions.** New Haven: Yale University Press

KANFER, F.H. and GOLDSTEIN, A.P. (eds) (1980) **Helping People Change.** Oxford: Pergamon

LANGSLEY, D.G., FLOMENHAFT, K. and MACHOTKA, P. (1969) Follow-up evaluation of family crisis therapy. **American Journal of Orthopsychiatry, 39,** 753-760

LAW, W.M. (1978) The concomitants of systems orientation in secondary school counsellors. **British Journal of Guidance and Counselling, 6,** 161-174

MASLOW, A.H. (1971) **The Farther Reaches of Human Nature.** New York: Viking Press

MEHLMAN, S.K. BAUCOM, D.H. and ANDERSON, D (1983) Effectiveness of cotherapists versus single therapists and immediate versus delayed treatment in behavioural marital therapy. **Journal of Consulting and Clinical Psychology, 51,** 258-266

MEICHENBAUM, D. (1977) **Cognitive Behaviour Modification.** New York: Plenum

MEICHENBAUM, D. and JAREMKO, M.E. (eds) (1982) **Stress Reduction and Prevention.** New York: Plenum

MITCHELL, K.M. (1971) Relationhip between therapist response to therapist relevant client expressions and therapy process and client outcomes. **Dissertation Abstracts International, 32,** 1853b

MITCHELL, K.M., BOZARTH, J.D. and KRAUFT, C.C. (1977) A Reappraisal of the Therapeutic Effectiveness of Accurate Empathy, Nonpossessive Warmth and Genuineness. In A.S. Gurman and A.M. Razin (eds) **Effective Psychotherapy.** Oxford: Pergamon

MITCHELL, K.M., TRUAX, C.B., BOZARTH, J.D. and KRAUFT, C.C. (1973) **Antecedents to Psychotherapeutic Outcome.** Arkansas: National Institute of Mental Health Grant Report (n.12306)

MURGATROYD, S. (1980a) Educational counselling and the disabled adult. **Adult Education, 53,** 159-165

MURGATROYD, S. (ed.) (1980b) **Helping the Troubled Child - Interprofessional Case Studies.** London: Harper and Row

MURGATROYD, S. (1983a) Counselling and the doctor. **Journal of the Royal College of General Practicioners, 33,** 323-326

MURGATROYD, S. (1983b) Counselling and the British Psychological Society - a caution. **Bulletin of The British Psychological Society, 35,** 452-453

MURGATROYD, S. (1983c) Training for crisis counselling. **British Journal of Guidance and Counselling, 11,** 131-144

MURGATROYD, S. and APTER. M.J. (1984) Eclectic psychotherapy - a structural-phenomenological approach. In: W. Dryden (ed.) **Individual Psychotherapy.** London: Harper and Row

NELSON-JONES, R. (1982) **The Theory and Practice of Counselling Psychology.** London: Holt-Saunders

PALLONE, N.J. and DI BENNARDO, F.R. (1967) Interview sequence in relation to counselor verbal mode, client problem related content and rapport. **Journal of Counseling Psychology, 19,** 523-525

PARKER, G.V. (1967) Some concomitants of therapist dominance in the psychotherapy interview. **Journal of Consulting Psychology, 13,** 313-318

PRICE, V.A. (1982) **Type A Behaviour Pattern - A Model for Research and Practice.** London: Academic Press

PROCTOR, B. (1978) **Counselling Shop - An Introduction to the Theories and Techniques of Ten Approaches to Counselling.** London: Burnett Books/Andre Deutsche

RACHMAN, S. and WILSON, G. (1980) **The Effects of the Psychological Therapies.** Oxford: Pergamon

RAPHAEL, B. (1977) Preventive intervention with the recently bereaved. **Archives of General Psychiatry, 34,** 1450-1454

RICE, D.G., FEY, W.F. and KEPECS, S.G. (1972) Therapist experience and 'style' as factors in cotherapy. **Family Process, 11,** 1-12

ROGERS, C.R. (1952) Client-centred psychotherapy. **Scientific American, 187,** 66-74

ROGERS, C.R. (1955) Personality change in psychotherapy. **International Journal of Social Psychiatry, 1,** 31-41

ROGERS, C.R. (1957a) A note on the nature of man. **Journal of Counseling Psychology, 4,** 199-203

ROGERS, C.R. (1957b) The necessary and sufficient conditions of therapeutic personality change. **Journal of Consulting Psychology, 21,** 95-103

ROSENTHAL, R. (1983) Assessing the statistical and social importance of the effects of psychotherapy. **Journal of Consulting and Clinical Psychology, 51,** 4-13

SHEEHY, G. (1981) **Pathfinders - How to Achieve Happiness by Conquering Life's Crises.** London: Sidgwick and Jackson

STEWART, W. (1983) **Counselling and Nursing.** London: Lippincott

SUNDLAND, D.M. (1977) Theoretical orientations of psychotherapists. In: A.S. Gurman and A.M. Razin (eds) **Effective Psychotherapy.** Oxford: Pergamon

SUNDLAND, D.M. and BARKER, E.N. (1962) The orientations of psychotherapists. **Journal of Consulting Psychology, 26,** 201-212

TRUAX, C.B. and CARKHUFF R.R. (1967) **Towards Effective Counselling and Psychotherapy - Training and Practice.** Chicago: Aldine

TRUAX, C.B. and MITCHELL, K.M. (1971) Research on certain therapist interpersonal skills in relation to process and outcome. In A.E. Bergin and S.L. Garfied (eds) **Handbook of Psychotherapy and Behaviour Change.** New York: Wiley

TYLER, L. (3rd edn, 1969) **The Work of the Counselor.** New York: Appleton-Century-Crofts

WALLACH, M.S., and STRUPP, H.H. (1964) Dimensions of psychotherapists activity. **Journal of Consulting Psychology, 28,** 120-125

WEISSMAN, H.N., GOLDSCHMID, M.L. and STEIN, D.D. (1971) Psychotherapeutic orientation and training. **Journal of Consulting and Clinical Psychology, 37,** 31-37

WELLS, R.A., DILKES, T.C. and TRIVELLI, N. (1972) The results of family therapy - a critical review of the literature. **Family Process, 11,** 189-267

WESSLER, R.L. (1983) A critical appraisal of therapeutic efficacy studies. **British Journal of Cognitive Psychotherapy, 1,** 39-46

WILE, D.B., BRON, G.D. and POLLACK, H.B. (1970) Preliminary validation evidence for the group therapy questionnaire. **Journal of Consulting and Clinical Psychology, 34,** 367-374

Note 1. Further details of these journals can be obtained from:

'British Journal of Guidance and Counselling'
NICEC
Bateman Street
Cambridge

'European Journal of Humanistic Psychology'/'Self and Society'
Vivian Milroy
62 Southwark Bridge Road
London

'British Journal of Cognitive Psychotherapy'
Dr W. Dryden
209 Belchers Lane
Little Bromwich
Birmingham

'Changes'
Dr Don Bannister
Department of Psychology
High Royds Hospital
Menston, Ilkley
Yorks

Note 2. Lazarus and his co-workers produces different coping models when the scores of Welsh and Californian subjects are factored and compared. Discriminant analysis suggests that the psychometric differences between these two samples accounts for significant variance between them in terms of their ways of coping scores. Further details from the author.

CONTEMPORARY APPROACHES TO THE UNDERSTANDING, ASSESSMENT AND TREATMENT OF DELINQUENCY

Norman Tutt

The question of whether the behaviour of individuals is largely determined by their internal states, that is, their drives, motivations, feelings, beliefs, etc., or by variables operating in their environment, that is, opportunity, relationships, peer influence, etc., is one which has absorbed psychologists for many decades.

This debate on the roots of behaviour is not of merely academic interest, since its outcome may have a very profound effect on social policy. An obvious example of this is the ways in which Burt's views on the nature and source of intelligence, the ability to measure intelligence accurately, and to make valid predictions of future performance, all affected the education policy of post-war Britain.

Currently, there is considerable interest in and acceptance of theories of behaviour which stress the influence of situational determinants. This chapter will examine evidence of the application of these theories to explanations of juvenile offending and will then discuss the influence such an application must have on both the policy and practice developed for controlling juvenile offending.

There is a wide range of empirical evidence which suggests that much behaviour is situation bound. Indeed, the approach has a long and respectable historical tradition. As long ago as 1928 two psychologists, Hartshorne and May, set out to investigate the constancy of certain traits in children (see Vernon, 1963).

They were interested in honesty and set up an experimental situation in which some 11,000 children could be dishonest, for example, steal pennies, cheat at table games, cheat at school work, and lie about cheating at school work. Their initial hypothesis was that children who were dishonest in one situation would also be dishonest in others. In fact they failed to find this and concluded that honesty is not a trait constant in all situations, but varies depending upon the individual's reaction to each situation.

In the past decade there have been a substantial number of studies which have re-emphasized the significance of situational determinants. These studies fall into three major categories:

1. MACRO-ENVIRONMENT STUDIES: studies in which crime figures are related to area or neighbourhood differences. For example, studies of crime differences between rural and urban areas, or privately owned and state housing schemes.

2. MICRO-ENVIRONMENT STUDIES: studies in which young people's behaviour is related to institutions or micro-environments in which they spend their lives. For example, studies of different school 'styles' and their impact on young people's behaviour, or participant-observation on the effects of streaming or gang membership.

3. IMMEDIATE-SITUATIONAL STUDIES: studies in which variables within the immediate situation can be related to specific behaviour of young people. For example, experimental designs to examine the modelling behaviour of young people, or post facto behavioural analysis.

1. Macro-environment studies

Studies based on crime statistics related to geographical area show that more crime is committed in cities than in small towns, which in turn have more crime than rural areas (McClintock and Avison, 1968). Although these studies are based on where the crime takes place, there is evidence that suggests the populations of these different areas illustrate different rates of emotional disturbance, family discord and adult criminality (Rutter et al., 1975). Other studies have shown that even within cities there is a wide variation in the crime rates by area. In general, high rates of delinquency are connected with high rates of adult crime, alcoholism and psychiatric disorder. Baldwin and Bottoms (1976) found high delinquency areas are those with a high proportion of low status individuals, low proportion of owner-occupied housing, high rates of overcrowding, shared accommodation and immigration. The correlation of these factors with high delinquency does not determine a causal relationship, but does suggest the macro-environment has some impact on individuals' and families' behaviour.

2. Micro-environment studies

A number of studies have demonstrated that if the intakes to schools are matched there are still different rates of delinquency and deviant behaviours demonstrated by pupils (Power, Benn and Morris, 1967; Reynolds and Jones, 1978). The implication of these studies is that the school environment is capable of either reducing or increasing the delinquency rate of pupils. Moreover the rates of delinquency correlated highly with other measures of student behaviour and poor levels of scholastic attainment. In other words a 'good' school was likely to produce good academic and sporting attainments and low levels of difficult behaviour, while other schools had the reverse effect (Rutter et al., 1979). Hargreaves (1967) as the result of a participant-observation study in one school, stressed the significance of rigid streaming in determining the 'delinquent' behaviour of the pupils.

The other micro-environment which has been the focus of much attention is the peer-group. Since a substantial amount of juvenile offending is conducted in groups it would seem reasonable to assume that the peer group somehow influences the behaviour of the individual. However, it is difficult to establish the causal relationship; is the young person delinquent and accordingly seeks out delinquent friends, or is the young person an innocent, 'corrupted' by the peer group? There have been few attempts to unpick this relationship. West and Farrington (1973) matched persistent recidivists with offenders who appeared to 'spontaneously remit', that is, had a history of offending, which suddenly ceased. Interviews with these two groups elicited from a number of the 'spontaneous remissions' the comment that disengagement from the delinquent peer group was an important feature in abandonment of delinquency. Whilst West and Parrington's evidence cannot be said to be conclusive, it does suggest that the peer group is influential in both initiating and maintaining delinquent behaviour.

3. Immediate situational studies

Bandura (1969) started his work on modelling to explain aggressive behaviour in children. He argued that patterns of behaviour are learned either by direct experience, governed by the rewarding and punishing consequences that follow any given action, or by observing the behaviour of others. Bandura's argument that children's behaviour arose from the immediate situation they observed or experienced led researchers to examine closely the effect of films and television on children's behaviour. Most reviewers appeared to be agreed that exposure to violent models of behaviour on film led to imitative aggressive behaviour on the part of the child (Brody, 1977). In a study of 12 to 17-year-old boys in

London, Belson (1978) claimed to show that high exposure to television violence was significantly correlated with frequent use of violence.

If films or television can influence behaviour immediately after the viewing, then it would seem reasonable to assume that 'real' models would be of even greater influence. A child who watches a high status peer shoplift might perhaps be influenced in his behaviour, especially if the peer is seen to receive rewards for the behaviour. Not only would immediate models of behaviour be significant, but other immediate situational variables would constrain or encourage the deviant behaviour. Each behavioural event will be the result of a number of specific factors. For example, if a young person breaks off a car aerial (criminal damage) it is important to explain the event by asking:

When did it occur? - There will be differences in meaning if in daylight compared with darkness.

Where? - A crowded shopping street is less likely than a deserted street.

Who with? - The event is less likely if the young person is with his parents than if with his peers.

What led up to it? - Were his peers 'daring' him to do it?

What was being planned? - Were the group only joking with no intent to 'force' the offender to act?

What did happen? - Did it break off more easily than expected?

Was it intended? - Was the intention a 'symbolic' twist of the aerial to answer the 'dare' of peers?

If not, why did it happen? - If not intended, what outcome was the offender hoping to achieve?

These subtle pressures in the immediate situation if changed may well change the outcome. An investigation of these situational factors is crucial before any plan of response is determined (Denman, 1983).

Obviously the three forms of situational factors interact. For example, if a young person lives in a high delinquency neighbourhood, and attends a 'delinquescent' school, then he will be exposed to many more deviant models and immediate situations likely to produce crime. On the other hand, as Wilson (1980) has shown, a child may live in a delinquent neighbourhood, but parental control of the immediate situation can reduce the likelihood of the child offending.

From these studies it would appear that delinquent behaviour is at least determined by situational factors. The implications for social policy and practice are profound, and the remainder of this chapter will examine these implications on various aspects of policy aimed at controlling juvenile crime or treating juvenile offenders, starting with the issue of crime prevention.

CRIME PREVENTION POLICY

Obviously, for the benefit of both the child and the community, prevention is the best strategy to adopt. But what should be the nature of that policy? There is a popular belief that general moral education programmes conducted in schools can inculcate appropriate moral attitudes in children and young people so that they may resist being drawn into crime. Alternatively and more specifically it is believed that young people commit crimes because of boredom, through lack of leisure facilities, or because youthful adventurous high spirits when acted out in an urban environment are likely to lead to conflict with the police. The provision of directed adventurous activities which channelled the energies of the young would therefore reduce crime.

However, research findings have shifted the emphasis of preventive work with juvenile offenders away from what could be termed 'social education', for example, provision of youth facilities, counselling services, activity leisure groups, etc., towards 'mechanical' forms of prevention, for example, the use of physical security of buildings, greater surveillance in shops and public transport, the introduction of 'vandal proof' building materials. The problem with the early identification of children 'at risk of delinquency' and the consequent taking of preventive action from state agencies is that any such process of identification would in fact identify more children at risk than would become delinquent. For example, although it is known from studies of offenders drawn from institutional populations (Tutt, 1974) that a disproportionate number of delinquents come from broken homes, many children from broken homes do not become delinquent. Consequently, if children were identified as 'at risk' on the basis of whether or not they come from broken homes, too many children would be identified. This remains true even if complication correlations and collations of numbers of factors are made. For example, West and Farrington

(1973) in the Cambridge study of delinquent development used data on five family background characteristics, collected before the boys in their sample were aged ten, to predict delinquency. The five factors were:

1. Low family income.

2. Large family size.

3. Having a parent with a criminal record.

4. Having parents considered to be unsatisfactory in rearing children.

5. Comparatively low intelligence.

On the follow-up they correctly identified 31 boys who were convicted before the age of 17. But 32 were incorrectly labelled, and 53 delinquents were missed, out of a sample of more than 400. Even if it were possible to identify accurately the criminogenic children and put them into deliquency prevention programmes, little would be gained. This is because, first, it is not known what action is preventive, and, second, such an identification may actually help create delinquent behaviour by labelling the child and giving him a self-identity as a 'problem', to which he then responds.

What is now advocated is a series of strategies aimed at reducing crime and not at preventing future delinquent behaviour. A Home Office Research Study entitled 'Crime as Opportunity' (Mayhew et al., 1976) gives a number of examples where the opportunity for delinquency appears to promote delinquent behaviour and where removal of the opportunity reduces the behaviour. For example, the wide-scale introduction of steering locks on cars reduces the opportunity for car theft and therefore the amount of illegal driving and taking away. The amount and type of supervision on buses influences the amount of criminal damage occurring. To take another example, the work of the housing planner Oscar Newman (1972) on 'defensible space' shows how environmental design may inhibit criminal acts so that housing schemes can be designed in such a way as to reduce vandalism and theft and enhance the personalized communal area.

Changes in operational services may also have an impact beyond that expected; for example, the truancy sweeps operated in the past by the juvenile bureau in various divisions of the Metropolitan Police, in which truants were picked up by patrolling officers and returned to school or home. In one division this action coincided with a 26 per cent drop in reported auto-crimes and a 36 per cent reduction in petty crimes, mainly theft (Metropolitan Police, 1978).

For a fuller discussion of the changed view of crime prevention, see the report from the All-Party Penal Affairs Group (1983), 'The Prevention of Crime Among Young People'. This report divides its recommendations between what it calls 'situational crime prevention' and 'social crime prevention'. The former includes physical and operational crime prevention strategies, the latter recommendations on unemployment, family, and youth and education service policies.

The policy and practice of diversion

The increased stress on the analysis of situational factors as causal variables in offending behaviour began rapidly to erode the rationale for individualized treatment of offenders. Indeed, if situational variables are so important it makes sense for policy-makers and practitioners to switch their attention away from the child or young person who 'owns' the problem to the administrative and professional processes which are brought to bear on these problems. This switch of attention is based on the assumption that the formal processing of the juvenile may serve to reinforce the problem. Thus the past two decades have seen a growing interest in the concept of 'diversion', that is, the deliberate turning away of the child or young person from the formally established processes, on the basis that enmeshment with these processes may contribute to the situational determinants which are reinforcing the deviant behaviours (Tutt, 1981). However, it would be misleading to present the development of diversion policies as being based solely on theoretical advances, and it is worth examining why this interest has arisen and why the concept has general support even from those groups who often hold very different views on how to deal with juvenile crime. The reason for the consensus is that diversion is supported by different groups for very different reasons. This section will start with an examination of these contradictory reasons.

Over the past twenty five years the apparent number of known juvenile offenders has increased rapidly. For the first 15 years the rise was consistent, but since 1974 the rise has been less consistent, showing wider fluctuations, and in some years actually declining. It should be stressed that the rise in juvenile crime has increased at approximately the same rate as adult crime and over this period the proportion of all crime committed by juveniles has remained constant at about 34 per cent (DHSS, 1981).

The rate of growth in juvenile crime has been substantial. For example, from 1965 to 1979 the increase in known juvenile offenders was 78 per cent, while the increase in population of 10 to 16-year-olds over the same period was only 19 per cent. Obviously such statistics are not only open to criticism on the basis of their reliability and validity - for example, they may merely reflect increased efficiency in recording methods - but are also open to a range of interpretations. What is significant is that this apparent increase in juvenile crime has led to pressure of numbers on the juvenile justice system which in turn has led to pressure for diversion from formal processing on the purely pragmatic grounds that the formal juvenile court process would have broken down under the sheer number of referrals. In addition, some observers pointed out that much juvenile crime was very trivial and involved petty theft or damage and that the sheer cost of formal processing was disproportionate to the crime (Tutt, 1974), more particularly since the vast majority of juveniles plead guilty when in court. It was, therefore, reasonable to seek a more cost-effective way of dealing with the case without formal processing.

Moreover, the continuous growth in juvenile crime provided indisputable evidence that the formal juvenile justice system was failing in its task of controlling or reducing crime. This led other groups to argue that informal diversion from the juvenile court was unlikely to lead to any worse outcome in terms of increased juvenile crime and would more likely reduce the chances of reconviction of individual juveniles by reducing the effects of labelling or stigmatizing the individual.

In addition, the increase in formal processing of juveniles, particularly those charged with trivial offences, led some observers to question whether in fact the justice system was over-reaching and entering the realm of legitimate family control of mischievous behaviour by children (Goldstein, Freud and Solnit, 1980).

This range of reasons - the growth of juvenile crime, the pressure of numbers, costs, labelling, and extensions of social control - led to an unlikely consensus amongst differing groups that diversion was a policy worth pursuing.

However, how the policy should be pursued was and still is open to a great deal of debate. In the United States of America the President's Commission on Law Enforcement and the Administration of

Justice, reporting in 1967, recommended the preferred policy of diversion. It used the term 'pre-judicial disposition' to refer to the unofficial handling of the problem youth prior to and in lieu of official juvenile court processing. The policy soon became a national strategy but with no clear definition or operational criteria. Fifteen years later, Rosemary Sarri was able to identify at least eight clearly differently defined forms of diversion (Sarri, 1983). In the United States random allocation experiments have been carried out to investigate the effectiveness of juvenile diversion schemes (Binder and Newkirk, 1977). Such research has led to more sophisticated attempts to improve the diversionary impact by improved assessment. For example, a diversion scheme which appears to have had some success in reducing recidivism is that carried out in California by Binder, Monahan and Newkirk (1976) which, largely based on contingency contracting within the families of arrested juveniles, utilizes a high degree of analysis and assessment of the situation by police officers and others.

In the United Kingdom a range of policies and practices has been called diversion. In certain circumstances the police are able to issue a formal caution to a juvenile offender rather than take proceedings against the juvenile through the court. The case has to meet certain criteria, and whilst there is some variation between police forces the criteria common to all forces are:

1. The evidence available is sufficient to support a prosecution in normal circumstances.

2. The juvenile admits the offence.

3. The parent or guardian agrees to a caution being administered.

In general the caution will be administered in formal circumstances at a police station in the presence of the parent or guardian, by a police officer in uniform not below the rank of Inspector. The introduction of cautioning, its widespread acceptance by the police and the continuous pressure to expand the use of the caution had led throughout the 1970s to it becoming the major established method for responding to juvenile crime. Thus by 1980 national criminal statistics showed that for 10 to 17-year-olds admitting, or found guilty of an offence, more than 51 per cent, an overall majority, of young offenders were cautioned.

Cautioning rates vary enormously between police forces. These variations do not seem to relate directly to expected levels of crime within areas, but to differences in police force procedures and practice. Criminal statistics for 1982 show that the rate of cautioning varies between a low of 32 per cent of males under the age of 17 cautioned in Cleveland to a high of 67 per cent in Suffolk. Areas of predictably equivalent crime however show marked differences in cautioning rates; for example, whereas the West Midlands police caution 50 per cent of male juveniles, Greater Manchester police caution only 40 per cent (Home Office, 1983).

Net-widening and research on cautioning

It is somewhat surprising that cautioning of juveniles has received continued encouragement, since recent research has suggested that police cautioning has a number of unintended negative consequences. The first is the phenomenon of 'net-widening'. Most research suggests that cautioning has not occurred in lieu of but in addition to prosecution. In other words, the number of young people being cautioned has increased rapidly but the number being prosecuted has not been reduced. This result could only have been achieved by drawing young people who would previously have been dealt with informally into the 'net' of the formal juvenile justice system.

Secondly, in 1978 the Home Office issued a guidance to police forces stating that previous cautions should be cited in the juvenile court. This citation is often taken as a statement of previous findings of guilt, and consequently the juvenile is given a higher tariff disposal than would be predicted on his previous court record. In support of this claim, the disposal patterns over the past decade suggest that young offenders are now less likely to receive conditional discharges or fines than formerly. This may be because magistrates discount these disposals, either because they are told or they assume that the offender has already had a police caution. The expansion of the use of cautions has in effect and on occasions eroded the lower levels of the juvenile court tariff.

Generally, the whole process of police cautioning has received little research attention. There has been only one major national study of cautioning, namely, that conducted by the Home Office Research Unit in 1976 (Ditchfield, 1976). That research suggested that at least part of the reason for the national phenomenon of an apparent vast increase in juvenile crime was that the pool of officially labelled juvenile offenders had increased as a direct result of changes in police practice since 1969. This view has been supported by Farrington and Bennett (1981). They examined the effect of the establishment of a Bureau within the Metropolitan Police Force. The setting up and operation of the Juvenile Bureau predated the implementation of the Children and Young Persons Act 1969. The researchers argued:

> The most important comparison is between 1968 and 1970, the latter being the first complete year in which every division of the Metropolitan Police was operating the scheme. During this period it can be seen that arrests increased 97 per cent for ten to thirteen year-olds, 88 per cent for 14 to 16-year-olds, ... After the introduction of the cautioning scheme there was a widening of the net of arrested juveniles, especially in the youngest (10 to 13) age group. It is implausible to suggest that there was anything approaching such a marked increase in juvenile offending, or any other marked change unconnected with the introduction of the cautioning scheme, during this short period. The same conclusion follows for the figures on official 'processing'. The figures on findings of guilt suggest that 10 to 13-year-olds were diverted, but not 14 to 16-year-olds. In all cases, the introduction of the Children and Young Persons Act 1971 had much less effect on arrests, findings of guilt and official processing of juveniles than the introduction of the Juvenile Bureau scheme.

Analysis of data for later years for the same police force areas carried out by Tutt (Tutt and Giller, 1983) supports some of the findings of Farrington and Bennett, most notably that it is the seriousness of the offence which is most closely related to the disposition decision. However, the massive increase in arrests described by the previous researchers did not persist into the latter half of the decade. In fact the number of arrests for 10 to 17-year-olds dropped back consistently from a peak in 1977 over the following two years, although the proportion cautioned remained surprisingly constant. In 1976, 32 per cent were cautioned; in 1977, 1978 and 1979, the figure was 34 per cent. Over this period the national cautioning average for police forces in England and Wales rose to over 50 per cent. A further example of 'net-widening' is provided by recent research from Edgar Jardine in Northern Ireland. He showed that whereas in Northern Ireland in 1977 there were only 549 cautions and 2,800 prosecutions, by 1982 there were 2,500 cautions but prosecutions had only dropped by 750 (Jardine, 1983).

True cautioning figures are notoriously difficult to establish since there are differential rates of cautioning for boys and girls and for younger and older children. Generally, younger girls (10-14 years) are more likely to receive a caution than all other groups; the cautioning rate for this group is over 80 per cent nationally. For younger boys the rate drops to approximately 65 per cent, for older girls (14-16 years) it falls to approximately 55 per cent and for older boys it declines to about 35 per cent.

The examination of the operation of police policy on cautioning illustrates two important points. Firstly, that theories of the 'normality' of delinquency, particularly within certain social situations, have become very influential, permeating, even if in a corrupted form, police decision-making processes. Secondly, the variations in cautioning policy highlight the difficulties and dangers of psychological research on identified delinquents, that is, those found guilty in court. Any group identified on this basis is more likely to reflect differences in local police practice than characteristics of delinquents. This is equally important for practitioners, since it is most likely that a psychologist will be asked to provide assessments either directly, or via school reports on children appearing in court. The police policy adopted in the local area will radically affect input to the juvenile court and therefore the baseline against which assessments are made.

This extremely important factor is nearly always forgotten in any discussion of assessment policy. Assessment can operate at three levels:

* assessment for the court;
* assessment after a court decision;
* assessment for treatment.

Assessment for the court

Each year many thousands of social inquiry reports are prepared for consideration in the juvenile court. Reports are prepared both in criminal and civil proceedings. Furthermore, substantial numbers are prepared for consideration by the full range of adult courts. In order to provide a crude estimate of the extent of this activity it is salutary to recall that during a year in one metropolitan authority nearly 600 social inquiry reports were prepared for the juvenile courts alone (Social Information Systems, 1984). If the production of such reports were distributed evenly across local authorities, which it is not, then in any one year 60,000 social inquiry reports would be prepared on juveniles alone. Because of the differential distribution across local authority and probation service areas, this figure is probably an under-estimate. If the work of the adult courts is added to this figure it becomes probable that the production of social inquiry reports is not only a significant consumer of time and resources but also has a profound impact on the working of the courts. In fact the numbers of social inquiry reports requested by the courts and prepared by the statutory services in 1983 was over 250,000.

The legislative provisions for the production of social inquiry reports in the juvenile court is spelt out in two sources which are now brought together under the Criminal Justice Act 1982. The first source is from child-care legislation. Section 9.1 of the Children and Young Persons Act (1969) states:

> It shall be the duty of the authority, unless they are of the opinion that it is unnecessary to do so, to make such investigation and provide the court ... with such information relating to home surroundings, school record, health and character of the person ... as appear to the authority likely to assist the court.

In criminal proceedings, the Home Office (1983) advise the report should follow the general guidance given by the Streatfield Committee in 1961:

1. An assessment of the offender's personality, character and family and social background which is relevant to the court's assessment of his culpability.

2. Information about the offender and his surroundings which is relevant to the court's consideration of how his criminal career might be checked (including his record while at any educational training or residential establishment).

3. His employment or prospects of obtaining employment.

4. Information about the circumstances of the offence in question and the offender's attitude to it.

5. An opinion of the likely effect on the offender's criminal career of probation or some specific sentence.

The legislation only provides a background for practice and it is left to the practitioners to determine the details of operation. It is fair to say that in putting the recommendations of the child-care legislation and the Streatfield Committee into operation, practitioners have concentrated on an assessment of the offender's personality, character and family and social background.

This concentration has come under much criticism both from a theoretical and an operational standpoint. The fact that the social inquiry report (SIR) assesses personality - even assuming such a process is easily achievable - implies that criminal behaviour is best explained by individual personality characteristics. By definition, these are enduring and will therefore determine the individual's future behaviour. In reality, there is now substantial evidence to suggest that much crime, particularly that committed by juveniles, is opportunistic and the result of the situation in which the offender finds himself rather than the product of specific personality characteristics.

Also, for some time psychologists have questioned the strength of correlation between expressed attitudes and actual behaviour. Anyone working within the criminal justice system will be familiar with the weak correlation between attitude and behaviour as they daily meet offenders, who express apparently strong conviction and attitudes that they will never re-offend and yet within a short time are back before the court charged with a further offence. The SIR is almost entirely dependent upon expressed attitudes since it rarely, if ever, samples actual behaviour. Thus it is the offender's attitude to his family, his work and his offence which is reported to the court. These reported views may not reflect his actual behaviour in any of these settings.

The factors stressed by the Streatfield Committee are to some extent merely a reflection of the wider social context in which the report is prepared, rather than a comment on the offender being assessed. Thus, Streatfield's heavy emphasis on the offender's record of employment and attitude to work could be significant at a time of relatively full employment since a record of unemployment may be indicative of instability of life style and predictive of rehabilitation. However, at a time of high unemployment frequent job changes may reflect the state of industry and the economy more generally than the personality and attributes of the individual. Similarly, with growing awareness and concern about the overcrowding in prisons, many probation officers are unhappy to recommend custody and very few indeed would argue for the reformative nature of prison. Yet twenty years ago the position was quite different. Thus the SIR, far from being a purely 'objective' evaluation, must per force be a reponse to certain social contexts. Finally, the SIR as envisaged by Streatfield was to contain some element of prediction; that is, the SIR author was to guide the court as to the likely outcome of certain disposals. The last three or more decades of criminology are littered with highly sophisticated attempts to develop predictive scales (Craig and Glick, 1963). Such attempts have proved to be inaccurate with a large sample. How much more inaccurate must be the predictions of an individual?

The fact that most SIRs are produced by individual psychologists or social workers working independently raises concern that inter-rater reliability; the chance of two or more individual workers coming to the same decision on the same case, is not high (Gelsthorpe, 1984). Moreover, as far as predictions of future behaviour are concerned, the best guideline would be the known 'failure rates' of certain disposals, (for example, the fact that 84 per cent of 15 to 17-year-old boys released from youth custody re-offend in two years) rather than factors known or assumed about the individual offender. Yet these rates are rarely quoted in SIRs. (For a full discussion of methods for reforming these crucial assessments, see Tutt and Giller, 1983.)

Assessment after a court decision

Given that some form of assessment is fundamental to any professional intervention, is it possible to define or refine the nature of assessment, and more specifically assessment of children? The definition offered in 'Observation and Assessment of Children' (DHSS, 1981) is, with additional explanation, a useful starting point.

Assessment is a continuous process whereby problems are identified and appropriate responses decided upon. It does not imply any particular organization, structure, institution or building. We identified the aims of assessment in intervention with children as:

1. To describe the problem presented or experienced by the child.

2. To make a judgement about the nature of the problem for which the child is referred.

3. To make recommendations about the form of intervention, if any, required to resolve or alleviate the problem(s).

Such a definition implies a clear consensus on a model of social intervention which may in fact not exist. Such a model is 'problem' focused and suggests intervention is appropriate when a problem has been identified either by the individual in the form of self-referral, his or her family, neighbours, or other informal social networks, or by the formal state and voluntary agencies, for example, police, education, health, NSPCC. Such a model rejects the view that social intervention is concerned with uncovering and identifying needs. This is rejected since there are major criticisms of the validity of needs theory. A problem focus allows for a wide variation of behaviour to be presented. For example, the child may be experiencing the problem (perhaps being ill-treated by the parent), or the community may be experiencing the problem when the child is committing a series of serious and dangerous acts.

Alternatively, the child may be experiencing the problem without any obvious external source, for example, suffering severe depression or phobic anxiety. Moreover, the child could be suffering unfortunate repercussions of the problem, possibly being received into care because the parents have been made homeless. So the homelessness is the problem, not the child.

Whatever the focus of the problem, no assessment can be made until that problem is identified in some way. Many thousands of children and their families suffer a range of problems which are never assessed; rightly so, because they do not present as visible problems to agencies. This is not to argue for an expansion of intervention but merely to illustrate that a problem is not a problem for psychologists until identified by some means and made accessible to the psychologist.

The problem having been presented, the psychologist, after a preliminary assessment, may well decide that it is not a 'real' problem for intervention or not one appropriately dealt with by the agency. The 'reality' of the problem depends upon the nature, frequency, and severity of its occurrence. Most children have occasional rows with their parents; therefore, a 'row with parents' is not necessarily a 'real' problem. However, rows which occur persistently over the adolescent's sexual behaviour and lead the parents to reject the child could well prove to be a 'real' problem. Whatever the reality of the problem, it may still not be an appropriate one for the agency. A child who has persistent problems at school because of apparent but unidentified learning problems certainly has a real problem but not one appropriately dealt with by social work intervention. The appropriate action in such a case may well be to ensure the child is retained in the educational service.

Assessment also aims to make recommendations concerning forms of intervention, if any. Any single problem may be helped by a range of interventions, many of which are contradictory and strongly disputed. It is possible to imagine a phobia in an adolescent which, theoretically, could be alleviated by a range of interventions from individual psychoanalysis through group-work, to individual behaviour-modification programmes. An assessment would make recommendations about which form or forms of intervention would be most effective. This presupposes an extraordinary and probably unattainable level of knowledge amongst workers. It also presupposes a range of clear-cut research findings on the effectiveness of various interventions, which frankly does not exist. The absence of this basic knowledge does not unfortunately allow the assessor the privilege of inaction. The assessor will have to continue to make judgements which often will be little better than random decisions. If this is so, it is crucial that 'no action' is one of the range of possible interventions, because, in many instances, after thorough and elaborate assessment the best decision may be that no intervention is less likely to be detrimental to the young person than ill-tested or inappropriate intervention. Psychologists should also content themselves with the fact that often their intervention will not resolve but may alleviate the problem. Many interventions in childhood will not produce a major conversion but may make a marginal improvement.

Current situation in the United Kingdom. No information is available on the numbers of children being referred to, and therefore assessed by, social agencies (DHSS, 1981) or about the numbers of children who, following a court appearance, are subsequently referred for further assessment. Numbers are not available for those being assessed in day centres or groups of various kinds either.

What is known is that on 31 March 1981 there were 96,9000 children in the care of local authorities in England and Wales (DHSS, 1981). Each of these will have been assessed by some means or another before a decision was taken to receive them into care. However, admission into care does not necessarily mean the child was removed from home for offending behaviour. Of the number in care approximately 15,000 were there following an offence.

Thus, while assessments of children with important outcomes are currently being made in large numbers in a range of settings, information is only available on a minority of children, the 5,000 being assessed in residential assessment centres.

On 31 March 1981, 4,900 children were in community homes with observation and assessment facilities. Given that the average turnover of children in these centres is four times per annum, this means that about 20,000 children are being assessed each year.

The centres often accommodate children from a wide age range; sometimes from under 2 to 17. However, a recent survey (1976) found the majority of children (70 per cent of all boys and 74 per cent of all girls) in assessment centres were in the 11-15 age range, and a minority (15 per cent of girls and 20 per cent of boys) aged 10 and under. The majority were in care following offending.

Although initially observation and assessment centres were envisaged as short-stay facilities, the survey indicated that nearly half the children remain in the centres over two months and that a significant minority (13 per cent) stay over 6 months. Alternatively, a number of children stay for a very short time indeed (about 25 per cent stay for less than 4 weeks).

The concentration on the stages of assessment in this chapter is justified, since it would be argued most processes of assessment are still based on a number of assumptions which have been questioned earlier in this chapter. The assumption that human personality is constant, enduring, measurable and predictable leads to a form of assessment which is likely to attract greater state intervention than is required or justified.

It is argued that these forms of assessment extend intervention, and as will be seen later the intervention may itself prove detrimental to the young person, reinforcing the deviancy. What therefore, would be the impact of reduced assessment? This question is being asked by increasing numbers of probation and social services, who are adopting policies whereby they do not routinely provide SIRs on first time offenders in the juvenile court. This policy originally adopted by the Greater Manchester Probation Service has been taken up by a number of social services departments within the Manchester area. A throughput study of one such area has provided a unique opportunity for rapid feedback on the impact of this policy (SIS, 1983). In the 6-month study, 291 cases were dealt with; of these, just over half (146 cases) entered the court without an SIR. The majority of these cases (73.3 per cent) involved juveniles who were appearing for the first time. In the deliberate absence of a report, the majority of those juveniles received a nominal penalty (that is, a fine or less in 87 per cent of cases - see Table 1). Only two custodial sentences resulted in a hearing where no report was available.

Table 1. Court outcome in the absence of an SIR

Withdrawn/dismissed	20	Fine	74
Absolute discharge	6	Attendance centre	15
Conditional discharge	24	Supervision order	2
Bound over	5	Detention centre	2
			146

It appears from this study that the absence of an assessment leads the Bench to assume that the offender is a 'normal' offender and therefore requires only a nominal penalty to rectify his behaviour, and not substantial long-term professional intervention.

Assessment for treatment

The thesis developed in this chapter is that delinquent behaviour results from specific situational determinants. The response from the police, courts and social agencies which make up the juvenile justice system will form a set of secondary situational determinants which can reinforce the delinquent image of the young person, thereby unintentionally maintaining the delinquent behaviour. By adopting a diversionary or minimal intervention stance, the juvenile justice system may reduce the likelihood of reinforcing the behaviour and therefore reduce the likelihood of recidivism.

The adoption of this approach has particular significance when assessing a juvenile offender for a treatment programme. Traditional treatment programmes have operated in generalized, if not grandiose, terms very often omitting any comment or concentration on the actual offending behaviour.

An alternative stance is to accept that offending behaviour is a result of specific situational determinants and rewarding after-effects. Such a stance leads to a treatment model in which a detailed analysis is made of:

the antecedents in the situation;
the actual offending behaviour;
the outcomes, both in terms of actual rewards and believed outcomes on the part of the offender.

Once this analysis has been undertaken a detailed 'attack' can be mounted on the behaviour in specific, strategic ways. For example, steps can be taken to reduce the possibility of the 'delinquent' situation being replicated, close surveillance may be provided to add a constraining determinant to the 'delinquent' situation, and new social skills which allow the offender to 'escape' without loss of status from delinquent situations can be taught. The actual and imagined rewards can be questioned publicly by the individual's peer group. There is nothing so effective for an offender who believes his actions have led to him achieving status among his peers than to be confronted by them and told he is a 'wanker' or 'wally' for committing the offence. Denman (1983) has produced a handbook for practitioners, which attempts to develop an individualized assessment of offenders and a programme of treatment objectives, as well as provide techniques for achieving these objectives. Denman's system is based on two guiding principles:

1. To discover, rather than attribute, 'reasons' or 'explanations' for a particular individual's specific delinquent action, in terms of phenomena at each different level, including situational phenomena.

2. To focus on private explanations and on individual accounts, which in effect means asking the offender.

Denman proposes a hierarchy of priorities for analysis and subsequent attack.

1. The behaviour and situation context - the specific details of the delinquent episode.

2. The reasoning behind the action - why did the offender decide to take part in this delinquent activity as opposed to other non-delinquent activities?

3. The general and more stable perceptions and philosophies held by the individual. The individual's account of specific phenomena (people, events, ideas, etc.) which arose in 2.

4. The past and present biographical events and situations which appear to be salient to 3.

Having constructed these priorities, Denman proposes using 'reasoning group work' based on knowledge from the social psychology of groups to:

1. Help the individual understand his own reasoning and belief system and how it influences behaviour.

2. Attack the beliefs which appear to be getting him into trouble.

3. Reinforce those beliefs which appear likely to stop him from getting into trouble.

4. Provide new beliefs which appear likely to stop him from getting into trouble.

5. Raise the importance he attaches to those beliefs which are likely to stop him from getting into trouble.

6. Lower the importance he attaches to those beliefs which appear to be getting him into trouble.

7. Raise and/or lower his certainty about outcomes as necessary.

Denman and others have implemented this programme with groups of juvenile offenders and are currently evaluating the impact on recidivism. Whatever the outcome of the evaluation, the programme is an interesting attempt to base a treatment model on the known evidence of situational determinants of crime. Moreover, it is an attempt to develop a treatment practice which also accepts minimal intervention. In Denman's programme, the 'professional' focuses attention solely on the individual's offending behaviour on the basis that state intervention is justified by that behaviour; other aspects of the offender's life-style, family, or belief-structure are ignored unless the offender declares them relevant to the offence. Such a degree of specificity strengthens both the position of the professional and the offender and would at least appear to have greater face validity than the generalized claims referred to earlier in this section.

METHODS OF EVALUATION

Much of the research under this heading was prompted by trying to discover what exactly was happening within the juvenile justice system, and therefore focuses on the operation of the system rather than the chidren entering it. Zander (1975) was one of the first to examine what was actually happening to those children made subject to care orders. Taking a sample of juveniles drawn from London boroughs and appearing before the London juvenile courts he discovered that 48 per cent of children made subject to a care order were actually admitted to residential care. The remaining children he divided into two groups - those who were returned home or to live with a relative as the result of a considered decision by social workers (18 per cent), and those who were returned home by default because no suitable institutions could be found (29 per cent). Three per cent were categorized as miscellaneous (rounding down in the original means the figures do not add up to 100 per cent). Following these children through their placement, he discovered that those sent home as deliberate policy were less likely to re-offend than those sent to treatment institutions, despite the fact that the opportunity to re-offend theoretically ought to have been greatly reduced for the latter group since the follow-up period commenced on the making of the care order. The group returned to the community by 'default' had the greatest likelihood of re-offending. This study suggests that deliberate minimal intervention may be effective, whereas just 'doing nothing' is detrimental to the young person.

Cawson mounted a large-scale study to examine what happened to juvenile offenders on care orders in England and Wales (Cawson, 1979). Using a postal questionnaire, Cawson followed up a sample of 497 children committed to the care of local authorities in the month of July 1975. Home Office records for the same period show 664 juveniles committed to care, whereas figures in the DHSS annual returns for the same period are only about 550. From the official statistics it is impossible to determine the completeness of Cawson's sample.

Although there were some regional variations in response rates, Cawson's work proved invaluable in laying some of the myths about the workings of the juvenile justice system.

Firstly, she showed that the level of delinquency of many children committed to care is not high: 30 per cent of her sample were committed to care on their first court appearance and almost 50 per cent were committed by their second. This was even more marked amongst girls, three quarters of whom were committed after their first and second appearances compared to 56 per cent of boys.

Thorpe, Green and Smith (1980) attempted to allow for cautioning prior to court proceedings as an explanation of the early use of care orders, and still found figures compatible with those of Cawson. In both studies, the vast majority of juveniles committed to care were committed following offences against property (82 per cent).

In contrast to the apparently marginal effect institutions have been shown to have on subsequent delinquent behaviour, cross-institutional studies have found them to have had a very powerful influence upon the behaviour of inmates while they were in residence. In his study of 23 probation hostels, Sinclair (1971) found that the proportion of boys who left prematurely because they had absconded or re-offended during their stay varied from 14 per cent to 78 per cent. Similar variations in 'drop-out' rates, ranging from 15 per cent to 66 per cent, amongst 15 community homes with education were found by Tutt (1976).

In Sinclair's study, this variation could not be accounted for by differences amongst intakes to each hostel nor by the more obvious difference of hostel size, age-range admitted, or location. A large amount of the variation in rates of premature leaving could, however, be accounted for by the different ways in which wardens ran their hostels. It was concluded that the hostel environment was the most important factor in determining its success while the boys were in the hostels, but had no effect upon post-release reconviction rates of the boys.

The importance of the institutional environment in determining current behaviour patterns was stressed by Clarke and Martin (1971) in their study of absconding from approved schools. Most of the considerable variation in absconding rates between schools (those in senior schools, for example, ranged from 10 per cent to 75 per cent) and much of the variability among individuals seemed to be due to the influence of the schools' environments; personal factors were largely unrelated to absconding behaviour. They also found that persistent absconding appeared to be a learned behaviour. Just as results from evaluative research have shown both the lack of evidence for differential effects and poor overall levels of effectiveness in reducing delinquent behaviour in the post-institutional environment, so evidence from Clarke and Martin's and Sinclair's work demonstrated the importance of the immediate environment in determining current behaviour.

Research into community-based projects has been carried out on a small local scale and often fails to achieve reasonable standards of evaluation. However, two important attempts at monitoring community-based programmes are worthy of comment. Hazel (1978) carried out an action research project to assess the viability of establishing foster care as an alternative to institutional placement of difficult and disturbed adolescents. Hazel's work led her to conclude that the placement in foster care of 14 to 15-year-old boys straight from the juvenile court could be an effective strategy. This research has had a far-reaching impact on the operation of social work (services) department, a substantial number of which have set up specialist family placement schemes following the success of Hazel's work. The practice developed by Hazel is firmly based on the theory that behaviour is situationally determined, and therefore, if offenders are placed in 'pro-social' situations, for example, foster families, their behaviour will be modified accordingly, whereas if placed in 'anti-social' situations, for example, institutions, in which their only direct contacts are the deviant sub-culture, then the young person's deviant behaviour will be reinforced.

The other community programme of a quite different nature is that organized by Community Service Volunteers (CSV), who in their Child Care programme place adolescents, many of them with serious histories of offending and being in care, as volunteer workers in local authority or voluntary placements. Placements have included work in playgroups, with the mentally handicapped, hospitals, homes for the physically handicapped and elderly. Millham et al. (1980) monitored the performance of the project and of the 432 young people referred to the scheme. Their results suggested that 'the CSV rates (of reconviction) compare well with the Borstal figures, although the numbers of young people involved are insufficiently large to make the comparison conclusive'. They continue:

> While we cannot be conclusive about the effectiveness of the CSV scheme for young offenders, it is clear from this evidence that this approach has helped some very serious offenders just as effectively, and perhaps more successfully, than institutional remedies. It has not only kept these young people in the community but seems to have also markedly reduced their delinquent tendencies. Indeed, the fact that only 6 per cent of the cohort were in penal establishments at the time of our follow-up study adds weight to this supposition. (Millham et al., 1980)

Finally, since the problem of juvenile offending is now seen, in part at least, as being defined by the interaction between the individual juvenile and the juvenile justice system, and since the nature of this interaction influences the outcomes for the individual's delinquent career, psychologists are being increasingly required to develop new methods with which to monitor the operation of the system.

Many attempts have been made to develop alternative programmes to custody for juvenile offenders. However, the introduction of such programmes has not succeeded in lowering rates of custodial sentencing, but merely in increasing the numbers of young people in such programmes - 'net widening'. This process occurs because it is not easy to determine whether or not any one delinquent referred to an alternative programme would in fact be a 'candidate' for a custodial sentence did that programme not exist.

One of the possible solutions to this problem is the development of information systems which can monitor the workings of local juvenile criminal justice systems and thereby evaluate the impact of changes in local policy and practice. Such a monitoring system works by separating out the characteristics of individual delinquents (in terms of their age, sex, area location, type of offence and delinquent career) from official reaction to their behaviour, whether police, education, social or probation service or juvenile court reaction. Therefore it becomes possible to examine in detail total populations of delinquents and the ways in which official reactions to them are constructed and vary. Such a monitoring system seeks to answer two questions:

1. What are the essential characteristics of the local delinquent population and how do they vary over time?

2. What are the official responses to these juveniles and how are these responses constructed in terms of the interactions of local agencies? For example, does an increase in police cautioning affect the decisions made in the juvenile court?

For the purpose of system monitoring as well as evaluating the impact of the implementation of new services, the questions are reduced to:

1. What changes have occurred in the delinquent population?

2. What changes have occurred in official reactions which can be accounted for by: (a) changes in the delinquent population; (b) changes in the services provided?

The characteristics which illustrate these changes are assembled locally and then subjected to computer analysis (Social Information Systems, 1983). Such monitoring allows key variables to be controlled. Thus, if a new service is introduced and then utilized by the court, is there a corresponding reduction in other 'target' sentences? If there is, can those two changes be causally linked? This is possible only if the juvenile population can be shown not to have changed substantially, nor other reactions changed, for example, no increase in police cautioning. Only with these variables controlled can the service be deemed on target.

This approach to monitoring clearly reflects the developments in psychological theory, since it attempts to tease out the significant factors which arise from the individual's behaviour and those which arise from the situation or reaction to that behaviour.

REFERENCES

ALL-PARTY PENAL AFFAIRS GROUP (1983) **The Prevention of Crime Among Young People.** Chichester: Barry Rose

BALDWIN, J. and BOTTOMS, A.E. (1976) **The Urban Criminal.** London: Tavistock

BANDURA, A. (1969) Social-learning theory of identificatory processes. In: D. Goslin (ed.) **Handbook of Socialization Theory and Research.** New York: Rand McNally

BELSON, W.A. (1978). **Television Violence and the Adolescent Boy.** Farnborough: Saxon House

BINDER, A., MONAHAN, J. and NEWKIRK, M. (1976) Diversion from the juvenile justice system and the prevention of delinquency. In: J. Monahan (ed.) **Community Mental Health and the Criminal Justice System.** New York: Pergamon

BINDER, A. and NEWKIRK, M. (1977) A program to extend police service capability. **Crime Prevention Review, 4,** 26-32

BRODY, S. (1977) Screen Violence and Film Censorship - Review of Research. **Home Office Research Study No. 40.** London: HMSO

CAWSON, P. (1979) **Children in Care - Some Preliminary Findings.** London: DHSS

CLARKE, R.V.G. and MARTIN, D.N. (1971) **Absconding from Approved Schools.** London: HMSO

CRAIG, M.M. and GLICK, S.J. (1963) Ten years' experience with Glueck Social Prediction Table. **Crime & Delinquency, 9,** 249-261

DENMAN, G. (1982) **Intensive Intermediate Treatment with Juvenile Offenders.** University of Lancaster: Centre of Youth, Crime and Community

DHSS (1981) **Offending by Young People: A Survey of Recent Trends.** London: DHSS

DHSS (1976) **Survey of 102 Assessment Centres by DHSS Social Work Service.** Unpublished

DHSS (1981) **Observation and Assessment of Children.** London: DHSS

DHSS (1982) **Social Services for Children in England and Wales 1979-1981.** London: HMSO

DITCHFIELD, J.A. (1983) **Police Cautioning in England and Wales.** London: HMSO

FARRINGTON, D.P. and BENNETT, T. (1981) Police cautioning of juveniles in London. **British Journal of Criminology, 21,** 123-135

GELSTHORPE, L. (1984) Taking care with the order. **Community Care, 495,** 19-21

GOLDSTEIN, J., FREUD, A. and SOLNIT, A.J. (1980) **Beyond the Best Interests of the Child.** London: Burnett Books

HARGREAVES, D.H. (1967) **Social Relations in a Secondary School.** London: Routledge and Kegan Paul

HAZEL, N. (1978) The use of family placements. In: N. Tutt (ed.) **Alternative Strategies for Coping with Crime.** Oxford: Blackwell

HOME OFFICE (1983) **Criminal Statistics 1982.** London: HMSO

HOME OFFICE (1983) **Social Inquiry Reports; General Guidance on Content; Circular No. 17/1983.** London: HMSO

JARDINE, E. (1983) Models of diversion in intervention with alienated adolescents. In: J. Harbison (ed.) **Children of the Troubles.** Belfast: Learning Resource Unit

MAYHEW, P., CLARK, R.V.G., STURMAN, A. and HOUGH, J.M. (1976) Crime as Opportunity. **Home Office Research Study No. 34.** London: HMSO

METROPOLITAN POLICE (1978) Personal communication

McCLINTOCK, F.H. and AVISON, J.H. (1968) **Crime in England and Wales.** London: Heinemann

MILLHAM, S., BULLOCK, R., HAAK, M., HOSIE, K. and MITCHELL, L. (1980) **Give and Take: A Study of C.S.V.'s Project for Young People in Care.** London: Community Service Volunteers

NEWMAN, O. (1972) **Defensible Space: People and Design in the Violent City.** London: Architectural Press

POWER, M.J., BENN, R.T. and MORRIS, J.N. (1972) Neighbourhood, school and juveniles before the Courts. **British Journal of Criminology, 12,** 111-132

REYNOLDS, D. and JONES, D. (1978) Education and the prevention of juvenile delinquency. In: N. Tutt (ed.) **Alternative Strategies for Coping with Crime.** Oxford: Blackwell

RUTTER, M., COX, A., TUPLING, C., BERGER, M. and YULE, W. (1975) Attainment and adjustment in two geographical areas. The prevalence of psychiatric disorder. **British Journal of Psychiatry, 125,** 493-509

RUTTER, M., MAUGHAN, B., MORTIMORE, P., OUSTON, J. and SMITH, A. (1979) **Fifteen Thousand Hours.** London: Open Books

SARRI, R. (1983) Paradigms and pitfalls in juvenile justice diversion. In: A. Morris and H. Giller (eds) **Providing Criminal Justice for Children.** London: Edward Arnold

SINCLAIR, I.A.C. (1971) **Hostels for Probationers.** London: HMSO

SOCIAL INFORMATION SYSTEMS (1983) **A Report on the Juvenile Justice System in Stockport.** Sheffield: Social Information Systems

SOCIAL INFORMATION SYSTEMS (1984) **A Report on the Juvenile Justice System in Newcastle.** Sheffield: Social Information Systems

THORPE, D., GREEN, C. and SMITH, D. (1980) **Punishment and Welfare.** University of Lancaster: Centre of Youth, Crime and Community

TUTT, N. (1974) **Care of Custody.** London: Darton, Longman and Todd

TUTT, N. (1976) Recommittals of juvenile offenders. **British Journal of Criminology, 16,** 355-358

TUTT, N. (1981) A decade of policity. **British Journal of Criminology, 21,** 246-256

TUTT, N. and GILLER, H. (1983) Police cautioning of juveniles: the practice of diversity. **Criminal Law Review, September,** 587-596

TUTT, N. and GILLER, H. (1983) **Social Inquiry Reports - Audio-training Cassette.** Kirkby Lonsdale, Lancaster: Information Systems

VERNON, P.E. (1963) **Personality Assessment: A Critical Review.** London: Methuen

WEST, D.J. and FARRINGTON, D. (1973) **Who Becomes Delinquent?** London: Heinemann

WILSON, H. (1980) Parental supervision: a neglected aspect of delinquency. **British Journal of Criminology, 20,** 203-235

ZANDER, M. (1975) What happens to young offenders in care? **New Society, July,** 185-187

ASSESSMENT PROCEDURES IN ORGANIZATIONS

Peter Herriot

The area of assessment is mostly concerned with how organizations select individuals to work for them; however, it also comprises the activity of appraisal, by which an employee's performance is assessed. This chapter will concentrate upon assessment for selection.

As in several other areas of applied psychology, there is a major divergence between what is recommended as sound professional practice and what actually happens on the ground. There are several different possible explanations for this divergence. One is typically favoured by academics and runs as follows:

> Personnel selectors in organizations are ill-trained. They do not understand the basic concepts of appropriate professional practice, and they have not acquired the skills necessary to carry out the requisite techniques. They pay no attention whatsoever to such vital questions as their selection ratio or how variable their criterion measures are.

Organizations might reply:

> These academics live in a perfect world - up their ivory towers. They do not understand the reality of personnel work - the politics involved, the pressure to cut costs, the fact that every job is different, the need to recruit in the organization's image. And they think we've got all the time in the world - they may have, but we definitely haven't.

Instead of taking the academic view caricatured above, I hope in this chapter to take things a little further - to explore why theory and practice diverge so much. This exploration will involve us in making explicit the underlying assumptions of the theory of assessment, and in asking whether assessment itself is the appropriate conceptual model to use. The structure of this chapter will therefore be as follows: first, we will consider the recommended professional theory and practice - how it ought to be done, according to the conventional wisdom. Next, we will look at how selection and appraisal actually are done, considering the evidence and applying the criteria of professional practice in our evaluation. Finally, we will try to explain the divergence, by analysing what is going on from an organizational and a social-psychological point of view.

PROFESSIONAL PRACTICE

The theory

Personnel specialists who engage in selection procedures have long had a bad press. They are stereotyped, if they have psychological leanings, as firing off a battery of tests in the hope that one or two of them will turn out to be effective. If they have no psychological orientation, they are criticized for using the same old techniques of application form, references and interview in such a way as to permit all their gut feelings to find ample expression.

Recently, considerable efforts have been made to construct a theoretical framework for selection procedures. It will not surprise the cynical to learn that this framework comprises in effect a recommendation on how to conduct scientific research. It is lucidly described in an excellent review article by Guion (1976). Guion outlines a sequential strategy for establishing a selection procedure, which runs as follows: Step One - decide what it is that you are trying to predict. What you are trying to predict is known as the criterion, a somewhat confusing usage since we also refer to selection criteria. This latter term denotes the data we use to make the selection rather than what it is we are trying to predict. It is assumed that the criterion will be some sort of assessment of how well the employee, once selected, performs at the job. Thus we might find that in many cases the criterion is job performance. However, 'job performance' is a construct, a theoretical concept. We cannot predict a construct - we have to operationalize it in terms of observations or measures.

Step Two, therefore, involves the task of operationalizing the criterion. Suppose we have decided that job performance is what we are trying to predict, how can we observe and measure it? Frequently used criterion measures are supervisors' ratings, often made annually as part of an employee's appraisal. Alternatively, more direct measures such as percent increase in sales (for sales persons) or number of patents applied for (for research and development scientists) are employed.

Now that we know what we are trying to predict, and have devised means of measuring it, the next step, Step Three, is to decide what is likely to predict the criterion. Guion (1976) suggests that this should be done 'on the basis of informed opinion'. This implies reliance on rule of thumb and authority rather than on a theoretically based body of scientific knowledge. However, sophisticated methods of job analysis have been developed in order to assist in the discovery of likely predictors. If the criterion is job performance, then the predictors are considered likely to be the skills and personal attributes needed for the job. Examples of these techniques are those of Dunnette (1976) and McCormick (1976).

Dunnette uses the critical incident technique made popular by Flanagan and Herzberg. He asks individuals doing a particular job to describe the critical or important incidents which resulted in successful or unsuccessful outcomes. He asks them to describe what it was that they were doing, and categorizes this behaviour under a more general dimension (for example, consideration towards subordinates or organizing and utilizing manpower resources). Then Dunnette infers the personal characteristics necessary to perform well on these dimensions (for example dominance, self-assurance, decisiveness). It is assumed that measures of these characteristics will predict a job performance criterion.

McCormick (1976), on the other hand, analyses jobs exhaustively, by means of his Position Analysis Questionnaire. The analysis is in terms of elements of jobs, which are reduced to job dimensions. There are 27 job dimensions, by some of which all jobs may be described: jobs differ with respect to their profile on these dimensions. Each dimension represents a type of behaviour which may in principle be observed and assessed by means of psychological tests.

This brings us to Step Four, which is to operationalize these predictors. That is, we have to discover means of measuring the personal qualities, attributes and skills which we have hypothesized will predict the criterion. Psychological tests of aptitude or personality present themselves as immediate candidates, but recently much emphasis has been laid on job sample tests (Asher and Sciarrino, 1974). Once a job has been analysed into its predominant tasks, samples of these tasks may be likely to predict future performance at them. Thus, applicants may be given one of the exercises that will be used to train them, if they are selected (trainability tests); or they may be given a typical in-basket of a middle manager, full of urgent problems requiring solution (work-sample test).

Thus we have, after Step Four, an hypothesis of a testable nature; for we have predictor constructs and criterion constructs, both operationalized in such a way that measures may be obtained and the extent to which they are related be ascertained.

However, professional practice requires more than this. First, we have to ensure that Steps Two and Four are soundly based; that is, we have to demonstrate that the measures obtained really do reflect the construct they are supposed to evidence. For example, are sales figures acceptable measures of a salesman's job performance? Are supervisors' ratings reliable? Are intelligence tests really measures of scientific creativity? The onus is laid upon the selector to demonstrate by theoretical argument and evidence that such measures do have construct validity, as it is called. Second, we have to take account of other constructs as well as predictor constructs at Step Three. We have, in fact, to look for moderator constructs. A moderator construct implies that the same selection instrument may be a better predictor for certain classes of persons than it is for others. So, for example, we might hypothesize that extraversion was an important quality for success at selling. But it might be the case that while men who scored highly on extraversion were much more successful than those who scored lower, the same was not so true of women. That is, the relationship between the predictor (a test of extraversion) and the criterion (a measure of sales performance) was greater for men than it was for women. In this case, sex is a moderator variable.

We have not finished yet. We still have to test our hypothesis on the organization for which employees are being selected. Only if the predictor variables do actually succeed in predicting the criterion variables does our procedure have criterion validity. Obviously, this is the way in which, in part at least, an organization should evaluate its selection procedure, though it will want to know its real cost effectiveness and utility in addition (Cascio and Sibley, 1979). The usual method of testing our hypothesis is to obtain predictor measures and criterion measures from presently employed workers in the organization. We can discover which measures add to the predictive power of our procedure and which do not by means of the multivariate technique of multiple regression. Having assured ourselves that our results are not specific to the sample of employees we used by cross-validating them on another sample, we will then retain the predictive variables only, and start using them to select applicants.

What we have done has been couched in the respectable terminology of scientific investigation. However, a correlation obtained between predictors and criterion is not of interest to the practitioner merely because it confirms his or her hypothesis. It is of far more practical value, for it reduces the number of errors in selection.

Consider Figure 1, which presents the relationship between a predictor variable (overall judgements of suitability, rated from 0 to 9) and a criterion variable (performance at a final test at the end of an initial period of training). Each cross represents an individual trainee. In box 1, the relationship between predictor and criterion is quite close, whereas in box 2, it is much less strong. Now assume two things: first, that selection was made at a cut-off point of 5 - those with a rating of 5 or above were selected; second, assume that those who scored 5 or above on the post-training test are capable of subsequent employment, whereas those who score below 5 are not. In box 3, we see the outcome for the result obtained in box 1. The top-right quadrant represents those who were selected and who passed the test; the top-left those who were not selected but who would have passed the test; the bottom-right those who were selected and who did not pass the test; and bottom-left those who were not selected and who would not have passed the test. Clearly those in the top-left and the bottom-left quadrants would not in practice have been selected or trained - their results would be extrapolated statistically from those of the applicants who were selected. Students of experimental psychology will recognize the instances in the bottom-right as 'false positives' - those who were selected but should not have been; and those in the top-left as 'false negatives' - those who were not selected but should have been. Now look at box 4, where we see the outcome for the result obtained in box 2. Clearly there are more errors, both false positive and false negative, since the relationship between predictor and criterion is weaker. Hence, any increase in predictive power of our procedure will reduce the number of errors. Organizations particularly concerned to select 'high fliers' will be very concerned if there are too many false negatives, while organizations for whom a false positive may result in extreme cost will be keen to avoid that type of error.

In recent years, it has been alleged that Step Five should be unnecessary. Suppose, for example, that we have employed McCormick's technique of job analysis described above. This will result in the hypothesis of a set of predictor variables consisting largely of psychological tests. These tests will already have been validated; for example, it will have been shown that people who score highly on a test of manual dexterity are more dexterous in a variety of tasks. Hence it is not necessary to validate the test each time it is used to select; what is important is to give the

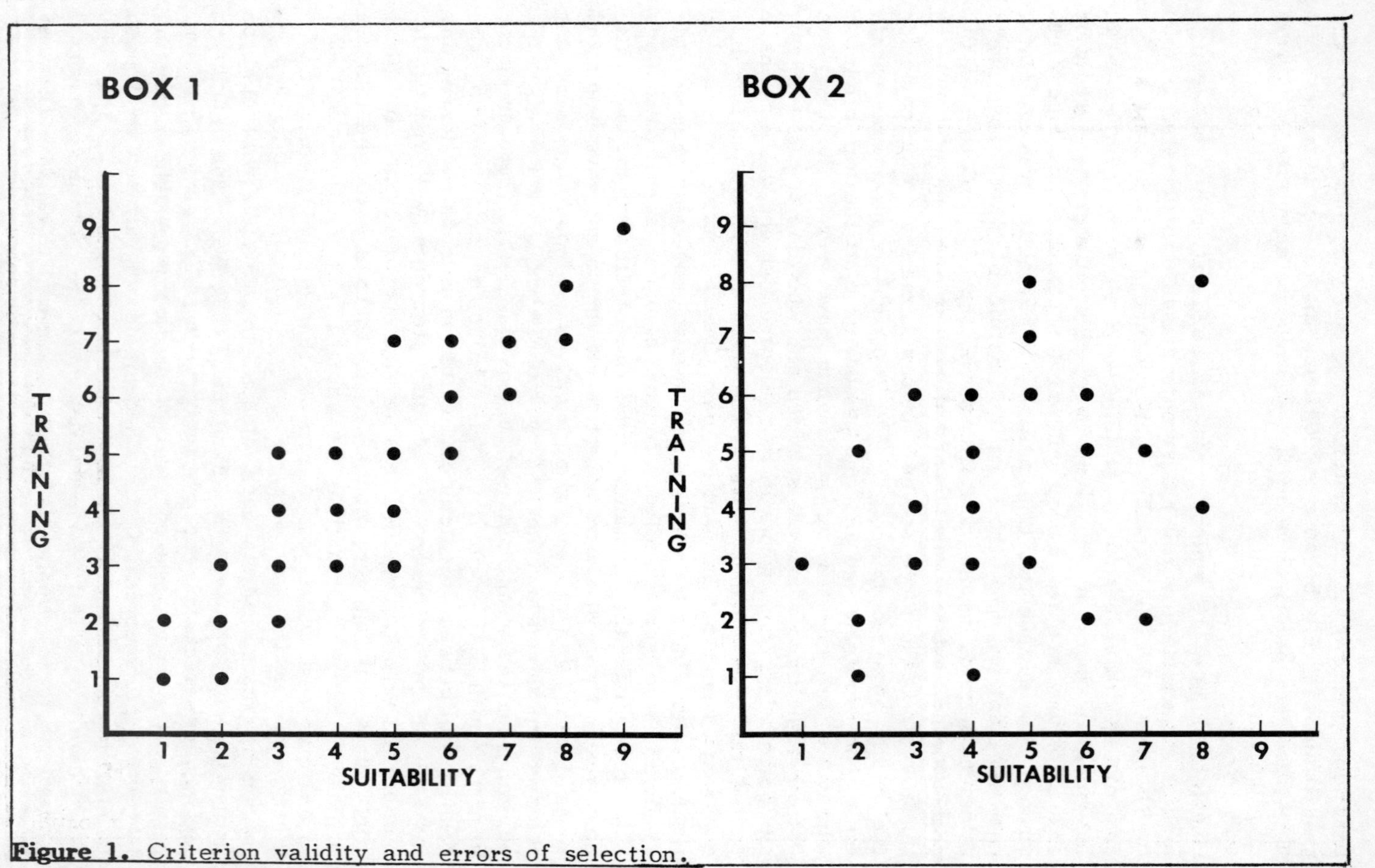

Figure 1. Criterion validity and errors of selection.

Figure 1 continued

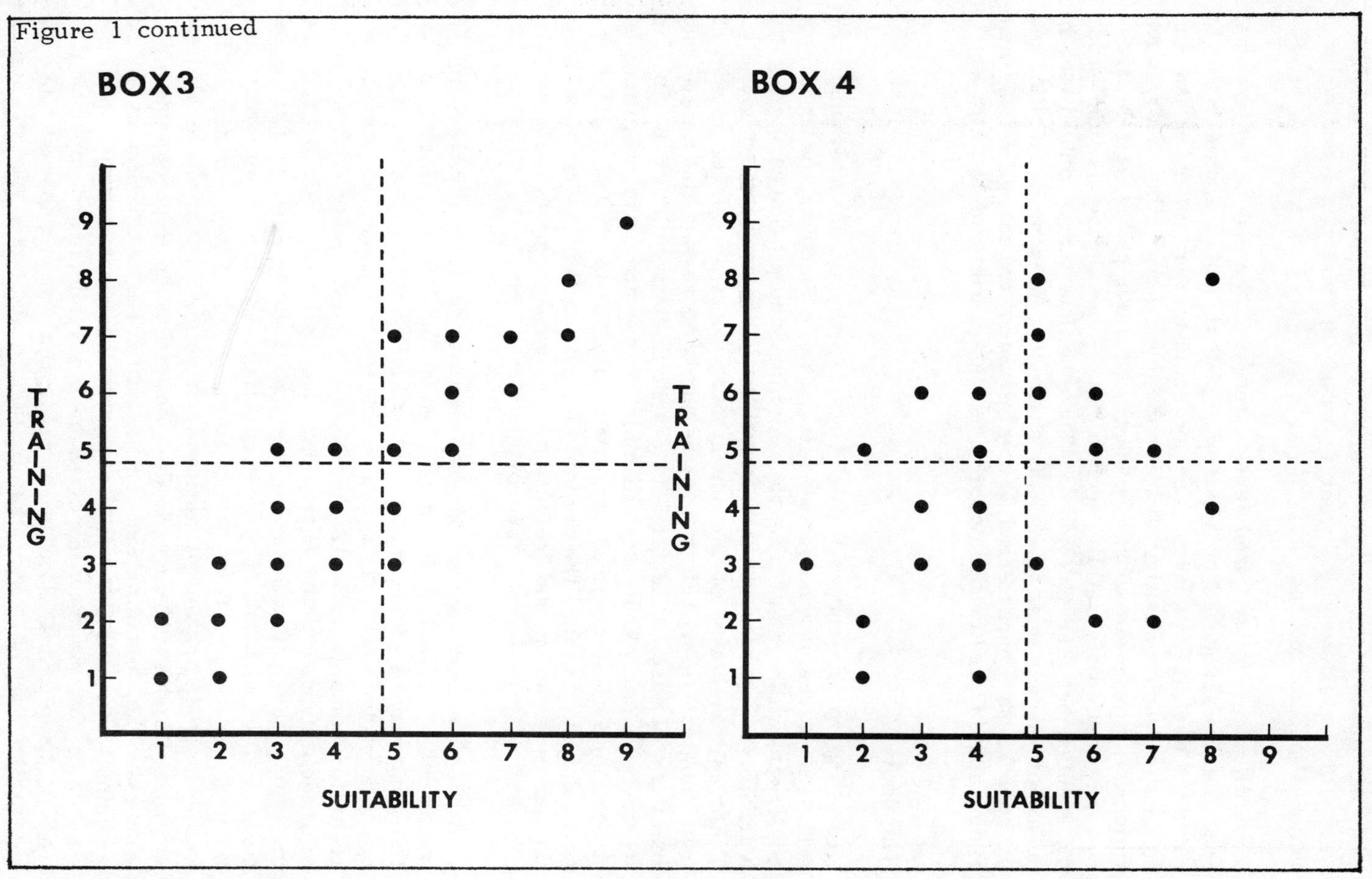

test the appropriate weight relative to other predictor variables. This will depend on the extent to which dexterity is found to be a major dimension of the job.

Regardless of these arguments, the recommended professional practice, as advocated by academics in text books, approximates to what is described above. The procedure is represented as the scientific one of devising and testing hypotheses; the theory upon which hypotheses are based is the set of assumptions held by those we may call differential psychologists - psychologists who study differences between individuals. They believe that people differ in terms of characteristics such as aptitudes, personality traits, and so on. These characteristics are assumed to change little over time, and to predict behaviour in a wide variety of situations.

The tools

According to the theory outlined above, the primary technique of selection is the psychological test. This is because the predictor constructs which result from the recommended procedure are usually attributes of persons - skills, aptitudes, personality traits, etc. The traditional way of measuring such constructs is by means of psychological test. This is not the place to review the nature and functions of tests - Anastasi (1982) does an excellent job. Suffice it to say here that the administration and interpretation of psychological tests has traditionally been the function of psychologists. Hence, the predominance of tests in the recommended procedure ensures that selection, at least in part, remains the preserve of professional psychologists.

Another favoured tool is the biographical data obtainable from an application form. These can be used as predictor variables in just the same way as psychological tests. For example, a selector might use the grade obtained in O-level mathematics as an operational predictor variable indicative of the predictor construct 'numerical aptitude', hypothesizing that numerical aptitude would predict the criterion (say, success in engineering training). We might argue that such a use would not have construct validity; in other words, there is little justification in treating an O-level mathematics grade as an indication of aptitude. It might be suggested that an aptitude implies capacity - what one is potentially capable of - whereas the examination grade indicates achievement. The examination result, it will be argued, depends heavily upon the quality of the education received by the applicant. A sophisticated user of biographical data might reply that he or she would use an interactive predictor - examination grade by type of school attended. This stratagem would enable him or her to utilize the valuable distinction between background factors and achievement factors. Such a procedure might serve to increase the predictive power of the variable and the fairness of the procedure; sociologists have obtained powerful evidence of the effects of the social opportunity structure upon academic attainment. Other aspects of biographical data which are typically used are previous relevant experience, positions achieved, etc.

A third selection tool frequently utilized is the reference form. Selectors assume that referees have observed the applicant performing in a variety of situations, and that they can therefore rate him or her on the various attributes necessary for such performances. Underlying this procedure is the idea that although referees may not have observed the applicant performing the tasks typical of the job, they can nevertheless infer from different behaviour the attributes necessary for it.

Also in the selector's armoury is the selection interview, although purists give it little attention as a psychometric tool. From the psychometric point of view, the interview is somewhat ambiguous. It could be viewed as a sample of the applicant's social behaviour, from which inferences about personal attributes are drawn just as they are from tests (which are also samples of behaviour, albeit taken in a controlled situation). Alternatively, the interview may be viewed as a means of verifying or expanding upon biographical data presented in the application form. Either way, it will be assumed that the products of the interview are ratings of attributes or biographical data which can serve as predictor variables.

Finally, we must consider the assessment centre, ably described by Finkle (1976). Assessment centres consist, in effect, of all the selection tools mentioned hitherto, together with exercises which are to a greater or lesser extent job-sample tests. Assessment centres differ from some other procedures, in that there are several selectors who observe the applicants and come to decisions as a group, and in that applicants are observed in a group, at least for certain of the exercises. After all the observations are made, the selectors agree upon ratings of a set of personal qualities, and also upon an overall assessment rating. These are the products of the assessment centre procedure which are typically used as predictor variables for selection purposes (it should be noted that assessment centres are also used for staff appraisal and development purposes).

The tools of the selector's trade therefore provide in theory precisely those predictor variables which are needed to test hypotheses, viz. measures of personal attributes. How well do they work?

THE REALITY

Criterion validity

An immediate and acid test of the recommended procedure is: does it work in its own terms? That is, do the predictors predict the criterion successfully? The nearest thing to a general answer to this question may be obtained from the superb article of Reilly and Chao (1982). These authors review the recent evidence on a variety of techniques, and confirm earlier findings with regard to their relative effectiveness. For a variety of criterion variables, biographical data and psychological tests are the best predictors. However, correlations between biographical data sets and criteria, and between individual psychological tests and criteria, do not often reach 0.5, explaining only 25 per cent or less of the variance. Other tools fare much worse. In their review of the selection interview, Arvey and Campion (1982) present a gloomy picture of poor criterion validity. Indeed, Reilly and Chao (1982) could find few recent studies which thought it worthwhile to test validity, and those that did had a mean correlation of 0.19 (explaining less than 4 per cent of the variance). Muchinsky (1979) found an even lower mean validity coefficient for the reference form (0.13). It should be said, however, that certain refinements have resulted in higher validity coefficients for the interview and the reference; specifically, when the applicant or the referee has been asked about observed behaviour in tasks or situations similar to those expected on the job, predictive power has increased.

One would hope that the assessment centre procedure, using as it does a battery of different techniques, might have superior criterion validity. It seems, however, that the obsession with arriving at assessments of a series of personal attributes decreases the potential predictive power of the procedure. If the different parts of the procedure were combined statistically, the validity coefficient would be considerably greater than that obtained by the overall rating (Wollowick and McNamara, 1969). Assessors tend to emphasize the highly salient exercises and interview (less valid predictors) at the expense of biographical data and tests (Gardner and Williams, 1973).

In sum, as tests of hypotheses, the criterion validities obtained in the published research are, to put it mildly, somewhat weak. As practical tools they are better than chance, although seldom explaining more than 25 per cent of the variance in the criterion variable.

Grassroots reality

Instead of looking at the results of the research literature which tests the criterion validity of examples of the best professional practice, it might be more appropriate to attempt to discover what really goes on and how best to describe it theoretically. After all, the construction of the selection procedure as the scientific testing of a predictive hypothesis is only one model of what is going on. There are others.

Let us first consider the psychological test, the lynchpin of the approved procedure. Sneath, Thakur and Medjuck (1976) received replies from 281 British organisations, of whom 72 per cent used tests in their selection procedures. Of these, only half had tried to estimate the validity of the tests in their situation, and only 5 per cent had employed any statistical method to do so. Thus, few organizations in Britain bother to discover whether the tests they employ are achieving their objective or not. There is a similar reluctance to follow the approved procedure in other elements of the selection process. Few organizations, for example, appear to do any empirical research on which biographical data are predictive. Many conduct unstructured interviews or request unstructured references, the outcome seldom being carefully constructed rating scales. The analysis of what they actually want to employ the applicant for is certainly seldom conducted in terms of the careful job analysis of Dunnette and McCormick (see p.399)

The nature of personal judgements

One response is to maintain that until the recommended practices are actually operated on a wider scale, it is unreasonable to criticize their effectiveness. However, it might be argued in response that it is usually good examples of professional practice which are investigated in the research literature, and even they (as we have discovered above) are not particularly valid. An alternative response is to try to explain why it is that selection procedures are not very successful according even to their own criteria: reliability and validity. Let us first consider ratings of personal attributes, since these are the products of interviews, references and assessment centres. Their use is buttressed by 'common sense', as our everyday language encourages us to believe that qualities reside in persons and determine what they do.

Rating scales are supposed to be psychometric instruments, in the sense that they are assumed to be measures of personal attributes. However, they have been plagued by a variety of 'errors':

the halo effect, whereby raters fail to distinguish between conceptually distinct and potentially independent attributes;

leniency or severity errors, whereby they assign a higher or lower rating than is warranted by the ratee's behaviour;

the error of central tendency, whereby they fail to use the extremes of the scale;

restriction of range, whereby ratings are all clustered around any particular point of the scale.

Immense effort has been spent in trying to improve the format of rating scales so as to reduce these errors. For example, behaviourally anchored rating scales have been developed, in which behavioural examples typical of each rating point are written on the scale. However, in their comprehensive review of the literature, Landy and Farr (1980) point out that typically only 4 to 8 per cent of the variance in ratings is explained by the format of the rating scale, while over 20 per cent is predicted by characteristics of the ratee (for example sex, race) which are irrelevant to the job. Landy and Farr ask whether it is behaviour and attributes of ratees which are actually being assessed, or whether it is not, rather, the implicit personality theories of raters. Rating scales may be telling us more about their users than their targets!

Why should this be so? The answer may lie in the nature and function of our perceptions and judgements of others. These form part of our modes of construing our social world. Individuals differ considerably in these respects. For example, some people have extremely complex conceptual systems for describing others, while others have relatively simple ones (Bieri, 1976). Some people tend to attribute what happens to them to their own efforts, while others attribute outcomes more to factors beyond their control (Rotter, 1966). Most of us are apt to attribute the causes of another's behaviour more to that individual than is justified, and less to his or her situation (Ross, 1977). We all bring such modes of construing the social world to our social experience, and cannot eliminate their effects.

Experimental psychologists will recall the failure to eliminate experimental subjects' knowledge of their language from the task of learning nonsense syllables. Knowledge of one's native language is relatively constant across individuals, however, whereas our implicit personality theories are likely to be much more varied. Thus we are left with the conclusion that, when they are asked to rate someone, raters' reliability will be poor. This will be due to their inevitable application of their differing personality theories to both the observed behaviour to be rated and the names of attributes and descriptions on the rating scale.

Social episodes

It is when we consider the function of our implicit personality theories, however, that we begin to understand the nature of selection procedures. Their function is the intensely practical one of enabling us to negotiate our social environment, in the same way that our modes of perceiving objects enable us to negotiate our material environment. Their purpose is to facilitate social exchange, not to assist 'objective' observation.

When we consider the separate components of selection procedures, it is clear how the social nature of the situation positively encourages the use of our implicit personality theories. Consider, for example, the application form. The ideal of psychometric assessment would be an actuarial calculation of the positive and negative items of information or, at least, a rating scale of attributes based upon relevant information. In fact, recruiters seem to use all sorts of information, including how the form was completed, in order to draw inferences about the applicant's personality, motivation and mobility (Wingrove, Glendinning and Herriot, 1984; Herriot and Wingrove, 1984). It is the inferences, more than the information, which predict the recruiters' decision.

Consider next the interview, a prime example of a social situation masquerading as an assessment tool. The interview is a social episode (Argyle, Furnham and Graham, 1981), with its own set of rules and with reciprocal roles which the parties play. Consider for a moment the unspoken rules of the interview - the list you produce is quite likely to be similar to the list of someone else. However, when the rules are broken, unfavourable inferences are often made about the person who breaks them! Herriot and Rothwell (1983) found that applicants who failed to speak much about certain topics which the interviewer expected them to cover were more likely to be rejected, illustrating the attributional principle that the violation of rules leads to attributions to personality.

In this research, however, an additional finding was that more attention was paid to personality inferences after the interview than before it (after merely reading the application form). Less attention was paid after interview to ability and interest factors. This implies that the interview behaviour of the applicant was used to infer personality features, exactly what we would expect of a social encounter. Considerable recent research on the interview supports this interpretation; for example, several studies have discovered that the nature of the non-verbal communication of the applicant predicts the interviewer's judgement (for example, McGovern and Tinsley, 1978).

Finally, let us review the crucial element of the assessment centre procedure - the final 'consensus discussion', as it is termed, when all the evidence from the different forms of assessment has been reviewed and the assessors have to arrive at an agreed series of ratings (or at a single overall rating of suitability). Like panel interviews, this group discussion may be construed as a social process rather than as an assessment procedure. The social-psychological literature on group decision-making would lead us to expect certain processes to be at work. In particular, we would expect the parties to be trying to persuade each other when they differed; and that they would be affected by social comparison processes such as the status of others in the group.

ORGANIZATION AND INDIVIDUAL

The self-concept

We have demonstrated that social-psychological processes such as person perception, attribution of the causes of behaviour and group influences are at work in situations which are supposed to permit objective assessment. This, it has been argued, is inevitable, since the situations are themselves social ones, and therefore our mental armoury for coping with social situations is inevitably brought into play. One alternative response to such an analysis would be to reduce the social contact between the parties in the selection process as much as possible; in other words, to rely very considerably upon psychological tests. Such a strategy fails to appreciate, however, that applicants may require a social exchange, and may treat impersonal test administration by the selector as a refusal to negotiate or offer information.

Moreover, the use of tests in this way reflects a very static view of the person. Most but not all psychological tests investigate types or traits of personality which remain relatively constant over time. For example, Eysenck's tests of extraversion-introversion and neuroticism-stability produce similar scores for individuals over periods of years (Eysenck and Eysenck, 1969).

However, these apparently relatively static forms of individual attributes may not be the best predictors of occupational and organizational adaptation. Instead, we may look to much more dynamic aspects of individuals, in particular their self-concept. If we include as part of this construct the idea of self-evaluation (self-esteem), and also one's notion of what one will become in the future (aspirations), we will stand a far better chance of such successful prediction. Self-esteem leads students to make occupational choices which are consistent with their notions of their own capacities, and they consequently are more satisfied in those occupations (Greenhaus and Sklarew, 1981). Aspirations and statements of what individuals intend to do interact with their interests to predict whether they will enter a job congruent with their studies or not (Holcomb and Anderson, 1978). For those entering their first job, of course, it is not merely a matter of entering a particular position in a particular organization. It is also a matter of entering an occupation and, indeed, of changing the theatre of one's life from the educational stage to the world of work (Super, 1980). Hence we would expect success in one's first position, especially, to be predicted by one's more general idea of one's self vis-a-vis job, type of organization, occupation, work and career.

The self-concept is not assumed to be a static aspect of the person. Rather, it is dynamic - a mode of adapting to one's environment (Bandura, 1978), by observing one's own behaviour and its consequences. Thus, the overall model of selection which we need to employ is not a static one of fitting the person to the job. This implies that people and jobs don't change much over time. Rather, the appropriate model is a dynamic one, of communication between applicant and organization with the applicant's self-concept playing a crucial part.

The social exchange model

We may, in fact, reconstrue the situation entirely as one of social exchange rather than as one of assessment by one party of the other. If we adopt this model, we find ourselves using the natural capacities of individuals to form social judgements and exercise social skills in the context for which they are developed (Herriot, 1984). Such a reconstruction recognizes that there are two parties to the selection procedure, both of whom wish to know things about the other. Applicants need to know what the organization will expect them to do; what are its plans for them in the longer term; what values it will expect them to espouse and what image to project; what life-style will be implied by their employment. This information is important since applicants will wish to establish the degree of congruence between what the organization expects of them and their own view of themselves, their aptitudes, values and aspirations. Applicants have to make decisions too, although this need may be temporarily obscured by the present employment situation.

The organization likewise needs to know about the applicants, not merely their aptitudes and achievements, but their notions of themselves, their values and their aspirations. It needs then to take a decision as to how congruent these are with the role it expects the applicant to play, immediately and in the longer term. It may also wish to estimate the probability that the role and the applicant's self-concept may become more congruent after employment (Katz and Kahn, 1978; Graen, 1976).

These decisions can only be taken meaningfully if the appropriate information has been communicated successfully. The selection procedure may be seen as a sequence of social episodes, in each of which one party sends information to the other. Hence, the organization may communicate what it expects in outline terms in the recruitment literature or job advertisement. The applicant will indicate his or her decision to continue the dialogue by responding with an application form. This could inform the organization of the applicant's past, present and future self. The organization may decide to terminate, or to continue the exchange by inviting the applicant for interview. Here the exchange sequence breaks down; both parties expect to learn more about the other, and the load on the interview may be too great (Herriot and Rothwell, 1983). In terms of a sequence of communication, it is the applicant's turn to receive information, since he or she has recently completed an application form, revealing much about himself and incidentally, risking rejection and loss of self-esteem. There is a case to be made for the organization making a presentation to the applicants before interview, in which realistic answers may be given to applicants' questions. The interview can then be used as the organization's turn to find out more about the applicant - probably by questioning him or her further on the contents of the application form. Thus the parties will have engaged in a two-way social exchange in which each party has had two opportunities of finding out about the other. After each of these episodes, each party has the opportunity of withdrawing from the social exchange - the process is as much one of self-selection in or out by the applicant as of selection of applicant by organization. The final episode might well be a negotiation, in which the organization makes offers and the applicant seeks to modify them more in accord with his or her own aspirations. Agreement by both parties implies commitment to a shared decision, and to mutual obligations.

Viewed in this way, the selection process is not an entirely separate preliminary to employment. It is rather the first stage of a continuing process - that of social exchange between organization and employee. If it is conducted ineffectively by organizations, then subsequent stages will be impeded. For example, if inaccurate information is given at the recruitment stage by employers, employees may subsequently leave, their false expectations having been shattered by experience (Wanous, 1977). Communication of role expectations, and their acceptance by the employee - or else attempts to modify them so that they are more in accord with his or her self-concept - are the building blocks of the relationship between organizations and their members (Katz and Kahn, 1978). So are the adaptations of the employee's self-concept and the organization's view of itself to their respective experiences.

There are many implications of this social exchange model of selection. One is that organizations are forced to analyse more carefully what it is they expect of employees. Such expectations are likely to extend way beyond the typical products of a job task analysis. It also forces applicants to ask themselves carefully what their intentions and aspirations are; and the extent to which organizations of different types are likely to meet those aspirations. Above all, it forces both parties to treat the situation as one of social exchange in which communication skills and the building up of a relationship of mutual trust based on accurate and freely exchanged information are paramount. The criterion for the success of such a process cannot conceivably consist of a measure of an individual employee's job performance. It must be treated in terms of the consequences of the selection procedure for the organization's functioning.

New models can serve several purposes at once. They can more adequately account for the evidence; they can guide planning and practice; and they can help people make sense of what they are doing. There is nothing more practical than a good model.

REFERENCES

ANASTASI, A. (5th edn, 1982) **Psychological Testing.** New York: MacMillan

ARGYLE, M., FURNHAM, A. and GRAHAM, J.A. (1981) **Social Situations.** Cambridge: CUP

ARVEY, R.D. and CAMPION, J.E. (1981) The employment interview: a summary and review of recent literature. **Personnel Psychology, 35,** 281-322

ASHER, J.J. and SCIARRINO, J.A. (1974) Realistic work sample tests: a review. **Personnel Psychology, 27,** 519-533

BANDURA, A. (1977) Self-efficacy: toward a unifying theory of behavioral change. **Psychological Bulletin, 84,** 191-215

BIERI, J. (1976) Cognitive complexity and personality development. In: C.J. Harvey (ed.) **Experience, Structure and Adaptability.** New York: Springer

CASCIO, W.F. and SIBLEY, V. (1979) Utility of the assessment center as a selection device. **Journal of Applied Psychology, 64,** 107-118

DUNNETTE, M.D. (1976) Aptitudes, abilities and skills. In: M.D. Dunnette (ed.) **Handbook of Industrial and Organizational Psychology.** Chicago: Rand McNally

EYSENCK, H.J. and EYSENCK, S.G.B. (1969) **Personality Structure and Measurement.** London: Routledge and Kegan Paul

FINKLE, R.B. (1976) Managerial assessment centers. In: M.D. Dunnette (ed.) **Handbook of Industrial and Organizational Psychology.** Chicago: Rand McNally

GARDNER, K.E. and WILLIAMS, A.P.O. (1973) A twenty-five-year follow-up of an extended interview selection procedure in the Royal Navy. **Occupational Psychology, 47,** 1-13, 149-161

GRAEN, G. (1976) Role-making processes in organizations. In: M.D. Dunnette (ed.) **Handbook of Industrial and Organizational Psychology.** Chicago: Rand McNally

GREENHAUS, J.H. and SKLAREW, N.D. (1981) Some sources and consequences of career exploration. **Journal of Vocational Behavior, 18,** 1-12

GUION, R.M. (1976) Recruitment, selection and job replacement. In: M.D. Dunnette (ed.) **Handbook of Industrial and Organizational Psychology.** Chicago: Rand McNally

HERRIOT, P. (1984) **Down from the Ivory Tower: Graduates and Their Jobs.** London: Wiley

HERRIOT, P. and ROTHWELL C. (1983) Expectations and impressions in the graduate selection interview. **Journal of Occupational Psychology, 6,** 303-314

HERRIOT, P. and WINGROVE, J. (1984) Decision processes in graduate pre-selection. **Journal of Occupational Psychology** (in press)

HOLCOMB, W.R. and ANDERSON, W.P. (1978) Expressed and inventoried vocational interests as predictors of college graduation and vocational choices. **Journal of Vocational Behavior, 12,** 290-296

KATZ, D. and KAHN, R.L. (2nd edn, 1978) **The Social Psychology of Organizations.** New York: Wiley

LANDY, F.J. and FARR, J.L. (1980). Performance rating. **Psychological Bulletin, 87,** 72-107

McCORMICK, E.J. (1976) Job and task analysis. In: M.D. Dunnette (ed.) **Handbook of Industrial and Organizational Psychology.** Chicago: Rand McNally

McGOVERN, T.V. and TINSLEY, H.E. (1978) Interviewer evaluations of interviewee non-verbal behavior. **Journal of Vocational Behavior, 13,** 163-171

MUCHINSKY, P.M. (1979) The use of reference reports in personnel selection: a review and evaluation. **Journal of Occupational Psychology, 52,** 287-297

REILLY, R.R. and CHAO, G.T. (1982) Validity and fairness of some alternative employee selection procedures. **Personnel Psychology, 35,** 281-332

ROSS, J. (1977) The intuitive psychologist and his shortcomings: distortions in the attribution process. In: J. Berkowitz (ed.) **Advances in Experimental Social Psychology, Volume 10.** New York: Academic Press

ROTTER, J.B. (1966) Generalised expectancies for internal versus external control of reinforcement. **Psychological Monograph, 80,** whole no. 609

SNEATH, F., THACKUR, M. and MEDJUCK, B. (1976) **Testing People at Work.** London: Institute of Personnel Management

SUPER, D.E. (1980) A life-span life-space approach to career development. **Journal of Vocational Behavior, 16,** 282-298

WANOUS, J.P. (1977) Organizational entry: newcomers moving from outside to inside. **Psychological Bulletin, 84,** 601-618

WINGROVE, J., GLENDINNING, R. and HERRIOT, P. (1984) Graduate pre-selection: a research note. **Journal of Occupational Psychology, 57,** 169-171

WOLLOWICK, H.B. and McNAMARA, W.J. (1969) Relationship of the components of an assessment centre to management success. **Journal of Applied Psychology, 53,** 348-352

INDEX

absent-mindedness 3-31
  and air disasters 22-23
  case studies 21-23
  and cognitive control 24-25
  diary studies 5-9
  and error-proneness 11-14
  and intelligence 13
  laboratory studies 16-21
  and lapses 3
  and mistakes 3
  and naturalistic studies 5-9
  place losing errors 20-21
  questionnaire studies 11-16
  and railway disasters 22
  and road disasters 22-23
  and shoplifting 14-16
  and slips 3
accidents
  and absent-mindedness 21-23
acculturation 171
acetylcholine
  information processing 130,132-135,146-148
achievement, indicators of 404
Activity (Osgood) 181
actor-observer difference 221-223
adrenaline 67,272
adreno-cortico-trophic hormone 266,269
affection 181
affective disorders
see depression
affective reactions 283
ageing
  and diurnal rhythms 80-81
  information processing 146-148,187,190
  and memory 21
  and neuro-chemical changes 147
  and place-losing errors 21
ahedonia 282
air disasters
  and absent-mindedness 22-23
algorithms
  computional theory 105,107,111-124
  and image redundancy 98
  and visual labelling 99
alpha activity 133
ambiguity
  and attribution 226
  authoritarians' intolerance of 249,252
amphetamines
  and memory 141-144
anger
  cognitive approaches 304
ANOVA cube 214
anti-anxiolytic drugs
  and memory 193
anti-semitism
  and personality factors 249,254
anxiety
  cognitive 283
  cognitive approaches 304
  and conditioning 192-193
  and extinction 192-193
  somatic 283
application forms
  and selection procedures 404
applied psychology
  and assessment 95
appraisal
  and assessment 397,398
aptitude
  indicators of 404
arousal
  autonomic 133-134
  behavioural 133-134
  and circadian changes 67-68,81-85
  diurnal variation in 67
  electrocortical 133-134
articulatory codes
  and reading aloud 32,48
articulatory loop 69-70
artificial intelligence 97
assessment
  and applied psychology 95
  and appraisal 397,398
  and delinquency 373,380-389
  and employment selection 397-414
  and inter-rater reliability 382
  and intervention 383-389
  and selection procedures 404-406
atropine
  and electrocortical arousal 134,135
  and information processing 130
attention
  and cholinergic drugs 129-132
  and cognition 13,292,298
  and consciousness 25
  and information processing 13
  limitation of 16,25
  and speech errors 18
attention, visual
  and language 163-167
attentional deficits
  and depression 302-303
attitudes, political
  and general intelligence 184
Attneave's cat 107
attribution
  and actor-observer difference 221-223
  and ambiguity 226
  and co-variance 214
  and cognition 211-217
  and learned helplessness 302-303
  and rating scales 225
attribution theory 210-234,24-245,408
  attribution process theory 210
  behavioural attribution theory 210,223-224
  dispositional 211,224-225
  and information processing 213
  and language 211
  and 'rules' 214
  situational 211,224-225
  and social psychology 210,214
Attributional Style Questionnaire 308
authoritarianism 239
  intolerance of ambiguity 249,252
Automatic Thought Questionnaire 307
automatic thoughts
  and depression 296,297
avoidance learning
  and neuroticism 192

babies
  sensitivity to speech 162
base-rate fallacy 217
Beck Depression Inventory 282,307
behaviour
  and cognition 310
  determination of 369

and maladaptive thought 299
neurochemistry of 129
stimulus-response theory 291
behaviour monitoring
and language 168-170
and neurochemistry 129
behaviour, verbal
and mental illness 168
behavioural change
and irrationality 300-301
behavioural disorders
and cognitive disorders 290
and reciprocal determinism 304
behavioural models
emotional disorders 290
behaviourism
methodological, compared to metaphysical 290-291
beliefs, irrational 355-357
Berkeley, George 97
beta activity 133
bilingualism
and cognitive development 168-169
binary constraint checking 100
binocular disparity 109
binocular stereopsis 119-124
block worlds 99,103,105
biographical data
and selection procedures 404-409
biological clocks 83
and sleep-wake cycle 84-85
and temperature 84-85
body temperature
and efficiency 66
and sleep 64-66
and sleep-wake cycle 65,82-83
brain
cholinergic systems 129
noradrenergic systems 129
brain damage
and dyslexia 50-55
Burt, Cyril 369

capacity theories
and information processing 134
capitalism
as an ideology 245
cardiovascular system
and stress 270,278
care
children in 385-386,389-390
care orders
and cautioning 390
careers counselling 350
catecholamines 67,265,171
categorization
and language 168
causal processes
and mental illness 333
causality
children's exploration of 166
and computer modelling 219
and explanation 224-225
perception of 210
cautioning
and care orders 390
and delinquency 377-380
chance
and stress 273
child rearing
and mental illness 333
children
language and thought in 156-174
Children and Young Persons Act (1969) 381
choline
and information processing 147-148
cholinergic drugs 129-132
cholinergic system
and memory 135-140
Chomsky, Noam (LAD) 163
circadian changes
and arousal 67-68,81-85
circadian rhythms 63,65
classification
and visual perception 97-99
clinical psychology
cognitive approaches 290-319
and counselling 346
and mediational factors 290
co-operative process
and visual representation 101-102
co-variation
and attribution 214
and trait psychology 177-209
cognition
and attention 13,292,298
and attribution 211-217
and behaviour 310
and clinical psychology 290-319
effects of deafness on cognitive development 159
and feed-back factors 293,298
and language 157
and memory consolidation 145-146
and mood changes 308-310
and reading 32
and relational factors 292-293,298
and response factors 293,298
and temporal isolation 83-85
and thought 157
and time of day effects 64
see also metacognition
cognitive approaches
anger 304
anxiety 304
depression 295-319
eating disorders 304
and empirical evidence 306-312
impulsive behaviour 304
pain 304
cognitive-behavioural approaches
and self-control 304
cognitive-behavioural therapy 291,355-357,359
cognitive control
and absent-mindedness 24-25
cognitive development 157-174
cognitive dissonance 221-223,244-245
cognitive distortion
and depression 306
cognitive dysfunction
and depression 295
pre-disposing factors 298
cognitive errors
systematic, in depression 296-297
cognitive factors
and clinical psychology 290-319
and counselling 352-357
and emotional disorders 290
cognitive failure
and coping strategies 13-14
and stress 12,13-14
Cognitive Failures Questionnaire 10-11
cognitive performance
and diurnal rhythms 63
and fatigue 64-65,86
cognitive psychotherapy 298

cognitive resource management 13-14
cognitive resources
  and neuroticism 192-193
cognitive schemata 296-297
Cognitive Style Test 307
cognitive therapy 290-319
communication
  and speech 158-160
see also non-verbal
  communication
communism 237
Communist party (UK) 238,254
Communist party (USA) 254
community-based projects
  and delinquency 391
Community Service Volunteers 391
community surveys
  and mental illness 320-321, 330
competing plans hypothesis 16
computational vision 95-128
  examples of 111-124
computer modelling
  and causation 219
concept object development 164
conceptualization
  distorted, in depression 297,308
  and language 168
conditioning
  and anxiety 192-193
conscience 181
consciousness
  and attention 23
consensus information
  and information processing 218
conservatism 237,242
Conservative party (UK) 238
consistency theory 244
conspiracy theory of politics 248
constraint satisfaction
  and visual representation 101
construct validity
  and selection procedures 400-407
conventional symbols 166-167
conversion, political 255
coping strategies
  and cognitive failure 13-14
correspondent inference 213-214
cortical desynchronization 133
corticosteroids 266,269,271
cortisol 271-272
counselling
  and clinical psychology 346
  cognitive components 352-357
  counsellor/client matching 350,358
  and cultural differences 361
  directive 349
  distribution of skills 347
  facilitative 349
  history of in UK 346-347
  and interaction studies 362
  and intervention 348-353
  necessary conditions for 351-353
  and organizational change 345-346
  outcome studies 356-357,360-362
  and personal change 345-346,362
  and personality theory 357-359
  and psychotherapy
  orientation 350
  research methods 357,360-361
  social components 352-356
counselling, careers 350
counselling psychology 345-368
  and clinical psychology 346
  and interaction studies 362
counselling, short-term 354-355
crime
  environmental influences 370-373
  and personality 382
crime, opportinistic 382
see also delinquency
crime prevention
  mechanical forms 373-375
  situational forms 374-375
  and social education 373
see also diversion
crisis intervention 360
criterion validity
  and selection 406-407
critical incidence technique
  and selection 399
custodial sentences
  alternatives to 392
cybernetics
  and metacognition 170

deafness
  effects on cognitive
  development 159
deduction
  and cognitive therapy 300
deep dyslexia 50,51
delayed memory
  and time of day effect 75-76
delinquency
  alternatives to
  custodial sentences 392
  assessment 373,380-389
  and care 385-386,389-390
  and cautioning 377-380
  and community-based
  projects 391
  and diversion 375-378
  effects of schools on 371
  and family background 373-375
  and foster families 391
  and institutional
  environments 391
  and intervention 384-387
  and justice 375-380,392
  and modelling behaviour 371-373
  and needs theory 383
  and net-widening 378-380,392
  and peer groups 371-372
  psycholgical research on 380
  and recidivism 387-389
  and social inquiry reports 381-382
  treatment model for 387-389

see also crime
depression
  and attentional deficits 302-303
  and automatic thoughts 296,297
  cognitive approaches 295-319
  and cognitive distortion 306
  and cognitive dysfunction 295
  and distorted
  conceptualization 297,308
  and memory 308
  and mood changes 308-309
  negative thought content 295-296,307
  and personality 298
  and pharmacotherapy 308
  and psychomotor retardation 310
  and self-control 301-302
  and stress 282
  and systematic cognitive
  errors 296-297
  treatment studies 310-312
  women's vulnerability to 321,336-337
development
  and language 157
  and thought 157

development, cognitive
  and deafness 159
developmental dyslexias 54-55
diary studies
  absent-mindedness 5-9
differential psychology 177
  and selection procedures 401
dispositional attribution 211,224-225
diurnal rhythms
  and ageing 80-81
  and cognitive performance 65
  and research methods 66
  and sex 81
  and Stroop test 86
diversion
  and delinquency 375-378
domgatism
  left/right wing, compared 252-254
Dogmatism Scale (Rokeach) 252-253
dreaming
  and memory 192-193
drugs
  information processing 129-155,193
Dysfunctional Attitude Scale 307
dyslexia
  and brain damage 50-55
dyslexia, deep 50,51
  phonological 50-54
  surface 50-54
dyslexias, developmental 54-55

eating disorders
  cognitive approaches 304
education
  social education and
  crime prevention 373
EEG 133
efficiency
  and body temperature 86-87
  and food 86-87
egocentric speech 158-160,169
emotional disorders 290
  and cognitive factors 290
  and irrational beliefs 300-301
empiricism
  and visual perception 97
employment selection 397-416
energy
  as a personality trait 181
episodic memory 19
equality 237-238
  and intelligence 190
error-proneness
  and absent-mindedness 11-14
  and obsessionality 13
ethogenists 247
evaluation
  and personality 181
evening types 79
exception words 49
explanation
  and causation 224-225
explanatory concepts
  and bio-social scientists 175
explanatory power of
  psychology 175
extinction 192-193
Extraversion-
  Introversion
  (Eysenck) 79-80,193
Exvia 180

F Scale (Adorno) 249,250,251,253
factor analysis 176-177,185
fallibility 3
false consensus 223
false negatives 401
false positives 401
family background
  and delinquency 373-375
family, foster
  and delinquency 391
family therapy
  outcome studies 360
fascism 237
fascist personality 248-252
fatigue
  and cognitive performance 64-65,86
feed-back factors
  and cognition 293-298
feminism
  and mental illness 320,334
food
  and performance efficiency 86-87
foster families
  and delinquency 391
Fourier transform 98
freedom 237-238
Freud, S.
  and 'Freudian slips' 4,8,24

Galton, Sir Francis
  twin studies 177
gender specific personality
  traits 334
gender stereotypes
  and mental illness 324,325-326,330-331
General Adaptation Syndrome 265-270
general intelligence
  as a personality dimension 183-209
  and political attitudes 184
gesture and symbol,
  distinguished 166
graphemes 36,38-39,43,55

habits
  see strong habit intrusions
Hamilton Rating Scales for
  Depression 307
'hassles' scales 276
Helmholtz, H. von
  and visual perception 97
helplessness
  and sex roles 336-337
help-seeking
  and sex differences 326-327
heritability
  and personality 177-209
heuristics
  and representation 219
homophones 44-49
honesty
  as personality trait 369
Hopelessness Scale 307
hyperactive children
  self-instructional
  techniques 304
hypertension 270

ideology
  definition 234-235
  ideological/non-ideogical
  thinking compared 241-242
  individual concept 238-240,243
  intellectual insecurity 252,253,254
  lack of in Western society 245,246
  Marx's theories of 235-236
  political 234,240-241
  social concept of 235-238,248
  and 'toughmindedness' 253
  and values 237-238

identity
women's/men's, compared 335,337
image processing
parallel 102
serial 102
image redundancy
and algorithms 98
immune response 272
impulsive behaviour
cognitive approaches 304
inconsistency
and neuroticism 191
individual differences
and intelligence 190
inference
and personality 409
and visual perception 97
information processing
and action slips 4-7
and ageing 187-190
and attention 14
and attribution 213
and capacity theories 134
and choline 147-148
and consensus information 218
and drugs 129-155
and intelligence 186-187
limitation of capacity 132-135
and methscopolomine 130-132,137
and physostigmine 135-140,148
and protein synthesis 145-146
and reading 32
and retrieval 76-79
and RU 24722 148
and smoking 131,134-135
and statistics 217-218
and stimulus manipulation 216
infradian rhythms 65
institutional environments
and delinquency 391
intelligence
and absent-mindedness 14
Burt's views on 369
and equality 190
and individual differences 190
and information processing 186-187
and social hierarchies 190
see also general intelligence
inter-rater reliability
and assessment 382
interaction studies
and counselling 362
interactive predictors
and selection procedures 404
intervention
and assessment 383-389
and delinquency 383-389
interviews
and selection procedures 405,406
inspection times 186
intrinsic images (Tenenbaum) 107
Introversion-Extraversion
(Eysenck) 79-80,193
IQ 186,187,191
irrational beliefs
and emotional disorders 300-301
irrationality
and behavioural change 300

job performance
as criterion 393
job sample tests 399
John Birch Society 252
justice
and delinquency 375-380,392

juvenile offenders
numbers of 376
situational determinants 369

Kana 42,47,50
Kanji 42,47,50

labelling, visual 99
laboratory studies
and absent-mindedness 16-21
Labour party (UK) 238
LAD (Chomsky) 163
language
and acculturation 171
and behaviour monitoring 169-170
and categorization 169
and cognition 157
and communication 158-159
and conceptualization 169
and development 157
and encoding systems 33
global characteristics 160
origins 162
and personality 179-209
and social relations 160,162,167,169
and symbols 166-167
and thought 156-174
and visual attention 164-167
and writing systems 41-42
language acquisition 157-174
lapses
and absent-mindedness 3
LASS (Bruner) 163
learned helplessness 295,302
learned hopelessness 295
learning
and maladaptive processes 292
learning, avoidance
and neuroticism 192
legibility
and word identification 39
lexical codes 33-62
lexicon
paths to: phonological 41-48,51,54
visual 41,48-49,54
Locke, John
theories of perception 97
logic
and thought-patterns 300
logogens 35,39-41,50
logographs
relation to sound 42
loneliness
and stress 282
Luria, A.R.
metacognitive theories 169-170

maladaptive thought
and behaviour 300
marital status
and mental health 330-332
Marx, K.
and ideology 235-236
Marxist-Leninism
as official ideology 245,248
meaning
and conventional symbols 166-167
scriptural representation 42
mediational factors
and clinical psychology 290
memory
and ageing 21
and amphetamines 141-145
and anti-anxiolitic drugs 193
and cholinergic system 129-140

consolidation
  cognitive process 144-146
  and depression 308
  disorders 146-149
  and dreaming 192-193
  episodic 19
  and methyldopa 143-144
  and neuroticism 192-193
  and nicotine 136-137
  and noradrenaline 141-144
  and orthography 19-20
  passive/active, compared 25
  and real-life actions 11-13
  and retrieval 76-77
  semantic 19
  and sleep-wake cycle 82,85
  and time of day effect 69-76
see also absent-mindedness
see also delayed memory
memory blocks
  induced 18-20
  tip-of-the-tongue states 3,8-9,19
memory lapses
  and orthography 19-20
memory load
  and performance rhythms 69,87
mental illness
  and causal processes 333
  and child-rearing 333
  community surveys 320-321,330
  and employment status 332
  gender stereotypes 324,325-326,330-331
  and marital status 330-332
  and sex differences 326-328
  and sex role 327-328
  and sex-typed traits 334-335
  and sexual inequality 335-337
  and social change 330
  social construction of 322,338-339
  and social stratification 335
  treatment rates 320-344
  and women 320-344
  and women's home role 329-332
mental rotation 109
mental tests
  and general intelligence 186
metacognition
  and cybernetics 170
  and verbal regulation
    of behaviour 169-170
methamphetamine
  and short-term memory 142-143
methscopalamine
  information processing 130,137-138
methyldopa
  and memory 143-144
Middlesex Hospital
  Questionnaire 12
mind
  existence, denied 291
mistakes
  and absent-mindedness 3
modelling behaviour
  and delinquency 371-373
moderator constructs
  and selection procedures 400
mood changes
  and depression 308-309
morning types 79
motion
  measurement of 117-118
motion parallax 107
multiple regession
  and selection procedures 400

National Front party (UK) 238,255
naturalistic studies
  absent-mindedness 5-9
  gender and mental health 324-325
Necker cube 100
needs theory
  and delinquency 383
net-widening
  and delinquency 378-380,392
neurochemistry
  and behaviour 129
neuroticism 176,181,190-194
  and avoidance learning 192
  and cognitive resources 192-193
  and inconsistency 191
  and memory 192-193
  and personality differences 191,193
  and stressors 191
nicotine
  and electrocortical arousal 133-134
  and information processing 131,134-135
  and memory 136-137
non-verbal communication
  and personality traits 409-410
  and young children 162-167
non-words 37-39,43,45,46,47,49,50,54
nonsense words 17
noradrenaline 272
  and memory 141-144

O-level
  as indicators of
    achievement/aptitude 404
object concept development 164
object recognition 98-99
obsessionality
  and error-proneness 13
occupational psychology 397-416
OLREC 98
orthograpy
  and memory lapses 19-20
  and phonology 42
outcome studies
  cognitive therapy 306-312
  counselling 356-357,360-362
  family therapy 360

pain
  cognitive approaches 304
Parmia 180
patient records
  and experimental studies 324-325
pattern recognition 97-99
peer-groups
  and delinquency 371-372
perceived control 273
perception
  and causality 210
perception, visual
  and classification 97-99
  and empiricism 97
  and inference 97
  theory of, John Locke's 97
  see also visual perception
performance rhythms
  and memory load 67,87
personal characteristics
  and rating scales 407-409
personal judgements
  and selection procedures 407-409
personal identity
  see identity
personality
  and consistency 177,200

and crime 382
and cultural differences 180
and depression 298
and evaluation 181,182
and general intelligence 183-209
and heritability 177-209
and inference 409
and language 179-209
and non-verbal communication 409-410
political attitudes 238-240,247-252
and sex differences 194-195
and social attitudes 238
personality theory 175-209
and counselling 357-359
and social episodes 409-410
personality traits
gender specific 334
and intellectual differences 181
and rating scales 407-409
pharmacotherapy
and depression 308
phonemes 36,42,48
phonological dyslexia 50-54
phonology
and orthography 42
and reading 42-43
and spoonerisms 16
physostigmine
information processing 135-140,148
Piaget, J.
and language/thought 157-159
political alienation 254
political attitudes
and general intelligence 184
and personality 200,238-240,247-252
and psycho-analytic theory 240
political conversion 255
politics
and ideology 234-264
Position Analysis Questionnaire 399
post-lunch dip 66-67
Potency (Osgood) 181,194
pre-articulatory editing 17-18
primal sketch (Marr) 107
pronunciation
and spelling 42
pseudohomophones 43-45
pseudo-words 37-38
Psychiatric Epidemiology Research Inventory 282
psycho-analytic theory
and political attitudes 240
psychodynamic theory 291
psychogenetics 175-209
psycholinguistics
and induced speech errors 16-18
psychological research
and delinquency 380
psychological tests
and selection procedures 404-407,410
psychology
explanatory power of 175
psychometrics 179-209,397-416
psychomotor retardation
and depression 310
psychopathology
history of 323
psychosomatic illness
and stress 267,268,281
psychotherapy
and counselling 350
cognitive 298
punishment
see justice

racism 246-247,254
unconscious motivations of 240
see also anti-semitism
railway disasters
and absent-mindedness 22
rating scales
and personal traits 407-408
Rational Emotive Therapy 295,300,355-357
reading
and cognition 32
and information processing 32
and phonology 41-43
reading ability
and brain damage 32
see also dyslexia
reading aloud
and semantic/articulatory codes 32-33
real world tasks 73-74
recall
and real world tasks 73-74
and time of day effect 69
recidivism
and delinquency 387-389
reciprocal determinism
and behavioural disorders 304
reference
linguistic/pre-linguistic 164-165
relational factors
and cognition 292-293,298
relaxation process
and visual representation 101
religion
and social reinforcement 190
representation, scriptural
and meaning 42
see also symbols
research methods
case studies 21-23
community surveys 320-321,330
counselling 357,360-361
diary studies 5-9
and diurnal rhythms 64
in-depth interviews 243
laboratory studies 16-21
naturalistic 4-9
qualitative 247
quantitative 247
questionnaire studies 11-16
response factors
and cognition 293,298
retrieval
see information processing
see memory
road disasters
and absent-mindedness 22-23
RU 24722
and information processing 148

schemata, cognitive 296-297
schools
and delinquency 371
scopolamine
information processing 130-131,137-139
selection, employment 397-416
selection procedures
and application forms 404
and biographical data 404-409
and construct validity 400-407
and differential psychology 401
and interactive predictors 404
and moderator constructs 400

and personal judgements 407-409
and psychological tests 404-407,410
and self-concept 410-413
as social episodes 409-413
see also assessment
self-concept
and selection procedures 410-413
self-control
and depression 301-302
self-instructional techniques
and hyperactive children 304
self-reports
and error-liability 12
semantic codes
and reading 32-33
semantic memory 19
senile dementia 147
sex and diurnal rhythms 81
sex differences
and help-seeking 326-327
and mental illness 327-328
and personality 194-195
men's/women's compared 335,337
sex differentials
in treatment statistics 320,322
sex roles
and helplessness 336-337
and mental health 327-328
sex specific disorders 321
sex-typed traits 334-335
sexual inequality
and mental illness 335-337
shift-work 64,82
shoplifting
and absent-mindedness 14-16
sign
and symbol, distinguished 166-167
situational attribution 211,224-225
skills, counselling 357
Skinner, B.F.
and stimulus response
theory of behaviour 291
sleep
and body temperature 64-65
sleep deprivation 65-66,84-85
sleep-wake cycle
and body temperature 65,82
and memory 82-83,84-85
slips
and absent-mindedness 3
slips of action 4-6
and place-losing errors 20-21
smoking
information processing 131,134,135
social attitudes
and personality 238
social change
and mental illness 330
social education
and crime prevention 373
social enquiry reports
and sentencing 381-382
social episodes
and personality 409-410
and selection procedures
social hierarchies
and intelligence 190
social interaction
and speech 160,162,167,169
social psychology
and attribution 210,214
Social Readjustment Rating
Scale 275
social reinforcement
and religion 190
social relations
and language 160,162,167,169
social representations 236,246
social stratification
and mental illness 335
socialism 237
sociology of knowledge 236
sound
and logographs 42
scriptural representation 42
Soviet psychology 168
Spearman, C.
factor-analytic method 177
speech
and communication 158-160
social interaction 160,162,167,169
speech, egocentric 158-160,169
speech errors
induced 16-18
spelling
and pronunciation 42
spelling-to-sound
correspondence 32-33
Spoonerisms of Laboratory-
Induced Predisposition 16
state
and trait, compared 191
statistical information
and information processing 217-218
statistics
of juvenile offenders 376
stimulus manipulation
and information processing 216
Streatfield Committee 381
stress
and ahedonia 282
and cardiovascular system 270,278
and chance 273
and cognitive failure 12,13-14
and coping techniques 281-282
and cultural differences 276-277
definition 265-266
and depression 282
and economic factors 277
and loneliness 282
and psychosomatic illness 267,268,281
and self-esteem 278
and sensation-seeking 280
subjective response to 281
and vasoconstriction 269-270
stress, chronic 267
self-created 280
social 277
stressors 269-272
and neuroticism 191-193
psycho-social 274-277
strong emotion intrusion 8
strong habit intrusion 8,19,24
Stroop test
and diurnal rhythms 86
surface contours
and visual perception 109
surface dyslexia 50-54
symbolic development 158
symbolic interactionists 247
symbols
and gesture, distinguished 166-167
and language 166-167
and sign, distinguished 166-167
symbols, conventional
and meaning 166-167
and visual perception 109
symbols, natural
and visual perception 109
see also representation

systematic errors
and daily life 3-4

tachistoscopic identification
task 35
television violence
and violent behaviour 371
temperature
and biological clock 84-85
temperature, body
and efficiency 66
temporal isolation
and cognition 83-85
Test-Wait-Test-Exit cycle 10
texture and shading
and visual perception 109
therapy, cognitive 290-319
thought
and cognition 152
and development 157
and language 156-174
verbal 160,169
thought, negative
and depression 295-296,307
thought-patterns 300
ticket thinking 249,251
time cues
synchronization of 83-85
time of day effects
and cognition 64
and delayed memory 75-76
and memory 69-76
and recall 69
time-zone transition 64,82,83
tip-of-the-tongue states
and memory blocks 3,8,10,19
trainability tests 399
trait
and state, compared 191
trait psychology 175-209
trait reliablity 191
treatment rates
and mental illness 320-344
treatment studies
and depression 310-312
twin studies 177
Two Value Model (Rokeach) 237
Type As 278-280

ultradian rhythms 63
Unconscious, the
as key concept 175
unintended actions
and environmental factors 16

validity, construct
and selection procedures 400-407
validity, criterion
and selection procedures 406-407
Value Survey (Rokeach) 237
values
and ideology 237-238
instrumental 237
terminal 237
vasoconstriction
and stress 269-270
verbal thought 160,169
violent behaviour
and television violence 371
vision, computational 95-128
visual attention
and language 164-167
visual input
and articulatory codes 32-33
visual perception
and binocular disparity 107
and binocular stereopsis 119-124
and boundary finding 111-113
and brightness 103-105
and conventional symbols 109
left/right eye
correspondence 122
and measurement of motion 117-118
and motion parallax 107
and natural symbols 109
and neural mechanisms 105-106
object-centred 107
receptive fields 117
and surface contours 109
and texture/shading 109
and vergence eye movement 124
viewer-centred 107
and word identification 38-39
Vygotsky, L.
and language/thought 159-161

Western Collaborative
Group Study 278
will 181
women
and depression 321,336-337
and mental illness 320-344
women's home role
and mental illness 329-332
word
and non-word, compared 35
word identification 33-64
word superiority 36-38
work sample tests 399
writing systems
and language 41-42

Zeitgeber
see time cues